THE
CRISIS
OF
LIBERAL
DEMOCRACY

A Straussian Perspective

SUNY Series in Political Theory: Contemporary Issues
John G. Gunnell, Editor

THE
CRISIS
OF
LIBERAL
DEMOCRACY

A Straussian Perspective

edited with an introduction by
KENNETH L. DEUTSCH
and
WALTER SOFFER

Foreword by Joseph Cropsey

State University of New York Press

Published by
State University of New York Press, Albany

© *1987   State University of New York*

All rights reserved

Printed in the United States of America

For information, address State University of New York
Press, State University Plaza, Albany, N.Y., 12246

Library of Congress Cataloging in Publication Data

The Crisis of liberal democracy.

　　(SUNY series in political theory. Contemporary issues)
　　Includes index.
　　1. Strauss, Leo—Contributions in political science.
2. Liberalism. 3. Democracy. I. Deutsch, Kenneth L.
II. Soffer, Walter, 1941–
JC251.S8C75   1987　　　320.5′1　　　86-5908
ISBN 0-88706-388-8
ISBN 0-88706-387-X (pbk.)

10   9   8   7   6   5   4   3   2

Contents

Foreword

Leo Strauss's work continues to engage the attention of serious students of political philosophy. In the period of more than a decade since his death, the interest in his work, evinced in translations, posthumous publications and republications, and, not surprisingly, controversy, has had a degree of intensity that presages a long prospect of continued recognition of his achievements. The present volume takes its place among the evidences of interest in Strauss's work in a particularly fitting way. Its authors include people who sat in his classes, people who did not, those who are more and those who are less self-identified as "Straussians," those who are not so identified at all, and for the most part people of a generation rather younger than Strauss's. The breadth of his own scholarly and political concerns deservedly finds a response in the width of the spectrum of reaction to his work.

It would be entirely incredible if Strauss's work were to be or to have been received with universal approval. His thought was intensely critical, not only in a scholarly sense or with a view to texts but also in a more immediate sense and with a view to the human environment that is our dwelling and that we sometimes call "modernity." There would be something seriously amiss among our congeners and contemporaries if they did not experience some resistance to the criticism of their very own—their own condition and their own understanding of that condition. Equally, there would be something small and deplorable about them if that resistance hardened into an intransigent rejection. It is to be hoped that this book will contribute to strengthening the openness of reflection and discourse about our condition as human beings and as modern beings that Strauss's work prepares.

Joseph Cropsey

Preface

In October, 1983 the coeditors set up a conference on "The Crisis of Liberal Democracy: A Straussian Perspective," which was held at S.U.N.Y. at Geneseo. The conference was made possible by a S.U.N.Y. Conversations in the Disciplines grant. The occasion of the conference was the commemoration of the tenth anniversary of Professor Leo Strauss's death.

The present volume contains the papers presented at the conference as well as contributions by Robert Eden, Roger Masters, and Michael Platt. The purpose of the book is threefold: to provide an overview of Strauss's political thought, to provide a critical evaluation of Strauss's teaching, and to show the way in which the Straussian perspective is brought to bear on selected topics in European and American liberal theory.

We wish to acknowledge the contribution of our department secretaries, Mrs. Cathy Lewis and Ms. Pam Wyant. The successful completion of this book owes much to their tireless efforts in organizing and coordinating the conference to which this book owes its existence. Special thanks is owed to John Gunnell and William T. Bluhm for their helpful suggesstions concerning the content and organization of the book.

We dedicate this book to the memory of Leo Strauss.

Kenneth L. Deutsch
Walter Soffer

Introduction

The crisis of liberal democracy is best understood as a crisis of moral foundations. Many contemporary political theorists are skeptical about the validity of the principles of liberal democracy and their moral consequences. Some of these theorists advance either a neo-Marxist view of human perfectibility, a concept of the "neutral" state, or the resurrection of the social contract symbolism to defend economic equality or individual freedom. None of these positions, however, adequately provide a theory of the regime as a moral force and statesmanship as the exercise of moral prudence.[1]

To be sure, liberal democracy has been a many-faced and variously interpreted phenomenon; however, it is possible to identify the core of modern liberal political philosophy in the notion that the most nearly just social arrangement is one that secures the right of individuals to pursue their interests fairly. Liberalism attempts to achieve political peace in a morally pluralistic and fragmented society. The advantage of liberal democracy is the removal from the political arena of issues that tend to be deeply divisive of the citizenry. The disadvantage of liberal democracy is that government has become morally neutral on the very issues that matter most to people. At its most fundamental level, liberal democracy is morally neutral concerning choices of ways of life. It presides over, rather than prescribes, such choices, intervening only to adjudicate conflicts and to prevent any particular way of life from dominating others. In John Rawls's view: "The liberal state rests on a conception of equality between human beings as moral persons, as creatures having a conception of the good capable of a sense of justice. . . . Systems of ends are not ranked in value."[2] For Ronald Dworkin, the liberal state "must be neutral on. . . the question of the good life; political decisions must be, so far as it is possible, independent of any particular conception of the good life, or of what gives value to life."[3] Such moral neutrality reflects the crisis of liberal democracy by raising the following question: Does not the liberal democratic ideal of moral neutrality sanction the dedication to individual freedom over any other individual or social good?

To relegate certain moral issues to individual choice is in fact a public moral judgment in need of scrutiny. An indication of the need for such scrutiny on the practical level is the recent injection into law and politics

1

of moral issues that many politicians and political thinkers would prefer to keep out. The abortion controversy, for example, forces all of us to ask whether an "impartial" liberal democratic system, presiding with what Chief Justice Warren Burger has called "benevolent neutrality," still serves the nation best.

Liberal democrats have traditionally provided two kinds of defenses for moral neutrality as a justification for the liberal state. First, it has been argued that there is no rational basis for choosing among ways of life. Assertions about the good are noncognitive, radically personal. The neutral state is consequently considered desirable because it is the sole nonarbitrary agency in public life. Second, there is the claim that individual freedom is the highest value. Freely chosen errors are to be preferred to a coerced pursuit of the good. State neutrality is justified as the public safeguard of this priority of individual freedom over the "social good."[4]

It cannot be denied that liberal democracy has had great success in achieving its goals of political liberty, limited government, and due process of law. Many ills nonetheless flourish. Along with political liberties we find atomization, alienation, and anomie. The premiss of individual freedom as the absolute value jeopardizes public spiritedness. Tales of political and corporate corruption have become commonplace. Anomic violence and the daily development of new forms of therapy and self-help testify to the loss of a sense of order. Politically, an important symptom of liberal democracy's crisis is the increased manipulation of the public agenda and policy making by special interest groups. Such dominance has become the accepted pattern of public life.

Liberal democratic regimes have failed to develop standards of political morality by which to judge and influence actions that affect the character and preservation of the regime itself. This failure has contributed to the diminished conviction that there are certain moral obligations that are binding on all who are committed to a free society. Liberal democratic regimes have tended to act as if private behavior affecting public life either will be "miraculously guided by a standard of the good or will be good merely because free."[5] Contemporary liberal democracy has been constrainted by its negative view of the political realm and as a consequence has been ineffective at establishing a public vision of the good that could help preserve the regime. Although liberal ethics has contributed significantly to political principles drawing the line on government authority, it has not sufficiently recognized the connection between the exercise of private freedom in a limited or constitutional state and the virtues the public must exercise to remain free from oppression.

In the absence of a standard of political ethics, early liberal democratic regimes have relied upon peoples' commitments to personal and social morality, which fostered a consensus of the common good. During periods of crisis, such regimes have relied upon the actions of statesmen to revive a sense of public dedication. Contemporary developments have shown the decay of the earlier ethos and the failure of political leaders to learn a philosophy of statesmanship that could provide guidance. These two developments have made it difficult for liberal democratic regimes to contend effectively with such problems as defining the role of technology in the public and private realms, managing economic dislocation, and countering the influence of perfectibilist ideologies that pose a threat to the conservation of liberal democratic/constitutionalist regimes.[6]

Tocqueville characterized the dilemma the American liberal democratic regime faces when he asked:

> Do you wish to raise mankind to an elevated and generous view of the things of this world? Do you want to inspire men with a certain scorn of material goods? Do you hope to engender deep conviction and prepare the way for acts of profound devotion?
>
> Are you concerned with refining mores, elevating manners, and causing the arts to blossom? Do you desire poetry, renoun, and glory?
>
> Do you set out to organize a nation so that it will have a powerful influence over others? Do you expect it to attempt great enterprises and whatever be the results of its efforts, to leave a great mark on history?
>
> If in your view that should be the main object of men in society, do not support democratic government: it surely will not lead you to that goal.
>
> But if you think it profitable to turn men's intellectual and moral activity toward the necessities of physical life and use them to produce well-being, if you think that reason is more use to men than genius, if your object is not to create heroic virtues but rather tranquil habits, if you would rather contemplate vices than crimes, and prefer fewer transgressions at the cost of fewer splendid deeds, if in place of a brilliant society you are content to live in one that is prosperous, and finally, if in your view the main object of government is not to achieve the greatest strength or glory for the nation as a whole but to provide for every individual therein the utmost well-being, protecting him as far as possible from afflictions, then it is good to make conditions equal and to establish a democratic government.[7]

Given the history of American liberal democracy, Toqueville's concerns should be our concerns. Liberal democracies need to learn standards of excellence that exert an "upward pull" against the demands of physical gratification in order to establish a creative tension between "the necessities of physical life" and "the elevated and generous view of the things of this world." It is this tension that modern liberal democratic theorists and regimes have often ignored in favor of a neo-Epicurean doctrine of human nature.[8] This tension between physical needs and moral excellence requires that politics go beyond "interest articulation" and the employment of leaders as "referees."

The failure of liberal democracy to understand and to respond to the current crisis suggests its philosophical limitations. Perhaps some of liberalism's assumptions preclude it from serving as a comprehensive theory of the good public order. Perhaps such a comprehensive theory must rest on premises more fundamental, more defensible than ethical noncognitivism and individualism. A profound examination of the need for and the possibility of such premises informs the thought of Leo Strauss.

The larger context for Strauss's analysis of liberal democracy was what he understood as the crisis of modernity stemming from the rejection of Greek antiquity and biblical religion in the name of the new sciences of nature and politics. The goal of the modern project, the improvement of the human condition through the technical mastery of nature, was formulated by modern political philosophy. What predominates today are a morally neutral methodology in the form of the fact-value distinction of positivist social science (which "may be said to be more dogmatic than any other position of which we have records") and an historicist ideology.[9] The dominance of positivism and historicism is, according to Strauss, tantamount to the demise of political philosophy as traditionally understood—the search for the naturally best regime. There is thus lacking a philosophical grounding or justification of the central values of contemporary liberal democracy. The one thing needful, argues Strauss, is a viable notion of natural right. In the absence of a concept of natural right, the alternative confronting liberal democracy is nihilism:

> The majority among the learned who still adhere to the principles of the Declaration of Independence interpret these principles not as expressions of natural right but as an ideal, if not as an ideology or a myth. Present-day American social science. . .is dedicated to the proposition that all men are endowed by the evolutionary process or by a mysterious fate with many kinds of urges and aspirations, but certainly with no natural right. . . .But the mere fact that we can raise the question of the worth of the ideal of our society shows that there is something in man that is not altogether in slavery to his society, and therefore that we are able, and hence obligated, to look for a standard with reference to which we can judge of the ideals of our own as well as of any other society. That standard cannot be found in the needs of the various societies, for the societies and their parts have many needs that conflict with one another: this problem cannot be solved in

a rational manner if we do not have a standard with reference to which we can distinguish between genuine needs and fancied needs and discern the hierarchy of the various types of genuine needs. The problem posed by the conflicting needs of society cannot be solved if we do not possess knowledge of natural right.[10]. . .If our principles have no other support than our blind preferences, everything a man is willing to dare will be permissible. The contemporary rejection of natural right leads to nihilism— nay, it is identical with nihilism.[11]

In the face of such a nihilism Strauss was forced to consider a reexamination of the principles of premodern political philosophy. The crisis of liberal democracy is thus a continuation of the quarrel between the ancients and the moderns. Strauss's return to ancient philosophy is neither nostalgia nor an exercise in intellectual history. It is required by the present crisis since the progression in the history of the West from nature to reason to history to will as the standard of thinking and acting has produced an intellectual and moral vacuum.

Strauss argues that in order to rehabilitate natural right there must be a restoration of the notion of the "beneficence of nature or of the primacy of the Good." This requires no less than a rethinking, through the tradition of political philosophy, of the fundamental experiences responsible for its emergence. To say that there are universal characteristics of human experience especially relevant for political philosophy is to say that there are experiences, intelligible at a pretheoretical level, that serve to demarcate politically significant from politically insignificant phenomena.

The fundamental experience of politics, whose perspective is that of the involved citizen rather than that of the scientific observer, is that of men who must decide courses of action on the basis of competing claims. Such competing claims, when made explicit, serve as criteria or principles of justification. The implicit notion of the good in politics is made thematic when it is recognized that political action involves either preservation or change and, therefore, "must be guided by some thought of better or worse." In this way political philosophy as a sustained reflection about the merits of the competing claims emerges from pretheoretical political experience. The moral neutrality of contemporary social science renders such a genesis invisible by concealing the fact that the ever present experience of political life at all times and places is an experience imbued with unavoidable moral discriminations and judgments. Politics is a world of value rather than a compendium of morally neutral facts or theoretical constructs. In order to see the natural development of political philosophy from political opinion, we must take as our point of departure political opinion itself, that is, political disagreements concerning good and bad actions, types of men, and types of law and governments.

For Strauss the origin of natural right is inseparable from the origin of philosophy. Ordinary political experience, whether concerned about a change for the better or about preventing a change for the worse, contains an awareness of the distinction between how men ought to live and how they in fact live. All men justify their actions and preferences in terms of what they "look up to" as worthy of respect and emulation. It does not matter whether what is looked up to is high or low, spiritual or material. Every person and every regime is what it is by virtue of what it regards as true or good in itself. In this sense the imitation of what is understood as the naturally good applies to contemporary as well as to ancient man.

The historical genesis of natural right depends on the search for a norm whose validity is secured by being grounded in the transhistorical, rendering it immune from the vicissitudes of human affairs and opinions. The decisive step was the discovery of the idea of nature as opposed to art and convention, and its supplanting of the ancestral and the holy. The discovery of nature as the standard meant the intelligibility of a human essence revealed to prescientific and prephilosophic experience as a natural hierarchy of ends. To understand this hierarchy is to evaluate and order the respective goals of human action. The establishment of a sound regime requires the cultivation of a noble way of life. This must be done if a regime is to become an object of respect and loyalty. As Strauss points out, the regime "depends decisively on the predominance of human beings of a certain type" and is "simultaneously the form of life of a society, its style of life, its moral taste, form of society, form of state, form of government, spirit of laws."[12]

The dominant contemporary claim is that political science and its empirical analyses must replace the prescientific experience of traditional political philosophy because of the conviction that genuine knowledge in all areas, the human as well as the nonhuman, is scientific knowledge. As a result, the old political universals—the various regimes and their respective notions of the human good—have given way to new empirical ones—such as freedom, coercion, and legitimacy. As Strauss points out, however, it is impossible to ground such an empiricism empirically, since the scientific study of politics must derive its concepts from the common sense understanding it wishes to circumvent. This is because the only way to grasp the sense and utility of scientific discourse (whether it be theory of perception or theory of politics) is to translate it back into the terms of prescientific experience, which is both its genesis and arbiter.

The methodological reduction of the political to the nonpolitical is a consequence of a prior metaphysical denial of natural political wholes in favor of prepolitical parts. That is to say, in the absence of the primacy of the common good, the good society has become the open society of radical individualism. Since there cannot be any goal unanimously approved, political science teaches the absence of a substantive public interest. And in the absence of a knowledge of human nature whose perfection or exellence produces happiness, liberal democracy is forced to abandon the notion that happiness can be an object of knowledge and thus of statecraft. The foundation of the liberal regime is thus restricted to the conditions for the pursuit of happiness—individual rights to life and liberty. From this results a cleavage between the public and private realms, whereby idiosyncratic happiness rather than virtue or piety becomes preeminent. Liberal democracy thus undermines, according to Strauss, what it truly requires, a dedication to civic virtues, patriotism, and religion. The successes of liberal democracy paradoxically expose its shortcomings, since the more universal the realization of the pursuit of private happiness becomes, the more liberal democracy conceals from itself the roots of its public crisis.

The relationship between liberal democracy and ideology is also paradoxical according to Strauss. The fact-value distinction fosters the notion that men can live without ideology. The nonideological society is egalitarian and permissive, a society in which all values are equal before the tribunal of reason. However, contrary to the idea of the fact-value dichotomy, the nonideological society "rationally" justifies the preference for the liberal democratic regime and thus denies the possibility of an ideology-free society. The new political science and a preference for liberal democracy thus go hand in hand since the alleged value-free analysis of political phenomena is guided by a frequently unacknowledged commitment to liberal democracy.

Understanding that what has no nature can have no meaningful goal, the modern state claims to be the regime demanded by the nature of man. The fixity of human nature is taken to be the firm and lasting foundation of the modern project. However, as Strauss observes: "The characteristic assertion of liberalism seems to be that man and hence also morality is not 'a fixed quantity'; that man's nature and therewith morality are essentially changing; that this change constitutes History."[13] Since the essentially changeable is the essentially malleable, we confront yet another paradox. Human nature is simultaneously the political norm and that which is to be altered and controlled by rulers and proper institutional and legal arrangements. Strauss points out that this paradox of the fixity and changeability of human nature has persisted throughout the production of the liberal democracies of the West. Gone is the conception of the soul as a natural hierarchy of parts. By teaching the equality of all values, by denying the distinction between the naturally high and intrinsically low, and by denying an essential difference between man and animal, the new political science, argues Strauss, unwittingly contributes to the victory of the low.

Strauss saw liberal democracy, especially in America, as solidly within the modern tradition of moral and political realism inaugurated by Machiavelli. Whereas the ancients envisioned the naturally best regime, the moderns envision the practically best, achievable regime. Strauss wrote to Löwith concerning ancient wisdom:

> I really believe. . .that the perfect political order, as Plato and Aristotle have sketched it, *is* the perfect political order. Or do you believe in the world-state? If it is true that genuine unity is only possible through knowledge of the truth or through search for the truth, then there is a genuine unity of all men only on the basis of the popularized final *teaching* of philosophy (and naturally this does not exist) or if all men are philosophers (not Ph.D.'s, etc.)—which likewise is not the case. Therefore, there can only be closed societies, that is, states. But if that is so, then one can show from political considerations that the small city-state is in principle superior to the large state or to the territorial-feudal state. I know very well that it cannot be restored; but the famous atomic bombs—not to mention at all cities with a million inhabitants, gadgets, funeral homes, "ideologies"— shows that the contemporary solution, that is, the completely modern solution, is *contra naturam*.[14]

Strauss favored the theoretical politics of the ancients, but was also appreciative of the practical wisdom of the Founding Fathers. He wrote, concerning America, that "liberal or constitutional democracy comes closer to what the classics demanded than any other alternative that is viable in our age."[15] Strauss agreed with the ancients on the chance realization of the naturally best regime. The modern *contra naturam* regime becomes the best regime possible by eliminating chance through a lowering of standards. Strauss's qualified praise of the Declaration of Independence is therefore a praise of the foundations of the practically best contemporary political alternative as a matter of political urgency. At first sight such foundations are clearly at odds with the ancient principles. Nowhere in Plato's or Aristotle's writings do we find unqualified acceptance of self-evident, natural human equality and individual rights on a universal scale; life, liberty, and pursuit of idiosyncratic happiness as the purpose of the regime; guidance by the *is* rather than than *ought* character of human nature; the overcoming of chance; the dominance of private interest in the form of property and commerce; and political institutions rather than character development to promote political success.[16] But because political life demands an articulation and defense of the best regime possible given the circumstances and available alternatives, Strauss respected liberal democracy. In this sense his thought is in keeping with the practical judgment of Plato and Aristotle in the light of the unrealizability of the naturally best regime. Strauss agrees with Aristotle's notion of the changeability of natural right—the distinction between the feasible or legitimate regime, as opposed to the best regime, given the heterogeneity of political communities and circumstances.

Strauss agrees with the Founding Fathers that the American regime cannot represent the complete human good. Yet he respected American liberal democracy for its stability and durability when led by prudent statesmen. However, in his own experience he witnessed an increasing decline of such stability and durability due to the absence of such men from public life. He also recognized that the increasing technological control over both man and nature was losing its way and that such power would generate a massive technological confrontation between liberal and despotic regimes. The deeper problem for the liberal democracies of the West in such a confrontation is the loss of resolve concerning the value of their mission. Liberal political science clings to the fact-value distinction, according to which only factual judgments can be objective or true. The justification of values is relegated to political philosophy (construed as ideology) on the ground that any justification of values can derive only from facts and that such a derivation is illegitimate. The attempt to trace values to fateful or radically free historical decisions fares no better. Whether it be due to an allegiance to positivistic political science or to historicism, the teaching of the nonrational character of all value judgments means that it is contrary to reason to expect a rational defense of the value of liberal democracy. Such a consequence is concealed behind a ritualistic adherence to method, which is itself indicative of the crisis. Because the positivist and historicist political scientist is a neutral spectator, he must remain neutral and thereby ineffectual in the conflict concerning the superiority of liberal democracy or its adversaries.

Strauss's preference for the ancients is connected with his contention that the quarrel between the ancients and the moderns has not been settled at the most profound level, at the level of first philosophy. He maintained that so long as nonteleological and nontheistic modern philosophy and science do not provide an intelligible and comprehensive account of the whole (and this is demonstrated by the failure to adequately understand "the human things"), they rest on a dogmatism presenting itself as merely methodological or hypothetical. At the same time, Strauss agrees with Plato and Aristotle that a knowledge of the human essence, as a part of the whole, does not require a comprehensive account of the whole. For Strauss, since natural teleology and biblical revelation remain as possibilities, the status of natural right remains an open question. In this way the process of liberal democracy as the most recent expression of western political wisdom participates in the unfinished dialogue that is philosophy—the nondogmatic grappling with the fundamental questions. No contemporary thinker exemplifies the spirit of philosophical inquiry more so than Leo Strauss.

The book is composed of three parts: an appraisal of the work of Leo Strauss, Straussian approaches to major issues of liberalism, and liberalism and the American experience.

Part One deals with an explication and evaluation of Strauss's political teaching as it finds expression in what Strauss considered the most pressing issue: the question of natural right.

In "Leo Strauss: Three Quarrels, Three Questions, One Life," Michael Platt suggests that while Leo Strauss devoted himself to at least three questions (of poetry and philosophy, of revelation and reason, and of the ancients and the moderns), his tentative answers to these questions made him write and teach political philosophy. If the questions could not be answered, still the quarrels might be settled. Strauss's life was one. In him as in the love of his life, Socrates, *eros* and *thymos* acted harmoniously. (Great men should be forgiven for their disciples.) In Socrates, Strauss found the best answer to the Nietzschean question of truth and life.

In "The Problem of Natural Right and the Fundamental Alternatives in *Natural Right and History*," Victor Gourevitch analyzes Strauss's most comprehensive statement regarding natural right. Strauss rejects what he calls "historicism" in the name of what he refers to as "the permanent framework of fundamental problems and alternatives." He recognizes two, and only two, philosophical alternatives, "Platonism" and "Epicureanism," and their nonphilosophical or "vulgar" variants. Within that framework, the problem of natural right proves to be the problem of the relationship between the philosophical alternatives and their nonphilosophical variants.

In "Evolutionary Biology and Natural Right: Leo Strauss, Natural Science, and Political Philosophy," Roger Masters takes issue with Strauss's contention that the idea of natural right is no longer tenable due to the victory of the nonteleological view of the universe of modern physics. Strauss' claim is false, argues Masters, since for Aristotle the teleological presuppositions of natural right were derived from biology, not physics. Given recent teleological trends in biology, whatever the implications of contemporary physics, Strauss's "basic problem" may be soluble provided that the ends of living beings are derived from twentieth century biology rather than from modern physics.

John G. Gunnell's essay, "Political Theory and Politics: The Case of Leo Strauss and Liberal Democracy," takes the position that Strauss's view of the crisis of liberal democracy can be intelligible only in terms of his characterization of the crisis of the West and that this can be understood only by examining his account of the decline of the tradition of political philosophy. By viewing critically Strauss's approach as an example of political theory as evocation, Gunnell seeks to present his own views of the conditions and limits of contemporary political theory.

In Part Two the Straussian approach is applied to the following issues of liberalism: liberality, freedom and equality, consent, and nihilism.

Hilail Gildin explores how modernity and its crisis provide the context for Strauss's analysis of liberal democracy. His essay on "Leo Strauss and the Crisis of Liberal Democracy" presents Strauss's view that modern times lacks a political philosophy to ground and support those aspects of contemporary liberal democracy that make it preferable to any alternative that is viable in our time.

Richard Cox, in "Aristotle and Machiavelli on Liberality," argues that the crisis of liberal democracy is most apparent concerning the "nature and purpose of the ownership of private property." The origin of such a crisis is traced to Machiavelli's critique of the classical teaching on the virtue called liberality. As Cox explains, what is at issue is a new definition of human nature and a new understanding of politics. The present forgetting of the Aristotelian teaching on liberality, a teaching that is a reflection of the "potentialities and limitations of human nature," testifies to the success of Machiavelli's portrait of human nature as acquisitive. The moral justification of acquisitiveness is based on a transformed notion of prudence in the name of practical political truth.

In "Aristotle and the Moderns on Freedom and Equality," Laurence Berns explains the reasons for the modern departure from classical notions of freedom and equality and suggests a basis for a reconciliation between classical and American political thought. The transition from classical virtue to modern freedom was due to the replacement of purposive nature as the ground of moral and political standards with the negative standard of the "condition of nature," which indicates what in nature is to be avoided or overcome, and the final repudiation of nature altogether as any such ground. The basis for the reconciliation between American and classical politics, according to Berns, is the discovery of classical principles implicit in the thought of the American Founders, their mutual respect for political prudence given the limitations of politics and their common appreciation of the need for enlightenment through liberal education.

Leo Strauss' claim that "the political problem consists in reconciling the requirement for wisdom with the requirement for consent" is the basis of Judith Best's discussion of John Locke. In her piece, "The Innocent, the Ignorant, and the Rational: The Content of Lockian Consent," Best shows how Locke's collapse of the distinction between reason and consent may make men forget that consent has a content and that rationality and consent are very different things.

In "Nihilism and Modern Democracy in the Thought of Nietzsche," Thomas Pangle discloses Nietzsche's historical philosophy of man as a reflection on "the fate of man as that fate unfolds in time." The "Super-man" is Nietzsche's antithesis of what human life eventually becomes if contemporary egalitarian goals are realized. The root and persistence of such goals is traced to contemporary democratic man's "increasing lack of capacity for self-contempt—and thus for self-transforming love" and servitude to "culture" and "educated opinion." This fosters in democratic man the complacency and pride responsible for the recalcitrance to Zarathustra's message. As Pangle explains, Nietzsche's purpose is to force us to face and take responsibility for the choice between "Last Man" and "Super-man."

Robert Eden in his essay "Why Wasn't Weber a Nihilist?" shows that Strauss's critical analysis undermines those social scientists who looked to Weber for support for the distinction between facts and values. Eden claims that Strauss could not have questioned Weber's moral resistance to nihilism at the level of science so relentlessly had he not broken the spell of Weber's insistent moral concern. Eden attempts to show, though, that Weber remains a question mark for Strauss. Weber ultimately was not able to tell us why he was not a nihilist and why vulgar nihilism thrives in a constitutional democracy.

Part Three discusses liberalism in America in terms of the problem of private interest and the public good.

Steven Salkever in his essay "The Crisis of Liberal Democracy: Liberality and Democratic Citizenship" claims that the dilemma of the radical incoherence of liberal democracy—the problem of getting an aggregate of free individuals to accept a political agenda that conflicts with the preferences of a majority of their number—persists and flourishes in our time. Similar difficulty attends to the attempt to overcome the tension between liberty and democratic equality. However, Salkever feels that "crisis" is not the appropriate diagnosis of contemporary liberal democracy. Rather than the thought of Aristotle, Tocqueville and the authors of the *Federalist Papers* should serve as the basis for an alternative conception of liberal democracy marked by the quiet virtues of liberality and moderation. Salkever views our real crisis as not characterized by insufficient energy but by inadequate self-regard.

In his essay on "Liberalism as the Aggregation of Individual Preferences: Problems of Coherence and Rationality in Social Choice," William T. Bluhm concerns himself with one of the major issues within liberal democratic political culture, namely, how individual utilities or "preferences" can be aggregated in a fair and efficient way in the creation of public policy. Bluhm provides us with an analysis of problems in the theory of social choice and alerts us to the questionableness of assuming that the primary problem of government is the summation of given and infinitely various preference orderings into a fair and meaningful whole. We need, instead, according to Bluhm, a political science that is concerned with the *formation* of preferences—a discipline concerned with the definition and implementation of the common good.

K.L.D.

W.S.

Notes

1. Leo Strauss, *What is Political Philosophy? And Other Studies* (New York: Free Press), 92.

2. John Rawls, *A Theory of Justice* (Cambridge, Mass.: Harvard University Press, 1971). 19.

3. Ronald Dworkin, "Liberalism," ed. Richard Wasserstrom, *Morality and the Law* (New York: Cambridge University Press, 1978), 127.

4. William Galston, "Defending Liberalism," *American Political Science Review*, vol 76, no. 3 (Septembe 1982), 621–22.

5. Joseph Cropsey, "Political Morality and Liberalism," *Political Philosophy and the Issues of Politics* (Chicago: University of Chicago Press, 1977), 138.

6. Alan Pino, "Classical Sources of American Values," *Political Traditions and Contemporary Problems* 2, ed. Kenneth W. Thompson (Washington, D.C.: University Press of America, 1982), 3–13; Herbert Storing, "Bureaucracy and Statesmanship," *Bureaucrats, Policy Analysts and Statesman*, ed. Robert Goldwin (Washington, D.C.: American Enterprise Institute, 1979), 64.

7. Alexis de Tocqueville, *Democracy in America*, ed. J. P. Mayer (New York: Macmillan, 1969), 245.

8. Francis Canavan, "Liberalism in Root and Flower," *The Ethical Dimension of Political Life: Essays in Honor of John H. Hallowell*, ed. Francis Canavan (Durham:

Duke University Press, 1983), 41–42. For an excellent discussion of how modern liberalism has consciously appropriated the principles of ancient hedonism, making hedonism the major motive force in the rise of the modern liberal-democratic state, see Frederick Vaughan, *The Tradition of Political Hedonism: From Hobbes to J. S. Mill* (New York: Fordham University Press, 1982).

9. Leo Strauss, *Liberalism, Ancient and Modern* (New York: Basic Books, 1968), 26.

10. Leo Strauss, *Natural Right and History* (Chicago: University of Chicago Press, 1953), 2–3.

11. Ibid., 4–5.

12. Strauss, *What Is Political Philosophy?, And Other Studies,* 34.

13. Strauss, *Liberalism, Ancient and Modern,* 34.

14. Letter to Karl Löwith, 18 August 1946, "Correspondence Concerning Modernity: Karl Löwith and Leo Strauss," *Independent Journal of Philosophy* 4 (1983): 107–8.

15. Strauss, *What Is Political Philosophy?, And Other Studies,* 113.

16. John Agresto, "Leo Strauss And The Resurgence Of American Conservatism" (Paper delivered at the annual meeting of the American Political Science Association, Washington, D.C. September 1983), p. 10.

Part 1

THE WORK OF LEO STRAUSS
AN APPRAISAL

First Section

AN OVERVIEW

Michael Platt

LEO STRAUSS: THREE QUARRELS,
THREE QUESTIONS, ONE LIFE

Leo Strauss devoted himself to understanding three quarrels or questions: the quarrel of the ancients and the moderns, the quarrel of
philosophy and biblical religion, and the quarrel of philosophy and
poetry. Since the first is most prominent in his writings, it is easiest to
begin with it.

In those of his writings whose scope, selection of texts to be read, and
issues to be treated are deliberately limited to the political, that is, the
vast majority of what he published, Strauss argues for the clear superiority of the political wisdom that flowed from the philosophic inquiries
of the ancients (Socrates, Xenophon, Plato, and Aristotle) over the cunning, fearful, cautious, compassionate, or daring political teachings that
flowed from the philosophic inquiries of the moderns (Machiavelli, Hobbes, Locke, Rousseau, and Nietzsche). However, he did so without
declaring that the struggle of the ancients and moderns had been settled
at the highest level, at the level of first philosophy. At the level of a conversation between Nietzsche and Socrates, or between Heidegger and
Aristotle, the question of the ancients and the moderns remained
unanswered. In order to test the claim of radical creativity as presented
by Nietzsche and the claim of radical historicism as presented by
Heidegger and therewith the claim of modern philosophy fully
developed, to best understand the whole, Strauss studied the ancient
philosophers, for he thought they offered the most cogent alternative to
the moderns. (It seems that he did not regard the attempt of German
idealism, of Kant and especially Hegel, to overcome the moderns as
satisfactory.)[1] Yet, while Strauss never ceased to concern himself with
first philosophy, what he thought is not easy to learn from his writings.
They are primarily concerned with political things.[2] Primarily, but not
exclusively, and perhaps not fundamentally, for Strauss used many
devices and indirections to indicate his thoughts to those of his readers
who read Heidegger and Nietzsche and who also read those books of

17

the ancients not primarily devoted to political things.[3] In this way he remained true to the twofold character of the quarrel of the ancients and
the moderns as he saw it: the superiority of the first questions to the
answers given by either the ancients or the moderns. The quarrel was
settled; the questions remained. An understanding of this twofold
character of the relationship of the ancients and the moderns and the
manner of writing Strauss adopted to be true to it brings to sight two
other quarrels or questions to which Strauss devoted his thoughts.

No less important, if less prominent, in his writings, was the quarrel
of poetry and philosophy.[4] Strauss knew this in ancient poetry and
philosophy itself, as the quarrel of Aristophanes and Socrates, the
Platonic attack on poetry, the philosophic subordination of poetry, ad-
vocated by Plato and legislated by Aristotle, and the reconciliations practiced by Thucydides and Plato himself. He also saw this quarrel transformed by the moderns. In his one published piece on Nietzsche he
tacitly observes what he stressed explicitly in several courses on Nietzsche: the connection between the quarrel of poetry (or making) and
philosophy and the quarrel of the ancients and moderns.[5] At work in the
break with the ancients effected by Machiavelli was the preference for
activity over thought; for doing, making, and founding over knowing
and wondering; for making a less noble but more possible city rather
than striving for a city that might be founded only with the cooperation
of chance. This preference finds expression in the modern concern with
freedom, with rights, with creativity, and with the will. The nature, or
alleged nature, of the will is most fully and splendidly elaborated in the
thoughts and the poetry of Nietzsche and can be expressed in the thesis:
Truth itself is the product of willful creation, not the reward of intellec-
tion, of the pure mind knowing ("Von der unbefleckten Erkenntnis,"
Zarathustra II). According to Nietzsche's elaboration, the philosophers,
especially Socrates, misunderstood themselves; what they called
"thinking" was really "making." They were as much poets as the poets
they attacked, without being as good, for their poem of the "true
world" was less true, less noble, less loving, less loyal to the earth than
the poems of the tragic poets. *Zarathustra* is meant to seek and bring
nearer a poetic wisdom, which will, however, not be a restoration of ancient tragedy, for its strong pessimism will be post-Socratic rather than
pre-Socratic. (Heidegger would seem to argue that Hölderlin is the post-
Socratic poet; Strauss noted Heidegger's turn to poetry, but took no
notice of the choice of Hölderlin in his writings.)[6] In any case, Strauss
found more truth in the view that truth is discovered than in the view

that truth is made and accordingly favored the subordination of poetry to philosophy.

For the student of poetry the consequences of this subordination are to be understood in the light of Strauss's maxim: Always assume that there is present a silent someone "who is by far superior to you in head and heart," for this teaches the reader of poetry to regard the poet as his superior, as one who says exactly what he meant to, every sentence, every sound, rather than as one who is human and weak and for whom allowances must be made. Such a poet could easily correct one's misinterpretations but prefers to guide the soul silently, through images, knowing that such silent guiding has the advantage of perfecting the reader's mind, by exercising it. The wisdom that comes from such a superior cannot be assumed to accord with what one already knows from previous study, however rigorous and satisfying, for, as Strauss emphasized, the disagreements of the wise and our unfitness to judge them are as apparent as the fact that between the wisdom of the wise and the folly of the foolish there is a vast gulf.

From such maxims flowed his manner of reading. The remarkable way he combines caution and boldness, counting and imagination, submission and interrogation, simplicity and suspicion gives the reader no method and no theory of hermeneutics.[7] It gives, instead, virtues to imitate. The best that the best theory could do would be to defend already good readers from bad theories, whereas a good example will sometimes arrest a youthful misreader and turn him around, for the young are more impressed with examples than arguments.

What Strauss thought of another modern manifestation of the quarrel of the makers (poets) and knowers (philosophers), namely, modern natural science, whose maxim "we know only what we make" unified making and knowing to the present point where the physicists have become unacknowledged Nietzscheans and where their project threatens the planet, must be divined from the few places where he indicates how Bacon qualifies, but does not oppose, Machiavelli's break with Socrates: how *fortuna* becomes a nature to be conquered, how the founder becomes an inventor, how the prince becomes a college of scientists, and how *virtù* becomes method, while all along the sights of human life are lowered still further; not virtue or wisdom or holiness, but security, convenience, and longer life are now to be counted as the proper relief of man's estate. In pointing to Bacon as the father and Machiavelli as the godfather of this project of knowing through experimental making and of doing so in order to master and remake nature, Strauss differs from Heidegger, who names Plato as the founder of the attempt to master Being and who, while able to show that this project cannot understand Being, seems unable to oppose it, for Being may as well choose to speak through the destruction of all forests as through a thinker walking quietly on a forest path.[8]

The quarrel of poetry and philosophy is connected to another that occupied the young Strauss and never ceased to concern him, one as old as philosophy and hard for moderns to understand: the question of piety, or of the relation of reason and revelation, or of Jerusalem and Athens, as Strauss often called it.[9] As Strauss observed, most men of today who like to call themselves thinking men would say, "We know there is no God." Strauss thought they presumed too much, that while it might be true that there were no sound proofs of God's existence, there were also no sound disproofs. For philosophy to become wisdom and give a complete account of the whole would be *the* disproof. Strauss said that philosophy had yet to do so. The connection of this question with the previous ones lies this way. According to Strauss, the ancient philosophers, most of them, realized that the city can never dispense with opinions, can never leave the cave, and hence cannot dispense with religion or the gods. Since the gods are the theme of the poets, at least the ancient poets, this means that the city will always need poetry, and since the philosophers cannot get along without the city, they must try to tame the poets. The moderns differ. They thought that not only could men live together without poetry, but that they would be more peaceful in public and more contented in private if they tried to. Strauss was aware of the fact that the ancient philosophers had to deal with the gods (and therefore with the poets), while the moderns had to deal with God. He also studied the biblical piety commanded by the God of the Jews, the God of the Muslims, and the God of the Christians, and the different fate of philosophizing in the communities formed by these three pieties, but he does not appear to have accepted the thesis that the origins of modernity can truly be traced to a supposed rebellion from Christianity that left the rebels still Christian at heart. In a striking phrase he speaks of Machiavelli, whom he regarded as the true founder of modernity, as being animated by "antitheological ire."[10] This might well be illustrated by the famous fifteenth chapter of the *Prince*: Is not Machiavelli's animus against ancient ideal republics really an animus against an excessive and unpolitical understanding of virtue, which flows from Christian teaching; Machiavelli allows anger at God to become anger at the good. In this want of discrimination Strauss saw a failure of philosophy to be philosophic. Duly ratified by later generations, this error has had immense and not wholly beneficial effects. It led to modern political philosophy and ideology and the modern scientific project. Each represents a unification of Jerusalem and Athens. Machiavellian teaching knows no higher admiration than admiration for the founder of whom it will later be said, "He had a divine preceptor." Unlike an ancient founder, but like the creative biblical God, he will treat every occasion as a material or chaos to be shaped as he pleases. Similarly, modern natural science presents a unification of Jerusalem and Athens. The highest being known to the former is a creative being; the highest being known to the latter is a knowing being. Modern science imitates both at once, for it makes in order to know and knows in order to remake better. Turning to the question of poetry and philosophy, here too Strauss thought that the modern union of admiration for the biblical God and admiration for reason (itself no longer understood as it had been by the ancients) had had a deleterious effect. Instead of being understood as imitation of nature, poetry came to be understood as creation and even creation *ex nihilo*. And in Nietzsche philosophy too became creative, and the fundamental and highest human activity, creative contemplation. In other words, the poet/*Übermensch* will be creative like God on the first six days and contemplative like Socrates, only all at once. Or rather contemplative like God on the seventh day, for he will contemplate what he has made; hence he cannot really be like Socrates. This last correction illustrates a point Strauss often stressed: All attempts to unify Jerusalem and Athens do at some decisive point sacrifice one or the other. Yet the struggle to unify them is the secret of the vitality of the West.

It would seem that the thing that unites all three of these quarrels or questions is philosophy, but this observation does not tell us which question was more fundamental for Strauss, perhaps because these questions are not finally separable. In a conversation between ancient Socrates and modern Nietzsche, the modern has the idea of the biblical God lurking in his teaching of will-to-power or creative contemplation. Likewise, in a conversation between Heidegger and Aristotle, the modern thinks of Being as creative and mysterious like the Holy God. In these moderns the quarrel of the ancients and moderns become a new form of the quarrel of philosophy and poetry; they take the side of poetry, Nietzsche championing tragic wisdom and later his own Zarathustra against Socrates, Heidegger championing Hölderlin and the pre-Socratics against the two thousand years of oblivion of Being inaugurated by the Greeks. How Strauss stood towards these thinkers is hard to say precisely. Perhaps the following thought accords with the commonsensical or rather erotic character of his thinking. The ancient Jews live in obedient fear of their Lord and Creator; the early moderns live in low fears, fear of death (Bacon) and fear of violent death (Hobbes); Nietzsche's joyful affirmation of becoming seems desperate; Heidegger lives first in dread and later in expectation; but the ancients lived in wonder. Wonder seems to be a mean between wisdom and stupidity; it seems to combine lacking and having; it knows too little to be wise and too much to stop loving. The *eros* in wonder cannot be an utter lack; just as dread must presuppose a knowing attachment to something, so wonder presupposes a knowing affection. If wonder is combined with certainty of Creation, it implies or becomes gratitude. In any case, wonder implies knowledge and for the philosopher such wondering includes the knowledge that the way of life which is devoted to it is the best. In this way ignorance of answers to the first questions is combined with certainty about the vital question of the best way of life and thereby with politics, for lives are lived with others and are either promoted or impeded by the various political regimes, which are all answers to the question: What is the best way of life?

If this account of these three quarrels or questions and their relation in Strauss's work is accurate, then those who wish to pursue first philosophy will find in Leo Strauss someone already conversing with them. They will, however, miss what he is saying if they are impatient with his attention to human, and therefore political, things, including such things as the crisis of the West, or if they discount his attention as a gift-giving, more charitable than true. His contention that political philosophy is the kernel of philosophy explains his attention and his way of writing not as exoteric but as philosophic; in attending to human things he, like Socrates, did not become less philosophic, but more so. Or as he writes at the end of the "Restatement" in the first edition of *On Tyranny* (1954, in French):

> In our discussion, the conflict between the two opposed basic presuppositions has barely been mentioned. But we have always been mindful of it. For we both apparently turned away from Being to Tyranny because we have seen that those who lacked the courage to face the issue of Tyranny, who therefore *et humiliter serviebant et superbe dominabantur*, were forced to evade the issue of Being as well, precisely because they did nothing but talk of Being.[11]

"Those who lack the courage" would seem to refer to Heidegger and include Sartre. The "we" he speaks of is himself and Alexander Kojève. A footnote of Strauss's to a book he published in 1936 tells us that he and his friend "M. Alexandre Kojevnikoff" intend to write something together.[12] That this friendship and this writing together became their exchange on tyranny[13] underlines something peculiar about Strauss, something he shares with Nietzsche and a few others: He never convinced any of his coevals to share his momentous discoveries. Becoming the Strauss who was Strauss meant parting from the friends of his youth and young manhood.

What made Strauss Strauss? Perhaps the least misleading answer will emerge if we ask who Strauss loved most. The answer must be Socrates. Strauss devoted more books to Socrates than to any other figure. Although he devoted his mature energies to the moderns and seemed to turn to Socrates late, in his old age, Socrates is present in his books on the moderns as a silent onlooker, superior in heart and in mind, whom Strauss knew he would meet up ahead, because he had met him before at the beginning of his ascent. When did Strauss become Strauss? When did Strauss discover Socrates?[14] Perhaps a clue is supplied by the story of how the young Strauss, after a day of reading in the Prussian State Library, would go to a cafe on Unter den Linden and pronounce the name "Nietzsche" loud enough to be heard at the other tables.[15] Was the young Strauss a Burckhardt with pranks? Did he decide to become a Basel Professor rather than a god? Did he lack the nerve to become a Nietzsche? Or did he always remain a Nietzschean, mild-mannered and politic by day, in prefaces and epilogues, but burning with immoderate thoughts in the deep, deep night, a Nietzsche with the mask of Burckhardt? It is hard to say. Such chimerical formulas fail to grasp his ipsissimosity. In Nietzsche, Strauss surely discovered the immoderation of philosophy, but in Nietzsche, especially the late Nietzsche, he also met the love of his life, Socrates. According to Nietzsche, Socrates saw Athens sickening, administered the new medicines of logic and dialectic, but in the end confessed life itself the sickness. Socrates tried to reconcile the city and the philosopher, but he failed. He wanted to reconcile truth and life, but instead he lived esoterically, not saying to others what he said to himself. In this esoteric Socrates of Nietzsche, Strauss could have discovered the clue to esoteric writing;[16] it is hard to say that he did, for his later studies of the Jewish and Islamic philosophers emphasize persecution and the art of writing, whereas the esotericism of Nietzsche's Socrates has nothing to do with either persecution or writing. What Strauss certainly found in Nietzsche and his Socrates is the Socratic question of truth and life. But the most satisfying answer, the Socratic answer, which may only be a better way of putting the question, Strauss found only later in the ancient Socrates, especially as described by Xenophon. The ancient Socrates is superior to Nietzsche and to his Socrates in both practical wisdom and solitude because he has found the least unsatisfactory reconciliation of philosophy and the city.

Once Strauss became Strauss there was no chance he might become a Nietzsche. And yet Strauss said the secret of the West was the tension between philosophy and theology, not the tension between philosophy and poetry.

Although the Strauss who was Strauss had no friend—at the level of someone he would have considered writing together with—he had an extraordinary number of devoted students, especially after his move to the University of Chicago; according to one estimate they now, including devoted students of his students unto a third generation, number over a thousand. The man who convinced none of his coevals convinced an extraordinary number of the brightest and most manly, indeed changed their lives. How much is a philosopher responsible for his students or disciples? A hard question. In answer to a related question, "How much are you responsible for the transcripts of your classes?," Strauss replied to me, "About as much as God is said to be responsible for evil or a world with evil."[17]

When one thinks of Strauss's books on politics, of how he was so careful in his courses to keep within departmental limits, how he battled against positivism in the political science profession, how he read Hegel's *Science of Logic* at home at night, how he admired the great statesmen, especially Churchill, how his description of the Battle of the Ancients and the Moderns stirs a young man's fighting spirit and how ready one is to fight for the Liberty of the West, to go down "guns blazing and flags flying," then one is inclined to slight his abiding concern for first philosphy, for "Being", as he says; one is inclined to remember Strauss's Quarrels and forget his questions, to join the City and forget about man.

And when one follows the manly path of his sentences, his steady ascents, his sudden dashes to a peak, or his equally sudden descents to some depth, when a single remark of his goes to the very heart of a matter that has long puzzled one, or when he makes something simple remarkable as well, when reading Strauss makes one get up and walk about the room, when all cares vanish in the bliss of thinking, and one is attached only to detachment, then one is inclined to ask the Questions and forget the quarrels, remember Man and forget all cities, men, and meals.

Although Strauss is responsible for both these feelings in his reader, he is not to be held responsible for any quarrel in which his *thymos* is set against his *eros*.[18] Neither "Let Socrates drink hemlock" nor "Let Athens perish" were his maxims. He never forgot the Questions for the Quarrels or the Quarrels for the Questions; he never slighted the Man for the City or the City for Man. He encouraged both interpretation and statesmanship. He studied Nietzsche and admired Churchill.[19] Without mistaking it for Athens or Sparta, he supported America. Socrates, the first political philosopher, has had important modern admirers: Montaigne, Hegel, Kierkegaard, and Nietzsche; but none who was a political philosopher, like Socrates, until Strauss.

Perhaps this accounts for an extraordinary omission in his work; Strauss never wrote on tragedy or on a tragedy, only on comedy and comedies. Was this because life is never a tragedy to a philospher, who is more likely to laugh twice or thrice at life than to cry twice or thrice over it. Did Strauss never weep? His discovery of natural right shines against a darkening night that makes his reticence brave. Strauss did not write of tragedy because he always wrote of it. The Battle of the Ancients and the Moderns was for him a Peloponnesian War of the West that he, like Thucydides, both recorded and fought in. The West became the West when Socrates warned the city what it owes the philosopher and the philosopher what he owes the city, with a single deed that summed up his life: his death. The Socratic reconciliation of the city and man is tragic, for it is naturally right that natural right shine brightest in a deed most contrary to natural right; that Socrates killed and had himself killed so as to found the West shows that natural right is the ground not only of practical wisdom and esotericism but of tragedy.

Quid sit deus? Although we do not know God, we do know that the best way of life for man is philosophy. We do not know the whole; in the dark, dark night our sun is a speck, yet this speck sheds enough light for a man to guide himself, to see donkeys, dogs and mules, and the difference between the one and the many. Indeed, against the darkness of the whole, what is visible shines brighter, just as our virtues shine brighter in defeat or adversity, like the campfires of the Greeks before Troy, where the West began by recognizing that we are our virtues. One people may bury, another may burn their dead, but fire burns Troy as it may burn Ithaka. The recognition of the essentially human character of the virtues is based upon the distinction of natural kinds, first noticed in the West by Homer when in the *Odyssey* he has his Hermes show Odysseus the nature of the *moly* that will protect him from losing his human shape despite the charm of Circe. Leo Strauss was fond of pointing to this passage as the beginning of philosophy.[20]

Notes

1. His thoughts on these things appear in his argument with Kojève in *On Tyranny* (Ithaca: Cornell University Press, 1963). See also their letters being published in the *Independent Journal of Philosophy*. Photocopies of the thirty-eight missives from Strauss to Kojève, which Michael Roth found in Kojève's library,

are said to have been deposited in the Strauss Archive at the University of Chicago Library (Regenstein).

2.   His deliberate emphasis on the political would remind one of Machiavelli if it were not for the fact that he may be described as a counter-Machiavelli, for his emphasis is always guided by an admiration for Socrates, something that makes him resemble Xenophon, whose taciturnity he increasingly imitated in his later works.

3.   Consider those places in his *Natural Right and History* (Chicago: University of Chicago Press, 1953), where he speaks of radical historicism; by it he means chiefly Heidegger, as Hilail Gildin has noted in his Introduction to *Political Philosophy: Six Essays by Leo Strauss* (Indianapolis: Bobbs-Merrill, 1975); see also Strauss's essay "Philosophy as Rigorous Science and Political Philosophy," *Interpretation* 2:1; his essay on "Kurt Riezler" *What Is Political Philosophy?* (New York: Free Press, 1959); and his unpublished lectures on "Existentialism" and on the "Problem of Socrates." Both Richard Kennington's "Strauss's *Natural Right and History*," *Review of Metaphysics* 35 (September 1981) and Seth Benardete's "Leo Strauss' *The City and Man*," *Political Science Reviewer* (1979) interpret the mentioned works according to the canons of interpretation they learned from Strauss.

4.   This theme is treated in his *Socrates and Aristophanes* (New York: Basic Books, 1966), but might be somewhat better appreciated if Strauss's classes on Plato's *Symposium* and on Nietzsche's *Zarathustra* were published. Strauss wrote on only one poet, Aristophanes; though he thought about others, especially Shakespeare, it is hard to know what he thought of their contribution to the question of poetry and philosophy. Is not Shakespeare a greater champion of poetry than Aristophanes? Did he not write both comedy and tragedy, as Socrates affirmed possible? And did he not write history as well? Does not the fact that he never quarrelled with Socrates or, for that matter, with the city, indicate that he at least brought the quarrel of poetry and philosophy to an end, one as sweet as noble, to employ his favorite adjectives?

5.   See also the essay, "The Three Waves of Modernity," which he wrote for the Gildin collection mentioned above in note 3.

6.   Unless what he says about nationalism in his essay on Kurt Riezler allows us to infer his view.

7.   In this respect his view accords with the ironic title of Hans-Georg Gadamer's *Wahrheit und Methode* (Tubingen: Mohr, 1960); for differences see their correspondence in *The Independent Journal of Philosophy* vol. 2 and Gadamer's later response to Strauss in his second edition, second appendix.

8.   Strauss admired *The Abolition of Man* (New York: Macmillan, 1947) by C. S. Lewis; the arguments Lewis offers in its third part against the coming biological engineering seem to accord with Strauss's thought; these arguments figure importantly in the work, currently addressed to such innovations, of Paul Ramsey, Hans Jonas, and Leon Kass. See especially the latter's *Toward a More Natural Science* (Free Press, 1985).

9. See his *Philosophie und Gesetz* (1935) translated into English by Fred Bauman (New York: Jewish Publication Society, 1987). See his "On the Interpretation of Genesis" published in *L'Homme*, vol. 21, no. 1 (January-March 1981), pp. 5–20, his "Mutual Influence of Theology and Philosophy," *Independent Journal of Philosophy III* (1979), and his "Progress or Return?: The Contemporary Crisis in Western Civilization," *Modern Judaism* 1: 17–45.

10. *What Is Political Philosophy?*, 44.

11. One would like to know why this paragraph did not appear in the English version (1959). The whole last two pages of the "original" French version did not appear in the English published later. The "original" French is not, it seems, original, for it is said to be translated from the English by Hélène Kern. Here is the whole passage:

Tout ce que je puis espérer avoir démontré en m'opposant à la thèse de Kojève en ce qui concerne la relation entre la tyrannie et la sagesse, c'est que la thèse de Xénophon sur ce grave sujet n'est pas seulement compatible avec l'idée de la philosophie, mais réclamée par elle. Ceci est très peu de chose, car la question se pose immédiatement de savoir si l'idée de la philosophie n'a pas elle-même besoin de légitimation. La philosophie au sens strict et classique est la recherche de l'ordre éternel ou de la cause ou des causes éternelles de toutes choses. Je suppose alors qu'il y a un ordre éternel et inchangeable dans lequel l'Histoire prend place, et qui n'est, en aucune manière, affecté par l'Histoire. Cela laisse supposer, en d'autres termes, que tout «royaume de Liberté» n'est pas plus qu'une province qui dépend du «royaume de la Fatalité». Cela présuppose, dans les termes de Kojève, que «l'Être est essentiellement immuable en lui-même et éternellement identique à lui-même». Cette hypothèse n'est pas évidente par elle-même; Kojève la rejette en faveur de l'idée que «l'Être se crée lui-même au cours de l'Histoire», ou que l'Être le plus élevé est la Société et l'Historie, ou que l'éternité n'est rien que la totalité du Temps historique, c'est-à-dire limité. Sur la base de l'hypothèse classique, une distinction radicale doit être faite entre les conditions et les sources de la compréhension, entre les conditions de l'existence et de la poursuite de la philosophie (sociétés d'une certaine sorte, etc.) et les sources de la connaissance philosophique. Sur la base des hypothèses de Kojève, cette distinction perd sa signification la plus importante: le changement social ou le hasard affectent l'être s'il n'est pas identique à l'Être, et, par là, il affecte la vérité. Sur la base des hypothèses de Kojève, un attachement absolu aux intérêts humains devient la source de la connaissance philosophique: l'homme doit se sentir absolument chez lui sur la terre; il doit être absolument un citoyen de la terre, sinon un citoyen d'une partie de la terre inhabitable. Sur les bases des hypothèses classiques, la philosophie exige un détachement radical des intérêts humains: l'homme ne doit pas être absolument chez lui sur terre, il doit être citoyen de l'ensemble. Dans notre discussion, le conflit entre les deux hypothèses fondamentales opposées a à peine été mentionné. Mais nous y avons toujours été attentif, car nous nous détournons tous deux, en apparence, de l'Être pour nous tourner vers la tyrannie, parce que nous avons vu que ceux qui manquent de courage pour braver les conséquences de la tyrannie, qui, par conséquent *et humiliter serviebant et superbe dominabantur*, étaient forcés de s'évader tout autant des conséquences de l'Être, précisément parce qu'ils ne faisaient rien d'autre que parler de l'Être.

12.   *The Political Philosophy of Hobbes* (Oxford: Clarendon Press, 1936), 58n: "M. Alexandre Kojevnikoff and the writer intend to undertake a detailed investigation of the connection between Hegel and Hobbes."

13.   Not that becoming "best enemies" means you are no longer friends.

14.   In a letter to me, Nahum Glatzer says that Strauss exchanged "classes" on Plato for "classes" on Abravanel in 1924 in Frankfort.

15.   Leo Strauss, "An Unspoken Prologue to a Public Lecture at St. John's," *Interpretation*, vol. 7, no. 3, 1–2.

16.   Consider *Jenseits von Gut and Böse*, 30, a passage Strauss dwelt on in at least one of his courses and did not dwell on, or even mention, in his "Note on the Plan of Nietzsche's *Beyond Good and Evil*," *Interpretation*, vol 3, nos. 2 and 3. I have reserved for separate study this very rhymed, reasoned and numbered piece. In considering the place of Nietzsche in Strauss's thought and in the formation of that thought, one should note that it is Nietzsche and not Heidegger who is the third of "The Three Waves of Modernity," an essay that appears in the Gildin collection mentioned above. That Nietzsche is there characterized as the deepest, the richest, and perhaps the last of the moderns suggests that Strauss' relation to him is his relation to modernity. Certainly one is provoked by this sketch to ask how Strauss understood his relation to the third wave.

17.   I would like to thank the Dartmouth College Research Committee for allowing me to count meeting a scholar as my scholarly meeting for 1970. By the next year, when they refused, meeting Strauss had made the distinction between a philosopher and a scholar sufficiently evident.

18.   For a marvelously simple, instructive, and subtle discussion of *eros*, *thymos* and their relation, I am indebted (so I hope) to Steward Umphrey's "*Eros* and *Thumos*," *Interpretation*, vol 10, no. 2 and 3, 353–422.

19.   The connection Strauss saw between Nietzsche's criticism of modernity and Churchill's great-souled virtue is most explicit in his unpublished lecture "German Nihilism" delivered at the New School on 26 February 1941.

20.   If so, then philosophy begins in comedy and yet upon emerging quarreled with its origin; by pitting Socrates against Achilleus, Plato distracts us from the contrast between Odysseus, who prefers home and a mortal woman to immortality, and Socrates, who says he does not. Comic Odysseus seems to achieve a reconciliation between man and the city that Socrates cannot. A draft of a portion of this essay was circulated in the *Newsletter* of the Politics Department at the University of Dallas in 1978. It was completed on a fellowship from the Humboldt Foundation.

Second Section

ON NATURAL RIGHT

Victor Gourevitch

THE PROBLEM OF NATURAL RIGHT
AND THE FUNDAMENTAL ALTERNATIVES
IN *NATURAL RIGHT AND HISTORY*

I

Natural Right and History,[1] Strauss's most comprehensive and complete statement of his views, takes "the crisis of liberal democracy" as its point of departure (pp. 1–8). I therefore turn to it in the hope of achieving a measure of clarity about the theme of this conference.

The surface structure of the book is straightforward and simple. It very naturally divides into three sections, with two chapters in each section: The first section deals with the modern challenge to natural right and to philosophy in the traditional sense; the second examines the classical reflections on the premises of philosophy and of natural right; the last reviews the modern reinterpretation of philosophy and of natural right, and the difficulties that attend these reinterpretations. The dramatic pattern is clear: An overview of present problems introduces a flashback to the beginnings, followed by an account of the reversal that apparently inevitably brought about the present plight. The book thus forms a circle: The first chapter begins where the last chapter leaves off, with the crisis of modern natural right.[2]

Strauss sees that crisis manifesting itself first in the thought of Rousseau and of Burke, developing through a stage of what he calls "theoretical historicism," that is, the teaching of the "historical school," and coming to a head in what he calls "radical (existentialist) historicism," namely, the teachings of Nietzsche and especially of Heidegger (pp. 26–32). Historicism holds that "all philosophizing essentially belongs to a 'historical world,' 'culture,' 'civilization,' 'Weltanschauung.'" (p. 12). The evidence for this view is said to be provided by "the experience of history," the recognition that people in different times and places have differed about what is true or good or just. Yet that much has clearly always been known. What is called "the experience of history" is, then, not a new experience, but is rather a new and specifically philosophical interpretation of a universal and thoroughly

30

familiar experience (pp. 10, 19f., 32, 33, and consider pp. 97–101). Whereas theoretical historicism appeals to "the experience of history" to deny the relevance of universal principles or norms (pp. 14, 15), radical historicism appeals to it to deny even their existence (pp. 17f.). It thus rejects the very possibility of philosophy in the traditional sense of the term (pp. 29f.), and hence it in particular rejects the possibility of natural right. It holds that philosophy, as it was traditionally understood, rests on the presumably arbitrary premise that "the whole" or "being" is at least in principle knowable, and that this premise, in turn, rests on the presumably arbitrary premise that "to be" in the emphatic sense means both "to be always" and "to be intelligible" (pp. 30f.). Radical historicism rejects these premises. It denies that "to be" can mean "to be always," because it holds that where there are no human beings there can be no being; in addition, it denies that "to be" preeminently means "to be intelligible," because it holds that all thought is ultimately under the sway of a blind or, in any event, inscrutable fate (pp. 32, 19f., 21, 26–31).[3]

Strauss rejects these radical historicist conclusions. He does not so much defend the premises which it challenges as he challenges the premises on which it proceeds. "The experience of history" does not , in his view, provide an adequate starting point. It is too derivative and too ambiguous for that. He thinks it less problematic to start with "our common-sense or natural understanding of our common-sense or natural world" and instead of speaking about "being" or about the "whole" which is "always" or "intelligible," to speak about a "framework" of "fundamental riddles" or "fundamental problems and alternatives," which is "unchanging" or "coeval with human thought." Nothing more is required for philosophy "in the original, Socratic sense."[4] Strauss does not deny the persistent disagreements to which historicism calls attention. He does deny that these disagreements warrant the historicist conclusion that they could not be resolved or that the problems at issue in them could not be elucidated. On the contrary, it seems to him that any disagreement clearly implies that the parties to it in effect agree that they are disagreeing about the same problem and that, therefore, such disagreements establish at least the presumption that clarity about that problem and the possible solutions to it can be achieved. Philosophy understood as the quest for clarity about the persistent, fundamental problems and alternatives is manifestly a form of scepticism. But precisely because it is a form of scepticism, it remains open to the possibility that the problems can be solved, and it therefore continues to strive for their solution (pp. 29f.). Historicism, and especially radical historicism, appears also to be a form of scepticism. But that appearance is misleading. For radical historicism categorically rejects the very possibility of an "unchanging framework" of "fundamental problems" that might, at least in principle, be always and everywhere accessible; it *a fortiori* rejects even the in-principle possibility that the problems admit of solution (pp. 21, 29). Historicism, but especially radical historicism, proves to be a form of dogmatism, "the form in which dogmatism likes to appear in our age" (pp. 22, cp. 20).

One may, of course, accept the antihistoricist suggestion of an "unchanging framework" of permanent problems and yet reject the suggestion that these problems must, at least in principle, admit of resolution. That is the alternative which, in Strauss's view, Max Weber adopted (p. 36). The heading of the chapter he devotes to Weber, "Natural Right and the Distinction Between Facts and Values," might lead the reader to expect a discussion of the view which together with existentialist historicism, was widely regarded as the major contender for philosophical notice, namely positivism. But Strauss does not discuss positivism in *Natural Right and History*. He traces Weber's influential view that we cannot resolve what he calls "conflicts of ultimate values" to his conviction that the most fundamental of these conflicts is the conflict between reason and revelation. Reason cannot resolve that conflict, for reason is a party to it. Reason can therefore also not resolve any of the other conflicts of values, for they are ultimately only forms of that most general conflict. The very appeal to reason is thus made to appear arbitrary (pp. 62f., 66, 70–76). On Strauss's reading, Weber's "irreconcilable conflict of ultimate values" proves to be only the most influential recent form of the fundamental and "permanent" problem of "Athens or Jerusalem." Weber poses that problem in a particularly radical form. However, Strauss refuses to be drawn into a discussion of it. For, quite independently of the possibility of revelation, we may and must seek to understand our life and our world as they are known to common sense, and he charges Weber with not even attempting to do so.[5]

Strauss criticizes Weber on essentially the same grounds on which he criticizes Heidegger: Both men fail to attend to our prescientific or prephilosophical understanding of our natural world. That understanding is not always and everywhere fully and immediately accessible. For the world in which we now live is permeated through and through by philosophy and science. Yet science and philosophy presuppose the prescientific or prephilosophic understanding. The attempt to recover that understanding must therefore take the form of historical studies of a sort. They will be nonhistoricist historical studies precisely because they will remain open to the possibility of a common sense or natural understanding of our common sense or natural world. By remaining open to that possibility, they also remain open to the possibility of philosophy. For philosophy is "the perfection of the natural understanding." The nonhistoricist study of the prephilosophical understanding is, then, directly continuous with the nonhistoricist study of the history of philosophy. A nonhistoricist history of philosophy would lay bare that "unchanging framework" of the "fundamental problems and, therewith, of the fundamental alternatives regarding their solution that are coeval with human thought" (pp. 32, cp. 23f., 35). In other words, a nonhistoricist history of philosophy would, for all intents and purposes, be a taxonomy of the permanent problems and alternatives. Such a history might, for example, take as a model the "history" of philosophy in the first book of Aristotle's *Metaphysics* (p. 28 n. 10).

As soon as *Natural Right and History* is viewed in the light of that program, the systematic structure underlying its dramatic surface becomes visible. The "fundamental problem" of natural right is: "what—if any—are the universal and unchanging standards of justice accessible to the unaided human reason?" The necessary condition for even raising that problem is that, at least, in principle, it be possible to achieve universally valid knowledge; and the necessary condition for asserting natural right is that at least this one fundamental problem can be definitively solved in a universally valid way (pp. 24, 28). In the first section of the book, Strauss reviews two reasons for rejecting the very possibility of natural right: radical historicism and revelation, albeit revelation very idiosyncratically interpreted. More specifically, radical historicism rejects the possibility of natural right by rejecting the premise of a permanent framework of problems and alternatives and hence the possibility of philosophy in the traditional sense. Weber, on the other hand, rejects the possibility of natural right by rejecting the possibility of solving the problem of right on the grounds that any rational solution of that problem could be invalidated or overridden by revelation. Strauss does not specifically say or argue that these are the only or even the most serious reasons for rejecting the possibility of philosophy and hence of natural right. He does not need to do so. For clearly they are: They exhaust the alternatives.

II

In the second and central section of *Natural Right and History*, Strauss goes on to detail the taxonomy of the problem of right on the premise that philosophy and hence natural right may be possible. He begins by drawing a distinction between the prephilosophical world and the world in which there is philosophy. The natural, prescientific world is ordered in terms of the different beings' "ways" or "customs." Characteristically, a special privilege attaches to "our" customs and ways, especially to our most authoritative, because oldest, customs and ways, and to their roots or causes, the gods (pp. 83f.). In the prescientific, prephilosophic or common sense world, no distinction exists, or at least no tension arises between the good and the right or just. The ancestral or divine things are the first things, and the right and the good are accordingly equated with the ancestral or the divine. With the "discovery" of nature and hence the "emergence" of philosophy (pp. 81, 82, 90, 93; 91), the philosophers cease to understand the beings in terms of their ways or customs and come to understand them, instead, in terms of the distinction between nature and convention (p. 90, cp. 7). Philosophy radically reinterprets the prephilosophic understanding. But it does not originally break with the themes and concerns of the prephilosophic understanding, and Strauss takes pains to indicate the continuity between the two: The philosophical quest for the first things is continuous with the privilege that the prephilosophic understanding attaches to the ancestral and the divine; the philosophical understanding of nature in terms of kinds refines the prephilosophic understanding in terms of the beings' ways; the philosophical distinction between nature and convention develops the prephilosophic distinctions between the evidence of things seen in contrast to hearsay and that between man-made things in contrast to things that are not man-made (pp. 86–89, 91–93). Philosophy may thus be said originally to be "the perfection of the natural understanding" (pp. 78f., 124 cp. 174f., 179). The expression might suggest that the prephilosophic understanding will, by some natural necessity, invariably discover nature and hence philosophy, and so "perfect" itself, that philosophy is the actualization of a potentiality. Strauss very clearly refuses to go that far. He refuses to speak of philosophy as a potentiality. He speaks of it as no more than a possibility, and he refuses to subscribe to the classics' understanding of it as a permanent possibility.[6] He evidently sees the discovery of nature and of philosophy as most exceptional, if not unique, and he would regard any assurance that if they were lost they would be rediscovered as a very grave threat to them. But regardless of whether and in what sense philosophy might be said to be a permanent possibility, the prephilosophical understanding of the prephilosophical world, and especially its equation of the good and the right with the ancestral or divine, certainly does remain, in one guise or another, a permanent alternative and, indeed, a permanent given. The prephilosophical understanding may be affected by the discovery of nature and of philosophy (pp. 82, 90, 91), but it is not eliminated by that discovery. On the contrary, the prephilosophic and the philosophic understanding now reveal themselves as rivals, the opposing terms in the alternative authority/reason (p. 92) or, in a modified form, in the alternative Jerusalem/Athens.[7] As the philosophers reinterpret what it means to be "first," they replace the received equation of the good with the ancestral or divine, with the equation of the good with the natural. All, or nearly all, of the philosophers further agree that the good life is the life according to nature (p. 95), and they agree that the life according to nature is the philosophic life (pp. 11f., 151; 164; 110, 112, 113). The philosophers thus agree in effectively demoting the life traditionally regarded as the good life, the life of the citizen-gentleman with its distinctive excellence, justice. However, the philosophers evidently disagree about the relation between the two ways of life; they evidently disagree about the place of justice in the good life; in particular, they evidently disagree about whether justice is inherently good and desirable or not, about whether it is natural or conventional (pp. 93, 95).[8]

Strauss distinguishes between two forms of conventionalism: philosophic conventionalism, i.e. the position of the pre-Socratics and of the philosophical Epicureans, to which he sometimes simply refers as "Epicureanism";[9] and vulgar conventionalism, i.e. the position represented by the Sophists (pp. 114–17). Among the philosophical proponents of the view that right is natural or, more precisely, that there is natural right, he discerns three distinct tendencies: the Socratic-Platonic-Stoic (p. 146), the Aristotelian (p. 156), and the Thomist (p. 163). As he notes, each of these tendencies asserts natural right more unconditionally than did its predecessor.[10] Sometimes he, for simplicity's sake, ignores these differences and refers to all forms of adherence to natural right as "Platonism."

In sum:

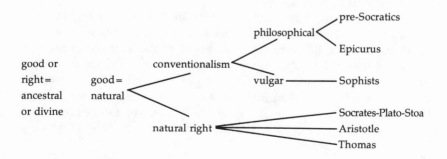

The two most general criteria by which Strauss here sorts the alternatives are: the presence or absence of philosophy, and the affirmation or denial of natural right. His first cut therefore distinguishes between the prephilosophical and what might by contrast perhaps be called the philosophical condition. No further distinctions are called for in the prephilosophical condition, since here the relation between the good and the right is unproblematic. It becomes a problem in the philosophical context. His second cut therefore distinguishes between the philosophers who deny natural right or that the just is good, i.e. the "Epicureans," and the philosophers who affirm natural right, i.e. the "Platonists." Although the Epicureans or conventionalists deny natural right, they do not deny philosophy; they thus deny natural right on essentially different grounds than do the historicists (pp. 11f., 177 n.11). The distinction between "Epicureans" and "Platonists" results from sorting in terms of "the problem of natural right." Strauss does not indicate whether sorting in terms of some other "fundamental problem" would result in the same classification. It certainly seems likely that it would. For the "secular struggle" between Epicureanism and Platonism (p. 170) is, after all, also "the secular struggle between materialism and spiritualism" (p. 174). Strauss evidently thinks that *both* positions are exposed to insuperable objections.[11] But he does not discuss this issue. Nor does he discuss the possible order or economy of the problems, except as it appears in the perspective of the problem of justice. Now the first distinction, that between the pre-philosophical and the philosophical condition, also applies *mutatis mutandis* within the philosophical condition or context, and Strauss accordingly distinguishes between philosophical and vulgar conventionlism. However, he does not draw a parallel distinction regarding the natural right doctrines. It is not immediately evident how that omission is to be understood: Is there no philosophical classical natural right teaching, or is there no vulgar classical natural right teaching?

Before considering that question it may be helpful to complete this brief summary of the action of *Natural Right and History*. The next episode also marks the peripeteia: Hobbes effects a synthesis of the two classical philosophical alternatives, Platonism and Epicureanism (p. 170), and "thus became the creator of political hedonism, a doctrine which has revolutionized human life everywhere on a scale never yet approached by any other teaching" (p. 169). Strauss devotes the third and final section of the book to the study of this reversal and of its most immediate consequences.

Strauss understands Hobbes as being primarily concerned with over-coming the exceedingly demanding and tentative, in short the "uto-pian" character of the classical natural right teaching, and with pro-viding instead a "realistic" or "Machiavellian" natural right teaching firmly buttressed by a science proof against "the cavils of the sceptics" (pp. 171–75, 178, 179, 190). The principle of this science is the equation of knowing with making: Knowledge is man's free construction in the service of his needs and desires (pp. 175, 176f.). By reducing knowledge or science to construction and by placing it in the service of man's needs and desires, that is to say, by subordinating reason to the passions, Hob-bes radically breaks with the one feature that the alternatives he is syn-thesizing have in common: the view that nature is the standard and that theory—and hence the theoretical or philosophical life—enjoys un-qualified priority (pp. 11, 177 n. 11). Hobbes's denial of the traditional priority of nature and of theory goes hand in hand with his denial of the traditional priority of the good in relation to the right.[12] With these moves, Hobbes effectively "politicizes" philosophy. One consequence of this politicization was that the crisis of his natural right teaching became a crisis of philosophy as such.[13]

As told in *Natural Right and History*, the history of philosophy since Hobbes is either an elaboration of Hobbes' teaching—for example by Locke—or a succession of attempts to come to terms with difficulties to which it gives rise—first by Rousseau, then by Burke, then by the historical school, and finally by the radical historicists. A fuller study of Strauss's critique of historicism, and in particular of his premise that the fun-damental alternatives are in principle always accessible, would have to attend especially carefully to the final chapter of *Natural Right and His-tory*. In that chapter Strauss presents Rousseau and Burke as severe critics of what they see as the defects in Hobbes's natural right teaching, critics who make every effort to correct these defects by returning to classical models, but who only succeed in exacerbating the crisis they had set out to resolve. The failure of even great thinkers to achieve what they set out to achieve does not prove that they set themselves an impossible task. But it does lend a certain plausibility to the radical historicist claim that the bases of our thought may not be fully accessible to us. The story or argument that Strauss unfolds in *Natural Right and History* in refuta-tion of historicism thus tends to bear strong witness in its behalf. Be that as it may. The clear aim of the book remains to illustrate and to articulate at least one fundamental problem within the—but most particularly within its—permanent framework: natural right, or the relations between the good, the pleasant, the noble, the just; and insofar as the problem of natural right bears on them, the relations between nature and convention; to articulate the fundamental philosophical and non-philosophical alternatives with respect to that problem, i.e., Platonism and Epicurianism, and their vulgar variants, to situate these alternatives within the broader alternative, i.e., prephilosophical, philosophical, and antiphilosophical understanding; and to show that the problems and the alternatives are, in principle, always and everywhere accessible.[14]

The question thus inevitably arises, "Is the Hobbesian synthesis a new alternative, is it a 'discovery,' or is it an 'invention'?" Strauss raises the question twice, and both times he leaves it open (pp. 173, 174, cp. 172). The mere fact that he is clearly critical of Hobbes's teaching is, of course, not a sufficient reason to disqualify it as an alternative, and the case *for* regarding it as one is very strong indeed. For Strauss's Hobbes sees the task of philosophy in terms very similar to those in which Strauss himself sees it: to overcome the alternative "Platonism"/"Epi-cureanism" while preserving and, if possible, putting on a firmer footing both philosphy and natural right. Yet Strauss rejects the Hobbesian synthesis. It is not a "discovery" or a third alternative. It cannot account for itself. Its account of the relationship between the prephilosophical and the philosophical understanding is inco-herent and so, therefore, is its account of the whole. Any account based on the subordination of nature is necessarily incoherent (pp. 173 n. 9, 201, 230, 271 n. 37, 272). The subordination of nature is, furthermore, ultimately responsible for the politicization of philosophy (pp. 11, 176f.). He gives no hint of any sympathy with Hobbes's or with Hobbes's suc-cessors' efforts on behalf of a natural right that might stand as a hedge against man's inhumanity to man. The price for such efforts was and, he appears to believe, necessarily is the politicization of philosophy. It is an excessive price. For in the last analysis, man's humanity consists in "the humanizing quest for the eternal order," and the subordination of that quest to even noble aims inevitably leads to a dehumanization (p. 34). Strauss fully recognizes what, on this view, his effort to depoliticize philosophy entails. He fully recognizes that to maintain, as he does, that Hobbes's defense of natural right at the expense of philosophy is not a permanent alternative, but that Epicurus's defense of philosophy at the expense of natural right *is* one, is tantamount to saying that when faced with the choice between the two, he chooses the latter. As if to underscore the point, he concludes his Hobbes discussion with the "philosophic poet's" warning that try as we may to drive out nature, it always returns victorious (pp. 201f.).[15] That philosophic poet was an Epicurean.

III

What, then, is Strauss's view regarding natural right? Or, more cautiously and precisely, what is the status of natural right in *Natural Right and History*? The only natural right alternative left standing is classical natural right or "Platonism." Classical natural right takes its bearings by man's ends or perfection. It views how men live in the light of how they ought to live. It therefore attends to duties more than it attends to rights. It takes its clue regarding men's natural end or perfection from the hierarchy of the wants. It proceeds on the assumption that the hierarchy of the wants corresponds to the hierarchy of the ends (p. 127). Strauss recognizes that that is a most problematic assumption. It is most immediately problematic because men's wants do not obviously form a clear, single hierarchy. The perfection of man as a rational being, the philosophic life and its distinctive virtue—wisdom or the pursuit of wisdom—is one thing; the perfection of man as a sociable being, the political life and its distinctive virtue—justice—is another. If, then, "natural right" is the name for "the rules circumscribing the general character of the good life" (p. 127), the question arises whether the rules circumscribing the general character of a life oriented toward wisdom are the same as the rules circumscribing the general character of a life oriented toward justice; in other words, the question arises whether the term *natural right* is not equivocal. Now Strauss, following his classical models, consistently maintains that, according to the natural hierarchy of wants or ends, the perfection of man as a rational being, wisdom or the pursuit of wisdom, and hence the philosophic life, is highest. For the fundamental problems are accessible to man as man, and "man is so constituted that he can find his satisfaction, his bliss, in free investigation, in articulating the riddle of being" (p. 75, cp. 164, 143). Insofar as articulating the riddle of being constitutes man's humanity, one might even speak of "cosmic support" for man's humanity.[16] The question regarding the status of natural right then takes the form: does wisdom or the pursuit of wisdom require a just civil order or moral virtue? Strauss, following his classical models, repeatedly indicates that it does not (pp. 151f., 164). If it does not, the further question arises: Has justice, narrowly and properly so called, a natural basis independent of the place it may occupy in the economy of the philosophic life? Strauss evidently does not think that it has.[17] He evidently thinks that the relation of justice to the philosophic life is as that of the useful or needful to the good.[18] He does not therefore simply subordinate the political life and justice to the requirements of the philosophic life and of wisdom. To do so would, as he observes, be utterly destructive of political life (pp. 92f., 143, 152f.). Rather, he shows his classical models tempering or diluting natural right in order to accommodate the requirements of political life.[19] They recognize that the good is one thing, and the needful or urgent another. They therefore recognize no unconditional duties and no unconditional rules of natural right (p. 162). Even if the good should always and everywhere be the same and always and everywhere be sovereign, it may, in practice, here and now, have to yield to the urgent or the needful. It may always have to yield. Strauss comes closer than does any one of his models to claiming that the good and the just order is unlikely ever to be actualized (consider pp. 139, 145f.). The forms which the accommodation between the good and the useful must in any given case take defines the province of prudence (pp. 162, 152, 66–70). Clearly, then, no discernible differences divide "Platonism" and Epicureanism" regarding prudence or natural right understood as the rules governing the life engaged in the pursuit of wisdom. Yet Strauss holds that Epicureanism denies natural right. Hence, when he speaks about natural right in *Natural Right and History,* he must be understood to be for the most part speaking about the rules governing the life oriented toward justice in contrast to the rules governing the life oriented toward the pursuit of wisdom.

On the classics' view, the best or highest form of the life oriented toward justice is the life of the gentleman. The gentleman "is the political reflection, or imitation, of the wise man" (p. 142).[20] Natural right understood as the rules governing the life oriented toward justice would, then, be the rules circumscribing the life of gentlemen and the regime that fosters and is ruled by gentlemen. Natural right so understood is, then, "natural" insofar as gentlemanliness may be said to be natural; that is, it is "natural" insofar as the moral virtues may be said to be natural. Strauss evidently does not think that they can unqualifiedly be said to be so. He evidently does not think that justice narrowly and properly so called can be said to have a natural basis independent of the place it may occupy in the economy of the philosophic life. He evidently makes his own the view expressed by Plato or by his Socrates that gentlemen, the very embodiments and exemplars of the moral virtues, are, given the opportunity, most likely to choose the life of the tyrant.[21] Moral or political virtue as such is "vulgar" virtue; only moral virtue in the service of the philosophic life is "genuine" virtue (p. 121). Contrary to the initial impression created by *Natural Right and History* that philosophy is the necessary condition of natural right because only philosophy can ground and validate universal moral and political principles, it now appears that Strauss regards philosophy as the necessary condition of natural right because philosophy is the only pursuit men engage in for its own sake alone, and it therefore is the only natural ordering principle of men's passions and pursuits, and hence of the virtues.

We noted earlier that Strauss draws a distinction between philosophical and vulgar "Epicureanism," but that he does not draw a comparable distinction between philosophical and vulgar "Platonism." It is now apparent that the corresponding "Platonist" distinction is the distinction between natural right in the service of the pursuit of wisdom, i.e. "philosophic" or "genuine" virtue on the one hand, and natural right in the service of the political life and of its excellences, i.e. "political" or vulgar" virtue, on the other. From the point of view of "Platonism," the "Epicurean" denial of natural right can, then, equally accurately be described as the failure of "Epicureanism" to provide for its responsible vulgarization. That is not to say that there could not be—or that there were not—civic-minded and responsible Epicureans. Strauss expressly calls attention to Cicero's friend Atticus who, as an Epicurean, did not accept natural right, i.e., political natural right, or natural right in the strict sense of right, but who, as a Roman citizen, defended natural right so understood as politically salutary (p. 154). There is, however, no Epicurean teaching to justify or to undergird Atticus's conduct.[22] The fact that there is not, points to at least one respect in which Epicureanism failed to be sufficiently mindful of opinion, and in particular of the distinction which opinion draws between the pleasant and the noble (pp. 108f., 110, 126). "Platonism," on the other hand, attends to opinion and so composes with the concerns and the judgments of political life.

The issue, then, once again revolves around the status of opinion, of the "natural," "common sense" understanding of the "natural," "common sense" world in the name of which Strauss had criticized Heidegger, Weber, and the state of nature doctrines of Hobbes and his successors (pp. 9f., 33f., 97–101, 124, cited in n. 16). Now opinion—the awareness of the praiseworthy and the noble, as well as of "those simple experiences regarding right and wrong" (pp. 31f., 105)—points to natural right in the narrow or strict sense of right. More precisely, it points to the possibility of natural right in the strict sense of the term. The fact that it does may establish a presumption in favor of natural right so understood. But it can do no more. "Platonism" recognizes the claim of that presumption. It recognizes that "one must go through the stage in which justice presents itself as identical with citizen-morality, and one must not merely rush through that stage" (p. 150 n. 24). Upon reflection, it appears that Strauss fails to make allowance for a distinctive vulgar classical natural right teaching because it would be redundant to do so.

Contrary to the initial impression that the alternatives are:

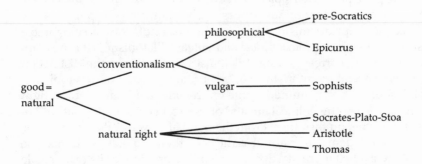

it now appears that Strauss classifies the alternatives as follows:

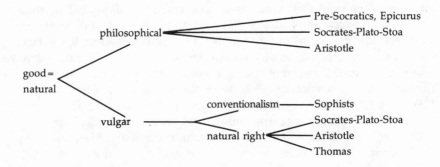

Setting aside, then, the views he may defend in the spirit of natural right so understood, of "diluted" natural right, or of Atticus the Epicurean, it is clear that Strauss makes no concessions whatsoever to any conception which claims to find in reason or in nature a firm foundation for principles of right narrowly and properly so called. His essentially sceptical conclusion is, of course, entirely consistent with the view that there is a permanent framework of permanent problems which the unaided reason may not be able to solve once and for all, and, hence, that there are fundamental alternatives between which the unaided reason may not be able to decide once and for all. At the same time it is entirely consistent with the assertion that there can be natural right only if the problem of natural right—unlike the other fundamental problems—admits of a definitive solution (pp. 24, 28, 35); in other words, only if knowledge is ultimately knowledge of ignorance.[23]

Notes

1. (Chicago: University of Chicago Press, 1953); otherwise unidentified page references throughout the present essay are to this book.

2. As Richard Kennington has noted: "Strauss's Natural Right and History," *Review of Metaphysics* 35 (1981): 57–86, 62.

3. "Nur solange Dasein *ist*, d.h. die ontische Möglichkeit von Seinsverständnis, 'gibt es' Sein. Wenn Dasein nich existiert, dann 'ist' auch nicht 'Unabhängigkeit' und 'ist' auch nicht 'Ansich'." Martin Heidegger, *Sein und Zeit* (Halle: Max Niemeyer, 1927), 212; see also pp. 183, 226, 230. Twenty years later Heidegger interpreted or reinterpreted this remark as follows: "In 'S.u.Z' (S. 212) ist mit Absicht und Vorsicht gesagt: il y a l'Etre: 'es gibt' das Sein. Das il y a übersetzt das 'es gibt' ungenau. Denn das 'es', was hier 'gibt', ist das Sein selbst. Das 'gibt' nennt jedoch das gebende, seine Wahrheit gewährende Wesen des Seins." A page below he adds: "Dieses 'es gibt' waltet als das Geschick des Seins. Dessen Geschichte kommt im Wort der wesentlichen Denker zur Sprache. Darum ist das Denken, das in die Wahrheit des Seins denkt, als Denken geschichtlich." Martin Heidegger, "Brief über den 'Humanismus' ", in *Platons Lehre von der Wahrheit, mit einem Brief über den 'Humanismus'* (Bern: A. Franke, 1947), 80, 81.

4. "Far from legitimizing the historicist inference, history seems rather to prove that all human thought, and certainly all philosophic thought, is concerned with the same fundamental themes or the same fundamental problems, and therefore that there exists an unchanging framework which persists in all changes of human knowledge of both facts and principles." (pp. 23f). "In particular, 'the experience of history' does not make doubtful that the fundamental problems, such as the problems of justice, persist or retain their identity in all historical change, however much they may be obscured by the temporary denial of their relevance and however variable and provisional all human solutions to these problems may be. In grasping these problems as problems the human mind liberates itself from its historical limitations. No more is needed to legitimize philosophy in the original, Socratic sense. Philosophy is knowledge that one does not know; that is to say, it is knowledge of what one does not know, or awareness of the fundamental problems and, therewith, of the fundamental alternatives regarding their solution that are coeval with human thought." (pp. 32, 35, 99–101) The qualification "coeval with human thought" appears to echo the passage from Heidegger's *Sein und Zeit* cited in the preceding note.

5. "He certainly could not deny that there is an articulation of reality that precedes all scientific articulation: that articulation, that wealth of meaning, which we have in mind when speaking of the world of common experience or of the natural understanding of the world. But he did not even attempt a coherent

analysis of the social world as it is known to 'common sense,' or of social reality as it is known in social life or in action. The place of such an analysis is occupied in his work by definitions of ideal types, of artificial constructs which are not even meant to correspond to the intrinsic articulation of social reality and which, in addition, are meant to be of a strictly ephemeral character. Only a comprehensive analysis of social life as we know it in actual life, and as men always have known it since there have been civil societies, would permit an adequate discussion of the possibility of an evaluating social science. Such an analysis would make intelligible the fundamental alternatives which essentially belong to social life and would therewith supply a basis for responsible judgment on whether the conflict between these alternatives is, in principle, susceptible of a solution" (pp. 77f). The parallels between the last sentence of this passage and the last sentence of the passage cited in the preceding note are striking.

6. "The discovery of nature is identical with the actualization of a human possibility which, *at least according to its own interpretation*, is trans-historical, trans-social, and trans-religious." (p. 89, italics added). This is one of the very rare instances in which Strauss so explicitly distances himself on so important a point from his classical sources and models.

7. "The Old Testament, whose basic premise may be said to be the implicit rejection of philosophy, does not know 'nature': the Hebrew term for 'nature' is unknown to the Hebrew Bible" (p. 81). "By calling nature the highest authority one would blur the distinction by which philosophy stands or falls, the distinction between reason and authority" (p. 92). "Revelation is always so uncertain to unassisted reason that it can never compel the assent of unassisted reason" (p. 75). "This is not to deny that, once the idea of natural right has emerged and become a matter of course, it can easily be adjusted to the belief in the existence of divinely revealed law" (p. 85).

8. "However indifferent to moral distinctions the cosmic order may be thought to be, human nature, as distinguished from nature in general, may very well be the basis of such distinctions. To illustrate the point by the example of the best-known pre-Socratic doctrine, namely, of atomism, the fact that the atoms are beyond good and bad does not justify the inference that there is nothing by nature good or bad for any compounds of atoms, and especially for those compounds which we call 'men.' In fact, no one can say that all distinctions between good and bad which men make or all human preferences are merely conventional. We must therefore distinguish between those human desires and inclinations which are natural and those which originate in conventions. Furthermore we must distinguish between those human desires and inclinations which are in accordance with human nature and therefore good for man, and those which are destructive of his nature or his humanity and therefore bad. We are thus led to the notion of a life, a human life, that is good because it is in accordance with nature. Both parties to the controversy admit that there is such a life, or, more generally expressed, they admit the primacy of the good as distinguished from the just. The controversial issue is whether the just is good (by nature good) or whether the life in accordance with human nature requires justice or morality" (pp. 94f.).

9. For Strauss's understanding of philosophical Epicureanism see the text cited in the preceding note, as well as pp. 109–113; for philosophical Epicureanism's "ascetic" teaching about pleasure and its "high demands on self-restraint," see

pp. 188f., as well as Victor Brochard's classic study, "La théorie du plaisir d'après Epicure," in *Etudes de philosophie ancienne et moderne*, (Paris: Vrin, 1912), pp. 252–293.

10. ". . . while the best regime is possible, its actualization is by no means necessary. Its actualization is very difficult, hence improbable, even extremely improbable. For man does not control the conditions under which it becomes actual. Its actualization depends on chance. The best regime, which is according to nature, was perhaps never actual; there is no reason to assume that it is actual at present; and it may never become actual. It is of its essence to exist in speech rather than in deed. In a word, the best regime is, in itself - to use a term coined by one of the profoundest students of Plato's *Republic* - a 'utopia'" (p. 139). "The Thomist doctrine of natural right or, more generally expressed, of natural law is free from the hesitations and ambiguities which are characteristic of the teachings not only of Plato and Cicero, but of Aristotle as well. In definiteness and noble simplicity it even surpasses the mitigaged Stoic natural law teaching. No doubt is left, not only regarding the basic harmony between natural right and civil society, but likewise regarding the immutable character of the fundamental propositions of natural law; the principles of the moral law, especially as formulated in the Second Table of the Decalogue, suffer no exception, except possibly by divine intervention. The doctrine of *synderesis* or of the conscience explains why the natural law can always be duly promulgated to all men and hence be universally obligatory. It is reasonable to assume that these profound changes were due to the influence of the belief in biblical revelation." p. 163; see also pp. 155, 177.

11. On the one hand, ". . . the corporeal mind, composed of very smooth and round particles with which Epicurus remained satisfied, was an inadequate solution." p. 172; on the other hand, there is ". . . the difficulty with which every teleological physics is beset. . ." p. 172. Yet "[n]atural right in its classic form is connected with a teleological view of the universe. All natural beings have a natural end, a natural destiny, which determines what kind of operation is good for them . . . . The teleological view of the universe, of which the teleological view of man forms a part, would seem to have been destroyed by modern natural science. From the point of view of Aristotle—and who could dare to claim to be a better judge in this matter than Aristotle?—the issue between the mechanical and the teleological conception of the universe is decided by the manner in which the problem of the heavens, the heavenly bodies, and their motion, is solved. Now in this respect, which from Aristotle's own point of view was the decisive one, the issue seems to have been decided in favor of the non-teleological conception of the universe. Two opposite conclusions could be drawn from this momentous decision. According to one, the non-teleological conception of the universe must be followed by a non-teleological conception of human life. But this 'naturalistic' solution is exposed to grave difficulties; it seems to be impossible to give an adequate account of human ends by conceiving of them merely as posited by desires or impulses. Therefore the alternative solution has prevailed. This means that people were forced to accept a fundamental, typically modern, dualism of a non-teleological natural science and a teleological science of man" p. 7f.

12. "Hobbes's notion of the state of nature presupposes the rejection of both the classic and the conventionalist view, for he denies the existence of a natural end, of a *summum bonum*" (p. 185 n. 23); compare the distinction Rawls draws between "utilitarianism" and his own contractarianism; John Rawls, *A Theory of justice*, Cambridge, Mass.: Harvard University Press, 1971, 24–32.

13. " . . . the whole scheme suggested by Hobbes requires for its operation the weakening or, rather, the elimination of the fear of invisible powers. It requires such a radical change of orientation as can be brought about only by the disenchantment of the world, by the diffusion of scientific knowledge, or by popular enlightenment. Hobbes's is the first doctrine that necessarily and unmistakably points to a thoroughly 'enlightened,' i.e. a-religious or atheistic society as the solution of the social or political problem" (p. 198, cp. pp. 34, 58, and consider the new meaning the Enlightenment attached to the name *philosophe*); see also pp. 171–77, esp. 173 n. 9, and cp. 201, 230, esp. n. 95, 271 n. 37, 272; also, 192.

14. Strauss goes to considerable lengths in his effort to establish that the ancients canvassed the fundamental alternatives. After pointing out how, under the influence of biblical faith, natural right doctrines ceased to be what they had primarily been for the classics, doctrines regarding the best regime, he adds: "Still, even this modification of the classical teaching was in a way anticipated by the classics. According to the classics political life as such is essentially inferior in dignity to the philosophic life" (pp. 144f). See also on the relation of theory and practice as it bears on slavery and on technology (pp. 22f) and on natural equality (p. 118).

15. Horace, *Epistles* I, x, line 24.

16. Consider p. 175; also: "Socrates started in his understanding of the natures of things from the opinions about their natures. For every opinion is based on some awareness, some perception with the mind's eye, of something. Socrates implied that disregarding the opinions about the natures of things would amount to abandoning the most important access to reality that we have, or the most important vestiges of the truth which are within our reach. He implied that 'the universal doubt' of all opinions would lead us not into the heart of truth, but into a void" (p. 124; see also pp. 78f.).

17. "If striving for the eternal truth is the ultimate end of man, justice and moral virtue in general can be fully legitimated only by the fact that they are required for the sake of that ultimate end or that they are conditions of the philosophic life. From this point or view the man who is merely just or moral without being a philosopher appears as a mutilated being. It thus becomes a question whether. . . justice and morality in general, in so far as they are required for the sake of the philosophic life, are idential, as regards both their meaning and their extension, with justice and morality as they are commonly understood" (p. 151).

18. In this connection, consider: "Certainly, the seriousness of the need of natural right does not prove that the need can be satisfied. A wish is not a fact. Even by proving that a certain view is indispensable for living well, one proves merely that the view in question is a salutary myth: one does not prove it to be true. Utility and truth are two entirely different things" (p. 6).

19. "Diluted" in contrast to "secondary" natural right: in Plato, pp. 153f., and in Aristotle, pp. 156f.

20. "Gentlemen have this in common with the wise man, that they 'look down' on many things which are highly esteemed by the vulgar or that they are ex-

perienced in things noble and beautiful. They differ from the wise because they have a noble contempt for precision, because they refuse to take cognizance of certain aspects of life, and because, in order to live as gentlemen, they must be well off" (p. 142).

21.   It is a question "whether the moral or just man who is not a philosopher is simply superior to the nonphilosophic 'erotic' man" (p. 151), where "the non-philosophic 'erotic' man" clearly refers to the tyrannical man (cp. Plato, *Republic* 573b–c, 619b–d).

22.   "Whoever concludes from the seeming tendency of this opinion [i.e., that no passion is, or can be, disinterested] that those who make profession of it cannot possibly feel the true sentiments of benevolence, or have any regard for genuine virtue, will often find himself, in practice, very much mistaken. Probity and virtue were no strangers to Epicurus and his sect. Atticus and Horace seem to have enjoyed from nature, and cultivated by reflection, as generous and friendly dispositions as any disciple of the austerer schools; and among the moderns, Hobbes and Locke, who maintained the selfish system of morals, lived irreproachable lives, though the former lay not under any restraint of religion which might supply the defects of his philosophy." David Hume, *An Inquiry Concerning the Principles of Morals*, "Of Self-Love" (par. 3).

23.   "It is true that the successful quest for wisdom might lead to the result that wisdom is not the one thing needful. But this result would owe its relevance to the fact that it is the result of the quest for wisdom: the very disavowal of reason must be reasonable disavowal. Regardless of whether this possibility affects the validity of the Socratic answer [to the problem of natural right], the perennial conflict between the Socratic and the anti-Socratic answer creates the impression that the Socratic answer is as arbitrary as its opposite, or that the perennial conflict is insoluble" (p. 36).

Roger D. Masters

EVOLUTIONARY BIOLOGY AND NATURAL RIGHT

Leo Strauss: Natural Science
and Political Philosophy*

The Intention of Leo Strauss

Although it is both fitting and pleasant to celebrate the memory of Leo Strauss, one cannot do so by passive recollection (in the manner of some college reunions). Rather, the only celebration worthy of such a teacher is an active and critical study of the issues he kept alive while others—to use his metaphor—"hid their heads in the sand." And of these issues, none was more central to Strauss than the contradiction between modern natural science and the tradition of natural right.

Whatever Leo Strauss's contribution to our understanding of individual political thinkers—Plato, Xenophon, Machiavelli, Rousseau, Kant, Locke, and Hobbes immediately come to mind—his greatest contribution was probably his single-minded insistence that *the* fundamental question of our time is the status of natural right. This concern, even more than his awesome intellect and his astonishing ability to practice close textual analysis, animated his writings, focused his classes, and stimulated his students. Today neither natural nor social science pretends to offer rational answers to the vital questions of how humans should live; as a result, we see technical rationality in the choice of means, whereas ends or goals are relegated to personal "value," whim, or historical inevitability. For Strauss, particularly after the events of the first half of this century, failure to reflect on this situation was the highest imaginable folly.

I cannot say with certainty what Strauss's *conscious* intention was; I was not privileged to have the kind of intimate relationship that would

*This paper was originally presented at a panel on the theme of "The Intention of Leo Strauss," organized by the Claremont Institute for the Study of Statesmanship and Political Philosophy as part of the 1983 Annual Convention of the American Political Science Association, Palmer House, Chicago, Illinois.

permit an assertion based on private confidences. But insofar as one can judge intentions from public deeds and from speeches (whether written or oral), clearly this focus on natural right was the intention of Leo Strauss. Hence, it is fitting to use this occasion for a reexamination of the issue with the kind of respect and critical independence that Aristotle long ago showed toward Plato.

Perhaps Strauss's best statement on the question is the passage that concludes the preface to *Natural Right and History*. Although well known, the text deserves to be cited again so that we will have before our minds Strauss's emphatic statement that a definition of natural right depends primarily on the relationship between the natural and the social sciences. Having pointed out that the contemporary inability to give "our ultimate principles" any other support "than our arbitrary and hence blind preferences" is tantamount to "retail sanity and whole-sale madness,"[1] Strauss goes on to say:

> The issue of natural right presents itself today as a matter of party allegiance. Looking around us, we see two hostile camps, heavily fortified and strictly guarded. One is occupied by the liberals of various descriptions, the other by the Catholic and non-Catholic disciples of Thomas Aquinas. But both armies and, in addition, those who prefer to sit on the fences or hide their heads in the sand are, to heap metaphor on metaphor, in the same boat. They are all modern men. We all are in the grip of the same difficulty. Natural right in its classic form is connected with a teleological view of the universe. All natural beings have a natural end, a natural destiny, which determines what kind of operation is good for them. In the case of man, reason is required for discerning these operations: reason determines what is by nature right with ultimate regard to man's natural end. The teleological view of the universe, of which the teleological view of man forms a part, would seem to have been destroyed by modern natural science. From the point of view of Aristotle—and who could dare to claim to be a better judge in this matter than Aristotle?—the issue between the mechanical and the teleological conception of the universe is decided by the manner in which the problem of the heavens, the heavenly bodies, and their motion is solved.* Now in this respect, which from Aristotle's own point of view was the decisive one, the issue seems to have been decided in favor of the nonteleological conception of the universe. Two opposite conclusions could be drawn from this momentous decision. According to one, the nonteleological conception of the universe must be followed up by a nonteleological conception of human life. But this 'naturalistic' solution is exposed to grave difficulties: it seems to be impossible to give an adequate account of human ends by conceiving of them merely as posited by desires or impulses. Therefore, the alternative solution has prevailed. This means that people were forced to accept a fundamental, typically modern dualism of a nonteleological natural science

---

*Aristotle, *Physics*, 196a25ff, 199a3–5.

and a teleological science of man. This is the position which the modern followers of Thomas Aquinas, among others, are forced to take, a position which presupposes a break with the comprehensive view of Aristotle as well as that of Thomas Aquinas himself. The fundamental dilemma, in whose grip we are, is caused by the victory of modern natural science. An adequate solution to the problem of natural right cannot be found before this basic problem has been solved.

Needless to say, the present lectures cannot deal with this problem. They will have to be limited to that aspect of the problem of natural right which can be clarified within the confines of the social sciences. Present-day social science rejects natural right on two different, although mostly combined grounds; it rejects it in the name of History and in the name of the distinction between Facts and Values.[2]

Strauss, Natural Right, and Aristotle's Physics

A careful reading of the passage just quoted suggests three observations of great importance: (1) Contrary to the assertions of some, Strauss aligned himself with neither the Thomists nor the "liberals"; rather, he argued that *all* "moderns," whether of the left, the right, or the center, face the same "predicament" with regard to natural right. (2) Far from claiming to have resolved the issue, Strauss did no more than to pose it with clarity and vigor; while keeping open the possibility of a solution consistent with ancient *social* science (what he called "classic natural right"), he insisted that the critical difficulty arose due to the findings of modern *natural science*. (3) This text seems to be based on a faulty interpretation of Aristotle's *Physics*; indeed, Strauss's view of the incompatibilty of modern natural science and classical natural right could more appropriately be derived from Nietzsche than from Aristotle or other writers in the ancient tradition.

Since this last remark will surprise, if not scandalize, many, some explanation is due. Strauss asserts, in the passage cited above, that no one could be a "better judge" of "the issue between the mechanical and teleological conception of the universe" than Aristotle and cites two passages in the *Physics* that presumably show that, for Aristotle, "the problem of the heavens, the heavenly bodies, and their motions" is the "decisive" issue for establishing whether "all natural beings have a natural end, a natural destiny, which determines what kind of operation is good for them." Leaving aside the puzzling fact that this is an argument from authority (i.e., the kind of argument Strauss taught us to treat with utmost suspicion), let us go back to the texts (as he so well taught his students how to do). If we consult *Physics*, 196a25ff and 199a3–5 (the citations in *Natural Right and History*, p. 8, n. 3), it becomes apparent that something is amiss.

The first of these passages occurs in the discussion of whether "chance" and "spontaneity" are "causes" (*Physics*, Bk. II, chap. iv). Aristotle has noted that some (nameless) thinkers have said that "nothing happens by chance," whereas others—like Empedocles—say that chance or spontaneity account for natural phenomena (196a). In the first passage to which Strauss refers (196a25ff), Aristotle then expresses surprise that "there are some too who ascribe this heavenly sphere and all the worlds to spontaneity" even though they also hold that "chance is not responsible for the existence or generation of animals and plants"; this is an absurd view, according to Aristotle, because the motions of the heavenly bodies have greater regularity than the motions of living bodies on earth.[3]

Comparing Aristotle with Strauss's supposed account of Aristotle, we find: (1) Aristotle is not contrasting a teleological natural science with a mechanistic one; he is comparing causality (including material and efficient causes as well as formal and final ones) with chance and spontaneity. (2) Aristotle doesn't claim that the explanation of the motions of the heavenly bodies is "decisive" for the principle of natural right or teleology with regard to living beings; if anything it is the reverse, and teleology in animals and plants is used to demonstrate the absurdity of attributing astronomic motion to chance (see also *Parts of Animals*, Bk. I, chap. i, 641b, where the same argument recurs). (3) Rather than treating chance or spontaneity and teleology as mutually exclusive alternatives, in the immediate sequel Aristotle gives a human example showing that they coexist in the same phenomena;[4] hence, chance can be defined as "an incidental cause in the sphere of those actions for the sake of something which involves a purpose" (*Physics*, 196b–197a).

If we turn to the second passage cited by Strauss (*Physics*, 199a3–5), our perplexity increases. Far from deriving teleological principles with regard to living bodies (biology) from the motions of the heavenly bodies (physics), Aristotle has just posed a difficulty that implies that natural purpose is even more likely to exist in biology than in physics: "Why should not nature work, not for the sake of something, nor because it is better so, *but just as the sky rains, not in order to make the corn grow, but of necessity* (*Physics*, 198b, italics added). Following a detailed rejection of Empedocles' account of the origin of species by a process seemingly akin to Darwinian natural selection, Aristotle concludes: "If then it is agreed that things are either the result of coincidence or for an end, and these [sc., "frequency of rain in winter," "heat in the dog days"] cannot be the result of coincidence or spontaneity, it follows that they must be for an end" (*Physics*, 199a3–5).

Once again, Strauss cites a passage distinguishing between "spontaneity" and nature in the sense of things occurring "for the sake of an end," as if the passage distinguishes between teleology and mechanical necessity. But in 199a3–5, Aristotle is explicitly *excluding* necessity as a distinct explanation ("if then it is agreed that things are either the result of coincidence or for an end"). As in *Parts of Animals* (I, i, 639a–642b), where a similar argument recurs, Aristotle assumes that teleology and necessity are simultaneously predicates of natural things (*Physics*, 200a–b) and that both are opposed to "spontaneity" or "chance" (which is viewed as an "incidental cause" in the sphere of teleology). These texts, as well as similar arguments in other scientific writings in the Aristotelian corpus, are far from fitting Strauss's description of Aristotle.[5]

The canons Strauss used in reading others thus demand of us that we consider his own statement of the predicament facing all modern men with more effort than has normally been done. In particular, why does Strauss speak of a "mechanical conception of the universe" (a phrase that brings to mind the physics of Galileo and Newton), while citing passages in Aristotle that refer to "chance" or "spontaneity" (phenomena that call to mind the physics of Bohr and Heisenberg)? In antiquity the doctrine that all things happen by necessity might seem to correspond to the nonteleological and mechanistic world view of the seventeenth century physicists; Aristotle also discusses this determinst view, yet the key statement in *Natural Right and History* refers only to apparently inappropriate passages concerning chance and spontaneity. Could Strauss have intended to direct our attention to quantum mechanics rather than to Newtonian mechanics? Despite appearances that the modern "predicament" is due to a nonteleological view of physics like that of the seventeenth century (laws of nature exist, but do not provide a natural ground for human purpose since they establish mere regularities of motion), isn't our "dilemma" caused by the twentieth century's nonteleological view of physics (laws of nature are man-made creations, imposed on a chaotic and meaningless process of chance and spontaneity)?

It will be objected that I am reading too much into the juxtaposition of Strauss's reference to a "mechanistic conception of the universe" with his citation of an Aristotelian discussion of chance. Isn't it enough to say that both are nonteleological? Clearly not: Strauss spent his entire life criticizing those who read texts in this way and thus ignore apparent contradictions as avenues to understanding the most serious themes in the most serious authors. And here we are discussing the statement of *the* most serious issue—natural right and natural science—as posed by a most serious man.

Without the challenge of twentieth century physics, moreover, Strauss's characterization of the "modern predicament" makes no sense. A nonteleological but mechanistic physics, like that of Galileo, *is* readily consistent with a modern conception of natural right like that in Hobbes, Locke, and Spinoza. In the critical passage from *Natural Right and History* under discussion, we learn that such a view "is exposed to grave difficulties" because "it seems impossible to give an adequate account of human ends by conceiving of them merely as posited by desires or impulses." But *how* do we know that the political teaching of Hobbes, Locke, and Spinoza is not an "adequate account"? Clearly Aristotle's discussion of chance and spontaneity is insufficient evidence for rejecting the seventeenth century conception that a new, mechanical formulation of laws of nature would be capable of conquering natural necessity. Neither Hobbes nor the modern psychologists from Hull to Skinner who share Hobbesian premises have admitted that it is "impossible to give an adequate account of human ends by conceiving of them merely as posited by desires or impulses."[6]

Lest it be thought that I have manufactured a difficulty from a footnote, consider how Strauss elsewhere described Aristotle's understanding of the articulation between physics and human ends in politics: "Aristotle's cosmology, as distinguished from Plato's, is unqualifiedly separable from the quest for the best political order."[7] How could Aristotle hold that the proper ends of human life are "unqualifiedly separable" from cosmology if the motions of the heavens are as decisive for natural teleology as the Preface of *Natural Right and History* pretends? A thinker of Strauss's stature does not make such blunders. And he taught us to beware of readers who pretended otherwise.

Twentieth Century Physics as a Challenge to Seventeenth Century Natural Right: Strauss and Nietzsche

Given the extreme rarity of Strauss's discussion of scientific matters, it is hard to know exactly what he meant by "the victory of modern natural science" or why this "victory" demonstrated the impossibility of modern as well as ancient concepts of natural right. But I submit that the footnote citing Aristotelian texts concerned with spontaneity and chance provides a clue: Unlike the seventeenth century physics of Galileo and Newton, the twentieth century physics of Einstein, Bohr, and Heisenberg does ultimately challenge a teleological conception of the universe on the basis of sheer "chance" and "spontaneity."

Even granting the logical possibility of this interpretation, many of those who studied with Strauss or have read his works extensively will be tempted to dismiss it as absurd. Had Strauss discussed the philosophic implications of twentieth century physics, either in his writings or his classes, one might be authorized to read an allusion to recent natural science into *Natural Right and History*. As it is, how can we dare explain the puzzling citation of Aristotle's *Physics* (196a25ff and 199a3–5) as a covert reference to physical teachings whose very existence Strauss seemed to ignore?

As a matter of fact, however, my interpretation of the Preface to *Natural Right and History* need not assume that Strauss had any detailed knowledge of the physics of Einstein, Bohr, or Heisenberg. On the contrary, Strauss's concern that a nonteleological conception of the universe, based on mere chance, caprice, or spontaneity, presented "grave difficulties" for all natural right doctrines, both ancient and modern, can be traced to a text that we *know* he read: Nietzsche's *Beyond Good and Evil*. Paradoxically enough, Nietzsche—writing in the late nineteenth century—outlined an argument that foreshadows the findings of twentieth century physics and explicitly relates such a view of nature to human ends. As a result, we are confronted with the even greater paradox that Strauss's formulation of the modern predicament seems to be derived substantially from Nietzsche rather than from Aristotle.

The idea that Nietzsche explored the human implications of theories of subatomic physics, elaborated only after Nietzsche's death, is only an apparent anachronism. Here, as in many issues of political philosophy, we have been led astray by superficiality when considering strictly scientific matters. It was, of course, quite impossible that Nietzsche's *Beyond Good and Evil* be a reaction to Bohr's radical insistance on chance and spontaneity in rejecting Einstein's view of an ordered universe: The debates of the 1920s surrounding quantum mechanics could not possibly have influenced a text written in the 1880s. But Nietzsche already knew of a physicist who had taken a position pointing in this direction, had cited him, and had explicitly linked such an understanding of nature to the impossibility of *all* doctrines of natural right, including those based on nonteleological or mechanical "laws of nature."

In the text I have in mind, Nietzsche proclaims:

> About material atomism: it belongs among the best refuted things that exist. Perhaps no one among the scholars of Europe today is still so unscholarly as to attach serious significance to it (other than employing it

as a handy means of expression), thanks mainly to the Dalmatian, Boscovich, who, together with the Pole Copernicus, has turned out to be the greatest and most successful opponent of 'eye-witness' evidence. Whereas Copernicus persuaded us to believe, contrary to the evidence of all our senses, that the earth is *not* standing still, Boscovich taught us to disavow our belief in the last thing which remained 'fast' on earth—namely our faith in 'substance,' in 'matter,' in the final residue of the universe, the little clod of atom.[8]

According to Nietzsche, confidence in the evidence of the senses (which had been so crucial to Aristotle) was ultimately destroyed by a once famous eighteenth century Jesuit astronomer and physicist. No longer widely known, Boscovich seems to have developed a version of field theory long before the giants of twentieth century physics demolished the notion of atomic particles as the indivisible building blocks of matter. More important, Nietzsche tells us explicitly two things about modern physics that are of supreme importance. First, scientific discoveries like those of Boscovich have revealed that *all* theories of natural phenomena are *merely* human constructs: "Today it is dawning on perhaps five or six minds that physics, too, is only an interpretation of the universe, an arrangement of it (to suit us, if I may be so bold!), rather than a clarification" (*Beyond Good and Evil*, aphorism 14). Second, a physics like that of Boscovich destroys not only the belief in *physical* atoms as the bedrock of a natural science of moving bodies, it also destroys the belief in the human soul as the *atomon* or basic unit of the social sciences: "We must next declare relentless war onto death, as we did with that better known 'need for metaphysics,' on that other and more fateful atomism which Christianity has best and longest taught: *psychic atomism*" (*Beyond Good and Evil*, aphorism 12).

Nietzsche thus refers to a physics of motion (including the motions of heavenly bodies—Boscovich was an astronomer) that is explicitly treated as "decisive" evidence against any form of natural teleology in human affairs. Moreover, for Nietzsche this physics understands nature as capricious rather than lawlike, exposing all theories of "laws of nature" (including those of Galileo and Newton, *or* of Hobbes, Locke, and Spinoza) as purely man-made fictions. Whereas Aristotle derives the need to study the soul from biology (*Parts of Animals*, 641a–b), Nietzsche uses physics to argue that it is impossible to study the soul as it has traditionally been understood.

Strauss clearly knew Nietzsche and those whose understanding was formed by Nietzsche. To unravel the riddle of the preface to *Natural Right and History*, all we need assume is that Strauss understood the "victory of modern natural science" to mean that twentieth century physics had confirmed the Nietzschean account. Based on Boscovich's radical theories, Nietzsche thus anticipated the contemporary view that physical theories are matters of convenience or "interpretation," and hence there is *no* possibility of either natural or rational standards for human affairs.

Biology, Physics, and Classic Natural Right

The foregoing excursus into the relationship between physics and natural right may seem totally irrelevant to the title of this paper. Reconsider, however, Strauss's argument that since the teleological view of man "forms a part" of the teleological view of the universe, "the manner in which the problem of the heavens, the heavenly bodies, and their motion is solved" is "decisive" both for natural teleology in general and for human teleology in particular. We have just seen that Strauss's apparent reliance on Aristotle for such a linkage between natural right and physics is questionable; even if Strauss himself blundered grossly in writing the Preface to *Natural Right and History* (which I personally doubt), his reference to Aristotle forces us to reconsider the kind of argument exemplified by Nietzsche. Let us therefore go back to Strauss's statement of the "fundamental dilemma" facing "all" of us as "modern men."

As Strauss puts it, "natural right in its classic form" was related to the view that "all natural beings have a natural end, a natural destiny, which determines what kind of operation is good for them." Aristotle called such final causes or ends "that for the sake of which," and asserted that natural operations "for the sake" of a purpose, goal, or "function" are logically prior to material or motor causes (*Physics*, 194b–199b; *Parts of Animals*, 639a; *Politics*, 1252b–1253a). But if we read the *Physics*—not to mention Aristotle's other works—with a modicum of care, we find that this principle is applied differently to animate and inanimate bodies. Broadly put, Aristotle uses natural teleology as a precise analytical tool when discussing animate beings, whereas teleology is more logical or metaphorical in the discussion of inanimate beings.

To put the central point more simply, Aristotle bases the concept of natural right on the principle of teleology in *biology*, rather than on a teleological *physics*. This point has been obscured by two errors in reading Aristotle. First, many commentators have failed to consider his biological writings with the seriousness they deserve (especially in relation to the Aristotelian concept of "natural ends" as it applies to human life). Second, when moderns do read Aristotle's biology, they tend to look for a teleological account of the "origin of species," whereas Aristotle is usually speaking of the form and function of existing species (e.g., *Parts of Animals*, 640a); in contemporarly terms, Aristotelian accounts of *ontogeny* are mistaken for evolutionary theories of *phylogeny*. A word on these errors, both of which can ultimately be traced to the difference between Greek paganism and our monotheist traditions, is in order.

The imprecise reading of Aristotle's scientific writings, symbolized by the general failure to question Strauss's apparently odd reference to the *Physics*, reflects the priority often given to that work (or to the *Metaphysics*) compared to his biological writings. But it is a manifest anachronism to read back into Aristotle the nineteenth century hierarchy of the sciences, according to which physics, chemistry, and biology are arrayed in a descending order based on "scientific " rigor. According to such a hierarchy, one could well say that physics is the "decisive" foundation of natural right since the motions of all animal beings are ultimately reducible to the motions of inanimate beings. It remains to be seen, however, whether Aristotle treats biology as reducible to the physical motions of inanimate bodies, not to mention whether he views physics rather than biology as the realm in which the natural ends of humans must be grounded.

In the *Physics* itself, just after the second of the passages to which Strauss referred, Aristotle presents an argument in exactly the opposite order; final causation in human art is used to explain final causation in nature: "If, therefore, artificial products are for the sake of an end, so clearly also are natural products. . . .This is most obvious in the animals other than man: they make things neither by art nor after inquiry or deliberation" (199a). Aristotle's evidence for natural teleology is thus primarily drawn from human intentionality, *then* from animals and other animate beings, and only *finally* from inanimate ones. Moreover, this understanding is explicitly divorced from the view that there must be an "agent deliberating" in order for purpose to exist: "It is absurd to suppose that purpose is not present because we do not observe the agent deliberating. Art does not deliberate. . . .If, therefore, purpose is present in art, it is present also in nature. The best illustration is a doctor doctoring himself: nature is like that" (*Physics*, 199b). Aristotle's concept of natural teleology, unlike that of Thomas, has no need of an active, purposive God as creator of the universe.

We find the same emphasis on natural teleology in the animal world consistently expressed throughout Aristotle's biological works. There, for example, Aristotle frequently elaborates on the criticism of

Empedocles' doctrine in the *Physics*. Empedocles had derived the form
of animals from a combination of chance and what has come to be called
natural selection: "Wherever then all the parts came about just what
they would have been if they had come to be for an end, such things sur-
vived, being organized sponteneously in a fitting way; whereas those
which grew otherwise perished and continue to perish, as Empedocles
says his 'man-faced ox-progeny' did" (*Physics*, 198b). This challenge to
natural teleology on the ground that it is a consequence of chance can be
rejected, according to Aristotle, because it cannot account for the generation and persistance of animals (*De Caelo* 300b–301a; *On Generation and
Corruption*, 333b; *Parts of Animals*, 640a; *Generation of Animals*, 722b).

Moreover, if it were correct that Aristotle derived the natural ends of
humans from physics, we might expect to find such a derivation in his
great works of "political science"—namely, the *Nicomachean Ethics* and
Politics. On the contrary, in these works we find the concept of natural
teleology related primarily to animals (e.g., *Politics*, I, 1253a, 1254a–b;
Ethics, V, vii, 1134b). Indeed, in both of these contexts, we find an explicit reference to the inexactitude of arguments derived from inanimate
beings in determining that which is natural for humans (*Politics*,
1254a–b; *Ethics*, 1134b). It follows that we must reconsider Aristotle's
scientific argument more precisely and reverse Strauss's argument on
the possible grounding of natural teleology. If so, the crucial question
becomes the following: Has modern *biology* discredited Aristotle's
biology as thoroughly as modern physics has discredited his physics?

Before turning to this issue, it is important to mention the second error
in reading Aristotle. For many nonspecialists, it is presumed that Aristotle's account of natural teleology in the animal world is an explanation
of the coming to be of the different species we see today. From that
perspective, modern biology seems to have sided with Empedocles' account of animals coming to be spontaneously, with the "fittest" surviv-
ing on the basis of adaptations that are merely the result of chance. But,
as was mentioned above, Aristotle does not seem to be arguing primarily in terms of the *origins* of species at all; on the contrary, he takes
the existence of animals largely for granted and stresses the need for a
principle   explaining   why   offspring   resemble   their   parents:
"Empedocles, then, was in error when he said that many of the
characters presented by animals were merely the results of incidental
occurrences during their development; for instance, that the backbone
was divided as it is into vertebrae, because it happened to be broken owing to the contorted position of the fetus in the womb. In so saying he
overlooked the fact that propagation implies a creative seed endowed

with certain formative properties. Secondly, he neglected another fact, namely that the parent animal pre-exists, not only an idea, but actually in time. For man is generated from man" (*Parts of Animals*, 640a).

In contemporary terms Empedocles' biology—a serious contender to that of Aristotle in antiquity—implies an evolutionary account akin to that of Lamarck (i.e., a position generally shown to be inadequate today). In contrast, Aristotle does not, as first appears, deny the existence of chance variations like those required in neo-Darwinian evolutionary theory: "Clearly mistakes are possible in the operations of nature. . .monstrosities will be failures in the purposive effort. Thus in the original combinations the 'ox-progeny' [of Empedocles] if they failed to reach a determinate end must have arisen through the corruption of some principle corresponding to what is now the seed" (*Physics*, 199a).

Paradoxically enough, Aristotle would have no difficulty adapting his biology to modern evolutionary biology. Indeed, as the molecular biologist Max Delbruck has argued, Aristotle could well be viewed as the discoverer of DNA, since he, alone of the biologists of antiquity, saw that a seed or principle of generation carried with it the information for the form and function of the adult animal.[9] The addition of random variations in the form of mutation or recombination—required by neo-Darwinian theory—is readily found in Aristotle's understanding of chance as an "incidental cause" in the "sphere" of natural teleology; that is, mutants are only mutants as a deviation from the previously existing "natural end" of the species.

We have tended to overestimate Aristotle's errors in biology (and such errors obviously exist) due to our tendency to focus on the issue of the origin of species. As has been noted, this is not usually Aristotle's main concern (*Parts of Animals*, 640a). It has become, however, the fundamental issue for modern man because of the importance attributed to the biblical account of creation. Clear enough in Darwin's own writing, this need to counter the Judaeo-Christian explanation of the origin of species is nowhere more evident than in the writing of Nietzsche. Hence, for most moderns the intellectual question posed by evolutionary biology has been theological rather than philosophical: If humans have evolved, then the account in *Genesis*, chapters 1 through 3, is at best a metaphor and at worst a myth. And in either case, evolutionary biology destroys the biblical faith in an omnipotent and caring God, whose creation of nature is the guarantee of the natural ends of human life.

It is obvious—but critical to stress—that Aristotle was a pagan. Classical natural right did not presume a creative God; indeed, Aristotle teaches that the universe is eternal (e.g., *Physics*, 253a–266a). Hence, the extent to which modern biology undermines theological or Thomistic accounts of natural right cannot be used to impute a similar challenge to Aristotle, or, more broadly, to the classical Greek view. It follows that the critical issue for us needs to be restated. Whatever the findings of modern physics, classical natural right—at least in the eyes of Aristotle—stands or falls by the status of final causation among animate beings. Therefore, contemporary biology, and not physics, is critical to the resolution of Strauss's question.

Contemporary Biology and Human Nature: The Return to Natural Right

For the last fifteen years I have devoted extensive research to contemporary biological science in order to reconsider the question Strauss posed in the Preface to *Natural Right and History*. Without pretending to explain the results of this work in detail, an outline should indicate that the modern "predicament" need not be as intractible as it appears if viewed from the Nietzschean perspective. (For the sake of simplicity, in the remainder of this paper, I will use the scientific form of brief references.)

Popular prejudices notwithstanding, the concept of reducing biology to physics now seems to be "absurd" (Simpson, 1969; Masters, 1979a); biological systems at the level of the organism, the species, and the ecosystem are distinct levels of phenomena that differ from inanimate or physical systems (Anderson, 1972). Contemporary natural science is not automatically hostile to a doctrine of natural right based on the assumption that living beings differ in decisive ways from inanimate bodies (Masters, forthcoming).

To be sure, most biologists resist the concept of "teleology," suggesting as it does the Thomist understanding of divinely ordained "natural ends" or purposes. But in every respect but the term, biologists argue in terms of "functional" analysis that is like Aristotelian teleology (Masters, 1976b); to avoid confusing this approach with Christian theology, however, biologists speak of "teleonomy" and "teleonomic processes" as characteristic of living species (Mayr, 1974; Corning, 1983). In particular, current evolutionary theories based on the distinction between the visible body (phenotype) and inherited information (genotype) imply that the animals we see are merely means by which DNA perpetuates itself; as one leading biologist has put it, an animal is simply a "vehicle" for "replicating" genes (Dawkins, 1976). "The hen is the egg's way of making another egg."

Recent theories of natural selection—notably the class of models described as "inclusive fitness theory" (Hamilton, 1964; Wilson, 1975; Barash, 1977)—have therefore analyzed the social behavior of animals as a means to the end of perpetuating genes. Despite claims to the contrary, such an approach is not vitiated by political or sexist bias (Masters, 1982a). On the contrary, it can be shown that the traditional questions of political philosophy are formally isomorphic with the theoretical problems posed by contemporary biology (Corning, 1977; Somit, 1981). More important, from this perspective the major political theorists appear to have elaborated "archetypical" models of *the* fundamental issues facing any social animal (Masters, 1977, 1982b, 1983a).

Contemporary biology can therefore be used to indicate the extent to which the understanding of a political philosopher like Rousseau has been confirmed or challenged by modern natural science (Masters, 1978b, 1983b). In this light, evolutionary theory points to a return to the notion of "natural right" (Masters, 1981b) and, to be specific, "classic natural right" (Masters, 1978a). Whereas moderns like Hobbes and Marx adumbrate a theoretical model of importance only under quite specific empirical conditions, the tradition of Plato and Aristotle shows a surprising relevance in the light of the latest research (Masters, 1975, 1978c, 1983b).

While this argument can be based on general theoretical considerations derived from neo-Darwinian models of natural selection, it can equally be based on more direct observation. For example, the ethological tradition represented by Konrad Lorenz and Niko Tinbergen suggests that the stimulus-response model of behaviorist psychology, ultimately derived from its Hobbesian tradition, is simply false (Masters, 1976c). More particularly, the Lockean "tabula rasa" is no longer adequate to account for observed human behaviors (von Cranach, 1979; Masters, 1976a); rather, humans can be seen to integrate culturally learned and innate or "natural" behavioral elements in ways that are constrained by prior human evolution. As Aristotle puts it, "the purpose of education, like that of art generally, is simply to copy nature by making her deficiencies good" (*Politics* VII, 1337a).

My own research has included participation in an empirical study illustrating this new, "naturalistic" approach to "human nature" akin to that of classical political philosophy. Humans communicate not only by languages more complex than the signals of other species (*Politics*, I, 1253a; Masters, 1970), but with nonverbal facial gestures akin to the displays of other primates (Masters, 1976c, 1981a). Recent experiments conducted by an interdisciplinary group at Dartmouth indicate that when Americans watch political leaders on television, their responses are a complex integration of "natural" responses (like those of primates) and learned political attitudes (Sullivan et al., 1984; Lanzetta et al., 1985; McHugo et al., 1985; Masters et al., 1986).

When human social behavior is analyzed from a biological perspective, therefore, it is evident that Aristotle was correct to describe our species as the *zoon politikon* (Masters, 1978a). Having lived in small, face-to-face bands for over 3.5 million years, hominids have developed a social repertoire of behavior that is amenable to description and empirical study (Masters, 1976a, 1981a). Elements of this behavior can be observed in primates (e.g., Morris, 1969; de Waal, 1983) or in preschool children (e.g., Montagner, 1978; Barner-Barry, 1981; Strayer, 1981). As a result, attempts to deprive humans of constituent components of the human repertoire of social behavior—while sometimes explicable in terms of what Aristotle calls "necessity"—can clearly be described as "contrary to nature" (Masters, 1983c, 1983d, 1983e).

Many political philosophers have long avoided direct study of the natural sciences; the attitude expressed by Strauss may have misled some to fear that the *only* defense of natural right is a humanistic rejection of the pretensions of sciences to explore human behavior. Aristotle, however, did not share such a view: "If any person thinks the examination of the rest of the animal kingdom an unworthy task, he must hold in disesteem the study of man" (*Parts of Animals*, I,v,644a). Since classical natural right was based on a polytheistic religious tradition consistent with the eternity of the universe, it does not presuppose that uniform teleological principles must govern both inanimate and animate beings; hence, "modern natural science" *can* be compatible with "classic natural right"—albeit at the cost of abandoning biblical or Thomist versions of natural law.

This conclusion may be cold comfort to many of those who have taken Strauss's deepest concern to heart. But it was only to be expected that neither of the "armed camps" Strauss describes as dominating the modern "predicament" could ultimately claim the victory that seems to have been won by natural science: Neither Thomism nor conventional "liberalism" have been particularly concerned to base their principles on the foundation of research in the physical and biological sciences. Hence, it may be only justice that scientific findings point in the direction of a need to abandon both Thomist theology and the "liberal" faith in a secular conquest of nature (Masters, 1982a, 1983e, forthcoming).

Even if my argument is correct and a solution to the problem of natural right is possible, such a solution will thus cost us dearly. Of the three principles—modern natural science, revealed religion, and classical natural right—it may only be possible to sustain two at any one time.

The ultimate paradox of Strauss's treatment of the impact of natural science on political philosophy could well be that what Strauss called the tension between Athens and Jerusalem may determine whether or not our civilization returns to a natural teleology like that of classic natural right.

Notes

1. Leo Strauss, *Natural Right and History* (Chicago: University of Chicago Press, 1953), 4.

2. Ibid., 7-8, and note 3.

3. For convenience, all citations will be to the translations in *Basic Writings of Aristotle*, ed. Richard McKeon (New York: Random House, 1941).

4. "A man is engaged in collecting subscriptions for a feast. He would have gone to such and such a place for the purpose of getting the money if he had known. He actually went there for another purpose, and it was only incidentally that he got his money by going there" (*Physics*, 196b, 33ff). This example *must* have been well known to Strauss: he often used it in the classes I attended as his favorite illustration of the difference between human purpose and accident.

5. Were it necessary, the case could be made more strongly: Not only does Aristotle *not* say that the problem of natural right stands or falls according to the solution of the problem of the motions of the heavens (e.g., *De Caelo*, 268b–270b, 293a–298a), but he *explicitly* rejects the argument that the analysis of necessity and purpose is identical in observational "natural science" and in the "theoretical sciences" like mathematics and theoretical physics (*Parts of Animals*, I, i, 639b–640a).

6. See R. S. Peters and H. Taijfel, "Hobbes and Hull—Metaphysicians of Behavior," *Hobbes and Rousseau*, ed. Maurice Cranston and Richard S. Peters (New York: Doubleday, 1972), esp. 165–66; B. F. Skinner, *Beyond Freedom and Dignity* (New York: Alfred A. Knopf, 1971).

7. Leo Strauss, *The City and Man* (Chicago: Rand McNally, 1964), 21.

8. Marianne Cowen (trans.) *Beyond Good and Evil*, aphorism 12 (South Bend: Regnery-Gateway, 1955), 14. All citations to Nietzsche are to this edition. For information on Boscovich, see American Council of Learned Societies, *Dictionary of Scientific Biology* 2 (New York: Scribners, 1970): 326; *Encyclopedia of Philosophy* 2 (New York: Macmillan and Free Press, 1967): 715-16. I am greatly indebted to Robin Jacobsohn, "Nietzsche's View of Human Nature and the Implications for Democracy" (Unpublished Honors Thesis, Dartmouth College Department of Government, 1983) for bringing these references to Boscovich to my attention.

9. See Max Delbruck, "How Aristotle Discovered DNA," *Physics and Our World: A Symposium in Honor of Victor F. Weisskopf*, ed. Kerson Huang (New York: American Institute of Physics, 1976), 123–30; Max Delbruck "Aristotle-totle-totle," *Of Microbes and Life*, ed. J. Monod and E. Borek (New

York: Columbia University Press, 1971), 50–55. For further evidence of the modernity of Aristotle's biology—and of its relevance to politics—see Anthony Preus, "*Eidos* as Norm in Aristotle's Biology," *Nature and System* 1 (1979): 79–101, and "Intention and Impulse in Aristotle and the Stoics," *Apeiron* 15 (1981): 48–58.

Bibliography

Anderson, P. W. August 1972. More is Different, *Science.* 177: 393–96.

Barash, David. 1977. *Sociobiology and Behavior* New York: Elsevier.

Barner-Barry, Carol. Longitudinal Observational Research and the Study of Basic Forms of Political Socialization. *Biopolitics: Ethological and Physiological Approaches.* Ed. Meredith Watts. New Directions for Methodology of Social and Behavioral Science. No. 7. San Francisco: Jossey-Bass. 51–60.

de Waal, Frans. 1982. *Chimpanzee Politics.* London: Jonathan Cape.

Durham, William. 1979. Toward a Coevolutionary Theory of Human Biology and Culture. *Evolutionary Biology and Human Social Behavior.* North Scituate, Mass.: Duxbury Press. 39–59.

Hamilton, William. 1978. The Genetical Evolution of Social Behavior, *Journal of Theoretical Biology.* 7 (1964): pp. 1–16. Reprinted in Arthur Caplan, ed., *The Sociobiology Debate.* New York: Harper & Row. 191–209.

Lanzetta, John T., Denis G. Sullivan, Roger D. Masters, and Gregory J. McHugo. 1985. Viewers' Emotional and Cognitive Responses to Televised Images of Political Leaders. In Sidney Kraus and Richard Perloff, eds. *Mass Media and Political Thought.* Beverly Hills, Calif.: Sage Publications, Pp. 85–116.

McHugo, Gregory J., John T. Lanzetta, Denis G. Sullivan, and Basil G. Englis. 1985. Emotional Reactions to a Political Leader's Expressive Displays. *Journal of Personality and Social Psychology.* 49:1513–1529.

Masters, Roger D. 1970. Genes, Language and Evolution, *Semiotica.* 2: 295–320.

Masters, Roger D. April 1975. Politics as a Biological Phenomenon, *Social Science Information.* 14: 7–63.

Masters, Roger D. December 1976a. Exit, Voice, and Loyalty in Animal and Human Behavior, *Social Science Information.* 15: 78–85.

Masters, Roger D. 1976b. Functional Approaches to Analogical Comparisons between Species. *Methods of Comparing Animal and Human Behavior.* Ed. Mario von Cranach. The Hague: Mouton. 73–102.

Masters, Roger D. 1976c. The Impact of Ethology on Political Science. *Biology and Politics.* Ed. Albert Somit. The Hague: Mouton. 197–233.

Masters, Roger D. 1977. Nature, Human Nature and Political Thought. *Human Nature in Politics.* Ed. J. Roland Pennock and John W. Chapman. New York: New York University Press. 69–110.

Masters, Roger D. 1978a. Classical Political Philosophy and Contemporary Biology. Paper presented to Conference for the Study of Political Thought, Chicago, Ill.

Masters, Roger D. 1978b. Jean-Jacques is Alive and Well: Rousseau and Contemporary Sociobiology. *Daedalus.* 93-105.

Masters, Roger D. 1978c. Of Marmots and Men: Human Altruism and Animal Behavior. *Altruism, Sympathy and Helping.* Ed. Lauren Wispé. New York: Academic Press. 59-77.

Masters, Roger D. 1979a. Beyond Reductionism. *Human Ethology.* Ed. Mario von Cranach et al. Cambridge: Cambridge University Press. 265-84.

Masters, Roger D. 1981a. Linking Ethology and Political Science: Photographs, Political Attention, and Presidential Elections. *Biopolitics: Ethological and Physiological Approaches.* Ed. Meredith W. Watts. New Directions for Methodology of Social and Behavioral Science. No. 7. San Francisco: Jossey-Bass. 61-80.

Masters, Roger D. 1981b. The Value—and Limits—of Sociobiology. *Sociobiology and Human Politics.* Ed. Elliott White. Lexington: Lexington Books. Chap. 4.

Masters, Roger D. September 1982a. Is Sociobiology Reactionary? The Political Implications of Inclusive Fitness Theory. *Quarterly Review of Biology.* 57: 275-92.

Masters, Roger D. 1982b. Evolutionary Biology, Political Theory, and the Origin of the State. *Law, Biology and Culture—Journal of Social and Biological Structures.* Ed. Margaret Gruter and Paul Bohannan. 5: 453-50.

Masters, Roger D. January 1983a. The Biological Nature of the State, *World Politics.* 35: 161-93.

Masters, Roger D. 1983b. The Duties of Humanity: Legal and Moral Obligation in Rousseau's Thought. *Constitutional Democracy: Essays in Comparative Politics.* Ed. Fred Eidlin. Boulder, Colo.: Westview. Pp. 83-105.

Masters, Roger D. 1983c. Ostracism, Voice and Exit: The Biology of Social Participation. Paper presented at Symposium on Ostracism, Annual Meeting of Law and Society Association, Denver, Colorado, June 3-5. Revised version in M. Gruter and R. Masters, eds. *Ostracism.* New York: Elsevier, 1986. Pp. 231-47.

Masters, Roger D. 1983d. Social Biology and the Welfare State. *Comparative Social Research, 1983.* Ed. Richard F. Tomasson. Greenwich, Conn.: JAI Press. Pp. 203-41.

Masters, Roger D. 1983e. Explaining Male Chauvinism and Feminism: Differences in Male and Female Reproductive Strategies. *Women and Politics.* Ed. Meredith Watts. Binghamton, N.Y.: Haworth Press. Pp. 165-210.

Masters, Roger D., Denis G. Sullivan, John T. Lanzetta, and Gregory J. McHugo. 1986. The Facial Displays of Leaders: Toward an Ethology of Human Politics. *Journal of Social and Biological Structures,* 9:319-43.

Masters, Roger D. forthcoming. *The Nature of Politics.*

Mayr, Ernst. 1974. Teleological and Teleonomic, A New Analysis, *Boston Studies in the Philosophy of Science.* 14: 91–117.

Montagner, Hubert. 1978. *L'Enfant et la Communication.* Paris: Stock.

Morris, Desmond, Ed. 1969. *Primate Ethology.* Chicago: Doubleday.

Simpson, George Gaylord. 1969. *Biology and Man.* New York: Harcourt Brace Jovanovitch.

Strauss, Leo. 1953. *Natural Right and History.* Chicago: University of Chicago Press.

Strayer, F. F. 1981. The Organization and Coordination of Assymetrical Relations Among Young Children: A Biological View of Social Power. *Biopolitics: Ethical and Physiological Approaches.* Ed. Meredith Watts. New Directions for Methodology of Social and Behavior Science. No. 7. San Francisco: Jossey-Bass. 33–50.

Sullivan, Denis G., Roger D. Masters, John T. Lanzetta, Basil G. Englis, Gregory J. McHugo. 1984. The effect of President Reagan's facial dispays on observers' attitudes, impressions, and feelings about him. Paper presented at the annual meeting of the American Political Science Association.

von Cranach, Mario et al. 1979. *Human Ethology.* New York: Cambridge University Press.

Wilson, Edward O. 1975. *Sociobiology.* Cambridge, Mass.: Harvard University Press.

Third Section

A CRITIQUE

*John G. Gunnell**

POLITICAL THEORY AND POLITICS:
THE CASE OF LEO STRAUSS
AND LIBERAL DEMOCRACY

Leo Strauss was the greatest writer of epic political theory in our century. Yet what he was saying, what he was doing by saying what he said, and what he hoped to accomplish remain open issues. If there is a single theme that gives coherency to his work, it is his account of the decline of the tradition of political philosophy and the entailed crisis of the West that is manifest in the crisis of liberal democracy. To understand Strauss requires locating his work within the literary genre to which that account belongs, but this is complicated by the fact that Strauss was one of the creators of that genre.[1] Furthermore, the form of discourse that characterizes this literature is far from explicit. It cannot be categorized as historical, exegetical, philosophical, or political, even though it may employ or partake of each.

I will argue that Strauss's work can best be understood as rhetorical and that it should be approached as an example of political theory as evocation. As such, it raises, at least by implication, questions about the conditions and limits of academic political theory and its relationship to politics. Although these questions were vivid for Strauss, they have become obscure within the contemporary enterprise of political theory.

For Strauss, as for many of the other scholars who immigrated to the United States in the 1930s and contributed to reshaping the character of political theory as an academic discipline, the dilemmas inherent in the relationship between intellectuals and politics and between academic and public discourse were matters of great concern. Strauss insisted that the "crisis of modernity" was "primarily the crisis of modern political philosophy," and he meant that they were in some sense at once causally linked and identical. Yet, he asked, was it not "strange" that "the crisis of a culture [should] primarily be the crisis of one academic pursuit

*An earlier version of this paper appeared in Political Theory, Volume 13, Number 3/August 1985, pp. 339-61, and is reprinted with the permission of Political Theory.

among many?'' His answer was, in part, that "political philosophy is not essentially an academic pursuit: the majority of great political philosophers were not university professors."[2] But even if it were not "essentially" such a pursuit, it had historically become one, and this was one of the problems that defined the situation within which a solution must be sought.

This issue is an important element in the context for understanding Strauss's work, and it is one that is crucial for a critical analysis of much of contemporary political theory. The difference is that Strauss, as well as many of the other emigrés, were profoundly aware of the problem and sensitive to the pathos of academic political theory and its relationship to politics. Yet in various ways their work served to sublime and intellectualize the dilemma and contribute to the alienation of political theory.[3]

Politics, political theory and theorizing, the political theorist, *and* the relationship between theory and practice have become conceptual objects constituted by academic discourse. Despite its allusions to practical issues, the bulk of academic political theory has little to say about the particularity of politics and even less about what (in Strauss's language) might be called "the nature of political things" or the ontology of political phenomena. Whether it could or should do otherwise is another matter. My immediate concern is with the authenticity of an activity that fails to confront the fact that speaking academically about politics is not the same thing as speaking politically.

In examining Strauss we can understand something of the origins of the problem and gain some new insight into its present manifestations. I will interpret in detail one essay by Strauss that I believe is of special importance for explaining his general intellectual project and his argument about modernity. The essay merits a careful treatment in light of its pivotal place in Strauss's work, but I am also approaching it as a vehicle for exploring his notion of the relationship between political theory and politics. Before turning to that essay, it is necessary to look more generally at Strauss's use of the concept liberal democracy.

I

It would be a mistake to assume that liberal democracy refers to any political phenomena that can be authoritatively disclosed. For Strauss, as for many political theorists who came to prominence in the late 1930s and early 1940s, the crisis of modern liberalism was a practical and historically situated problem, but the relationship between the concept of liberalism or liberal democracy and particular political ideas and institutions is far from unproblematical in his work. Liberal democracy is basically part of a constellation of symbols that play a crucial role in his evocative prose, and it is within that configuration that the principal meaning can be found. My analysis is confined to distinguishing four basic characteristics or aspects of usage: (1) the historical dimension of his symbolism; (2) his paradoxical account of liberal democracy; (3) the abstract nature of his treatment; and (4) the intellectualist emphasis that attaches to his claims.

Sometimes for Strauss, "liberal democracy" has a specific historical reference. One significant instance is his description of Germany and the Weimar regime of the late 1920s; he evokes parallels with, and connections between, Weimar and the contemporary crisis of the West. Weimar was already internally "weak" and exemplified justice without power and will, but at a "critical moment the victorious liberal democracies discredited liberal democracy in the eyes of Germany by the betrayal of their principles through the Treaty of Versailles." Strauss attributes both the "precarious" situation of the Jews and the social disillusionment that prepared the way for the Third Reich to the "weakness of liberal democracy."[4]

From the ruins of Weimar sprung the only regime in history based on a principled and "murderous" hatred of the Jews and dedicated to the destruction of both public rights and private freedom. Liberal democracy contained not only the seeds of its own destruction but the basis of a regime that negated its defining values. Strauss argues that the idea of tolerance in liberal democracy not only conceals possibilities of intolerance but leads to the abdication of a basis for defending its own principles. "Absolute tolerance is altogether impossible," and when liberal democaracy becomes relativistic it leads to an "abandonment of all standards including its own."[5]

The other significant historical manifestation of liberal democracy is the United States. This is the most immediate and practical object of Strauss's political commentary. Although the United States is the "bulwark of freedom" in the face of a "contemporary tyranny" that "has its roots in Machiavelli's thought," the shadow of Weimar hangs over it.[6] The fate of liberal democracy and the West as a whole resides in the confrontation between the United States and Russian communism. But the nation is now in danger, though modern social science and other influences, of accepting the "yoke" of German historicism and rejecting the very idea of natural right as well as the rarefied but salvageable ideal embodied in the Declaration of Independence.[7]

Strauss's discussion of liberal or "constitutional" democracy is studiously paradoxical. On the one hand he claims that it may be the best practicable form of regime and the best hope of the modern world.

It has historical connections with such elements of "pre-modern thought" as classical republicanism and the notion of the mixed regime in Aristotle's philosophy and "comes closer to what the classics demanded than any alternative that is visible in our age."[8] On the other hand its intellectual origins are in part the same as those of modern totalitarianism with which it shares certain principles and tendencies. In Strauss's dramatic historical cycle recounting the decline of the tradition of political philosophy and the rise of contemporary political institutions, "the theory of liberal democracy, as well as of communism, originated the first and second waves of modernity."[9] Strauss insists that liberal democracy and communism are not the same, even though, from a distance, they look very much alike. But one of his aims is to demonstrate that they are more alike than we might tend to assume. Furthermore, the historical degeneration of liberal democracy, with its growing "conformism" and "invasion of privacy," into something akin to communism is an eminent, imminent, and immanent danger.[10] Sometimes Strauss depreciates the difference—suggesting that it is largely just a matter of degree or a difference in means (since they are both dedicated to the creation of a "universal and homogeneous state") and that what separates the two are such particular factors as the freedom under liberal democracy to "to criticize the government."[11] But at other times he nurtures the image of opposition and claims that the future of liberal democracy rests on a choice between "true" and "perverted" liberalism.[12]

Apart from limited and ambivalent historical symbols, Strauss offers little in the way of concrete institutional and ideological analysis. Liberal democracy appears largely as a bundle of abstact qualities. It is presented as a political manifestation of the demonic humanism that animates the hubristic "modern project" of attempting to master and control nature, including human nature, for the purpose of serving the material needs and desires of humankind.[13] As close as he comes to specifying substantive attributes of liberal democracy are references to such things as "mass culture," the rule of an uneducated majority, and the belief in the freedom of individuals to live according to their private passions.[14]

At times, Strauss educes the image of liberal democracy by way of a contrast model based on classical ideas and institutions. The ancients, he claims, had little hope that an aristocracy or rule by the best citizens would, or could, come into existence. They settled for the idea of a practical solution whereby either the best, the "gentlemen," would be elected by the people or the constitution would be a mixed regime. Strauss indicates that there are historical connections between these notions and modern liberal democracy, but the connections have become attenuated. "Modern republicanism," starting from the principle of natural equality and popular sovereignty, seeks, for example, to guarantee prepolitical natural rights and achieve material prosperity, and its elite is commercial and industrial. From at least Locke through the *Federalist Papers*, there was a generally steady decline of the principles of classical republicanism into those of liberal democracy that, Strauss implies, was paralleled by similar institutional tendencies.[15] Modern democracy (which Strauss seldom distinguishes from liberal democracy) presupposes a "distinction between state and society" with the former an instrument of the latter, "a fundamental harmony between philosophy and the people" as well as between philosophy (or science) and politics, and "egalitarianism."[16]

Strauss's description of liberal democracy is basically ideational. The problem of its crisis is located within a cosmic battle of "isms," and the causes of the crisis, both historically and in the present, are attributed to the ideas of certain individuals. The solutions are of the same character. Liberal democracy may in some sense be the best hope of the West, but if it is to fulfill this function, and even survive, it requires purification. This is not a matter of any simple choice between liberalism and conservatism. Even though conservatism may represent some of its better tendencies,[17] liberal democracy encompasses both poles.

This intellectualist emphasis indicates what for Strauss was a matter of great concern, but a concern that he seldom discussed very directly or fully. This was the problem of the relationship between the intellectual (particularly the academic) and politics. Intellectuals had betrayed politics, but politics had also shunned and betrayed them. Strauss's dramatic rendition of the past is complemented by a projection of this relationship onto the present and into the future, and in an important sense it is this problem that informs his enterprise.

Strauss often speaks of Machiavelli as the turning point not only in the tradition of political thought but also in the whole development of modern institutions. Hobbes is portrayed as one of the "founders" of the modern project, and Rousseau and Nietzsche mark the crests of the last two waves of modernity. But it was Spinoza, through his restatement of "classical republicanism," who was "the philosopher who founded liberal democracy, a specifically modern regime. Directly and through his influence on Rousseau, who gave the decisive impulse to Kant, Spinoza became responsible for that version of modern republicanism" and was the "first philosopher who was both a democrat and a liberal."[18] It is far from apparent how, exactly, one could respond to Strauss's claims about this intellectual patrimony, let alone its impact on political thought and practice in the contemporary world.

The initial problem is to grasp precisely what kinds of claims are involved. Just as the origins and character of liberal democracy are highly intellectualized, so is its contemporary predicament. The Cold War, Strauss argues, came down to a "qualitative difference, which amounts to a conflict, between liberal democracy and communism."[19] Although (American) liberal democracy possesses characteristics and tendencies that make it potentially regenerate, social science, the most important intellectual and educational force in the modern world, has not only failed to nourish these better elements but also has reflected and reinforced "the most dangerous proclivities of democracy." Strauss suggests that this is no accident. The two are historically and culturally entwined and "there is then more than a mysterious pre-established harmony between the new political science and a particular version of liberal democracy."[20] Social science, with its "generous liberalism" or excessive tolerance, which is only a step away from nihilism, not only fails as a critical force but also constitutes part of the modern project and serves as both its apologist and impetus.[21]

Strauss argues that to a large degree the "new political science" teaches doctrines that are simply incorrect. But it also teaches what might be understood as "inappropriate" truths when it blurs the line between liberal democracy and communism. Although Strauss himself acknowledges that "there is only a difference of degree" between the two,[22] social and political science allows this knowledge to enter the public mind and, worst of all, neither provides nor admits a standard of comparative judgment. Through its propagation of the fact-value distinction and the idea of the equality of all values, it denies the very possibility of any such standard. But the uncritical "methodological" character of social science is not the end of the problem. It incorporates a tacit, substantive commitment to a vision of "rational society" that is coincidental with that of liberal democracy.

Strauss argues that the new political science, typified by Lasswell and the behavioral movement, "came into existence" as "a revolt against" an earlier "democratic orthodoxy" that failed to recognize "the irrationality of the masses and the necessity of elites." It could, he suggests, have learned from classical political science that there was "no compelling case for liberalism (for example, for the unprincipled freedom of such speech as does not constitute a clear and present danger) nor for democracy (free elections based on universal suffrage)."[23] But political science had such an "unfaltering commitment" to liberal democracy that, rather than facing up to the implications of its criticism, it merely declared that no rational or objective value judgments are possible and that "no iron-clad argument in favor of liberal democracy ought in reason to be expected." Thus, "the crisis of liberal democracy" has been concealed by "almost willful blindness." It is, he says, "no wonder then that the new political science has nothing to say against those who unhesitatingly prefer surrender, that is, the abandonment of liberal democracy, to war" and that it merely "fiddles" while the West writhes in the throes of crisis.[24]

Since Strauss describes the crisis of liberal democracy in basically intellectual, and even academic, terms, it is not surprising that his solution falls into the same category. It would be a mistake, however, to fail to recognize that he was poignantly aware of the gap between thought and action or between the academy and politics. For this reason alone it is necessary to be somewhat wary of taking too literally his attribution of great efficacy to the ideas of past thinkers. But although distance between philosophy and politics is inevitable, and even desirable, Strauss does not deny important relationships or the possibility of contact. His purposes were far from merely scholarly, and many of his arguments can only be understood as rhetorical moves that are, at least in purpose, "political" and not simply a form of symbolic action.

Strauss sympathized with Weber regarding the tension between the vocations of science and politics. His own reluctance about joining theory and practice reflects some of the same concerns that informed Weber's distinction between fact and value. It is rooted less in his exposure to classical wisdom (which serves to justify his claims) than in experiences indicating what happens when intellectuals get involved in politics. Marx's and Lenin's dreams of making ideals a reality ended in totalitarianism, and Heidegger violated the philosophical calling by giving intellectual legitimacy to the Nazi regime.[25] Strauss's tale about the modern project being created by philosophers who believed in the practicality of their millenarian schemes is designed to tell us something about theory and practice and the unresolvable conflict between them. To cross the line is to cease to be a true philosopher, and this is the fate of modern philosophy.[26]

The answer to the crisis of liberal democracy, in the sense of what should be done, is not for philosophers to become political actors. There are natural and eternal structures and demands that are impervious to human action and convention and prevent the direct translation of theory into practice. Philosophy cannot become esoteric and forget practice, but neither can it become politicized and submerged in life without corrupting both philosophy and politics.[27] The just city is one that reflects philosophy, but politics cannot bear philosophical rule without mutal destruction. At least this is how Strauss reads the *Republic*.

Strauss's solution to the modern crisis is the development of an "antidote" that consists of what he understood himself as doing—maintaining the basis of a liberal education, in the classical sense, in a society that devalues it. Part of the purpose of this liberal education would be to reawaken the conservative elements in liberal democracy that are most akin to classical philosophy. Such an education would in some measure help "to found an aristocracy within democratic mass society."[28] Wisdom must in part speak the language of politics, since it is neither insulated from the city nor irrelevant to it. But those who possess this wisdom and teach it should not be part of that practical aristocracy. Theoretical and prudential wisdom are, and must be, two different things. Only through the medium of propagating liberal education can the intellectual achieve a hearing in the "market place," and thus the intellectual "seeks light and therefore shuns the limelight." Strauss points to what he considers to be the "grandiose failures" of Marx, "the father of communism," and Nietzsche, "the stepgrandfather of fascism." These individuals had an exemplary liberal education in the best sense, but they did not link their wisdom to "moderation," which, in practical terms, means "loyalty to a decent constitution and even the cause of constitutionalism," that is, to liberal democracy, whose crisis is the crisis of our time.[29]

II

In discussing Strauss's essay on "the crisis of our time,"[30] my emphasis is on Strauss's emphasis, and my purpose is to bring his argument into full view where it can be examined and understood in terms of structure, content, and type. The first part of his essay deals with the character of the modern crisis and its origins; the second part focuses on the confrontation between the old and new political science or between political philosophy and social science; the third part is devoted to Aristotle and a discussion of the relevance of his teaching for understanding and dealing with the crisis.

Strauss argues that at the "core" of the modern crisis is the "doubt of what we can call the 'modern project.'" Part of the crisis, or at least a catalyst, is the external threat of communism, but the basic problem is the internal disability of modern liberal democracy. The character of the modern project is defined by its rejection of classical notions of natural right and their replacement by an attempt to dominate nature for the purpose of creating a universal society dedicated to material advancement. Strauss claims that this project was "originated by modern political philosophy," but along the way led to the decline of political philosophy itself and its transformation into "ideology or myth." Thus, any solution must begin with a "restoration" of political philosophy.

This requires a historical exercise in destruction, recollection, and recovery and particularly a return to the point of that crucial quarrel between the ancients and moderns so that the "old answers" can be given an opportunity now that the "modern answers" have failed.

Strauss urges that the existence and symptoms of the crisis are self-evident and require no detailed description or "proof." All the little crises that, he suggests, we note and experience everyday are merely manifestations of "one great crisis" that was first diagnosed by Spengler. The problem is in large part psychological—a failure of nerve and a crisis of confidence. The West has "become uncertain of its purpose." Strauss is not in any unqualified way committed to that purpose or its ultimate validity, but he maintains that the loss of "faith" has left society "completely bewildered." The West, as demonstrated in the "famous declarations made during the two world wars," had understood itself as the embodiment and "future" of mankind, and any society that understands itself in these terms cannot relinquish the vision without "despair" and "degradation." This universalism was, however, merely an expression of a "purpose stated originally by the most successful form of modern philosophy: a kind of political philosophy which aspired to build on the foundation laid by classical political philosophy, a society superior in truth and justice to the society toward which the classics aspired."

The goal of the modern project was to overcome the gap between theory and practice and remove "philosophy or science" from the realm of contemplation and employ it as an instrument in the service of human prosperity. This also meant that the philosopher became a scientist or social actor and descended into the cave. Strauss implies that this was early liberalism, Marxism, and the Hegelian dream of the coincidence of the rational and the real. The mastery of nature was to be the key to universalism, since it would make it possible for everyone to achieve their "natural right" to what Locke called "comfortable self-preservation." This would result in "freedom and justice" and would eventually lead to, and require, a society of global dimensions or at least a society of democratic nations.

Strauss argues that in recent years the "experience of Communism" has brought this project up short. It has demonstrated that, "in the foreseeable future, there cannot be a universal state" of any kind and that "political society remains what it has always been: a partial or particular society whose most urgent and primary task is self-preservation and whose highest task is its self-improvement." This confrontation with communism has only brought to light truths already accessible in classical political philosophy. Human nature is not infinitely malleable or perfectable, and there are natural limits on the scope of political society. The experience has not only provided a practical or political lesson but a "lesson regarding the principle of politics" that has cut deeply into the beliefs of the West, including its "belief that affluence is a sufficient or even necessary condition of happiness." The modern project, as opposed to the classical view of life, assumed that social progress could be achieved through external or institutional means rather than through "the formation of character" and that there could be a separation of law and morality. Such "heroes" of the project as Hobbes even suggested that morality could be supplanted by "enlightened absolute sovereigns." The lessons learned have been ones of means as well as of ends.

The general crisis of the West is, according to Strauss, "repeated" in the crisis of "moern liberal democracy." This kind of regime "claims to be responsible government," in the sense of government responsible to the governed and having "no secrets" (in Woodrow Wilson's sense of open covenants). Here Strauss is alluding to the democratic, or, in his view, egalitarian aspect of liberal democracy. It is also "limited government," with a sharp "distinction between the public and the private." This represents its liberal or permissive dimension, which in effect means that the private (and secret) is above (below, or outside) the law and, like the act of the indicivual voter, outside the realm of political responsibility in the classical sense. The contradiction within liberal democracy is that this "irresponsible individual" is also "sovereign," and Strauss's implication is that it is not really responsible government at all but something closer to a Hobbesian tyranny.

This, he claims, was not "the original notion of liberal democracy," which had entailed the idea of a "sovereign individual" who was "limited and guided by his conscience." But, as with Hobbes's despot who stood outside political society, there was no way to define, create, or provide for such qualities as conscientiousness. Just as Hobbes's despot would, in practice, probably not be enlightened, liberal democracy, which makes no place for moral education, has degenerated into "permissive egalitarianism," and "the change is well known to all." Strauss's account is abstract, and it is not clear whether this "moral decline," whereby the conscientious individual has been replaced by "the individual with his urges," is a theoretical or practical decline (or a movement from theory to practice). Strauss also suggests, without explication, that the decline is paralleled by or connected with the relativization and pluralization of the concept of culture. Its meaning has been transformed (largely through the medium of the social sciences) from "*the* culture of the human mind" to simply a designation for any mode of thought and action including that in a "lunatic asylum."

Strauss suggests, with obvious irony, that the modern sense of crisis "is not merely a strong but a vague feeling." It "acquired the status of scientific exactitude" when social science renounced its dream of a "universal and prosperous society" as "the rational solution of the human problem" because of practical difficulties and its avowed "inability to validate any value judgments." The modern project, the purpose of the West, and the core of liberal democracy were reduced to nothing more than an ideology. The "Olympian freedom" of social science "overcomes the crisis of our time" only by ignoring and subtly reinforcing it. The greatest paradox is that concern with scientific objectivity may in the end serve to "destroy the conditions of social science," since social science is more concerned with the "validity of its findings" than with the crisis of the West.

Unlike their contemporary progeny, the philosophers who created the modern project were sure of their purpose. They did not accept classical natural right, but they believed that their plan was "required by nature, by natural rights," and designed to serve "the most powerful and natural needs of men." But another paradox (in Strauss's increasingly paradoxical story) was that the conquest of nature also demanded the "conquest of human nature," which in turn meant "the questioning of the unchangeability of human nature" that had made it possible to define the ends of the modern project. Finally, science and philosophy were separated with the former dedicated to achieving power over nature, but at the same time precluded from making rational value choices about the exercise of that power. With reason limited to the objective "is," the goal or end of the project to which society had committed itself became merely an "ought" or "subjective ideal."

Strauss argues that social science is out of phase with the world of common sense and practical life. The average citizen does not, in everyday life, make a hard distinction between fact and value or feel unable to make rational value judgments. A problem emerges only when common sense is replaced by modern scientific understanding. Since science, however, depends on common sense and is a refinement of it, it should comprehend that "primary understanding" before modifying it. Strauss admits that it is not an easy task to achieve the primary understanding that is necessary for the social sciences to become "truly sciences, rational enterprises," but, fortunately, "the most basic work" was accomplished by Aristotle. Thus, a solution, or the basis of a solution, to the crisis is, in principle, accessible, but this requires escaping the dominance of modern scientific thought.

In the second part of his essay, Strauss takes up the problem of the relationship between social science and political philosophy. The decay of political philosophy into ideology has been accompanied by the replacement of "research and teaching in political philosophy" with the history of political philosophy. He does not disclose precisely how and when this took place or what was replaced, but he claims that since this transformation involves replacing a "doctrine" that claims to be true with a "survey of errors," it is "absurd" and really impossible. Although much of Strauss's own work might be characterized as such a survey, his point is to "demonstrate" how the position of modern social science is internally contradictory and necessarily turns back upon itself.

According to Strauss, what, functionally, has taken the place of political philosophy is "logic," which claims to show, on the basis of the invidious fact-value distinction, the impossibility of political philosophy. Many of the matters once considered by political philosophy are now the province of "non-philosophic political science." Its search for timeless general laws of political behavior identifies it, he claims, as part of a (Hegelian, neo-Marxist?) "comprehensive enterprise called universal history." Strauss, parenthetically, enters his doubts that history can be modeled on the natural sciences, but his basic purpose is to locate social science within this historicist framework and thereby suggest that if it followed its own inner logic, it would be forced to look not only at behavior and institutions but also at the "ideologies" that inform them. At this point Strauss's argument becomes conspicuously ironic.

He suggests that some ideologies (we may assume, at least, Marxism and liberal democracy) are "known to have been originated by outstanding men." To grasp the crude understandings, which are those that are in practice politically effective, one must understand the source from which they were derived, and, consequently, "it becomes necessary to consider whether and how the ideology as conceived by the originator was modified by its adherents." Since "one kind of ideology consists of the teachings of the political philosophers," it is necessary to understand them as they understand themselves in order to assess the effect of these ideas. "Surely," he says, "every one of them was mistaken in believing that his teaching was a sound teaching regarding political things," since "through a reliable tradition we know this belief forms part of a rationalization." But "in the case of the greatest minds," this "process" and the manner in which the ideas were understood (by adherents of various types, adversaries, and just plain observers) is worth studying. The activity of behavioral science requires, then, the study of history of political philosophy, and this, fortuitously, has been "rendered possible today by the shaking of all traditions" in the wake of the modern crisis. The crisis "may have the accidental advantage of enabling us to understand in an untraditional, a fresh manner what was hitherto understood only in a traditional, derivative manner."

According to Strauss's hypothetical account, modern political science would eventually be forced to conduct a study of the classics, and this, in turn, would require it to confront reflectively its own premises and "consider the possibility that the older political science was sounder and truer." It would, in this way, come to transcend its own limitations and even transform itself into a study of the history of political philosophy that would be more than a survey of errors. Such a revitalized understanding of classical political philosophy would not provide "recipes" for dealing with our "present-day predicament." The "success" of modern philosophy has resulted in a new type of society to which classical principles do not directly apply, but a grasp of these principles "may be the starting point for an adequate analysis, to be achieved by us, of present-day society in its peculiar character, and for the wise application, to be achieved by us, of these principles to our tasks."

After this exploration of the limits of social science, Strauss's next move is to confront objections that might be raised to seeking wisdom from the classics, and particularly Aristotle. This final section of the essay is sophistic and opaque, and it requires careful explication. Its intention, however, is basically to present an indirect critique of the image of liberal democracy that he has evoked and to call into question certain aspects of contemporary political thought and politics by associating them with this image.

Strauss does not say precisely who claims that Aristotle's political philosophy has been refuted, but the assumption of refutation is, he suggests, tied to the notion that Aristotle's cosmology has been discredited by modern science and philosophy. Strauss never claims that it has not been, or does not deserve to be, discredited, but he argues that the core *principle* of classical metaphysics has not been refuted. This is "the fact of essential differences" and the existence of "essences" as well as the entailed proposition that the "whole consists of heterogeneous beings." He suggests that we can, for example, deduce from this principle that there is an "essential difference between the common good and the private good." From this point, Strauss's text moves on like a Platonic dialogue with the interlocutors absent.

Strauss next takes up the belief "that Aristotle has been refuted because he was anti-democratic." Strauss does not want to argue that he was a democrat but rather to explain why he was not one. He preemptorily defines *democracy* as "majority rule" and notes Aristotle's claim that there are always two groups—the rich and poor—in every society and that the poor, or those who must "earn their living," constitute the majority and do not have the leisure to acquire the eduation to rule well. Strauss concedes that today "the economy of plenty" might make it possible for the majority to be educated, but he argues that these current circumstances are the product of modern technology and science. This 'new interpretation of science," as existing "for the sake of human power," which appeared in the "works of Bacon, Descartes, and Hobbes," rejected Aristotle's idea that science existed for the sake of "contemplation." Strauss maintains that we have now (e.g., because of the atom bomb) become "doubtful whether the unlimited progress of science and technology is something unqualifiedly good." If the modern notion of science is dubious, then so, he implies, is the status of the economy of plenty and majority rule. Aristotle's undemocratic principle of justice remains intact.

Another reason for considering Aristotle as something other than a democrat is his assumption that people are naturally "unequal in politically relevant respects." Strauss argues that this "can hardly be denied," as, for example, in the cases of "natural inequality regarding understanding." This aspect of the human condition is in fact still "recognized" in modern democracy and its idea of "equality of opportunity," which "implies" that people should pursue that for which they are best suited. The same idea is embodied in modern "representative," as opposed to "direct," democracy, "which elects people whom it believes are above average." It is difficult to be certain about what Strauss means here. He may, for example, be pointing to the residue of earlier republican principles in liberal democracy, or the force may be ironic and sardonic. Few would accept this as either an accurate or adequate interpretation of equality of opportunity and representative democracy.

Finally, Strauss considers the objection "that Aristotle's whole political philosophy is narrow, or provincial." He rejects this on the historical grounds that the concept of the "city-state" was neither merely nor essentially Greek and that *polis* is best translated not as *state* (which implies, for example, a distinction between state and society) but as *country*. He wants to stress the universal significance of Aristotle's analysis of the *polis* and his notion of happiness.

Strauss claims that Aristotle embraced a "reasonable" notion of happiness, which is still the "ordinary" one that "all men understand" (i.e., an "enviable" life or "reasonable contentedness"). Substantively, "happiness means the practice of moral virtue above everything else, the doing of noble deeds," and the "complete human good" that is the end of the city. Yet in "scientific circles," especially since the time of the seventeenth century "founders of modern political philosophy," this notion has been questioned on the basis that "happiness is entirely subjective." Since this threatened to destroy any basis of political judgment, individuals such as Locke and Madison substituted the "conditions" of happiness, such as "life, liberty, and pursuit of happiness," that they took to be objective. The end of political society or the state was to create and maintain these conditions or "natural rights of men." They forsook the idea of imposing public criteria of human happiness and maintaining its superiority over the private and subjective search for happiness in society. This inevitably implied that society was superior to the state, and the "solution" to the persistent "theoretical" ambiguity about this relationship was to conceive of "culture or civilization" as a "matrix for both."

Strauss insists on a sharp distinction between the modern (seventeenth and eighteenth centuries) concept of natural rights (or the rights of man) and the traditional (classic and medieval) teaching about natural law. The transformation was one in which the idea of rights was given priority over the ideas of law and duty in which " 'nature' was replaced by 'man'." This anthropocentric shift and the rejection of a "hierarchic order" corresponded to Descartes's epistemology.

In Aristotle's philosophy of the *polis*, political society was naturally limited in size and conformed to the nature of man by taking account of the limits on such human powers as "knowing" and "caring" for others. This philosophy, was also concerned with the *politeia* (constitution, political order, or regime), its types (which determined the character of society), and ultimately with the question of their ranking and the best form. "Aristotle is animated by the political passion, the concern for the best regime." But this led to "a grave political and moral problem" manifested in Aristotle's discussion of the difference between a good man and a good citizen.

The constitution (form) determines the character and end of society (matter), and every society (even a materialistic one) has a hierarchy of values, including one primary value that represents its character. In the case of democracy, this value is equality. Aristotle (according to Strauss) also claimed that there must be a "harmony" between the primary value and the regime or the "preponderant" or "authoritative" part of society (possibly, but not necessarily, the majority) that gives form or "tone" to society. Although it "runs counter to our notions," Aristotle held, and our "experience" confirms, that the identity of a city is a function of the regime. "Moderate and sober people reject" the "partisan" or "extreme view" that a city is only truly a city if it corresponds to a particular kind of regime, but "patriots" are also incorrect in insisting that a "change of regime is a surface event which does not affect the being of a city at all." Aristotle is "much more rational" than a patriot and "less radical" than a partisan. For Aristotle a change in regime does not, for example, necessarily cancel obligations, but it constitutes another city in its "most important respect." The highest possible value would be "human excellence," and nothing would be a greater change than to turn to "baseness." Aristotle is a "partisan of excellence."

Strauss suggests that Aristotle's "thesis regarding the supremacy of the regime" can be clarified in terms of the phenomenon of "loyalty." Loyalty should be directed toward not simply the "country" but also "the country *informed* by the regime." This principle would, for example, invalidate the argument of a fascist or communist who would claim to be a loyal citizen and set out to undermine the Constitution "out of loyalty to the United States." No one "who knows what he is doing" would, out of loyalty to liberal democracy, say or "teach" that the "Constitution should be changed constitutionally so that the regime would cease to be a liberal democracy." Strauss argues that a specific notion of justice (democratic, aristocratic, and soon) embraced by the "preponderant part of society" and, again, "not necessarily the majority," is the "principle of legitimacy" or "public or political morality," which is in turn the "source of all law." Even if a society (such as liberal democracy) should be "characterized by extreme permissiveness," this principle must be "established and defended." But this particular principle "necessarily has its limits," since "a society that permits its members every sort of non-permissiveness will soon cease to be permissive" and, in fact, will soon cease altogether. Strauss's message is once again that liberal democracy should be defended, but that it is, or has become, however, internally defective.

The variety of regimes and principles of legitimacy inevitably raises the question of the best regime. Aristotle said that the highest end of man, happiness, was the same for both the individual and society, yet the highest kind of happiness for the individual was contemplation and not politics or the "doing of noble deeds." The city can, at best, achieve a kind of analogous status. Strauss suggests that this "seeming self-contradiction" or "apparent result" is the consequence of the fact that the idea of the best regime is "an explicit abstraction. . .from the full meaning of the best life of the individual." Such an abstraction is "appropriate to a political inquiry, strictly and narrowly conceived," because it indicates the limits of political life and the life of the citizen. Strauss, also, by implication, indicates his notion of the limits of theory and philosophy in its relationship to political life.

Strauss claims that it is significant that Aristotle has examples "of men of the highest excellence" but no examples of such cities. There is always and everywhere a tension between philosophy and politics and between the good person and good citizen, but that tension is especially pronounced in the case of liberal democracy. An individual can only transcend this city through "what is best in him" or by pursuing "true happiness" as opposed to subjective happiness, but subjective happiness, Strauss has insisted, is at the core of liberal democracy. Not only is full self-realization impossible in such a regime, but there is a deep conflict between liberal democracy and both the pursuit and content of philosophical knowledge. Yet, for various reasons, philosophy must seek to sustain this kind of regime.

III

It should be apparent to a sensitive reader that the essay (in its discussion of loyalty, communism, the limits of the politics, egalitarianism, and various other matters) is not only a theoretical critique of the idea of liberal democracy, or its fallen condition, but a response to some of the concrete international and domestic political issues of the 1960s. We would surely fail to grasp the point, then, if we did not identify it in certain important respects as political commentary.[31] It is about politics; its intention and purpose are political; it is often ideological in tone and substance; it displays political passion; and it is intensely rhetorical and evocative. Furthermore, in view of the extensive educational influence and the latent political effects that might, and probably do in the recent administration of govenment in the United States, attach to Strauss's work, it must be considered politically consequential to an extent that goes well beyond most academic political theory. Yet, in an equally important sense, it cannot be understood as political unless the real difference and intricate relationship between public and academic discourse is obscured.

Strauss was more attuned to this disparity and complexity than much of contemporary political theory, which has largely translated this practical issue into a philosophical problem and treated it accordingly. But awareness and concern did not allow or impel him to achieve an authentic position. In the end, Strauss's analysis of liberal democracy and its crisis is only an intimation that can neither be part of either philosophical or political discourse nor some intelligible intermediate ground. The argument is as elusive as its object. It is consistently elliptical, consciously ambiguous, broken by aporian moments, moved forward by spurious allusions, characterized by a strategic or mock-strategic style, laced with irony and sarcasm, and held together by arcane thematic connections. It is a fascinating object of exegesis, but there is no clear basis on which it can be substantively engaged either politically or philosophically.

Evocation, rhetoric, and obscurantism are the stuff of politics, but there is a paradox when political speech is conducted in an academic context and addresses philosophical themes. The point is not that it is ultra *vires*. It does, however, lack or avoid a primary audience, unless it is assumed that dissembling is an acceptable form of education and scholarly exchange. And its nobility of purpose and belief in the ultimate service of truth cannot insulate it from subjection to critical description and analysis, which destroys it as a medium of expression. It seeks, without leaving the security of the academy, to speak politically in the language of philosophy and to philosophize rhetorically. It cannot in the end do either effectively or genuinely, but it justifies its antimonian pursuit in terms of some vague notion of a seamless web of social life that makes actual differences between philosophy and politics nugatory.

What, then is the status of philosophical claims to political knowledge that lack political authority? This was a great problem for Strauss, and even if he did not solve it, he understood it. Like Weber, he was committed to the autonomy of both politics and philosophy, yet he insisted on the relevance of philosophy and on rescuing political theory from academic impotence. The dilemma propelled his project into a kind of inauthenticity where philosophy held itself academically aloof, but compromised truth in the service of political purpose. More than once Strauss reveals his willingness to accept the noble lie not only in politics but also in the relationship between philosophy and politics. His saga of the decline of the tradition and the crisis of modernity falls into this category, but so do his claims about the existence and rediscovery of natural right.

Although Strauss talks a great deal about transcendental standards of political judgment and the need to accept this regulative assumption in both philosophy and politics, he knew that philosophy could posit no such transcontextual grounds. There was no philosophical solution to philosophical relativism and historicism. His claim that there was a tradition of thought and action that accepted these principles and his analysis of individuals such as Aristotle at best only make a case for a past belief in natural law. Even less convincing are his arguments for a version of pragmatic univeralism or the notion that evidence for such principles is indirectly accessible in the practice of everyday life where people make value judgments and assume criteria of validity. And his claim about the internal contradiction of value relativism is far from a compelling basis for embracing absolutism.

What cannot be doubted, however, is that Strauss recognized that political society required transcendental beliefs and a belief in transcendentalism. There must be a belief in truth in politics even if truth and politics were ultimately incompatible. His mistake was to assume that it was within the province and capacity of academic philosophy to save the appearances and underwrite political values either specifically or generically.

It was not so much that modern philosphy challenged transcendentalism that was at stake for Strauss as the fact that, in his view, society could not bear the fate of that challenge. He examines in detail the theoretical revolution produced by the three waves of modernity and culminates in Nietzsche's withdrawal of meaning from history and the universe and the call for its human reconstitution.[32] But he never really refutes or contradicts Nietzsche's revelation, nor does he quarrel with what he describes as Nietzsche's claim that

> the theoretical analysis of human life that realizes the relativity of all comprehensive views and thus depreciates them would make human life impossible, for it would destroy the protecting atmosphere within which life or culture or action is alone possible.[33]

It would seem that in an important sense Strauss's and Nietzsche's projects are identical.

Strauss believed, or would have some audiences believe, that modern philosophy contributed significantly to the rise of fascism. But although this particular political "implication" of modern thought had in practice been defeated by liberal democracy, Nietzsche's "critique of modern rationalism or of the modern belief in reason cannot be dismissed or forgotten. This is the deepest reason for the crisis of liberal democracy." The problem for Strauss was to keep the "theoretical crisis" from becoming a "practical crisis,"[34] This required a philosophical concealment of the truth. If the theoretical crisis was not once again to end in a practical catastrophe, philosophy must take up the task of helping to sustain those values that we in practice judge to be superior to communism, but which have been undermined philosophically and ideologically. Philosophy must aid in maintaining the legitimating values of political order that, like the authority of Oz, must remain sacred to be effective. Since, however, the claims of philosophy lack natural political authority, they must be supported by the authority of knowledge if they are to speak, even indirectly, to politics.

Strauss's discussion of the past, present, and future of liberal democracy and the meaning and accessibility of the classical teaching is part of a story that belongs to an ultimately paradoxical and impossible enterprise. It is an enterprise designed to maintain both the myths of political society and the myth of the special authority and ability of academic political theory to speak to such matters.

Notes

1. For a discussion of this genre, and Strauss in particular, see John G. Gunnell, "The Myth of the Tradition," *American Political Science Reivew*, 72 (March 1978): 122–34; and *Political Theory: Tradition and Interpretation* (Cambridge, MA.: Winthrop, 1979).

2. Leo Strauss, "The Three Waves of Modernity," *Political Philosophy: Six Essays by Leo Strauss* ed, Hilail Gilden (Indianapolis: Bobbs-Merrill, 1975), 82.

3. See John G. Gunnell, "Encounters of the Third Kind: The Alienation of Theory in American Political Science," *American Journal of Political Science*, (August 1981), 440–61; "In Search of the Political Object: Beyond Methodology and Transcendentalism," *What Should Political Theory be Now?*, ed. John S. Nelson (Albany: SUNY Press, 1983), 25–52.

4. Leo Strauss, *Liberalism, Ancient and Modern* 2(New York: Basic Books, 1968), 225.

5. Ibid., 63.

6. Leo Strauss, *Thoughts on Machiavelli* (New York: Free Press, 1958), 13–14.

7. Leo Strauss, *Natural Right and History* (Chicago: University of Chicago Press, 1953), 1–2.

8. Leo Strauss, *What is Political Philosophy?* (New York: Free Press, 1959), 113; Strauss, "The Three Waves of Modernity," 98.

9. Strauss, "The Three Waves of Modernity," 98.

10. Strauss, *What is Political Philosophy?*, 38.

11. Strauss, *Liberalism, Ancient and Modern*, v, vi.

12. Ibid., 64.

13. Strauss, *What is Political Philosophy?*, 55.

14. Strauss, *Liberalism, Ancient and Modern* 5, 12.

15. Strauss, *Natural Right and History*, 245.

16. Leo Strauss, *The City and Man* (Chicago: Rand McNally, 1964), 35, 37, 40.

17. Strauss, *Liberalism, Ancient and Modern*, 16–18.

18. Ibid., 241.

19. Leo Strauss, "Epilogue," *Essays on the Scientific Study of Politics*, ed. Herbert Storing (New York: Holt, Rinehart & Winston, 1962), 319.

20. Ibid., 326.

21. Strauss, *Natural Right and History*, 4–6.

22. Strauss, "Epilogue," 319.

23. Ibid., 326.

24. Ibid., 327.

25. Strauss, *Liberalism, Ancient and Modern*, 227.

26. Leo Strauss, *On Tyranny* (New York: Free Press, 1963), 218; Strauss, *Thoughts on Machiavelli*, 297–98; Strauss, *Natural Right and History*, 34.

27. Strauss, *Natural Right and History*, 26.

28. Strauss, *Liberalism, Ancient and Modern*, 5.

29. Ibid., 24–25.

30. This essay, "Political Philosophy and the Crisis of Our Time," was published in *The Post-Behavioral Era*, ed. George J. Graham and George W. Carey (New York: David McKay, 1972), 217–42. It was adapted from two lectures published in *The Predicament of Modern Politics*, ed. Herbert Spaeth (Detroit: University of Detroit Press, 1964), 41–54; 91–103. The first lecture was the "Crisis of Our Time" and the second was "The Crisis of Political Philosophy." Strauss is clear about the connection: "The crisis of our time as a consequence of the crisis of political philosophy" (p. 41). Portions of these essays also form the introduction to *The City and Man* in which the matieral on Aristotle appears in expanded form as the first chapter. The earlier versions have short but pointed sections that stress the failure of the Western powers in the early part of the century to take a firm stand against totalitarianism, the decline of the West, the Cold War, and the extent to which the crisis is manifest in a retreat from political "honor" and "purpose" in the face of communism. There are also additional short passages that represent characteristic arguments of Strauss regarding the importance of the classical teaching, the possibility of recovering it, and its status as "truer" and more original than modern thought. The essay is also thematically closely related to his essays on "What is Political Philosophy?" and "The Three Waves of Modernity."

31. See Gunnell, 1978, 1979; Deborah Baumgold, "Political Commentary on the History of Political Theory," *American Political Science Review* 75, (December 1981), 928–40.

32. Strauss, "The Three Waves of Modernity," 94–98.

33. Strauss, *Natural Right and History*, 26.

34. Strauss, "The Three Waves of Modernity," 98.

Part 2

ISSUES IN LIBERALISM

First Section

STRAUSS ON LIBERALISM

Hilail Gildin

LEO STRAUSS AND
THE CRISIS OF LIBERAL DEMOCRACY

The reflections that follow will take the form of an attempt to understand the concluding paragraph of Strauss's *The Three Waves of Modernity*. That paragraph reads as follows:

> I draw a political conclusion from the foregoing remarks. The theory of liberal democracy, as well as of communism, originated in the first and second waves of modernity; the political implication of the third wave proved to be fascism. Yet this undeniable fact does not permit us to return to the earlier forms of modern thought: the critique of modern rationalism or of the modern belief in reason by Nietzsche cannot be dismissed or forgotten. This is the deepest reason for the crisis of liberal democracy. The theoretical crisis does not necessarily lead to a practical crisis, for the superiority of liberal democracy to communism, Stalinist or post Stalinist, is obvious enough. And above all, liberal democracy, in contradistinction to communism and fascism, derives powerful support from a way of thinking which cannot be called modern at all: the premodern thought of our western tradition.[1]

Strauss does not affirm, in this passage, that the cause of democracy has been rendered hopeless by Nietzsche's criticism of it. Nietzsche has indeed made it impossible, according to Strauss, to rest the case for democracy any longer on the grounds previously furnished by modern political philosophy, although these grounds originally persuaded men to fight for it and for a time were an important part of the customary argument for it. I understand Strauss to mean that the radical historicism of Nietzsche and his most important successors has made it difficult to believe any longer in the state of nature or in the free self-legislation of practical reason or in the rationality of the historical process as a fundamentally progressive process that leads to and culminates in the universal recognition of human freedom and dignity. That the belief in the solidity of these grounds has been shaken is sufficiently demonstrated, for Strauss, by the continuing power of the fact-value distinction among social scientists. The deepest reason for the crisis of modern liberal democracy underlies the most obvious manifestation of it.

The theoretical crisis need not, Strauss says, lead to a practical crisis. (That it may do so under certain unspecified conditions is not ruled out.) Most striking and thought-provoking, however, is Strauss's concluding assertion. What powerful support can the nondemocratic, not to say antidemocratic, premodern thought of our western tradition possibly lend to liberal or constitutional democracy today?

Strauss rejected certain contemporary attempts to portray the classics as democrats: "The premises: 'the classics are good,' and 'democracy is good' do not validate the conclusion 'hence the classics were good democrats.' It would be silly to deny that the classics rejected democracy as an inferior kind of regime." The classics were aware, he acknowledges, that democracy, owing to its permissiveness, tolerated philosophy. The execution of Socrates by Athens confirms rather than refuses this contention if one takes into account the length of time during which Socrates was permitted to engage in the kinds of conversations for which he became so well known. "Yet Plato did not regard this consideration as decisive. For he was concerned not only with the possibility of philosophy, but likewise with a stable political order that would be congenial to moderate political courses; and such an order, he thought, depends on the predominance of old families."[2]

This would seem to leave the cause of liberal or constitutional democracy, as Strauss views it, in sorry shape. Liberal democracy would find itself between a tradition that supports it but is no longer tenable and a tradition that Strauss regards as still tenable but that never favored it, and this might lead some to suppose that Strauss's reasons for preferring constitutional democracy to its Communist antagonist is at bottom the same as the reason for Socrates' attachment to Athens. Since democracy, ancient as well as modern, treasures the freedom to live as one pleases, it tolerates philosophy, whereas Communist regimes do not. The extent to which Strauss's work reflects his concern with the contemporary crisis of philosophy—a crisis that, in his opinion, is at the bottom of the theoretical crisis of modern liberalism—seems to support the belief that his political preferences derive from his concern for the future of philosophy.

Yet it would be a mistake to conclude that Strauss cared about the fate of constitutional democracy only to the extent to which it was linked to the fate of philosophy. Like Socrates, he was just in more than one sense. His support of liberal democracy can be compared to his support of political Zionism. No one who knew Strauss ever doubted the depth and genuineness of his concern for Israel. Nor could anyone who knew him think that this concern was based on the belief that the fate of philosophy in some mysterious way depended on the survival of Israel. He thought no such thing. His support of political Zionism was unhesitating even though his approval of it was not unqualified:

> Political Zionism was concerned primarily with nothing but the cleansing of the Jews from millenial degradation or with the recovery of Jewish dignity, honor, or pride. . .

> . . .[B]y making its peace with traditional Jewish thought. . .it brought about the establishment of the state of Israel and therewith that cleansing which it had primarily intended; it thus procured a blessing for all Jews everywhere regardless of whether they admit it or not. It did not, however, solve the Jewish problem. It could not solve the Jewish problem because of the narrowness of its conception, however noble. . .in the religious sense, and perhaps not only in the religious sense, the state of Israel is part of the Galuth. Finite, relative problems can be solved; infinite, absolute problems cannot be solved. In other words, human beings will never create a society which is free from contradictions. From every point of view it looks as if the Jewish people were the chosen people, at least in the sense that the Jewish problem is the most manifest symbol of the human problem insofar as it is a social or political problem.[3]

In the immediate sequel, Strauss proceeds to contrast the solutions to the Jewish problem provided by liberal democracy and by Communism.

> Liberalism stands and falls by the distinction between state and society or by the recognition of a private sphere, protected by the law but impervious to the law, with the understanding that, above all, religion as particular religion belongs to the private sphere. As certainly as the liberal state will not "discriminate" against its Jewish citizens, as certainly is it constitutionally unable and even unwilling to prevent "discrimination" against Jews on the part of individuals or groups. To recognize a private sphere in the sense indicated means to permit private "discrimination," to protect it, and thus in fact to foster it. The liberal state cannot provide a solution to the Jewish problem, for such a solution would require the legal prohibition against every kind of "discrimination," that is, the abolition of the private sphere, the denial of the difference between state and society, the destruction of the liberal state. Such a destruction would not by any means solve the Jewish problem, as is shown in our days by the anti-Jewish policy of the U.S.S.R. It is foolish to say that that policy contradicts the principles of Communism, for it contradicts the principles of Communism to separate the principles of Communism from the Communist movement. The U.S.S.R. owes its survival to Stalin's decision not to wait for the revolution of the Western proletariat, that is, for what others would do for the U.S.S.R., but to build up socialism in a single country where his word was the law, by the use of any means, however bestial, and these means could include, as a matter of course, means successfully used before, not to say invented, by Hitler: the large-scale murder of party members and anti-Jewish measures. This is not to deny that Communism has not become

what National Socialism always was, the prisoner of an anti-Jewish ideology, but makes use of anti-Jewish measures in an unprincipled manner, when and where they seem to be expedient. It is merely to confirm our contention that the uneasy "solution of the Jewish problem" offered by the liberal state is superior to the Communist "solution."[4]

The reason why what benefits or harms philosophy was not, according to Strauss, the only thing the classics looked at in determining how good or bad a regime is can be seen from a passage we quoted earlier: Plato, he affirms, was concerned not only with the possibility of philosophy but also with political stability and political moderation. All these desirable things are not always found in the same city, as the well-known contrast between Athens and Sparta makes plain. But does this not point to the answer to the question we earlier raised? Does it not tell us what, in the classical teaching, supports the cause of liberal democracy? To the extent that the classical teaching concludes that the role of law is preferable to tyranny, it also provides a basis for preferring liberal or constitutional democracy to communism or fascism.

That Strauss and the classics, for all practical purposes, favored the rule of law rather than men and were averse to arbitrary government is not plain to all. That is because although their support of the rule of law was unhesitating, their approval of it was not unqualified. They believed that rule of law as such suffered from inescapable defects. They thought that it was important for the intelligent supporters of constitutionalism to support it with their eyes open to its serious defects precisely because constitutional government was the best one could reasonably hope for, practically speaking. In order to make their thoughtful readers aware of what these defects were, they on occasion spoke in praise of absolute rule by the wise or by men of surpassingly outstanding excellence or by virtuous and wise tyrants. In the case of Aristotle the passages concerning the circumstances under which absolute rule by the exceptionally virtuous individual is proper and just have not, by and large, misled his commentators into overlooking his support of constitutional regimes. Socrates, Xenophon, and Plato have not always been so fortunate. Although it did not escape the notice of scholars such as McIlwain and Sinclair that Plato's *Statesman* is a thoughtful defense of rule of law, for the most part certain unforgettable passages from the *Republic* have shaped opinion concerning what Plato's views were regarding the best regime: Plato's best regime, according to that opinion, is absolute rule by one or more philosopher-kings. In *On Tyranny*, Strauss points out that Socrates was accused of teaching his associates to be "tyrannical" and that Xenophon was suspected of adhering to and transmitting that "tyrannical" teaching as well. In our time we have witnessed a renewal of this misunderstanding. To the extent that Strauss was thought to favor a return to classical political philosophy and in particular to the political philosophy of Plato, he and his students were, on occasion, believed to prefer absolute rule by themselves to constitutional democracy. It was this, I believe, that led an eminent fool to proclaim that no Leninist or Straussian would ever be permitted to receive tenure at Yale. Alexandre Kojève for one, Strauss's philosophical adversary as well as his philosophical friend, never entertained any doubts concerning what the "tyrannical" reaching meant for Strauss:

> According to Strauss, Xenophon was perfectly well aware of the necessarily utopian character of the sort of advice given by Simonides. He thought that the "enlightened" and "popular" tyranny portrayed by the latter is an ideal which cannot be realized, and *his dialogue has as its goal to convince us that, this being the case, it is better to give up any idea of tyranny before even having tried to establish it.* Strauss and Xenophon thus seem to reject the very idea of "tyrannical" government.[5]

It is because Kojève disagreed with Strauss regarding this point that he took issue with Strauss's *On Tyranny* in a long review essay, to which Strauss later replied. Those seeking to gain an understanding of the practical implications of Strauss's political philosophy can do no better than to begin by reading that exchange and the work that gave rise to it.[6]

To see how the "tyrannical" teaching makes one aware of the limits of the political, it is useful to recall the well-known example of Churchill in the 1930s. In retrospect it is easy to see that England (and mankind) would have been spared an immense amount of suffering if his warnings had been heeded in time. The constitutional government of England was not, as later became apparent, very good or very wise at least in this very important respect. Yet who seriously believes that it would have been better for England to have been a tyranny during that period? The mere fact that the absolute rule of the wise is impossible does not keep men from sometimes having to pay a very high price for its absence. That price, in turn, helps explain why the temptation to resort to tyranny remains a peril coeval with political life. Classical political philosophy, which is "free from all fanaticism because it knows that evil cannot be eradicated and therefore that one's expectations from politics must be moderate," provides the best antidote to that temptation, according to Strauss.[7]

Grasping the classical tradition's approval of constitutional government and repudiation of tyranny is essential for understanding the support premodern political philosophy can give to the cause of constitutional democracy. It is not, however, sufficient. Constitutional government can take a variety of forms. There can be constitutional monarchies as well as constitutional democracies. What we have said up to this point does not explain the restriction to constitutional democracy. It does not explain why, according to Strauss, "at present democracy is the only practicable alternative to various forms of tyranny." In particular, it does not shed enough light on what Strauss means when he declares that "it would not be difficult to show that the classical argument cannot be disposed of as readily as is now generally thought, and that liberal or constitutional democracy comes closer to what the classics demanded than any alternative that is viable in our age."[8]

The principle to which Strauss appeals in outlining the classical argument for liberal or constitutional democracy is one familiar to every reader of Aristotle's *Politics*. At the same time it is known to the average person whether or not he or she has ever heard of Aristotle: "We too, even our communist coexistents, think that it is just to give equal things to equal people and unequal things to people of unequal merit."[9] We will be chiefly concerned with the answer implied by this principle to the question of who should rule. We will first consider its political implications in one unusual situation analyzed by Aristotle in the *Politics* and then examine its consequences for the situation created by modern technology.

In the last two Books of the *Politics*, Aristotle constructs an aristocratic utopia. Citizenship in this regime is limited to Aristotelian gentlemen, men whose youth was devoted to acquiring moral virtue and practical wisdom and whose adult lives are spent in their exercise. Aristotle raises the question whether they should be permanently ruled by the best among themselves or whether they should all take part in ruling and in being ruled. Let us make the plausible assumption that some of Aristotle's aristocrats will surpass the large majority of their fellows as much as, say, Burke or Churchill surpassed the large majority of their fellow members of Parliament. Why should Aristotle's aristocrats not be ruled by those among them who combine the best breeding with the best natural gifts? Aristotle's answer to this question deserves to be pondered. I quote it in the literal translation of Laurence Berns: "If therefore certain men were to differ from the others as much as we deem the gods and the heroes to differ from men, having first to begin with great superiority in body and then in soul so that the pre-eminence of the rulers was indisputable and evident for the ruled it is clear that it would be better for the same men always some to rule and some to be ruled."[10] Aristotle goes on to point out that superiority in virtue is not inseparably linked to bodily superiority and therefore is not easy to recognize. The conclusion Aristotle draws is that superiority in virtue, even great superiority in virtue, is not manifest even under the optimum conditions supplied by the best regime, though it may well be present

there. Aristotle's highest title to rule, outstanding superiority in practical wisdom and moral virtue, must be diluted by the requirement for
consent before it can become politically effective and salutary. Aristotle,
whose starting point seems to be so much more down-to-earth than
Plato's—Aristotle does not require theoretical wisdom of his rulers, but
rather integrity and practical wisdom—reaches the same conclusions
regarding the limits of the city from the standpoint of his more down-to-
earth principle that Plato had reached from the standpoint of his more
exalted one. Politically speaking, all citizens of Aristotle's aristocracy
must be regarded as equal. Justice requires giving equal things to those
who are equal in merit. Therefore, all must have the right to take part in
ruling and in being ruled.

The principle that leads to the equality of all citizens in Aristotle's best
regime does not always have egalitarian political consequences. It is appealed to by Aristotle when he justifies the absolute kingship, over willing subjects, by a man of surpassing virtue. Such kingships, however,
are, as Aristotle observes, very much a thing of the past, whereas rule by
the many, whether of the sound or unsound variety, is very much a
thing of the present. Kingship belongs to the dawn of political life when
cities were small and men who greatly excelled in virtue were rare and
unrivaled. Kingships don't occur now, Aristotle affirms, because cities
now are big and consist of men who are alike; none surpasses the others
sufficiently in the politically relevant virtues for it to be right for him to be
king over the rest.[11] It is even doubtful whether the politically relevant inequalities in virtue that remain are sufficiently great to justify aristocracy
in the strict sense, given the disappointing fact, noted by Aristotle, that
nowhere can as many as a hundred virtuous and nobly born men be
found.[12] Aristotle's aristocratic utopia seems to be no better suited than
his kingship to the cities of his time. In these cities, he says, stable
regimes other than democratic ones are difficult to establish. Moreover,
in these cities rule by the many would seem to be a requirement of
Aristotle's principles of right as well. Aristotle's eminently practical
solution to the political problem, in which the key role is assigned to the
middle class, is meant to show such cities how to establish what we
would call a sound and law-abiding democracy and what Aristotle calls
a "polity." Big cities have, for Aristotle, the disadvantage of restricting
what is feasible politically to rule by the many, whether of the sound or
unsound variety. But they do have one compensating advantage:
Because a large middle class is present in them, it is at least possible to
establish a polity there. The presence of a large middle class is said by
Aristotle to have a stabilizing influence even on unsound democratic
orders. [13] The equality that prevails among the citizens of Aristotle's

aristocratic utopia is on a much higher plane than the equality found among the citizens of his polity. The first is based on virtue. The second is based on a rough equality in merit that falls far short of virtue. The principle to which appeal is made in all these cases remains one and the same, however.

The principle that we have been discussing is not egalitarian. It requires giving unequal things to people of unequal merit. Yet because differences in merit must be manifest in order to be subject to law, a constitutional government will treat as equal those whose inequality is not manifest. The law ignores differences in merit that it cannot sink its teeth into. Under certain conditions, as we have seen, the principle does have egalitarian consequences. Strauss repeatedly asserted that the application of it to conditions under which economy of scarcity has been replaced by the economy of abundance would result in an argument for constitutional democracy. That replacement, it is true, presupposes "unlimited technological progress with all its terrible hazards," a development of whose beneficial character Strauss was far from certain.[14] It was not clear to him that the decision to emancipate technology from moral and political control was sound. "We have no right to applaud a situation that was created by a decision that, however well intentioned, was not evidently virtuous and wise." "But" he adds immediately, "we cannot escape from that situation; it is our duty to act virtuously and wisely on it."[15] If, in an economy of scarcity, the best that one can reasonably hope for is what Strauss calls aristocracy, open or disguised, then in an economy of abundance the best that one can reasonably hope for is liberal or constitutional democracy. The argument linking the two is supplied by the following important passage:

> It is a demand of justice that there should be a reasonable correspondence between the social hierarchy and the natural hierarchy. The lack of such a correspondence in the old scheme was defended by the fundamental fact of scarcity. With the increasing abundance it became increasingly possible to see and to admit the element of hypocrisy which had entered into the traditional notion of aristocracy; the existing aristocracies proved to be oligarchies, rather than aristocracies. In other words it became increasingly easy to argue from the premise that natural inequality has very little to do with social inequality, that practically or politically speaking one may safely assume that all men are by nature equal, that all men have the same natural rights, provided one uses this rule of thumb as the major premise for reaching the conclusion that everyone should be given the same opportunity as everyone else: natural inequality has its rightful place in the use, nonuse, or abuse of opportunity in the race as distinguished from at the start. Thus it became possible to abolish many injustices or at least many things which had become injustices.[16]

This passage reveals in interesting overlap between teachings one associates with modern political philosophers and the conclusions that, according to Strauss, follow from applying the classical—and the everyday—principle of right to a condition of increasing abundance. Important differences remain. Hobbes, for example, wishes the claim that all men are by nature equal to be an exact truth and not a rule of thumb. The difference between the conclusions drawn by Strauss and the modern teachings they remind one of is that the modern teachings are doctrinaire and inflexible. They are not presented as valid only in an economy of abundance. They are affirmed to be valid everywhere and always. Nevertheless, the overlap, as far as our age is concerned, remains. To my knowledge the work by a student of Strauss that explores this overlap most searchingly is Harry Jaffa's study of Lincoln and the Civil War in *The Crisis of the House Divided*.

If Strauss is right, then slavery is an excellent example of the kind of injustice that ceases to be tolerable in an economy of abundance. Its injustice had been denounced by classical writers in ancient times. Aristotle, who defends it as right in one extreme case, condemns the institution as it existed in practice in the overwhelming majority of cases. Yet no ancient thinker seriously proposed abolition because none of them expected that it could be abolished, owing to the prevalence of scarcity. Aristotle, without intending to utter a prediction, explains when slavery will vanish: When instruments will do their work at a word of command or by intelligent anticipation and when shuttles will weave of themselves and plectra do their own harp playing. Modern technology and increasing abundance make slavery an injustice that one no longer need tolerate and therefore an injustice that one no longer can tolerate. Jaffa tries to show, and in my opinion succeeds in showing, that the political philosophy of Aristotle in particular explains the rightness of Lincoln's speeches, deeds, and thoughts during the greatest crisis American democracy faced better than any modern political philosophy.

Strauss rarely speaks of the crisis of liberal democracy without reflecting on the problem of education. It was because ancient democracy meant rule by the utterly uneducated that it was viewed by the classics as an inferior regime. The hope entertained by modern proponents of democracy was that democracy could meet this criticism by educating its members. The quality of contemporary education, as measured by the standard of liberal education, is one of Strauss's chief concerns. It will surprise no one to learn that Strauss did not think modern democracy had lived up to its goal. In his courses he would sometimes contrast the presentation of democracy in Plato's *Republic* with de Tocqueville's description of it. Both regimes are said to be dedicated to freedom. But whereas the regime set before us in the *Republic* is multicolored and characterized by the greatest diversity, the one de Tocqueville describes exhibits a uniformity resulting from an invisible but almost irresistible propensity to conform. One result of that pressure is what Strauss calls mass culture. Liberal education is the effort to counteract it. The dignity of the cause of liberal democracy depends to a degree on whether that effort is at least partially successful. The essential difference between liberal democracy and communism is that liberal democracy regards some things as more sacred than itself. These things include not only art, religion, and philosophy but also nearly everything, high or low, that falls within the private realm. A Communist society cannot regard anything as more sacred than itself, except perhaps some future condition of itself. The plausibility of the case for liberal democracy depends on the extent to which there are to be found, among the things that it regards as higher in dignity than itself, things that truly are higher than it in dignity. Liberal democracy continues to be the troubled repository of the great western tradition at the same time that it harbors within itself tendencies that undermine it: Thoughtless conformism and mass culture are equally inimical to Biblical religion and to genuine philosophical thought. The mere fact that these destructive tendencies are the unanticipated and unintended consequences of the mass character of modern democratic society rather than the outcome of a malevolent intention to destroy the western tradition does not make them any less powerful or dangerous. Liberal democracy gives the effort to preserve the western tradition, in a manner worthy of that tradition, a fighting chance. This is another one of the essential differences between it and communism that made Strauss give liberal democracy his unhesitating support even though his approval of it was not and could not be unqualified.

Efforts to continue the western tradition in a manner worthy of it are complicated by the crisis of philosophy in the twentieth century, a crisis that calls into question whether philosophy, as it has been traditionally pursued, deserves to survive. Since philosophy is an essential part of liberal education as it was traditionally understood, a simple return to that tradition would seem to be manifestly unworthy of it. Strauss made this difficulty his theme. He did not simply assume that truth or reason or nature of God are discredited superstitions, although he was aware of how radically they had been challenged in the nineteenth and twentieth centuries. He was persuaded that a thoughtless surrender to this challenge was not the appropriate response to it. He sought to bring about a thoughtful confrontation between the views on which this challenge is based and the most important alternatives to them. Liberal education as he understood it, practiced it, and encouraged its practice consisted in this effort. It would be misleading not to add that in the course of a lifetime dedicated to liberal education as we have described it, Strauss found himself more powerfully attracted to the philosophical alternative examplified by the Socrates of Plato and Xenophon than to any other view.

Did Strauss believe that his efforts on behalf of liberal education would benefit the cause of constitutional democracy? He was careful not to promise anything of the kind. Liberal education, he thought, could not become and should not aspire to become a mass movement. Its effects on the political arena were, therefore, bound to be limited. What the political effects of a liberal education on the liberally educated would be is a different question. As the passage with which we will close makes clear, his answer to this question is not simple. Marx and Nietzsche, whom he cites as examples in it, were the greatest enemies liberal democracy ever had. Yet the horrors of the twentieth century have made an important difference, in his opinion. One cannot expect, he begins by saying,

> that the liberally educated will become a political power in their own right. For we cannot expect that liberal education will lead all who benefit from it to understand their civic responsibility in the same way or to agree politically. Karl Marx, the father of communism, and Friedrich Nietzsche, the stepgrandfather of fascism, were liberally educated on a level to which we cannot even hope to aspire. But perhaps one can say that their grandiose failures make it easier for us who have experienced those failure to understand again the old saying that wisdom cannot be separated from moderation and hence to understand that wisdom requires unhesitating loyalty to a decent constitution and even to the cause of constitutionalism. Moderation will protect us against the twin dangers of visionary expectations from politics and unmanly contempt for politics. Thus it may again become true that all liberally educated men will be politically moderate men. It is in this way that the liberally educated may again receive a hearing in the market place.[17]

Notes

1. Leo Strauss, *Political Philosophy: Six Essays by Leo Strauss* (Indianapolis: Bobbs-Merrill, 1975), 98. The Second World War eliminated fascism as a rival to constitutional democracy. That is why Strauss often speaks as though its only rival is communism.

2. Leo Strauss, *What Is Political Philosophy?* (New York: Free Press, 1959), 36.

3. Leo Strauss, *Liberalism, Ancient and Modern* (New York: Basic Books, 1968), 228–30. For the noble side of the modern project see *Liberalism, Ancient and Modern*, 255–56, Leo Strauss, *Thoughts on Machiavelli* (New York: Free Press, 1958) 297, and Leo Strauss, *The City and Man* (Chicago: Rand McNally, 1964), 89.

4. Strauss, *Liberalism, Ancient and Modern*, 230–1.

5. Alexandre Kojève, "Tyranny and Wisdom," in Leo Strauss, *On Tyranny* (Ithaca: Cornell University Press, 1963), 146, italics added; see also Strauss, *On Tyranny* 102–3.

6. The exchange is reproduced in *On Tyranny*, 143–226. For a thoughtful and thorough study, with some of whose conclusions I disagree, of the writings under discussion, see Victor Gourevitch, "Philosophy and Politics, I–II," *Review of Metaphysics*, 22 (1968):58–84, 281–328. My disagreement with Gourevitch stems from his interpretation of Strauss's understanding of the distinction between vulgar virtue and genuine or philosophic virtue. Gourevitch thinks that Strauss regards the two kinds of virtue as mutually exclusive and that no mixture of the two, no in-between, no "halfway house" is possible. (For this formulation of the difference between Gourevitch's interpretation of Strauss and that of some of Strauss's other students, I am indebted to Leonard Grey.) It follows that Strauss, according to Gourevitch, has no basis for discerning any difference in genuine merit between "the gentleman, the ruler or the founder" (*Philosophy and Politics*, 305): All three are merely examples of vulgar virtue and, as such, equally lacking in true merit. The denial by this interpretation of all genuine "intellectual virtue" to the outstanding statesman and founder fails, in my opinion, to do justice to the thought of Strauss. To give only one example, speaking of the *Republic* in *The City and Man* Strauss says (p. 139): "Seen in the light of the best polity, of the truly just order, of justice or philosophy, political life or political greatness loses much, if not all of its charm; only the charm of the greatness of the founder and legislator seems to survive the severest of tests." There would appear to be admirable human possibilities other than the most admirable human possibility. Part of the explanation of them is supplied by the teaching concerning *eros*, which accords to "the longing for immortality through fame" a rank higher than two other forms of *eros*, though not the highest rank (*City and Man*, 110). To achieve immortal glory, the founder must earn it. The glory of the founder presupposes the possibility of distinguishing between sound and defective, superior and inferior political orders. That possibility does not depend on regarding the gentleman as the highest human type, as is shown sufficiently by the examples of Machiavelli and Kojève, neither of whom regarded the gentleman as anything of the kind, and both of whom, like Strauss, had strong and perfectly genuine political preferences and convictions based on their understanding of the human condition. This is not to deny that the gentleman occupies a more important place in Strauss's preferred political solution for classical times than he does in the solutions of Machiavelli or Kojève.

7. Strauss, *What Is Political Philosophy?*, 28. Cf Strauss, *The City and Man*, 63, 131–32.

8. Strauss, *What Is Political Philosophy?*, 306–7; Strauss, *On Tyranny*, 207.

9. Strauss, *What Is Political Philosophy?*, 37.

10. Aristotle, *Politics*, 1332b12ff.

11. Aristotle, *Politics*, 1286b18–22, 1313a3–8, 1287b41–1288a6. See also Strauss, *The City and Man*, 37.

12. Aristotle, *Politics*, 1302a1–2.

13. Aristotle, *Politics*, 1296a9–18.

14. Strauss, *On Tyranny*, 207.

15. Strauss, *What Is Political Philosophy?*, 311.

16. Strauss, *Liberalism, Ancient and Modern*, 21.

17. Strauss, *Liberalism, Ancient and Modern*, 24.

Victor Gourevitch

A REPLY TO GILDIN

In a note to his contribution to the present volume, Hilail Gildin takes issue with my account of Strauss's distinction between "vulgar" and "genuine" or "philosophic" virtue in a review of *On Tyranny* published nearly twenty years ago (see 95, no.6). In that review I had tried to summarize Strauss's analysis of the *Hiero* and his debate with Kojève, and to point out some parallels between *On Tyranny* and Strauss's other works. *On Tyranny*, and in particular the reply to Kojève, happen to occupy a privileged place in Strauss's *oeuvre*, because in them he speaks of certain philosophical issues more fully and more explicitly in his own name than he does anywhere else.

Some of Gildin's comments can be answered quickly and easily. I fully recognize, and I recognize that Strauss recognizes, "admirable human possibilities other than the most admirable human possibility." Any one who did not would scarcely deserve a moment's serious consideration. Just prior to the few words from my article that Gildin quotes, I had stated that Strauss "[f]or all practical purposes. . .leaves the moral judgments and concerns of ordinary life undisturbed" ("Philosophy and Politics II," *The Review of Metaphysics* 22 [1968]: p. 305). He will therefore certainly leave undisturbed the perfectly ordinary judgment that for the most part rulers, or at least good rulers, rank higher than do gentlemen, or at least than do gentlemen who have no share in rule, and that founders, or at least good founders, rank higher than either. These ordinary judgments will be somewhat qualified by the equally ordinary judgment that while *noblesse oblige*, it is unseemly to seek rule. The appearance of being drafted for office is but one acknowledgment by ambition of the ordinary and decent opinion of mankind.

Gildin takes particular exception to my account of the distinction Strauss draws "between two different standards of human excellence, two senses of virtue or two kinds of virtue: political virtue, the virtue of the citizen, which finds its most complete embodiment in the moral ex-

cellence of the gentleman, the ruler or the founder; and the excellence of
the philosopher or the wise man." ("Philosophy and Politics II," 305)
He finds that my account of this distinction creates the misleading impression that "Strauss regards the two kinds of virtue as mutually exclusive and that no mixture of the two, no in-between, no 'halfway
house' is possible." If careful readers are, indeed, left with that impression, I regret it. But mixtures are, as the name indicates, only intelligible
in terms of the alternatives they mix. Thought therefore focuses on
the most distinctive features of these alternatives and, hence, on their
differences. Conduct, by contrast, will respect mixtures, in-betweens,
and halfway houses. To do so almost defines moderation. Moderation is
a virtue of conduct. It is not a virtue of thought, as Strauss makes sometimes shockingly clear. That is one reason why the two lives and their
distinctive virtues are, in his judgment, necessarily and permanently in
tension, even if they are not, strictly speaking, mutually exclusive.

According to Gildin it is more faithful to Strauss's understanding to
view the two lives as continuous, to recognize *eros* as their middle term
and "the outstanding statesman and founder" as its most representative embodiment. The statesman or founder is animated by *eros* for immortal glory. In order to earn it he must exhibit the capacity "of
distinguishing between sound and defective, superior and inferior
political orders." In other words he must exhibit a form of wisdom or intellectual virtue. He must therefore be acknowledged to exhibit a "mixture, in-between, or 'halfway house'" of vulgar and genuine virtue and
hence, presumably, of the two lives. What is more, his intellectual virtue
or wisdom would provide Strauss with a common measure for the two
lives, with that basis for discerning differences in genuine merit which
Gildin charges my account fails to allow him.

Let us begin by granting and echoing Gildin's important reminder of
how emphatically all of Strauss's writings convey his awareness of the
dignity and indeed the nobility of political life. But does he in fact speak,
as Gildin here has him do, of the "genuine 'intellectual virtue'" of
outstanding statesmen and founders? "Intellectual virtue is an ambiguous expression. Presumably that is why Gildin surrounds it with
quotation marks. Sometimes the expression refers to the possession and
exercise of the theoretical sciences; sometimes, and more properly, it
refers to the distinctive character and economy of all the virtues in a soul
possessing or bent on possessing theoretical wisdom. The statesman
and the founder, and certainly "the outstanding statesman and
founder," unquestionably possess intellectual virtue in the first sense. It
is not at all clear that Strauss thinks that they possess it in the second
sense, in the sense that Gildin attaches to his expression "genuine 'in-

tellectual virtue.'" Regardless of what may be his judgment in some particular case, he for the most part does not point to any "genuine" intellectual virtue among rulers and founders, nor does he for the most part so much as suggest that what intellectual virtue they do possess entails or points to intellectual virtue in the full and proper sense of the term. In reflecting on Strauss's presentations of this problem, the reader has to bear in mind that for Strauss wisdom or intellectual virtue in the full and emphatic sense—Gildin's "genuine 'intellectual virtue'"—is zetetic[11] or sceptic in the original sense" (*On Tyranny*, 210). Now Gildin supports his claim that Strauss attributes "genuine 'intellectual virtue'" to founders by citing the following passage: "Seen in the light of the best polity, of the truly just order, of justice or philosophy, political life or political greatness loses much, if not all of its charm; only the charm of the greatness of the founder or the legislator seems to survive the severest of tests" (*The City and Man*, 139). When Gildin cites this passage in support of his own interpretation, he evidently would have us take it to say that the charm of the founder or the legislator survives the test of philosophy. Yet that is not what it says. It says no more than that their charm *seems* to survive that test. Strauss is most sensitive to the difference between *seems* and *does* (*e.g.*, *On Tyranny*, 203). Moreover, in the chapter in *The City and Man* specifically devoted to a discussion of the *Republic*—on which the passage that Gildin here quotes is but a brief backward glance—Strauss categorically and without *seems* or other qualifications says: "Certain it is that the *Republic* supplies the most magnificent cure ever devised for every form of political ambition" (*The City and Man*, 65). There is no reason to believe that Strauss does not mean what he says here either, or that he thinks it undesirable to be "cured," or that he rejects the teaching of the *Republic* as he understands that teaching. One might nevertheless wonder whether, when he speaks as he does here of "every form of political ambition," he is really referring only to gentlemen and to rulers, but not to founders, to "outstanding" founders? Strauss speaks to that question more fully in another context:

> By suggesting to his young companions that they should together found a city, Socrates appeals from the petty end of the tyrant to the grand end of the founder: the honor attending the tyrant who merely uses a city already in existence is petty in comparison with the glory attending the founder and especially the founder of the best city. The founder however must devote himself entirely to the well-being of his city; he is forced to be concerned with the common good or to be just. Desire for glory appears to be that passion which, if its scope is broadened, transforms the lover of tyranny, to say nothing of the lover of bodily pleasures, into a lover of justice. In Plato's *Republic* this transformation proves to be only the preparation for the true conversion from badness to goodness, the true conversion being

the transition to philosophy, if not philosophy itself; this conversion is effected by the understanding of the essential limitations of everything political. [*Thoughts on Machiavelli*, 239]

According to Gildin, Strauss holds that the ambitions and excellences of rulers and founders point beyond the political realm, and must therefore, at least in part, be understood "by the teaching concerning *eros* which accords to 'the longing for immortality through fame' a rank higher than to other forms of eros, though not the highest rank" (*City and Man*, 110). The brief quote suggests that this is Strauss's point in that particular passage of *The City and Man*. Yet his point in that passage and throughout the entire chapter on the *Republic* is precisely the opposite: Namely, that what is most distinctive of the *Republic's* account of the political realm and life is that it abstracts from *eros*, and he concludes the chapter by pointing out that "this abstraction is necessary if justice as full dedication to the common good of a particular city is to be praised as choiceworthy for its own sake" (*The City and Man*, 138; see also 128, 135). This abstraction from *eros* is but one form in which the compulsion of thought by justice can manifest itself. Once again, Strauss makes the same point even more emphatically in *On Tyranny*:

> The ruler too. . .is prompted by love of some kind. Xenohpon indicates his view of the ruler's love in the *Education of Cyrus*, which is, at any rate at first glance, his description of the greatest ruler. Xenophon's Cyrus is a cold or unerotic nature. That is to say, the ruler is not motivated by true or Socratic *eros* because he does not know what a well-ordered soul is. The ruler knows political virtue, and nothing prevents his being attracted by it; but political virute, or the virtue of the nonphilosopher, is a mutilated thing; therefore it cannot elicit more than a shadow or an imitation of true love. The ruler is in fact dominated by love based on need in the common meaning of need, or by mercenary love. [*On Tyranny*, 216f].

Or yet again:

> The philosopher's dominating passion is the desire for truth, i.e., for knowledge of the eternal order, or the eternal cause or causes of the whole. As he looks up in search for the eternal order, all human things and all human concerns reveal themselves to him in all clarity as paltry and ephemeral. He has then the same experience regarding all human things, nay, regarding man himself, which the man of high ambition has regarding the low and narrow goals, or the cheap happiness, of the general run of men. The philosopher, being a man of the largest views, is the only man who can be properly described as possessing *megaloprepeia* (which is commonly rendered by "magnificence") (Plato, *Republic* 486a). Or, as Xenophon indicates, the philosopher is the only man who is truly ambitious. Chiefly concerned with eternal beings, or the "ideas," and hence also with the "idea" of man, he is as unconcerned as possible with individual and perishable human beings and hence also with his own "individuality," or his body, as well as with the sum total of all individual

human beings and their "historical" procession. He knows as little as possible about the way to the market place, to say nothing of the market place itself, and he almost as little knows whether his very neighbor is a human being or some other animal (Plato, *Theaetetus* 173c8–d1, 174b1–6). The political man must reject this way altogether. He cannot tolerate this radical depreciation of man and of all human things (Plato, *Laws* 804b5–c1). He could not devote himself to his work with all his heart or without reservation if he did not attach absolute importance to man and to human things. He must "care" for human beings as such. He is essentially attached to human beings. This attachment is at the bottom of his desire to rule human beings, or of his ambition. But to rule human beings means to serve them. Certainly an attachment to beings which prompts one to serve them may well be called love of them. Attachment to human beings is not peculiar to the ruler; it is characteristic of all men as mere men. The difference between the political man and the private man is that in the case of the former, the attachment enervates all private concerns; the political man is consumed by erotic desire, not for this or that human being, or for a few, but for the large multitude, for the *demos* (Plato, *Gorgias* 481d1–5, 513d7–8; *Republic* 573e6–7, 574e2, 575a1–2), and in principle, for all human beings. But erotic desire craves reciprocity: the political man desires to be loved by all his subjects. The political man is characterized by the concern with being loved by all human beings regardless of their quality. [*On Tyranny*, 211f]

So much may perhaps suffice to answer the question of how I was led to present Strauss's account of the two lives, of their respective virtues, and of the relations between them as I did. It would be tedious and, what is more, probably inconclusive to arraign further quotations on one side and the other. Perhaps Strauss indicates his understanding of the issue most clearly, even bluntly, by choosing to speak about "vulgar" and "genuine" virtue. He has no terms for anything in-between. Indeed, regardless of where one picks up the thread of his thought, one is led to the same conclusion: The political life in any of its forms, the philosophical life, and the relations between them, are understood better in terms of a disjunction than of a conjunction. It has to be so. For in his view the transition from the one to the other involves not only *eros* but also a conversion of the soul. In addition, as I have indicated in the body of my essay above, the disjunction, or at least the sharp contrast between the two lives is the basic premise of his understanding of the "fundamental alternatives" as well as what is primarily at issue in his quarrel with the Moderns (cp. pp. 37–38, 41).

Strauss most frequently returns to the relation between the two lives and their respective virtues, and hence in particular to the question of how compatible they might be, in the form: Is what Plato calls common or citizen virtue, what Aristotle calls moral virtue, and what he himself calls "vulgar" virtue, legislative, or is it merely ministerial? Is justice or practical wisdom "virtue entire," or is it instrumental to virtue more properly so called? And is justice under the two descriptions the same? As I understand Strauss and his classical models, it cannot be both equally, but is and properly ought to be ministerial to what they call the philosophical life or what Strauss sometimes also refers to as "genuine" virtue. *Tertium non datur* (cp. *Thoughts on Machiavelli*, 78).

Strauss speaks to the issue in a remarkably personal exchange with his life-long friend Jacob Klein:

> *Mr. Strauss:* . . .Mr. Klein and I differ regarding the status of morality.
>
> *Mr. Klein:* (Laughter) I am not entirely certain of that. That's all I can say. Well, I will add something to that. And that is again a question of a difference of emphasis. I think I wouldn't emphasize it so much, the morality of man, but I do think that man ought to be moral.
>
> *Mr. Strauss:* Yes—sure. I did not mean that when I spoke of our difference. I think that in your scheme of things morality has a higher place than in my scheme.
>
> *Mr. Klein:* I really don't think so. Why do you say that?
>
> *Mr. Strauss:* Because we have frequently had quite a few conversations. . . now and then, and one general formula which suggested itself to me was that you attach a higher importance to morality, as morality, than I do. Now, let me explain this. That the philosophic life, especially as Plato and Aristotle understood it, is not possible without self-control and a few other virtues almost goes without saying. If a man is habitually drunk, and so on, how can he think? But the question is, if these virtues are understood only as subservient to philosophy and for its sake, then that is no longer a moral understanding of the virtues.
>
> *Mr. Klein:* That may be. (Tape break)
>
> *Mr. Strauss:* . . .a statement by a modern extremist, but who had a marvelous sense for Greek thought, Nietzsche—in his *Genealogy of Morals*, third treatise, "What is the Significance of Ascetic Ideals," he explains, why is a philosopher ascetic? And he makes this clear, that he is ascetic. And, he says, that is not different from the asceticism of a jockey, who in order to win a race must live very restrainedly, but that is wholly unimportant to the jockey, what is important is to win the race. If one may compare low to high things, one may say similarly of the philosopher, what counts is thinking and investigating and not morality. Of course the word morality is a "bad word" because it has so many connotations which are wholly alien to the ancients, but, I think for provisional purposes, we can accept it.
>
> *Mr. Klein:* If there's something that I learned from Plato, or that I think that I learned from Plato, it is to understand that nothing can be—*nothing* can be —that isn't in some way—and that's very difficult—good. That's why I do understand why Mr. Strauss says that the philosopher is in a certain way superior to the concern about morality, but I can not agree that the ultimate

consideration of things, as far as one is capable of doing that, ever, *ever*,
frees men of the compulsion to act rightly.

Mr. Strauss: Yes, I think that you believe that. Yes, that is what I meant.
["A Giving of Accounts: Jacob Klein and Leo Strauss," *The College* 22
(1970): 4f]

Any attempt to understand what Strauss here says he meant, in other
words his account of the two lives, inevitably leads to the question of
why, to speak in terms of Plato's powerful metaphor, anyone outside
the cave, that is to say anyone striving to leave it, would spontaneously
return to it. He begins and ends his reflections on this question with the
observation that the wise do not wish to rule. He clearly shares his
classical models' view that if and when they nevertheless do participate in rule, they invariably do so under compulsion, never out of
eros. The way up and the way down are not one and the same; nor are
those who might happen to meet halfway as they make their way in opposite directions. The difference between them is apt to be particularly
pronounced if wisdom is understood, as Strauss understands it, to consist more in the clarifying of the fundamental problems and alternatives
than in answers and solutions. Wisdom so understood is most unlikely
to prove to be what even those who earnestly set out in quest of it expected. It is far more likely that, "in a sense" as Aristotle says, it will
prove to be the opposite of what they expected (*Metaphysics*, I, 2,
983a12; cp. Plato *Phaedo*, 89d1–90d7). The *eros* of those setting out in
quest of wisdom is therefore not likely to prove a particularly reliable
clue to what someone who has gone more than halfway may find or
be; or to how they may appear to him. None of this is to deny that
the best of Gildin's statesmen or founders are set and kept in motion
by *eros* for the righteous city. But, to repeat, there may not be any
idea of the city (*The City and Man,* 93), nor any basis for holding fast to
even "the simple teleology—anthropocentric or not—which at first
glance seems to supply the most rational solution to all difficulties"
(*Xenophon's Socratic Discourse*, 149). Strauss is ever mindful of how men
in earnest quest for the righteous city might react to that possibility. He
regards it as a sign of rare strength to be able to face up to it without
yielding to either misology or injustice. Therefore, "[i]t cannot be the
duty of a genuinely just man. . .to drive weaker men to despair of the
possibility of some order and decency in human affairs, and least of all
those who by virtue of their inclinations, their descent, and their abilities,
may have some public responsibility" (*The City and Man,* 137). Compulsion may clearly take many forms (ibid., 127f), as the examples Gildin
discusses in his essay also show.

Gildin's comments on the two lives appear in a note to an essay in which he argues that Strauss's prefered political solution for modern times is "liberal or constitutional democracy"; that, contrary to widespread misconceptions, his defense of classical political philosophy is entirely compatible with the defense of liberal or constitutional democracy as "the most viable political alternative in our age" (p. 96); and that, indeed, classical political philosophy provides the most powerful, if not the only, defense available to modern liberal constitutional democracy. The argument of the essay and of the note, taken together, would lead one to expect Strauss to say that liberal constitutional democracy, or at least its founders and outstanding statesmen, most adequately represent a reconciliation, mixture, or in-between of the two lives and of "genuine" and "vulgar" virtue. Yet Gildin repeatedly, and very fairly, characterizes the Straussian defense of liberal democracy as "unhesitating support" but not "unqualified approval" (pp. 93, 94, 100). The characterization points to tension more clearly than it does to reconciliation. The more closely one attends to his thoughtful presentation, the more evident it becomes how pervasive and intense that tension is. This is not the occasion to consider Gildin's argument with anything like the care that it deserves. We must confine ourselves to a few brief remarks that most directly bear on the issue at hand.

In its barest outline, his argument proceeds as follows: *The* principle of justice calls for giving equally to equals and unequally to unequals; and in all politically relevant respects, all men are equal. Formerly, political societies could not conform to this principle because of natural scarcity. They can conform to it now because technology, i.e., the conquest, mastery and control of nature has, for all intents and purposes eliminated scarcity and with it any justification for unearned social or political privations as well as for unearned privileges, for slaves as well as for gentlemen, in short for all social or political inequalities that are due to chance rather than to merit. The founder's glory, by contrast, is always and everywhere fully earned by his ability to distinguish between superior and inferior political orders. He is, therefore, properly and legitimately representative of the political life. It is not difficult to understand distaste for the name *gentleman* and even for some of those who lay claim to it, anymore than it is difficult to understand the wish that Strauss had not featured gentlemen quite as prominently as he did. Gildin goes so far as to say that the founder's ability to distinguish superior from inferior orders "does not depend on regarding the gentleman as the highest human type," as if any party to this discussion had ever maintained that the gentleman is the highest human type. The only question was and is whether Strauss regards him as representative of the political life, and if he does, why he does so. "The gentleman is . . . the political reflection, or imitation of the wise man" (*Natural Right and History*, 142; cp. the concluding paragraph of *On Tyranny*). He evidently provides Strauss with that basis for discerning differences in genuine merit which Gildin prefers to look for in the founder. And he is not easily read out of Strauss's preferred political solution for any age. Indeed, the principle that inequalities due to the natural or social lottery are unjust does not settle the issue in favor of constitutional democracy, not even among alternatives "viable in our age." For the principle of giving equally to equals and unequally to unequals, is also accepted by "our communist coexistents" (*What is Political Philosophy*, 37). Gildin sees the essential difference between the two to consist in the following: "liberal democracy regards some things as more sacred than itself," whereas Communist societies do not and cannot regard anything as more sacred than themselves. "The cause of liberal democracy" thus depends to a considerable extent on its success in educating its members to remain alive to what is truly higher in dignity than itself (p. 200). One cannot help wondering whether Gildin has not simply substituted a liberally educated portion of the democratic citizenry for Strauss's gentlemen, and whether the deep tensions to which he calls attention between liberal democracy and the liberal education that would point beyond it do not very faithfully mirror the deep tension that Strauss describes as the permanent and radical alternative between the two lives.

However, in the process of thus transposing Strauss's "preferred political solution" into a modern context and idiom, Gildin has been led to attribute to him views the main features of which are, as he acknowledges, for all practical purposes indistinguishable from those of the Moderns: that the conquest of *fortuna* and of nature is the necessary condition for bringing political reality into conformity with *the* principle of justice. The one major difference between their solutions to which Gildin calls attention is that, unlike at least some Moderns, Strauss remains undogmatic about applying principles; he has far graver reservations about the conquest of fortune and nature than any Modern, certainly than Machiavelli or Kojève, to mention only the names Gildin mentions. Gildin reports some of these reservations, but he gives no indication that they might affect Strauss's preferred political solution for our times. It is difficult to escape the conclusion that if the conquest of chance and of nature is the necessary condition of a political order that, in contrast to all ancient and modern alternatives, makes it possible to conform as fully as any political order can to the basic principle of justice, then it is our clear moral duty to do everything in our power to support and promote it, and hence to support and promote the technology which makes it possible and the material plenty which it creates. So that, in the name of justice, Strauss and his Ancient models may find themselves in the position of jettisoning not only gentlemen but also the politics of moderation and austere virtue; they may find themselves, instead, in the position of endorsing and even promoting technology and material plenty and, hence, of unleashing the passions that most contribute to them. It may have been at least in part in order to forestall such a reversal of his teaching that Strauss attended so much more carefully and constantly to the contrast between the two lives and their respective virtues than to their possible mixtures.

Hilail Gildin

A RESPONSE TO GOUREVITCH

One very important question remains unanswered in Victor Gourevitch's thoughtful and measured response to my criticism of his 1968 essay on Strauss. Does not the interpretation Gourevitch offers of how Strauss and his classical models understood the distinction between genuine virtue and vulgar virtue deprive these thinkers of any solid basis for distinguishing in truth and not merely in appearance between better and worse political orders? Does it not turn the teachings in which they develop these distinctions, teachings that claim to supply guidance to statesmen and legislators, into no more than elaborate self-protective pretenses? Does it not reduce the difference between them and the classical philosophical schools that were indifferent to the political, as the Epicurean school was believed to be, to one of mere show? One could easily grant that Aristotle regarded theoretical wisdom as higher than practical wisdom and that he would therefore have viewed his *Politics* as inferior in rank to many of his other works. But it is very difficult to read, say, Book 5 of the *Politics* and believe that the elaborate and penetrating analyses and judgments of the transformations of regimes found there is merely exoteric. To put it cautiously, much of Book 5 strikes this reader as being simply true. Strauss opened the essay in which he responds to Kojève by remarking that "a social science that cannot speak of tyranny with the same confidence with which medicine speaks, for example, of cancer, cannot understand social phenomena as what they are" (*On Tyranny*, 189). He criticized historicism and the fact-value distinction for denying the very possibility of supplying political life with the guidance it manifestly needs. One may disagree with Strauss's conclusions, but it is not easy to believe that, in the end, he secretly thought that classical political philosophy is no better suited to supply political life with guidance than are the two contemporary views that he criticized.

114

The startling claim that Strauss's indoor convictions are in the end far closer than they appear to be to the schools of contemporary thought he subjects to outdoor criticism is restricted to what are asserted to be his views concerning political life. (His praise of the philosophic life as represented by Socrates is generally acknowledged to be incompatible with either historicism or with fact-value positivism.) As far as I can see, that startling claim is based on two arguments: an interpretation of what is believed to be his critical analysis of the gentleman or of moral virtue and an interpretation of what is believed to be his radical depreciation of political life.

In "Progress or Return" Strauss provides a very clear and balanced statement of his understanding of morality and of the problem of morality:

> One can say, and it is not misleading to say so, that the Bible and Greek philosophy agree in regard to what we may call, and we do call in fact, morality. They agree, if I may say so, regarding the importance of morality, regarding the content of morality, and regarding its ultimate insufficiency. They differ as regards that "x" which supplements or completes morality, or, which is only another way of putting it, they disagree as regards the basis of morality. ["Progress or Return? The Contemporary Crisis in Western Civilization," *Modern Judaism* 1 (1981) 34]

For Greek philosophy, what completes morality is understanding or contemplation, Strauss says. "For the Bible, it is "humility, a sense of guilt, repentance, and faith in divine mercy" ("Progress or Return," 37). Now the view of morality ascribed to Greek philosophy would seem to give rise to the following difficulty. Morality as it is thought to be practiced by the moral man or the gentleman is practiced as an end in itself. The actions flowing from the moral virtues are supposed to be chosen by the gentleman because of their intrinsic nobility. To justify the moral virtues on the ground that they serve an end other than themselves, even if that end is higher than they are, and certainly if it is lower, would seem to rob them of that nobility. In numerous passages Strauss expounds sympathetically the view he affirms to be that of Greek philosophy. He argues that only the life of understanding can purify the soul and liberate it from secret but powerful unjust longings. Therefore, that life alone deserves to be characterized as the life of genuine virtue. Contrasted with that life, the life of the gentleman is said to be the life of vulgar, habit-bred virtue. In one striking passage in the *Republic*, a man of merely habit-bred virtue who had previously led an orderly life and had been rewarded for doing so in the afterlife, chooses, once given the chance to do so, the life of a tyrant for his next life. Some students of Strauss's thought have reasoned as follows from this reduc-

tion of the virtue of the gentleman to vulgar virtue. One of the key virtues, if not the key virtue, of the gentleman is justice. The depreciation
of the gentleman leads to a depreciation of justice. But the justice of the
gentleman is the common good. If the virtues of the gentleman are sham
virtues, then the common good is a sham good, and a sham good cannot
supply a basis for distinguishing better from worse political orders. It
therefore cannot supply a basis for what is ordinarily understood by
political philosophy. Any impression to the effect that what is ordinarily
understood by it is to be found in, say, the writings of Plato and Aristotle is the result of taking seriously what was never meant seriously by
these authors.

The reasoning that I have just sketched of some interpreters of
Strauss's thought in my opinion fails to do justice to the subtlety of his
account of the virtue of the gentleman. I shall return to this point in the
immediate sequel. For even apart from that inadequacy, the reasoning
suffers from another defect: It assumes that regarding the moral virtues
as ends in themselves is a precondition for having the right to strong,
principled, and perfectly genuine political preferences and convictions.
But is this the case? Do not the examples of Machiavelli and Kojève suffice to show that it is not the case—to mention two thinkers the authenticity of whose immoralism Strauss does not challenge and whose
perfectly genuine political preferences and convictions he analyzes and
questions without questioning their right to have them? The ends by
which Strauss asserted that most classical political philosophers took
their bearings in seeking an understanding of political life are indicated
by the following passage:

> Most classical political philosophers considered the city the most perfect
> form of political organization, not because they were ignorant of any other
> form, nor because they followed blindly the lead given by their ancestors
> or contemporaries, but because they realized, at least as clearly as we
> realize it today, that the city is essentially superior to other forms of
> political association known to classical antiquity, the tribe and the Eastern
> monarchy. The tribe, we may say tentatively, is characterized by freedom
> (public spirit) and lack of civilization (high development of the arts and
> sciences), and the Eastern monarchy is characterized by civilization and
> lack of freedom. Classical political philosophers consciously and
> reasonably preferred the city to other forms of political association, in the
> light of the standards of freedom and civilization. And this preference was
> not a peculiarity bound up with their particular historical situation. Up to
> and including the eighteenth century, some of the most outstanding
> political philosophers quite justifiably preferred the city to the modern state
> which had emerged since the sixteenth century, precisely because they
> measured the modern state of their time by the standards of freedom and
> civilization. Only in the nineteenth century did classical political

philosophy in a sense become obsolete. The reason was that the state of the nineteenth century, as distinguished from the Macedonian and Roman empires, the feudal monarchy, and the absolute monarchy of the modern period, could plausibly claim to be at least as much in accordance with the standards of freedom and civilization as the Greek city had been. [*What Is Political Philosophy*, 65]

Gourevitch claims that he does not deny that Strauss thought mixtures between the life of philosophy and the political life are possible. What he denies is that, according to Strauss, there are more than two ultimate ingredients in such mixtures—genuine virtue and political or vulgar virtue. If I am not mistaken, he has in mind such examples as Cicero and Xenophon. In my opinion Strauss thought that there could be a third ingredient according to his classical models—the intellectual virtue of practical wisdom, a virtue subordinate to theoretical wisdom yet other than it or than vulgar virtue and evidently essential to the enlightened statesman. Evidence for this is to be found in Strauss's lectures on the *Symposium*, lectures from which I am not reluctant to quote because Strauss approved them for publication with minor editorial changes. Speaking of the second kind of eros, the longing for immortality through fame, Strauss says:

The second kind of eros strives in the highest case for political, economic prudence. According to Plato there is no essential difference between city and household, a thesis with which Aristotle takes issue at the beginning of the *Politics*. Political, economic prudence is the highest [prudence] and is identified here with moderation and justice. There is a passage in the *Phaedo*, 82a-b, where it is said: "The vulgar and political virtue which men call moderation and justice and which arises from habituation without philosophy and intellect." That is not the same which he means here. There is no reference to habituation here, for example. We must take this as a much higher thing [p. 187].

Strauss goes on to explain that the immortal fame sought in the second kind of eros is achieved primarily by the good poets:

Love of honor, ambition, the highest form of love of one's own, namely, love of one's own immortality is concerned with the beautiful and noble to a much higher degree than procreation and offspring. This second form is essentially concerned with the production of the most beautiful prudence, namely, political prudence, the prudence of the statesman. This immortality is the preserve, above all else, of the good poets, who are immortal in their works. This implies poetry at its best generates political prudence, educates great statesmen and legislators [p. 190].

One example, for Strauss, of such a poet is Aristophanes, to whom Strauss devoted an entire book, *Socrates and Aristophanes*. At this point in the lectures on the *Symposium* Strauss raises for later consideration the question why Socrates should not also be considered an educator of statesmen and legislators.

The third kind of eros culminates in the vision of beauty that is said to alone engender true virtue. It is the preserve of the philosopher. The virtue produced by the poets, by contrast, "is no more than a shadow of true virtue. This political prudence which we so admire, and rightly up to a point, is only a shadow of true virtue, and this is the utmost that the poets can achieve" [p. 205].

Three kinds of virtue are distinguished in Strauss's lectures on the *Symposium*. First, there is merely vulgar or political virtue. Above this is the virtue or practical wisdom of great statesmen and legislators. Above that, in turn, is true, genuine virtue. The following remarks by Strauss on the occasion of Churchill's death furnish a beautiful example of his admiration for virtue of the second kind:

> The death of Churchill is a healthy reminder to academic students of political science of their limitations, the limitations of their craft.
>
> The tyrant stood at the pinnacle of his power. The contrast between the indomitable and magnanimous statesman and the insane tyrant—this spectacle in its great simplicity was one of the greatest lessons which men can learn, at any time. No less enlightening is the lesson conveyed by Churchill's failure which is too great to be called tragedy. I mean the fact that Churchill's heroic action on behalf of human freedom only contributed, through no fault of Churchill's, to increase the threat to freedom which is posed by Stalin or his successors. Churchill did the utmost that a man could do to counter that threat—publicly and most visibly in Greece and in Fulton, Missouri. Not a whit less important than his deeds and speeches are his writings, above all his *Marlborough*—the greatest historical work written in our century, an inexhaustible mine of political wisdom and understanding, which should be required reading for every student of political science.
>
> The death of Churchill reminds us of the limitations of our craft and therewith of our duty. We have no higher duty, and no more pressing duty, than to remind ourselves and our students, of political greatness, human greatness, of the peaks of human excellence. For we are supposed to train ourselves and others in seeing things as they are, and this means above all in seeing their greatness and their misery, their excellence and their vileness, their nobility and their triumphs, and therewith never to mistake mediocrity, however brilliant, for true greatness. [Spontaneous remarks by Leo Strauss on hearing of the death of Churchill, in class at the University of Chicago, January 25, 1965. I am indebted to Harry U. Jaffa for drawing my attention to these remarks.]

One cannot deny that there are passages in Strauss in which the only alternatives seem to be genuine virtue and vulgar virtue and in which the shortcomings of political life are forcefully displayed. There are also passages in which possibilities between the two are presented as possessing genuine merit. (We will consider one of these passages in the immediate sequel.) The conflict between the two sets of passages can, I think, be resolved as follows: When the aim is to establish the philosophic life at its best as the model of human excellence, an effort is made to show that all rivals to it fall short of human excellence in a decisive respect and do not deserve to be called by that name. Once the standard has been established and recognized, however, one can apply it in a more generous spirit and acknowledge that there can be various ways of approximating it to various degrees. What one faces here is not so much a simple continuum as a range of discrete possibilities that may well differ in rank, similar, say, to the range of possibilities of poetic excellence between Shakespeare and doggerel.

Speaking of moral virtue in *The City and Man*, Strauss observes, "For Plato, what Aristotle calls moral virtue is a kind of halfway house between political or vulgar virtue which is in the service of bodily well-being (of self-preservation or peace) and genuine virtue which, to say the least, animates only the philosophers as philosophers" (p. 27). Here moral virtue is not simply vulgar virtue either according to Aristotle or according to Plato. Why it is not is made clear in the sequel. For Strauss's views are not adequately reflected when the gentleman is equated with the potential believer, if by believer one understands someone characterized by habit-bred piety. Another characteristic of gentlemen as a class that is of great importance to Strauss is that they can be depended on to be sympathetic to philosophy. These two characteristics are not always compatible as the following passage makes clear:

> When the philosopher Aristotle addresses his political science to more or less perfect gentlemen, he shows them as far as possible that the way of life of the perfect gentleman points toward the philosophic way of life; he removes a screen. He articulates for his addressees the unwritten *nomos* which was the limit of their vision while he himself stands above that limit. He is thus compelled or enabled to correct their opinions about things which fall within their purview. He must speak of virtues and vices which were "nameless" and hence hitherto unknown. He must deny explicitly or tacitly that habits as highly praised as sense of shame and piety are virtues. The gentleman is by nature able to be affected by philosophy; Aristotle's political science is an attempt to actualize this potentiality. The gentleman affected by philosophy is in the highest case the enlightened statesman, like Pericles, who was affected by Anaxagoras. [*The City and Man*, 28]

Someone might object that Aristotle does not eliminate piety as a virtue. He replaces what his addressees might understand by piety with what he holds to be the true understanding of piety. True piety consists in making oneself as like as possible to God, the exemplar of theoretical wisdom. True piety is philosophy. Strauss would have no quarrel with this assertion. But would he consider piety in this sense vulgar virtue? Is the gentleman enlightened by philosophy an example of vulgar virtue? One defining characteristic of vulgar virtue is that it is "without philosophy" (*Phaedo*, 82b2-3; *Republic*, 619c7). The gentleman enlightened by philosophy may not be a philosopher, but can he be said to be without philosophy? As the example of Pericles indicates, he may possess gifts of intellect of a very high order, even if they are not the gifts of intellect that make the successful pursuit of theoretical wisdom possible. He may possess gifts of intellect that enable him to acquire practical wisdom and so become capable of being an outstanding statesman.

But are we not ignoring the radical depreciation of political life to be found in Strauss and his classical models? Are we not forgetting that the city is only the cave and statesmanship no more than a knack for finding one's way around in the cave? Much is made, by those who urge this objection, of the following passage in *The City and Man* in which Strauss analyzes the dramatic setting of the *Republic:*

> Xenophon tells us that Socrates, being well-disposed toward Glaucon for the sake of Charmides and of Plato, cured him of his extreme political ambition. In order to achieve this cure, he had first to make him willing to listen to him by gratifying him. Plato's Socrates may have descended to the Piraeus together with Glaucon who was eager to descend, in order to find an unobtrusive opportunity for curing him of his extreme political ambition. Certain it is that the *Republic* is the most magnificent cure ever devised for every form of political ambition [p. 65].

Strauss connects Socrates's conversation with Glaucon in the *Republic* with Socrates's conversation with Glaucon in the *Memorabilia*. He suggests that there is an agreement concerning it between Plato and Xenophon. In both, it is suggested, Socrates's intention is to overcome Glaucon's passionate desire to enter political life. The conversation with Glaucon is followed, in Xenophon, by a conversation with Charmides, one of the two people for whose sake Xenophon says that Socrates undertook to help Glaucon (the other was Plato). In that conversation Socrates tries to kindle Charmides's political ambition. He encourages Charmides to become aware of his outstanding abilities and to enter political life. One is entitled to wonder whether Socrates is as opposed to political ambition and as contemptuous of the virtues of the outstanding statesman as the last sentence of the passage we quoted might seem to imply.

The passage we have just quoted is from the chapter on the *Republic* in *The City and Man*. That chapter is followed by the chapter on Thucydides that is subdivided into ten sections. The first section is entitled "Political Philosophy and Political History." The title of the last section is "Political History and Political Philosophy." Thucydides's work presents a great variety of statesmen, generals and demagogues, and judgment is passed on their excellence, mediocrity or vileness. It abounds in examples of political greatness and its opposite. The first section of Strauss's chapter begins by contrasting Plato and Thucydides: "It suffices to remember how Socrates on the one hand and Thucydides on the other speak of Themistocles and Pericles, and how Plato on the one hand and Thucydides on the other present Nicias" (p. 139). Nevertheless, the section goes on to suggest that the teachings of Plato and Thucydides need not be incompatible; "they may supplement one another" (p. 140). In the final section of the chapter, what had been suggested as a possibility is asserted to be true: "If one does not limit oneself to contrasting easily quotable judgments of Thucydides and Plato on men like Themistocles and Pericles, if one considers that all these judgments are elliptical, and if therefore one ponders them, one realizes that the two thinkers are in fundamental agreement regarding the good and bad and the noble and base" (p. 237). I understand this to mean that for Thucydides, as for Plato, political greatness points beyond itself to something higher that itself, and that for Plato, as for Thucydides, the greatness of the statesman who is not a philosopher is genuine, although it is not the peak. For a better understanding of its relation to the peak, it is helpful to turn to some of Strauss's remarks on Plato's *Statesman:*

> the *Republic* did not make sufficiently clear the cognitive status of kingship or statesmanship. From the *Republic* we could easily receive the impression that the knowledge required of the philosopher-king consists of two heterogeneous parts: the purely philosophic knowledge of the ideas which culminates in the vision of the idea of the good, on the one hand, and the merely political experience which does not have the status of knowledge at all but which enables one to find one's way in the Cave and to discern the shadows on its walls, on the other. But the indispensable supplement to philosophic knowledge also seemed to be a kind of art or science. [Here Strauss in a note refers the reader to *Republic* 484d and 539e and asks him to compare it with 501a–c]. The Eleatic stranger seems to take the second and higher view of the nonphilosophic awareness peculiar to the statesman. Yet in the dialogues *Sophist* and *Statesman* he makes clear the nature of the sophist and of the statesman, i.e., the difference between the sophist and the statesman, without making clear the difference between the statesman and the philosopher. We are promised by Theodoros that the Eleatic

stranger will also expound (in a sequel to the *Statesman*) what the philosopher is, but Plato does not keep his Theodoros' promise. Do we then understand what the philosopher is once we have understood what the sophist and statesman are? Is statesmanship not, as it appeared from the *Republic*, a mere supplement to philosophy but an ingredient of philosophy? That is to say, is statesmanship, the art or knowledge peculiar to the statesman, far from being merely the awareness necessary for finding one's way in the Cave and far from being itself independent of the vision of the idea of the good, a condition or rather ingredient of the vision of the idea of the good? If it were so then "politics" would be much more important according to the *Statesman* than it is according to the *Republic*. [*History of Political Philosophy*, 42–43]

Strauss concludes his remarks on the *Statesman* by affirming what he suggests tentatively in the passage we have quoted. The knowledge of the statesman at its highest is practical and prescriptive, not contemplative or theoretical. It is the highest practical knowledge. It is essentially different from the highest theoretical knowledge that is humanly attainable, but it cannot be separated from it. Here once again we seem to have returned to the Platonic thesis concerning the philosopher as the model of human excellence. What is clearer now is the ingredient in that model that the excellence of the statesman approximates. It is no more impossible for there to be outstanding statesmen who are not outstanding philosophers than it is for there to be outstanding mathematicians who are not outstanding philosophers. Strauss and his classical models have a right to affirm this and mean it at the same time that they affirm the philosophic life to be the highest life.

In closing, I would like to comment briefly on some of Gourevitch's observations regarding my paper for this volume. These comments are not meant to imply that there is any pronounced disagreement between us concerning the points I will mention. They are intended only for clarification: (1) According to Aristotle, the principle that it is just to give equal things to equal people and unequal things to people of unequal merit is the principle that should govern the distribution of political authority. That principle, according to him, is in fact recognized and appealed to by all those who seek to justify their claim to rule. It is appealed to by democrats, by oligarchs, by mullahs, and by the well born, to mention only a few examples. Aristotle distinguishes what he regards as valid from invalid appeals to his principle and explains the grounds on which he does so. If Leninist regimes think that, practically speaking, all men are equal, there is very little evidence that they do in view of the way political power is distributed in their societies. (2) In my paper I tried to explain why, according to Strauss, constitutional democracy comes closer today to what the classics require than does any feasible alternative to it. This is very different from affirming that democracy is the simply just political order, a view that I do not think he held. (3) To the extent that something reminding one of the gentleman continues to play a role in Strauss's thoughts concerning the present, that role concerns the crisis of liberal education rather than the political arena. The most that Strauss permitted himself to hope regarding the political arena was that the liberally educated, free of grandiose and extravagant political expectations, might one day obtain a hearing in it. But receiving a hearing in the marketplace is not the same as ruling it. In this respect Strauss's preferred solution for the present is very different from his preferred solution for the classical city, a solution whose essential ingredient was the rule of gentlemen, direct or indirect.

No interpreter has denied that Strauss believed he knew some political orders to be inferior to others. Some students of his thought, however, (including some admirers) have held that he was an esoteric adherent of the teaching he calls philosophical conventionalism, and they understand the debate between philosophical conventionalism and classic natural right, which looms so large in *Natural Right and History*, as, in truth, little more than a debate over how to prudently communicate that somewhat shocking view. Now, according to Strauss's interpretation of the philosophical conventionalists, their analysis of political life is not essentially different from the one offered by Thrasymachus. It is different chiefly insofar as it infers, not that it is better to be hammer than anvil, but that it is desirable to be neither—by leading the philosophic life. But no more than Thrasymachus would be able to (or would want to be able to) declare a democratic hammer superior to an oligarchic hammer are the conventionalist philosophers able (or desirous of being able) to declare some regimes superior to others. As for tyranny, Thrasymachus praises it as beneficial not to the city, of course, but to the tyrant. The philosophical conventionalists do not praise the tyrannical life, as Thrasymachus does, but tyranny does bring out, with great clarity, the hammer/anvil situation present in all political life according to their view (at least as that view is reconstructed by Strauss). Now a few students of Strauss's thought believe that according to him there is only a verbal difference between the true, genuine teaching of Plato, Aristotle and Xenophon regarding political life on the one hand, and philosophical conventionalism on the other. And this has the consequence, not always perceived by those who hold this view, of denying that these thinkers (or Strauss) either can distinguish better from worse political orders or would want to do so. A genuine and important difference between conventionalism and classic natural right remains, even after one has grasped the significant areas of agreement, up to a point, between the two positions. One cannot understand Strauss's thought without understanding that difference.

Second Section

STRAUSSIAN APPLICATIONS

Richard H. Cox

ARISTOTLE AND MACHIAVELLI ON LIBERALITY

A prodigal king is nearer a tyrant
than a *parsimonious.*
—*FRANCIS BACON*

I

The word *crisis* evokes the sense of a crucial phase in a potentially fatal disease in a living body. To be precise, it is that phase when the greatest uncertainty exists as to whether the body will throw off the disease and return to health, or succumb and lose its essential quality, its life. By analogy, the phrase *the crisis of liberal democracy* evokes the sense of a crucial phase in a potentially fatal disease in a body politic whose regime is a liberal democratic one. The artful physician of the living body must correctly judge the symptoms of a disease in order to prescribe such remedies as may prove beneficial. And by analogy, the artful physician of the body politics must so act, *mutatis mutandis.* The questions then become: What is the disease afflicting liberal democracy in our time? What are its symptoms? What may be its remedies?

We are helped, here, by repairing for a moment to the etymology of *crisis.* Its root is a group of related Greek words which have the sense of "separating, distinguishing, judging." I suggest that the disease that afflicts our liberal democratic regime is a profound difficulty in "separating" or "distinguishing" and, perhaps most of all, a profound difficulty in "judging." I further suggest that one of the most revealing symptoms of the disease is the progressive inability, among those who are ostensibly the most educated, to judge thoughtfully concerning the nature and purpose of the ownership of private property. And I suggest, finally, that this inability is rooted in a growing forgetfulness concerning the nature and purpose of the specific virtue traditionally called "liberality."

Let us now turn our attention to the current political world. The decisive political fact is the existence of two superpowers, the United States and the Soviet Union. The first is, in common parlance, a "liberal democracy" and the second a "communist state." Or, in another version of common parlance, the first is a "capitalist state" and the second a "communist state." It is revealing that the latter version of common parlance comes closer to the nub of the conflict between the two kinds of regimes by throwing into vivid relief the fact that the United States appears to emphasize as its core principle the right to private ownership of that peculiar property called "capital," whereas the Soviet Union appears to emphasize the utterly common ownership of all property, including all that "capital" denotes. It is even more revealing that within liberal democracies there is a tendency for the phrase *liberal democracy* to be replaced by the phrase *capitalist state*, for the latter is rooted in the ascendancy within such democracies of the political vocabularly of Karl Marx and his epigones. The subtle but significant replacement of *liberal* with *capitalist* points to the root problem of the growing inability to separate, to distinguish, and to judge: "Liberal" evokes, however tenuously, the traditional sense of a human virtue, but "capitalist" evokes, quite powerfully, the image of immense wealth owned by a rapacious elite.

The issue here is not one of mere nomenclature; it is nothing less than whether public officers and citizens within the liberal democracies of the West have the intellectual, moral, and political health to withstand the relentless pressure that is exerted by Marxist doctrine backed by the formidable power of the Soviet Union and other Marxist regimes. Thomas West aptly states, "Marxism-Leninism exercises a tremendous attraction over Westerners disgusted by the crass display of greed and self-indulgence unleased by modern liberalism." And he persuasively argues that in seeking to come to grips with that power of attraction, we must go to the roots by again posing the question of the nature of man—in particular, the question whether ambition, desire for private gain, and preferences for one's own are sown in the nature of man.[1]

I think it exceedingly useful, as one aspect of such an inquiry, to return to the point at which the essentials of the moden project come most thoughtfully into being, and that is in the writings of Machiavelli. I think, in particular, it is exceedingly useful to turn our attention to Machiavelli's critique of the classical and Christian teachings on virtue, and most especially for present purposes to his critique of the classical teaching on "liberality" as enunciated in Aristotle's *Ethics*. I think so because what we today call "the crisis of liberal democracy" is but one manifestation of the drawing out of certain consequences that flow from Machiavelli's amazingly successful polemic against the classical teaching on "liberality."

II

I turn first to a sketch of Aristotle's treatment of "liberality." The treatment occurs primarily in two places. In Book II, Chapter 7 of the *Ethics*, Aristotle gives a list of the moral virtues, including a brief definition of each, and liberality is among them. In Book III, Chapter 6 he begins a series of little treatises on each of the moral virtues, wherein he elaborates, develops, and qualifies the preliminary definitions given in Book II. The crux of the argument concerning liberality is as follows: Liberality is, like all the other moral virtues or human excellences, a mean between two extremes which are vices, one a vice of excess and the other a vice of deficiency. Specifically, then, liberality is observance of the mean in regard to the "giving and getting" of useful physical goods, that is, goods whose value may be stated in monetary terms, hence of what we shall broadly call "property." The vice of excess corresponding to the virtue liberality is called "extravagance" or "prodigality": Prodigality consists in the lavish and even foolish giving of one's property to others and in the deficient attention to, or even heedlessness, concerning the getting of property. The vice of deficiency is called "stinginess" and is the converse of prodigality: stinginess consists in little or no giving and in avaricious getting of property. In sum, liberality is that peculiar human excellence that, when truly present in a human being, causes him to act virtuously in regard to both giving and getting property.

With this sketch of the bare bones of Aristotle's argument as the background, I wish now to draw attention to and to comment on three aspects of the more detailed form of his argument. These have been selected both because they are important with respect to Aristotle's own argument and, in addition, because they afford points of entry into Machiavelli's horizon in the *Prince*.

The first point is that the argument concerning liberality in the *Ethics* presupposes the existence of and even the rightness of the private ownership of property, for without such ownership the virtue in question would be nonexistent in reality. Whether that is a thoughtless or thoughtful presupposition is itself a good question. Suffice it to say, here, that the treatment of property in the *Ethics* is integrally linked to the parallel and further treatment in the *Politics*, especially Books I and II; that the latter treatment is both immensely profound and subtle; and that one of the crucial conclusions of the latter treatment is that the private ownership of property is a quality of the good political society.

The crux of the argument is that such ownership most fully corresponds to both the potentialities and limitations of human nature, given the irreducible fact that human beings are a compound of body and soul in which the pleasures and the pains are markedly individual. Liberality, then, is a human excellence in that it decisively transcends mere concern with one's own yet never supposes a human capability, in general, of utter transcendence as does Socrates' mad scheme in Plato's *Republic*.

A second point of critical importance is that liberality, like all the moral virtues, consists in a mean concerning the passions, that is, a kind of sustained and extensive moderation of the underlying and fundamental human passions such as fear, desire for pleasure, and anger. Correspondent and ministerial to such moderation of the passions is the indispensability of proper moral training from earliest childhood: as the twig is bent, so will it grow. Now given the importunate and potent character of the human passions—in particular, for example, the importunate and potent desire for all kinds of pleasure—the institution of such moral training for the citizens is both the greatest responsibility and the greatest difficulty for the statesman and the legislator. This is to say that, in practice, it is exceedingly difficult to make citizens liberal in the true sense of that term, just as it is exceedingly difficult to make them courageous or just.

This difficulty may be seen more concretely now by some reflection on the following arguments in the little treatise on liberality: the liberal man will give to others because it is noble; he will give only the right amount, to the right people, at the right time, in the right way, and do everything else that is entailed in right as distinct from haphazard and impulsive giving; and it will bring such a man pleasure to give, or at least cause him no pain. In a parallel way, the liberal man will never stoop to getting property of the wrong kind from the wrong sources in the wrong way, for "honest taking goes with honest giving, and any other kind of taking is contrary to it."[2]

Consider, then, for a moment the stipulation that the liberal man will give property only to the "right" people. As one looks closely at Aristotle's argument, both in the context of the treatment of liberality as well as elsewhere, it becomes clear that "right" people means those who are actually, or at least potentially, capable of a considerable degree of moral virtue, such as being able and willing to use property given to them for truly virtuous ends, such as engaging in citizen activities or in a life of study. Conversely, it is also painfully clear—to the essentially modern soul—that mere desire for property, or even sheer neediness, are not in themselves any moral claim upon the liberal man's propensity to give of his own property to others. And, finally, it is clear that to give to the "wrong" people means, in particular, to give to those who are actually, or at least potentially, vicious human beings—for example, to those who may use property given to them to lead lives of indulgence in base physical pleasures, whether on a small or a grand scale.

Reflection shows that the discrimination, the judgment, and the thoughtfulness required to separate the virtuous from the vicious prospective recipients of one's largesse and to give only to the former make great demands on the moral and intellectual character of the giver. Indeed, that is precisely why liberality, with respect to giving, is a virtue or human excellence. So far from being a spontaneous response of the passions to the importunity or neediness or attractiveness of others, it is, rather, a highly disciplined moral activity guided by *phronesis*, or "prudence," the reigning intellectual virtue concerning the political things.

Consider, also, the other side of Aristotle's argument, concerning the proper getting of property. Here the difficulties are, if anything, greater than those with respect to giving. For precisely because no property of the kind we are speaking of belongs by nature to human beings, but rather must somehow be acquired, directly or indirectly, it follows that the crucial problem is, in terms of the relationship of means to ends, the getting which makes possible the giving. What is more, the generally strong and persistent character of the desire to acquire property necessary for one's own sustenance, a desire closely connected to the fear of death or of painful neediness, makes it all the more probable that the getting will be for the keeping and not for the giving. This is a troubling fact that Aristotle recognizes in concluding the treatise on liberality with the acute observation that of the two vices related to property, stinginess is far more prevalent among humans than prodigality.

But stinginess itself may be further considered under the heads of deficiency in giving and excess in getting; and the latter, in turn, raises the question of the distinction not only of the amount gotten but also of the means by which it is gotten. It is worth noticing here that Aristotle is more concrete and emphatic in designating certain kinds of "wrong" getting than he is in designating "right" getting. With respect to "right" getting, he alludes to, but does not much expand upon, getting by inheritance and by business activity and praises the former but tolerates the latter. With respect to "wrong" getting, he is more concrete and explicit. Indeed, the ordering of the treatment of specific kinds of "wrong" getting, which occurs towards the end of the treatise on liberality, is worth closer attention.

The order and the nature of the examples of "wrong" getting prove, on reflection, to be both instructive concerning Aristotle's own argument and to afford an entry point for the polemic by Machiavelli. Aristotle orders the examples of "wrong" getting in three subgroups. First, Aristotle groups together two specific forms of rather petty and base getting from wrong sources: the activity of the pimp, who gets from the sordid merchandising of women's bodies to lustful men; and the activity of the usurer, who gets from the sordid merchandising of small sums of money at high interest. Second, Aristotle next contrasts petty "wrong" getting with monstrously "wrong" getting, for he turns briefly to the example of tyrants, who sack cities and plunder temples. He pauses, almost in passing, to note that such men commonly are not called "stingy," but rather "vicious, impious, and unjust." Third, Aristotle returns to petty and base getting and again gives two examples: the activity of the gambler and that of the stick-up man; the former willfully accepts reproach for taking from his friends rather than giving to them, and the latter willfully runs the risk of injury or death to acquire expendable property.

Aristotle's denunciation of pimps, usurers, tyrants, gamblers and stick-up men, and his distinguishing among them must be kept constantly in mind as we move forward to Machiavelli's polemic. For now it is sufficient to remark, first, that the brief argument concerning the tyrant, the second of the three subkinds of "wrong" getting, suddenly leaves the domain of discourse on the qualities of private men and enters that of discourse on rulers, or, to be more precise, of vicious rulers. The second of the three bad qualities commonly ascribed to tyrants is "impiety." The implication seems to be that common morality holds that "piety" in a ruler is the only thing needful, or at least the most critically important thing in deterring rulers from simply seizing the property of other cities and their citizens or from plundering temples.

A third point of importance concerning Aristotle's treatment of liberality is that it is part of a large, complex treatment of moral virtue in general, and of the specific moral virtues in particular. Two aspects of that treatment require comment here. First, Aristotle indicates but does not explicitly say that the moral virtues are comprised of a precise number of specific virtues, whereas he later in Book VI of the *Ethics* explicitly says that the intellectual virtues are precisely five in number. Aristotle thus leaves it to the reader to scrutinize the treatment of the specific moral virtues in order to determine their number. Such scrutiny indicates that the number is eleven. Second, Aristotle barely suggests that the order of the treatment of the specific moral virtues has been established with great care. Here, even more than is the case with the problem of the number of the moral virtues, Aristotle leaves it to the reader to try to uncover the ground of that order. Thus, for example, it is a good question why the treatment begins with courage and culminates with justice. And thus it is also a good question, given our present concerns, why liberality is the third moral virtue to be treated, preceded by courage and moderation and followed immediately by "magnificence" —a clumsy way, in English, to try to convey the sense of the Greek *megaloprepeia*, which means "greatness of fitting contributions to great civic ventures," such as sponsoring a sacred embassy. A careful investigation of this problem of the order of placement of liberality would lead us far afield. Suffice it to say, on this occasion, that the placement appears to be rooted in a profound reflection on the order of the human passions, their relationship, and their relative importance to the concerns of the statesman and the legislator. Thus, for example, fear of death in battle, desire for a variety and abundance of bodily pleasures, and desire for protection of the body through external possessions are passions that must be contended with in seeking to inculcate courage, moderation, and liberality respectively. As for the relationship between "liberality" and "magnificence," which to Aristotle are clearly distinct virtues concerning property, suffice it to say that the first focuses on private giving and getting in relations among private men, whereas the second focusses on private giving and getting with respect to great civic affairs.

III

As necessary background to Machiavellis' treatment of liberality, I must first make some observations concerning the nature of his project, his mode of discoursing, and his general treatment of virtue and vice. His project is no less ambitious than to reorder human life completely by bringing mankind "new modes and orders" that will rest on a new understanding of virtue. His mode of discoursing is a provocative combination of simple, explicit, and often morally repulsive prescriptions for founding and maintaining political rule intertwined with and undergirded by extremely subtle, covert, and profound moral and political reasonings. Indeed, since Machiavelli conceives of himself as a true prince of the mind who is in the process of founding a new order for men and since he urges every true prince to use the natures of both the lion and the fox in making war on his enemies, it is not too much to say that Machiavelli's mode of discoursing is an application of that principle to his guerilla warfare on the traditional teachings: The overt and morally repulsive prescriptions represent the lion; the covert and morally subtle reasonings represent the fox.

As for Machiavelli's general treatment of virtue and vice, I will sketch several points here as setting the framework for the particular treatment of liberality. Machiavelli begins the treatment of virtue in Chapter 1 when he says that dominion, or rule, is acquired either by arms, fortune, or virtue. The three modes of acquisition are then taken up thematically in clusters of chapters: arms in Chapters 12–14, virtue in Chapters 15–23, and fortune in Chapter 24–26. The thematic treatment, I observe, changes the initial order of the three modes such that virtue falls into the central position, flanked on the ends by arms and fortune. And I observe, further, that from the outset of his treatise, Machiavelli presents the treatment of virtue in the light of and in reference to a certain form of acquisitiveness.

The thematic treatment of virtue and vice begins with the title to Chapter 15, which reads: "Of Those Things for Which Men, and Especially Princes, Are Praised and Blamed."[3] The body of the chapter then falls into three parts: The first is a general statement of Machiavelli's intention, wherein he says that though he "knows" that others have written on his theme, he will depart in the greatest possible degree from the "orders" of those others by treating not the imagined but the effectual truth. The second part contains a list of the "things" referred to in the title. The third part states a general principle concerning the ability of the prince to adhere to what is held to be good. Chapter 16 begins a treatment of the list that is the central element of Chapter 15. In principle, it seems that each succeeding chapter should treat one set of "things" from that list. In fact, however, the initial, seemingly orderly, treatment gives way to confusing disorder, such that only Chapters 16, 17, 18, and 19 take up such sets. Machiavelli writes here particularly like the fox.

My basic premise is that Machiavelli covertly and quite deliberately models his treatment of virtue and vice on Aristotle's treatment in the *Ethics*. Thus, in particular, the list in Chapter 15 of the "things" praised and blamed corresponds to the list of the virtues and vices in Book II of the *Ethics*, and the treatment of particular "things," which begins in Chapter 16 and extends through Chapter 19, corresponds to the series of treatises on the specific moral virtues, which goes from Book III, Chapter 6, to the end of Book V of the *Ethics*. Since Machiavelli's treatment of liberality is an integral part of this covert modeling it is now necessary to consider certain features of how Machiavelli both imitates and radically departs from Aristotle.

The first important feature concerns differences in the treatment of virtue in general. I have already noted that, from the outset, Machiavelli treats virtue solely as a mode of acquisition of dominion, whereas

Aristotle treats it as the human mode of achieving the good. Further-more, Aristotle gives a lengthy discussion and a definition of the nature of virtue prior to presenting the list of the specific moral virtues, then a further lengthy discussion of certain aspects of virtue, such as what it means to do something voluntarily, prior to the thematic treatment of each specific moral virtue. Machiavelli, in contrast, gives no general discussion nor definition of virtue; he compels the reader to discover the argument concerning these points in the interstices of the web he weaves all through the *Prince*.

A second feature concerns differences in the treatment of the specific elements in each list. Aristotle clearly refers to the elements as virtues and corresponding vices and gives a succinct definition of each. Machiavelli, in contrast, is ambiguous and even evasive as to what the elements are to be called—a point to which I will turn for more extended treatment presently—and gives no definitions of the "things" praised and blamed.

A third feature, related to, yet different from, the second, concerns the triadic character of Aristotle's representation of virtue and vice in con-trast to the bipolar character of Machiavelli's presentation of the "things" praised and blamed. To be concrete: Aristotle begins by con-trasting courage, a virtue, to two vices, cowardice (the vice of deficiency) and fooldhardiness (the vice of excess). Machiavelli, in contrast, begins with a pair of "things," namely, to be reputed either "liberal" or "stingy." What this bipolar character ultimately signifies is unclear, but on its surface it stands in great tension with Aristotle's teaching that vir-tue is essentially a mean between two extremes.

A fourth feature concerns remarkable differences in the content and order of Aristotle's and Machiavelli's lists. Aristotle's list begins with "courage" and ends with "justice." Machiavelli's list begins with "liberality" and ends with "religion." Closer inspection shows that Aristotle's list is silent about "religion," whereas Machiavelli's list is silent about "justice." What Machiavelli means by so curious an inter-change is one of the most baffling problems of his teaching on virtue. And a related problem is why, though Machiavelli includes the sense of "courage" in certain sets of the elements in his list, he sees fit to place "liberality" first, thus elevating it to the primary position, occupied in Aristotle's list by "courage."

A fifth feature concerns the exact number of sets of elements in each list and the subsequent treatment of them. Neither Aristotle nor Machiavelli says how many sets are in his list, but scrutiny shows that each list contains eleven sets. Aristotle's treatises on the specific moral virtues treat each of the eleven sets, but Aristotle makes a most unob-

trusive change in the order of three of the sets, including one that concerns the virtue of speaking "truthfully." Machiavelli both imitates and
radically departs from Aristotle's changes and does so in two ways:
First, Machiavelli, without giving any explanation, unobtrusively collapses the treatment of the first two sets, both of which have to do with
the uses of property, into a single chapter, Chapter 16. Second,
Machiavelli at first suggests that he will treat each of the eleven sets in
order, a plan that would cause the sequential treatment to conclude with
Chapter 26, the last chapter in fact in his whole book; that would
furthermore cause the last chapter to be a thematic treatment of religion
and its contrary. The actual order of treatment is, however, much more
complex. For one thing Machiavelli treats the first four sets of his list in
three chapters, Chapters 16, 17, and 18, and he then suddenly collapses
the treatment of the remaining seven sets into Chapter 19. The most obvious feature of Chapter 19 is that it is the longest chapter in the *Prince*, a
feature that is meant, I suggest, to constitute a cunning and perverse imitation of the fact that Aristotle's treatise on justice is the longest treatise
on the specific moral virtues. One unobtrusive indication of this intention on Machiavelli's part occurs at the center of the chapter when
Machiavelli says that Marcus Aurelius, the only man ever to be called a
"philosopher" in the *Prince*, was among those who were "lovers of
justice." Machiavelli, himself a philosopher and a prince of the mind, is
also, in his strange way, a "lover of justice." The real question is
whether justice can be had without a grounding in what traditionally is
understood to be vice. That question, I will argue presently, comes most
sharply into focus concerning the getting and giving of property and
thus concerning the true nature of liberality.

A sixth feature concerns differences in the mode of presentation of
items in the two lists. In Aristotle's list the virtue nearly always is mentioned first, it is named, defined, and then its two corresponding vices
are similarly treated. Machiavelli's list, in contrast, is both puzzling and
strange. For one thing Machiavelli never explicitly identifies a given
"thing" praised or blamed as either a virtue or a vice. For another the
order of the "things" traditionally understood to be either virtue or vice
proves to be utterly chaotic—or at least seems to be so. Again to be concrete: Machiavelli begins with two pairs—the very two pairs that have
most to do with the use of property, namely, "liberal"/"stingy" and
"givers"/"rapacious"—wherein, in each pair, the "thing" traditionally
called a virtue is given first and the vice second. But the anticipation that
this order of virtue first and vice second is the fundamental order of the
entire set of pairs is rudely shattered with the third pair, "cruel" and
"full of pity." What is more, the rest of the pairs prove to be chaotic,

with the vice sometimes first and the virtue sometimes first. Reflection on the onset of the chaos draws attention, retrospectively, to the seeming order of the first two pairs; that is, one begins to wonder whether "liberality" and "giver" are, in Machiavelli's account of the effectual as distinguished from the imagined truth, in fact vices instead of virtues. And reflection on the onset of the chaos draws attention, prospectively, to the thematic treatment of "cruel" and "full of pity," which takes place in Chapter 17. Suffice it to say, for now, that what emerges in Chapter 17 is a troubling argument in which "full of pity" comes to mean, at times, "full of piety," by a play on the Italian and Latin ambiguity of the words used, and "full of piety" comes to mean, shockingly, "full of cruelty." A further problem thus emerges concerning the underlying relationship of Machiavelli's treatment of "liberality" to "piety" as "cruelty."

This aspect of Machiavelli's strange way of arguing leads to a final feature of importance and that is the nature of the choice of words for the items in each list. In Aristotle's list, words for the virtues, such as "courage" or "liberality," are taken, often with no comment, from ordinary moral discourse, and the same is true for the words for the vices. In Machiavelli's list, words for the "things" praised or blamed seem also to be taken, with no comment, from ordinary moral discourse. But there is one exception, and it proves on investigation and reflection to be an immensely revealing one. This very revealing exception occurs when Machiavelli briefly digresses, or at least appears so to do, in choosing the term to pair with "liberal." He rejects *avaro*, which seems to be a word in use in Florentine Italian, in favor of *misero*, which is explicitly said to be Tuscan. Machiavelli makes this choice on the grounds that *avaro*, or "avariciousness," "in our language still denotes one who desires to have by rapine; *misero* we call the one who abstains much from using his own." The singularity of Machiavelli's care in choosing the term to pair with "liberal" is but the first of many indications of the thoughtfulness of his entire treatment of virtue in general and of "liberality" in particular. Furthermore, the content of his seemingly digressive statement is intended to remind us of the nuances and distinctions of Aristotle's treatment of "liberality." For example, by reminding us of the distinction, so important to Aristotle, between what is "one's own" and what is "another's," Machiavelli, from the outset of his own treatment, raises the question of the very basis of that distinction. Similarly, by reminding us of the distinction, also very important to Aristotle, between vice in getting and vice in giving and their relative degrees of viciousness, Machiavelli from the outset of his own treatment raises the question of the very basis of that distinction as well. I suggest, in sum, that

Machiavelli is a worthy opponent of "the philosopher" and that his underlying polemic against Aristotle's treatment of "liberality" is one of the foundations of his new modes and orders.

In order to see better how deeply grounded in such a polemic Machiavelli's new teaching on "liberality" really is we have, next, to confront the deliberate, complex, and sometimes maddeningly oblique ambiguity of Machiavelli's terminology concerning virtue and vice. It may have been noticed that in the preceding remarks on Machiavelli I have repeatedly followed Machiavelli's usage in referring to the "things" for which men, and especially princes, are praised and blamed. That usage emanates from the title to Chapter 15. I am convinced that Machiavelli very deliberately uses the general word *things* there (in the Latin, it is *rebus*) instead of *virtues* and *vices*, which he very well could have done, and that he does so in order to raise the question, from the outset of his treatment, as to just what those "things" truly are that common moral discourse praises and blames and that it calls virtue and vice. So let us follow Machiavelli's way more closely now.

Machiavelli begins the title, as I have noted, with a Latin word that conveys the very general sense of "things" that are yet undifferentiated by definition into specific kinds. But then, in order to underscore further this purpose, Machiavelli twice changes the vocabulary of his discourse during the argument of Chapter 15. The first change occurs just prior to the list of pairs of what have been called "things" in the title. Machiavelli now changes to the use of the Italian *qualita*, or "quality," the Latin root of which suggests, very powerfully, the question of the "whatness" or the "nature" of a thing. Furthermore, to remind the reader of this first significant change, Machiavelli again uses *qualita* shortly after the list of pairs. Nor is that all: The second use of *qualita* occurs in the second of two sentences in Chapter 15 that begin with the phrase "I know." The first thing Machiavelli "knows" is that many have written on his subject, and the second is that "everyone will confess that it would be a most praiseworthy thing to find in a prince all the qualities written above which are held to be good." The desperate ambiguity of this sentence comes to light when one reflects on the chaos in the ordering of virtue and vice that has taken place in the list of "things" —now called "qualities." What is "held to be good" by "everyone" may not be held to be good by Machiavelli, to say the least.

The second decisive change in Machiavelli's vocabulary occurs shortly after the second use of "I know." For now, finally and belatedly, Machiavelli begins to use the traditional terms *virtue* and *vice*. Or to be more accurate, he begins by twice using *vices*, thus reversing the order of the title, which, by its order *praise* and *blame*, implies the order *virtue* and *vice*. Furthermore, as if to underscore the fact that he is in the course of turning traditional moral principles on their heads, Machiavelli twice categorically states that the prince must not concern himself with incurring "the infamy of those vices" that would make it impossible for him to hold his "state." And to further buttress this reversal, Machiavelli concludes the chapter by counseling the prince that what "seems virtue" will bring "ruin," and what "seems vice" will result in "security" and "the good" being his. The undermining of Aristotle's teaching on the nature of "the good," as that at which all human activity is naturally directed, is well under way.

The most decisive single indication that this is a fundamental aspect of Machiavelli's great project is his use, for the only time in Chapter 15, of the word *prudente*, or *prudent*, in conjunction with the first of the two statements that the prince must not concern himself with the infamy of vices that would lose him his state. That is to say, what Machiavelli the philosopher truly "knows," in contrast to what "everyone will confess," is that the truly "prudent" prince must accept not just the infamy but the actuality of being vicious as vice is understood in ordinary moral discourse and that this is so because "the human condition" does not permit the prince to do otherwise. This aspect of Machiavelli's teaching is the true foundation of the contemporary Marxist dogma that the elite, called the Communist Party, not only may but also must engage in the most heinous crimes in order to destroy capitalism and bring mankind into the promised land of communism, a condition of peace and plenty and harmony. The profound difference between the Marxist dogmatists and Machiavelli is that Machiavelli knows that he must come directly to grips with Aristotle's teaching on prudence and show its radical deficiency. For Machiavelli knows that the most acute classical reasoning concerning the nature and purpose of "prudence" is contained in Book VI of the *Ethics*; that Aristotle elevates "prudence" (*phronesis*) to the highest rank among the intellectual virtues in respect to the moral and political things; that Aristotle virtually equates "political science"(*he politike*) with "prudence"; and that Aristotle teaches that a given moral virtue, such as courage or liberality or justice, is essentially actual in the human soul only when it is guided by "prudence." Machiavelli decisively yet unobtrusively reminds us that he knows all these things about Aristotle's teaching on "prudence" by his own peculiar use of that term in Chapters 15–19. The single use and the singularly shocking sense of "prudence" in Chapter 15 pertain to virtue in general. But that single use and that singularly shocking sense adumbrate a single use and a singularly shocking sense that pertain to specific moral virtues in each of the four succeeding chapters. Stated generally, a radically new teaching on "prudence," one consciously though obscurely rooted in guerilla warfare against Aristotle's teaching, is at the basis of Machiavelli's new science of politics. It remains to consider, all too briefly, how that new teaching on "prudence" and that new science of politics come most crucially into blurred yet revealing focus in the new teaching on "liberality."

The decisive importance of liberality in Machiavelli's argument is indicated not just by his having silently replaced courage with liberality, in Aristotles' ordering, nor by his having taken great and singular care in choosing *misero* over *avaro* as the opposite of "liberal," but by the precision with which he speaks of "liberality" and its contrary in relation to the other "things" or "qualities" or "virtues." Thus, at the beginning of Chapter 17, having treated liberality and its contrary in Chapter 16, Machiavelli says, "Descending then to the other previously mentioned qualities. . . " And thus at the beginning of Chapter 19, having treated the first four pairs from the list in Chapter 15, Machiavelli says, "Since I have spoken of the most important qualities which have been mentioned above, I wish to discuss the others briefly with this generality." In short, the most important qualities are those treated in Chapter 16, 17, and 18, and first among the most important "qualities" is "liberality" and its contrary. We must then come to a sharper focus on Chapter 16 and its relationship to the list of "qualities" in Chapter 15.

The first thing that confronts us in Chapter 16 is, of course, its title: "Of Liberality and Parsimony." But according to the list in Chapter 15, it should be: "Of Liberality and Stinginess." What is more, given the singular care Machiavelli took to choose *misero* over *avaro* as the contrary of *liberale*, it is strange and puzzling that he should now, suddenly and with no word of explanation, replace *misero* with *parsimonia*. Is "parsimony," according to Machiavelli, subtly different from "stinginess"— different enough, that is, to require a change in nomenclature? If so, what is that difference, and why not explicitly state it? Indeed, why not choose *parsimonia* in the first instance over either *misero* or *avaro*, to be the contrary of *liberale*?

This stumbling block at the very threshold of Machiavelli's thematic treatment of liberality concerns, on the surface, the proper nomenclature for that quality that traditionally is held to be a vice contrary to liberality. But as I shall show in what follows, it concerns, much more profoundly, the proper understanding of the effective as contrasted to the imagined truth concerning "getting" in relation to "giving."

It is important, at this point, to recall the formulation in Aristotle's *Ethics*. Liberality has two corresponding vices, prodigality and stinginess. Both prove to be vices pertaining predominantly to "giving," the former an excess and the latter a deficiency, which is to say that neither vice pertains predominantly to "getting," or that the vices concerning "getting" are somehow obscured by the vices concerning "giving." It is in this area of moral analysis that Machiavelli will drive his salient. His initial choice of *misero* over *avaro* brings the problem to light by momentarily suggesting the possibility, which is then quickly rejected, that *avaro*, with its sense of "desiring to have by rapine," might be considered the contrary of *liberale*. His subsequent tacit and strange choice of *parsimonia* as the contrary, in the title of Chapter 16, reinforces the sense of a vice of "giving" contained in the first choice in Chapter 15. We are now confronted with a virtue and two names for the corresponding vice or vices, which is intended to remind us of the triadic formulation of Aristotle even while decisively departing from it, since both *misero* and *parsimonia*, though they refer to vices of "giving," are virtually synonymous. The tacit exclusion, by Machiavelli, of the vice that Aristotle calls "prodigality" points to a doubt on Machiavelli's part that humans are likely, given their natural acquisitiveness, to go to excess in "giving," or at least a sense that such a phenomenon is much less politically relevant than is its opposite, which is traditionally thought of as deficiency in "giving."

The status of, indeed the profound reflection on, natural acquisitiveness, is made even more manifest by what Machiavelli does with the second pair in his list in Chapter 15. That pair, we recall, is *donatore* and *rapace*. What is peculiar about the first term is that it, like *liberale*, refers to "giving," but unlike the difference between liberality and magnificence in Aristotle's *Ethics*, there is a difference of very insignificant degree between it and *liberale*. Machiavelli's tacit exclusion, through this device, of the virtue of magnificence, rests on the same line of thought as does the exclusion of prodigality. What is peculiar about the second term, *rapace*, is that, given the virtual synonomity of *liberale* and *donatore*, it is all the more strange that *donatore* should have *rapace* as its contrary. The exclusion of rapine, in the choice of *misero* over *avaro*, thus seems to have been only provisional. It remains to see what happens to *donatore* and *rapace*.

What happens most obviously, as I have noted above, is that, whereas Chapter 17, properly speaking, should treat *donatore* and *rapace*, it in fact treats *crudele* and *pietoso*. What happens, much less obviously, is that the treatment of *donatore* and *rapace* becomes integrated into the argument of Chapter 16 in a most intricate, strange, and yet ultimately revealing way. In order to see how and why this is accomplished, it is now necessary to look at the structure of that chapter.

The chapter falls into two nearly equal parts. The end of each part is signaled by the use of *"Pertanto. . . ,"* or *"Consequently. . . ,"* as

Machiavelli draws up his conclusion. The first part begins as a treatise, then momentarily becomes a speech in direct discourse using the familiar form of "you," and then concludes as a treatise. The second part is a little dialogue initiated by a "someone" who responds to Machiavelli's first part. In this part the "someone" and Machiavelli each have two speeches. This peculiar mixture of modes of speech—treatise interwoven with dialogue—echoes, and is intended to remind us of, the first such mixture in the *Prince*. That mixture occurs in Chapter 3. The chapter is, under the guise of being only a little treatise on "mixed principates," in reality the first chapter in a group of three that give open yet intimately phrased advice (the use of the familiar form of "you" is striking in this respect) on how to be successful at the conquest of others' lands and dominions. The group is, bluntly stated, advice on how to be rapacious, a "quality" that is, as Chapter 15 indicates, traditionally understood as a vice. Machiavelli's advice rests on the principle that humans are driven by natural necessity to seek to acquire, a principle obliquely recognized by the human admiration for men such as Alexander the Great, whose name appears twice in the title of Chapter 4— the only such occurrence in the *Prince*—and who is praised by Machiavelli at some point in each of the four main parts into which the *Prince* is divided. As we shall see, the image of Alexander and what he signifies is as much a link between Chapter 16 and the group of chapters on conquest as is the link indicated by the peculiar mixture of treatise and dialogue that characterizes Chapters 16 and 3.

We must now look more closely at certain aspects of the substance of each part in Chapter 16, keeping in mind that the first part is dominated by the sense of a treatise setting forth a body of established principles and the second by the sense of a dialogue setting forth a brief but trenchant discussion of principles themselves. Each part begins with a peculiar kind of praise of liberality and ends with a peculiar kind of praise of stinginess. Thus, the first part begins with Machiavelli speaking in his own name (*dico*: I say), saying that "it would be good to be reputed liberal." This is to say that goodness lies in the reputation not the possession of liberality and raises the question how one may obtain that reputation. The first part ends with Machiavelli's assertion that "a prince" ought "little to esteem . . . incurring the name of stinginess; because this is one of those vices which enables him to reign." This is to say that vice lies in being imprisoned by the traditional moral blame of stinginess, an imprisonment that will prevent one from reigning. The second part begins with "someone" replying to Machiavelli's praise of stinginess, saying "Caesar with his liberality obtained the imperium." This is to say that a certain seeming liberality, i.e., the bestowing of vast booty from conquering expeditions upon soldiers and citizens, is the in-dispensable means to that kind of rule that consists of "command in war."[4] The second part ends with Machiavelli's assertion that "it is far wiser to have the name of stinginess, which begets an infamy without hatred, rather than to be necessitated, by wanting the name of liberal, to incur the name of rapacious which begets an infamy with hatred." This is to say that given the potency of the desire to achieve "command in war," which is the essential aspect of "reigning," incurring the name of being stingy is more expedient and safer than incurring the infamy of being rapacious. In fact, this conclusion is a peculiar kind of praise not only in its preference of one vice over another but more so in its seeming oblivion of the rapacity of Caesar—a rapacity that was an intrinsic aspect of his greatness. We must therefore now try to see the path by which Machiavelli reaches this strange kind of wise praise.

Let us start from the way in which "someone" challenges Machia-velli's first conclusion, which is to say with the immediate adducing of the greatest conqueror of the greatest conquering polity of antiquity, Julius Caesar. This little section of the *Prince* proves, upon examination of it in relation to the rest of the work, to be Machiavelli's sole treatment of Caesar. Its fundamental purpose is to bring into focus, in the form of its singular example, the argument made on behalf of the primacy of con-quest at the very center of Chapter 3, for that argument spoke only generally of the excellence of Rome at conquest at the height of its republican expansion. Now Machiavelli is profoundly aware that the greatness of Rome's conquering abilities, hence of its greatest con-queror, is beset by classical philosophy's blame of rapacity—a blame, we have seen, that is strongly stated in the last part of Aristotle's treatise on liberality. What Machiavelli must do, then, is to show that that blame is without secure moral and intellectual foundations; to be more exact, he must show that classical philosophy's blame of that rapacity that is exer-cised against other polities is lacking in such foundations, for the available human alternative in practice, as opposed to what is available in the imagination, makes such blame unwise and imprudent.

The revolutionary character of Machiavelli's enterprise on this crucial point is indicated by a subtle contrast between the two parts of Chapter 16. The first part employs the traditional nomenclature of virtue and vice. Thus, in his momentary dialogic mode of speech early in the first part, Machiavelli says of liberality that "if it is used *virtuously* and in the mode one ought to use it"—that is, in the mode set forth in Aristotle's treatise on liberality—"one will not become known for it." He later rein-forces this with the assertion that a prince cannot "use this *virtue* of liberality" so as to become known for it "without harm," and thus, "if he is prudent," he will not care for being called stingy. And at the very end of the first part he asserts that stinginess "is one of those *vices* which enables him to reign." The second part is, in contrast, utterly silent about the traditional nomenclature of virtue and vice—and with good reason. For in this second part the undermining begun in the first part becomes radical: Machiavelli's wisdom concerning the true status of what Aristotle blames as the vice of rapacity in rulers lays the basis for a new nomenclature of virtue and vice. Let us see more specifically how and why.

In the first part it is unclear, at first, whether Machiavelli speaks of "men" or of "princes" or of both, an ambiguity that echoes the ambiguity of both the title and the body of Chapter 15, and that extends through Chapter 19. The difficulty underlying that ambiguity is that classical philosophy does not adequately recognize the difference between what a few rare men may seek and do and what most men in fact seek and do, nor the difference between private men and princes with respect to their respective fields of action. This double-edged difficulty permeates the argument of Chapter 16, but its articulation takes different forms in the two parts. In the first part the articulation is such as to raise grave doubts about the classical formulation while still remaining in important respects within the horizon of its nomenclature of virtue and vice and of its insistence on the self-restraint of men and princes. But in the second part the articulation is much more potently at odds with the classical formulation and, above all, with respect to the moral status of the rapine that results from foreign conquests. Let us see how this movement takes place.

Early in the first part, having acknowledged that there is such a thing as liberality in Aristotle's sense of that term, Machiavelli begins obliquely to criticize the political relevance of that phenomenon by turning to that "effectual truth" he has promised to set forth in Chapter 15. In particular, Machiavelli observes that "men" give the name of liberal not to those who give virtuously but to those who give "sumptuously." That is to say that men, taken essentially as their acquisitive nature necessarily makes them and not as Aristotle's virtuous man may become as the result of the fortunate combination of good nature, circumstances, and moral education, praise prodigal givers. They do so because what they truly desire is to be the recipients of lavish benefits even at the expense of others who may be, according to Aristotle's demanding standards, more worthy than themselves. Furthermore, among men it is the "few"—that is, the few potent political men, not the few truly virtuous men—who most expect lavish benefits even, and most especially, at the expense of the "many." What stands in the background here is the crucial distinction in Aristotle's *Politics* between "oligarchs" and "democrats," the two kinds of men who form the core of the two basic kinds of political regimes. What Machiavelli now seeks to show is that the "prince" is best by a fundamental problem: If he gives lavishly to the few, he must eventually get by taking ruthlessly from the many, either by harsh taxes or outright robbery or both. But if he virtuously chooses neither to give lavishly to the few nor to get ruthlessly from the many, he necessarily alienates the few more than he pleases the many and in that alienation lie many great dangers. The prince may, however, take the risk of that alienation in the expectation that his policy of virtuous action will, though being characterized by the few as mere stinginess, make it possible for his meager income to suffice for his political needs. At this point in the argument Machiavelli for the first time explicitly refers to specific areas of policy that require expenditures: to defend himself "from whoever makes war on him"; and to "undertake enterprises without burdening the people." Shortly after, he gives three modern examples that appear to be intended to support his argument: Pope Julius II, the King of France, and the King of Spain. With respect to the first two, Machiavelli mentions most particularly the need to make war and with respect to the last, the undertaking of enterprises. Thus, the prominence of war as a fundamental problem begins to emerge more distinctly. Machiavelli then reaches his conclusion: His recommended posture of princely stinginess will make it possible for the prince "not to have to rob his subjects," to "defend himself," "not to become poor and despised," and "not be forced to be rapacious." Reflection on this group of four things that the policy will facilitate shows that the first and the last are barely distinguishable, provided we construe not being forced to be rapacious to refer still to the prince's policy toward his own subjects. This repetition of a proscription against rapacity, while it accords formally with Aristotle's proscription, does so not on Aristotle's grounds, but on grounds of security for the prince's reign; prudent self-restraint with respect to robbing one's own citizens is simply sound insurance. On reflection, it is also noticable that with the reduction of the group of four things to three the central element becomes the problem of the prince's defending himself from external foes.

That this progressively more emphatic attention to the problem of foreign foes is Machiavelli's intention is borne out by the stunning implication of the immediate introduction by Machiavelli's "someone" of the example of Caesar, hence of Rome as personified by its most famous and rapacious prince. For though Machiavelli, arguing partially on the premises of classical philosophy in the first part, had recklessly assured the prince that the prescribed policy would enable him to defend himself against whatever foreign foe he might encounter, the single example of Caesar at once undermines the previous argument. For none of the modern examples offered would stand a chance against Caesar at the head of Roman legions. This sudden turn in the argument of Chapter 16 consists in enlarging the political horizon to take account of ancient political practice at its peak, as is shown by Machiavelli's own subsequent addition of Cyrus the Great and Alexander the Great to the example of Caesar that was so suddenly and unexpectedly obtruded by his "someone." Or to be more precise, the horizon now includes ancient political practice at its peak if one construes its peak to consist of excellence at conquest, which includes excellence in plundering, sacking, and ransoming. Consideration of this form of the effectual truth, as distinct from the imagined one, now opens the way for a more radical consideration of liberality and its contrary.

In the little dialogue with "someone," Machiavelli makes two sets of distinctions. The first is between one who is already a prince and one who is on his way to acquiring a principate. He argues that the latter necessarily must practice Caesar's kind of liberality, but that the former should not. He means that the rapine that makes possible this peculiar kind of liberality, which in turn makes possible the ascendant prince's rise, is to be conceived only in respect to that end, or that such rapine is the necessary means to an end that is not investigated as to its being good, but is simply accepted as being such. The horizon of Cyrus, Caesar, and Alexander is thus accepted as being a fundamental political fact, or an aspect of the effectual truth that is at the basis of the new teaching on virtue and vice.

In reply to "someone's" contention that even actual princes have practiced Caesar's kind of liberality and have been successful in doing so, Machiavelli gives a second distinction, that is, a distinction between spending "his own and that of his subjects" and spending "that which belongs to others." He argues that the prince ought to be "frugal" with respect to the first, using the word *parco*, the root word for the *parsimonia* of the title to Chapter 16. It thus appears that to be "stingy" in the strict sense pertains to princes who seek, unwisely, to confine their expenditures simply to what can be obtained by legal and fair means from their subjects, whereas to be "frugal" in the strict sense pertains to princes who seek wisely to take advantage of the availability of the property of others in order to make the expenditures that will satisfy both the "few" and the "many." Indeed, with respect to this latter kind of property, Machiavelli argues that the prince "ought not to omit any part of liberality," else "he will not be followed by his soldiers." But this is to suggest that the rapine that is carried out against others' lands and dominions and makes possible the strange sort of liberality practiced by a Caesar is simply necessary. Yet the political practice of many ancient and modern political societies seems to cast doubt, to say the least, on such an understanding of what is "necessary."

Machiavelli's rejoinder, spelled out at length and in subtle detail in many parts of the *Prince*, may be summarized as follows: We must start from man's utter neediness and his resultant natural and potent desire to "acquire," which, in its root sense, means "to get in addition to" previous possessions. Now man's previous possession is, by nature, nothing but his bare body, equipped with potent and relentlessly importunate desires, but no naturally designated property by which to satisfy those desires. The root problem then becomes whether convention or law can properly supply a firm basis for the differentiation between what is "one's own" and what is "another's." The difficulty with this supposition is that law itself is impotent without the ruthless application of force to back it up, at least on crucial occasions, and, furthermore, there are different natures among men, with some natures being naturally inclined and able to use that force ruthlessly in the pursuit of their ascendancy to rule as well as to maintain their rule; among humans as they really are, and not as they are imagined to be in works such as Plato's *Republic* or Aristotle's *Ethics*, those who most decisively delineate the problem of how to distinguish between what is "one's own" and what is "another's" are the Cyruses, Caesars, and Alexanders, great conquerors all. Their settling of such a boundary, which proves often to last over long periods of time, provides the basis for the private activity of "giving," but one should never forget that there had to be a prior and emphatically political "getting." Thus, to blame those who are most naturally capable of "getting," in the definitive sense of establishing the distinction between what belongs to a given polity and to another, is also to blame the root condition of "giving." True liberality, it thus turns out, must never lose sight of its roots in what traditionally is improperly called "rapine" since that very moral term presupposes a rightful prior ownership on the part of the one who is robbed. We thus come, as is fitting, to the question of the rightful ownership of the world or of any of its parts.

IV

That fateful question has been treated in the West since the advent of Machiavelli's daring new teaching always with that teaching more or less understood as the foundation. Thus, the project of a Bacon—to enable man to conquer nature for the relief of man's estate—and the

project of a Locke—to enable man to acquire virtually unlimited private
property (on the grounds that the impetus of such acquisition will
benefit mankind more than whole libraries full of treatises on liberality)
—redirect and qualify but in no sense fundamentally alter Machiavelli's
daring project of giving much greater moral respectability to sheer
human acquisitiveness than had classical philosophy or Christian doctrine. It certainly is true, however, that not a few people today contend
that Marx's unsparing critique of such acquisitiveness, especially in the
form in which it is identified with the ends and institutions of modern
capitalism, constitutes a decisive and immensely hopeful transcendence
of the projects of Locke, Bacon, and, more remotely, Machiavelli. I think
that that contention is essentially mistaken. For Marx's own argument
accepts and even praises the advent of modern natural philosophy and
modern science, which will enable man to conquer nature, and of
modern political philosophy and political economy, which will enable
man to produce enormous wealth, as necessary phases in the historical
process by which all men will finally be liberated from their ages-old
dual enslavement to nature and to other man. Furthermore, Marx's own
argument ultimately, if only obscurely, posits the historical inevitability
of Machiavelli's polemic against classical philosophy and Christian doctrine as the necessary precondition for Bacon's and Locke's projects; it
thus posits the historical inevitability of that daring reconstruction of
liberality on the basis of rapine rightly understood.

But the Marxist interpretation of Machiavelli's great project, as a stage
in the unfolding of the consciousness of "capitalism," simply does not
correspond to Machiavelli's own understanding of what he is about. To
Machiavelli, the investigation of liberality is no less a philosophic activity
than was that of his great predecessor and philosophic opponent,
Aristotle. Such philosophizing, praised by both Aristotle and
Machiavelli, consists in the desire to know for oneself and in the self-
consciousness of the freedom of the soul to think, to observe, and to
engage in dialogue. The cavalier reduction of such an investigation to
the banality of "ideology," in the Marxist sense, is itself a piece of
modern dogma of the most stifling kind.

As for whether Machiavelli truly has shown the deficiencies of Aristotle's teaching on liberality, that can only be decided by engaging in a
sustained and repeated confrontation of both their own arguments. It is
one of the grave symptoms of the crisis in liberal democracy that such a
confrontation, which was once understood in principle to be an essential
part of a liberal education, is no longer so understood. In its place we
have, for the most part, vulgar exhortations from right and left. Thus,
from the right we hear that the right to private property, and even the

right to immense accumulations of it, is the one indispensable condition of human freedom, and from the left we hear that private property, and especially its immense accumulation, is the very destruction of human freedom. Dimly in the background, as I have sought all too sketchily to show, is the problem of the nature of liberality. It is the mark of a liberal perspective to seek to bring that problem out of the shadows into the full light of day.

Notes

1. Thomas G. West, "Marx and Lenin," *Interpretation* (January 1983), 85.

2. Aristotle, *Nichomachean Ethics*, 1120b, 32–35. The text of the translation used is by Martin Ostwald: *Nichomachean Ethics* (Indianapolis: Bobbs-Merrill, 1962).

3. Niccolo Machiavelli, *The Prince*. The text of the translation used is by Leo P. S. de Alvarez, *The Prince* (Dallas: University of Dallas Press, 1980). I have also used the Italian text included in Mark Musa's bilingual edition, *The Prince* (New York: St. Martin's Press, 1964).

4. Cf. de Alvarez, *The Prince*, Chap. 1, n. 4.

Laurence Berns

ARISTOTLE AND THE MODERNS
ON FREEDOM AND EQUALITY

I

The modern notion of freedom as self-legislation was first expressly formulated as such by Rousseau.[1] But it is implicit at least in Hobbes's scheme of representation. Why should one obey the sovereign, according to Hobbes? Because through the social contract each of us has covenanted to allow his will to represent each of our wills, to take his will for our wills. He is our representative; his legislation through the social contract is, legally considered, our own self-legislation. In obeying him we are, legally speaking, obeying ourselves. The more fundamental principle necessitating this construction is expressed in the *Leviathan* as follows: "there being no Obligation on any man, which ariseth not from some Act of his own; for all men equally are by Nature free."[2] Rousseau and especially Kant are anticipated also in Hobbes's noticing that, according to this principle, injury and injustice are like self-contradiction, willing to do that which one has already willed through contract not to do.[3]

What does "equally" mean in the statement "all men equally are by Nature free"? It does not mean that all men are equal in natural abilities. In his discussion of the ninth "Law of Nature",[4] which declares that every man is to acknowledge every other man as his equal by nature if there is to be peace, Hobbes leaves it open as to whether nature has, in fact, made all men equal or not. One decisive equality in the state of nature is the nearly equal ability of all men to kill one another: Even the strongest man may be killed by the weakest when he is asleep. But this is not the equality being discussed here. Locke states very clearly what I take to be Hobbes's meaning: "Though I have said . . . *that all men are by Nature equal,* I cannot be supposed to understand all sorts of *Equality*: Age or Virtue may give Men a just Precedency: *Excellency of Parts and Merit* may place others above the Common level . . . and yet all this consists with the equality all men are in, in respect of Jurisdiction of Dominion one over another, which was the *Equality* I there spoke of . . . being that *equal Right* that every Man hath, to his *Natural Freedom*, without being subjected to the Will or Authority of any other Man."[5] As Jefferson once put it in the context of a discussion of natural talents: "Whatever be their degree of talent it is no measure of their rights. Because Sir Isaac Newton was superior to others in understanding, he was not therefore lord of the person or property of others."[6] This equality appears to be the negative condition for the positive ethical standard of freedom as self-legislation and the political standard that governments derive their just powers from the consent of the governed.

The development of the notion of freedom as self-legislation was inextricably connected with Rousseau's doctrine of the general will. As he put it in the *Social Contract*: " 'The problem is to find a form of association which will defend and protect with the whole common force the person and goods of each associate, and in which each, while uniting himself with all, may still obey himself alone, and remain as free as before.' This is the fundamental problem for which the social contract provides the solution.'"[7] The solution is a society in which all are subject to the general will that determines the law and at the same time each, as a constituent part of that will, contributes to the making of the law to which he is subject. All are subject to laws that each has in part imposed on himself.[8] For Rousseau and for Kant the process that makes the will general is also what makes it moral. Being compelled to express one's will in such a form that it can be made to coincide with the will of all others moralizes the will; that is, it frees it from the irrationality and immorality of selfish desire.[9] For example: I decide that I do not want to pay my taxes. In a republican manner I transform my wish into the form of a law. The form of law requires me to generalize my selfish desire: No one ought to pay taxes. But then I am compelled to consider that the police, the public schools, the courts, and so on would disappear, and I become aware of the irrationality of my original inclination. The form of general or universal law, then, not only guarantees the freedom of the subject but also keeps the will rational and moral. The idea is fully developed as a moral principle in Kant's doctrine of the categorical imperative, the one fundamental imperative laid down by the moral law: So act that you can will that the maxim of your action can become a universal law. For example, Kant says, a man is hard pressed. He asks himself: May I make a promise with the intention of not keeping it? The categorical imperative impels him to ask again: Would I want the maxim of my action, to get out of a difficulty by making a false promise, to become a universal law? Should everyone make false promises when they can extricate themselves from difficulties in no other way? I then come to see, Kant says, that indeed I can will to lie, but I can in no way will a universal law of lying. By such a law there could be no promises at all. No one would trust in any promise, and my maxim, as soon as it is universalized, would contradict and annul itself.[10]

In Kant the principle of freedom or autonomy (Greek *auto-nomia*, self-legislation) is no longer primarily a political principle, but has explicitly become a moral principle. I will say little here about Hegel, except that for Hegel freedom as self-legislation is extended through and beyond politics and morality to become a logical and metaphysical principle. The life of the concept, the life of that Spirit or Mind that forms and informs the human mind, human History, and the objects of human knowledge —if you will, the mind of God—proceeds in accordance with the principle of freedom, self-legislation.

When seen in contrast to the naturalistic ethics and politics of Plato and Aristotle, the legalism, egalitarianism, formalism, and emphasis on will common to the moral and political doctrines of Hobbes, Rousseau, Kant, and Hegel can be understood as rooted in their common depreciation or rejection of purposive nature as the ultimate source of political and ethical standards. The watchword of classical ethics is virtue, not freedom. Freedom itself becomes meaningful as the path to virtue. The classical notion implies that we can discern a natural hierarchy of human desires, culminating in the desire for the highest happiness. This, in turn, presupposes a natural hierarchy of human faculties or powers. The soul is the natural ruler of the body and the intellect or mind is by nature the ruling part of the soul. As Leo Strauss noted, it is on this basis that thoughtful men are said to be the natural rulers of the less thoughtful.[11] The modern notion, with one eye to nonteleological mathematical physics,[12] presupposes no such order of ends, an order that might allow for one man who understands it to decide what was better for another who does not understand it.

The depreciation of nature is, of course, implicit in the idea of the conquest of nature.[13] In Hobbes the goals and character of moral and political life are still determined by reference to nature, especially human nature, but in a way very different from the way of the classical tradition. The "condition of nature" is miserable; its only redeeming feature is the possibility of exit and, by means of the social contract entering into its opposite, the state of civil society. Instead of serving as a positive guide to human goodness, the condition or state of nature clarifies the *summum malum*, what in nature is to be overcome or avoided. Nature is a source of negative standards. Hobbes's emphasis on negative standards is continued and refined by Locke in his making "uneasiness" because of the possible loss or absence of what we desire, the chief spur to human activity.[14] In Chapter 5 of the *Essay on Civil Government*, the subject is treated playfully by his making the part that nature (compared with that which labor) contributes to the value of things shift from 1/10th, to 1/100th, to 1/1000th, to the "almost worthless materials." Less dramatically than the notion of the conquest of nature, this labor theory of value points beyond depreciation to the negation of nature. Natural defect, refined fear and pain, not merit or virtue, become the point of departure for the guidance of human activity. The negating activity of labor, "the pain which removes pain," replaces the classical notion of the art that completes, imitates, and perfects nature.[15]

The depreciation of nature culminates in Kant and Hegel by its complete disqualification as a source of ethical and political standards. For Kant, the student of Newton, nature must be understood as a mechanism. If morality is to be saved, it is to be traced to a source or sources altogether independent of nature, namely, practical reason. Only as a moral being, acting in accord with practical reason and knowing himself to be the cause of what he does, can man see himself (and therefore other men) as a noumenon, as a thing in itself, as outside the chain of mechanical causation, as free. Kant claims to have proved that moral reason and theoretical reason, which sees everything, including man, under the aegis of mechanical cause and effect, do not contradict one another; like Euclidian parallels, they simply do not meet. This thoroughgoing separation of the realm of nature from the realm of freedom then becomes a special problem for Kantian philosophy. How can natural man and moral man coexist in one and the same man? How are the realm of nature and the realm of freedom related in one and the same world? Kant wavered between two solutions to the problem of the unification of nature and freedom, a philosophy of religion or a philosophy of history. The philosophy of religion was his more fully elaborated solution. But in his reflections on history he might be said to have been the Kepler for Hegel's Newton.[16] The way two of his essays on history, *Conjectural Beginning of Human History* and *The End of All Things*, are keyed to the book of *Genesis* on the one hand and *Revelations* on the other, points to how the theory of history was intended to become a secular substitute for Biblical faith.[17] While for Kant philosophy of religion comprehends philosophy of history, for Hegel philosophy of history comprehends philosophy of religion. For Hegel nature is mere externality, the "not real"; morality moves on a lower plane than History, and all morality and History, in fact all meaningfulness in things and in minds, is ultimately traced to the free self-legislating movements of Spirit.

The essential connection between the philosophy of freedom and the philosophy of history was discussed by Leo Strauss as follows: "The so-called discovery of history consists in the realization, or in the alleged realization, that man's freedom is radically limited by his earlier use of his freedom, and not by his nature or by the whole order of nature or creation."[18] That men are limited, even in their freedom, in myriad ways is obvious to any perceptive observer. Limits that appear to a scientific or philosophic observer as rooted in human nature and circumstance, or to a religious observer as following from the will or providence of God, according to the philosophy of freedom, must be interpreted nonheteronomously, that is, in a way not inconsistent with human autonomy.[19] Moral man, in his freedom, is understood to be essentially dependent neither on nature nor on God, but on History or historical conditions, which are themselves understood as the products of human freedom. Speaking loosely, freedom is shown to be ultimately dependent only upon itself.

To sum up, the nature uncovered by modern science, which in Bacon, Descartes, Hobbes, Spinoza, Locke, and ambiguously in Rousseau is still to be obeyed, in Kant and Hegel is found altogether incapable of supplying man with ethical and political principles.[20] The classical dependence of morality on nature and of practice on theory is replaced ultimately by an exaltation of human "creativity," coupled with despair of finding a rational source of ends to guide that creativity. The most impressive recent philosophic expression of that coupling is Heidegger's coupling of authenticity with Angst.

II

The supposition, that is, the reason for being, of the democratic polity is freedom, says Aristotle.[21] One sign of such freedom is political equality that is, a system of ruling and being ruled in turn, an equality that is in accord with number, treating each man as one unit and apportioning political authority according to number, not merit. Majority rule then is considered to be just rule. In effect it means rule by the poor, because they always happen to be in the majority. The other great sign of freedom is living as one likes. Living as one likes turns out to be not merely a sign of freedom but also the function or end of freedom. The slave must live as another likes; the freeman can live as he himself likes.

What are the relations between freedom, equality, poverty and living as one likes? Which is more fundamental, freedom or equality? Leo Strauss, whose interpretations of these passages I am following, argued that claims to rule are made in terms of freedom, a distinguishing mark, a superiority, not in terms of a merely shared quality, like equality, and certainly not in terms of an acknowledged defect, like poverty. If living as one likes is the end, how can politics conduce to that end? By providing the conditions for, or removing the impediments from, each to pursue as much as possible what he likes without interfering with the like pursuits of others. Those conditions of uninterferability point in the direction of what comes to be called individual rights.

But is living as one likes a reasonable end? In the *Metaphysics* (1075a19ff.), where the order of the household is presented as an analogy for the clarification of the order of the cosmos, Aristotle says, "in a household it is the free for whom it is at least of all permitted to do what they please but everything or most things are ordered, while slaves and beasts who contribute little to the common good for the most part act at random."[22] Those democrats evidently do not know what true freedom is. In Book VIII of the *Politics*, free or liberal works and deeds are distinguished from the unfree, illiberal, or vulgar: "and that task as well as that art and study ought to be deemed vulgar which renders the body or the soul or the intelligence of free men useless for the practices of virtue." Freedom is neither license nor indetermination.[23] Freedom gets its character from the end it serves, that is, virtue.

The political implications of this view are spelled out in Book III, Chapter 9, of the *Politics*, which could be viewed as an anticipation of Hobbes and Locke. What is the end for the sake of which the political association is constituted? What makes a society a political society? It is not an alliance for protection against criminals and foreign invaders simply for the sake of self-preservation. It is not for the sake of exchange, trade, and commerce, the guaranteeing of contracts. It is not constituted to serve negative standards, what must be prevented, minimum guarantees of what each is entitled to, or rights instead of duties. Nor is it for the sake of intermarriage, social pastimes and religious communion, living together, or the practices of friendship. All these things are necessary if there is to be a political community, but they are not sufficient. The end of the political association is virtuous living, the sharing of a good life, a communion of mutual concern for one another's wellbeing, which means primarily a concern for one another's qualities, one another's character. The purpose of the polis is the formation of virtue in the citizens. Care or friendship that does not reach to a concern for what kind of human beings one's fellow citizens are is not yet political care or political friendship. Having said all this, however, it is useful to remind ourselves that Aristotle is here speaking of what he calls "political virtue," and political virtue is not complete virtue or virtue unqualified.

What is the practical sense of this emphasis on ethics? Aristotle tells us sadly that very few regimes actually do devote themselves primarily to fostering a certain state of character in the citizens, and when they do, as Sparta and Crete did, it is usually training for war. But since war is for the sake of peace and practical action ultimately for the sake of those activities that are ends in themselves, that is, leisure (*scholē*), explicit political formation of virtue usually misses the mark.[24] On the other hand, the very notion of regime, or polity, implies that every political order has ethical consequences for those that live within it.

No political society exists without some way of distributing the rewards and punishments entailed in living together, without some ranking of the relative values of goods to be exchanged. Implicit in these distributions and exchanges is a ranking of the activities and the men that received the distributions and produced the goods exchanged. Some notion of distributive justice, no matter how defective, is operative in every political community.[25] The most important distributions for set-ting the style or tone of society, according to Aristotle, are the distribu-tions of political offices, especially the highest offices.[26] The ways of those who receive the highest honors are the ways most likely to be followed in society. Political society forms character whether it purpose-ly aims at it or not. Since the most common regimes are defective regimes, it would seem that for Aristotle political formation of character is often malformation. Aristotle's policy is, on the one hand, to raise our political and ethical sights as high as they can reasonably go and, on the other, to make it perfectly clear how limited are the possibilities for actu-alizing our goals.

III

The founders of the American polity in their philosophic thinking were in large part followers in the tradition of the "new science of politics" of Hobbes and Locke. To what extent, and how, might their political thinking be reconcilable with the ethical approach to politics of Aristotle? If we assume that philosophers cannot live with inconsisten-cies, or at best cannot be untroubled by inconsistencies, then the founding fathers were not all philosophers, although they were a remarkably philosophic group of men.

As Strauss put it in connection with *The Federalist*: "These writings reveal their connection with the classics simply enough by presenting themselves as the work of one Publius."[27] It has been argued that when Publius says, "The aim of every political constitution is, or ought to be, first to obtain for rulers men who possess most wisdom to discern, and most virtue to pursue, the common good of the society," he only appears to be espousing classical principles, because he concludes the sentence by indicating that the "virtue" he speaks of is only instrumental not classical virtue: "and in the next place, to take the most effectual precautions for keeping them virtuous."[28] But Aristotle and Plato, too, use the word *virtue* to describe ordinary, or political, virtue as well as virtue in the full sense of the word, the steady habit of acting well, knowingly and with pleasure.[29] In his discussion of the best form of democracy, a judicious mixture of democracy, oligarchy, and aristocracy, where an agricultural populace elects and audits the performance of their officials, and where the highest offices are held by large land holders or those most fit for them,[30] Aristotle says:

> Necessarily those governed in this way are governed well: for the ruling offices will always be held by the best men with the consent of the people and without their being envious of the good men.

The arrangement is satisfactory also to the latter, for they will not be ruled by inferiors,

> and they will rule justly because others are authoritative over calling officials to account. For to be dependent and not to have license to do everything that one decides to do is advantageous: for the license to do whatever one wants is not capable of guarding against the base in every human being.[31]

Arrangements "in defect of better motives" (*The Federalist*, No. 51) did not have to wait for modern times to be discovered.

There are even intimations of Publius' genuinely new argument, the argument for enlarging the orbit of the representative republic with a view to making "factious combinations less to be dreaded" (*The Federalist*, No. 10).

> Wherever the middle class is large factions and dissensions arise least. Large *poleis* too are more without faction for the same reason, because the middle class is large. In small *poleis* it is easy to divide everyone into two groups, so as to leave no middle, and almost everyone is either poor or rich. Democracies too are more safe than oligarchies and last for a longer

time through the men of the middle class. . .they partake more of offices in the democracies than they do in the oligarchies. . .without the men of the middle the multitude of the poor fare badly and are destroyed.[32]

The men of the middle class are more likely to listen to reason, Aristotle argues, more likely to avoid the domineering arrogance of the very well-to-do and the servile envy of the poor.

The most impressive attempt known to me to combine classical thought with the principles of the American polity is to be found in the work of Harry V. Jaffa. I will for the most part confine myself here to his discussion of the Declaration of Independence in the essay, "What is Equality? The Declaration of Independence Revisited."[33] Jaffa builds on George Anastaplo's observation that the references to God in the Declaration of Independence portray him in terms of the three powers of constitutional government.[34] "All men are created equal" is interpreted by Jaffa in an Aristotelian mode placing man between beasts and God. The respects in which men are equal or the same is understood "as much by understanding what he is *not*, as by understanding what he *is*. . .man is not either beast or God." The three powers of government are properly united in God, but never in human hands; that is, they are properly united in a being that is the perfection of reason, justice, and mercy. It is the very definition of tyranny to unite them in fallible creatures like men, whose partial perfections are subject to corruption by passionate self-love and other such influences. "The equality of mankind is an equality of defect, as well as an equality of rights." The qualitative distinction between animals that possess reason and beasts that do not is more fundamental than any distinction of quantity or intensity of possession between the possessors of reason. Just government presupposes sufficient enlightenment among human beings to recognize that no rational animal is the proper subject of despotic rule, and no man is sufficiently godlike to be entrusted with despotic rule. Reciprocal with these equalities of superiority and defect is the notion that consent is the only just basis of government. Jaffa anticipates the objection that consent is not an adequate replacement for wisdom as the ground upon which rule can be legitimated. The claims of wisdom have dubious political value because of "the fact that it is not the wise who advance under the banners of wisdom but rather pretenders to wisdom." Strauss's account of the classical position in a way admits this last point. The classics favored the rule of gentlemen, that element of society that through its wealth and leisure had the greatest opportunities to acquire a liberal education, which means an education that among other things fosters civic responsibility. This points to the ultimate justification of the rule of gentlemen: The rule of gentlemen is the political reflection of the, for almost all political purposes, impossible rule of the philosophers, the rule of "the men best by nature and best by education."[35] Jaffa is aware of the impoverishment that would attend the removal of such political reflections.

An interesting contrast to the classicism of Harry Jaffa is to be found in the classicism of George Anastaplo. While Jaffa emphasizes the natural equalities of superiority and defect upon which the moral principles governing the American polity are based, the central consideration for Anastaplo's "Constitutionalist" are the blessings of liberty. He reviews Jaffa's *Equality and Liberty* in an article entitled "Liberty and Equality."[36] Civil liberties, in contrast to civil rights, make for popular influence over, as well as protection against, government. But most importantly during "a time of effective popular rule," they provide for the protection of minorities from the encroachments of majorities, for the protection within democratic government for natural aristocracy.[37] While Jaffa's rhetoric emphasizes the transformation of self-evident truth into "living faith," the sacramental character of our moral and political principles,[38] Anastaplo recurs to the distinctions between human being and citizen, politician and scholar, thoughtful man and partisan, and nature and circumstance.[39] The inevitable partiality and relativity of any effective political statement point to prudence and moderation as indispensable political virtues—even in the pursuit of justice.[40]

The most useful way of beginning to account for these differences may well be in terms of different judgments about the needs of our situation, about "the crisis of liberal democracy," about the political conditions for philosophizing, on the one hand, and the reliability of nature, on the other.

The moral fervor of the political savior is not usually associated with the cool deliberation of the man of prudence. And yet both Jaffa and Anastaplo find their paradigms in Abraham Lincoln. After a careful line-by-line analysis of the Emancipation Proclamations, "recreating" the complex of problems Lincoln had to deal with, Anastaplo reflects on prudence in general:

We see, of course, what prudence can mean in a particular situation—and hence what prudence itself means. One must adjust to one's materials, including the prejudices and limitations of one's community. Such adjustment often includes settling for less than the best. But the most useful adjustment is not possible unless one *does* know what the very best would be . . . .how important chance is in human affairs—and hence how limited we often are in what we can do, even when we know what should be done.

We should . . . guard against that fashionable opinion which dismisses what is reasonable and deliberate as cold-blooded and calculating. It is also important, however, if one is to be most effective as a reasonable, deliberate and deliberating human being, to seem to be other than cold-blooded and calculating. . .it is important to be a good politician. . . .we are reminded of the importance in political things of appearances, of a healthy respect for the opinions (and hence the errors as well as the sound intuition) of mankind.

Certainly self-righteousness should always be held in check, but not always a show of indignation. Still, indignation even in a good cause should be carefully watched. Consider, for example, the famous Abolitionist William Lloyd Garrison's 1831 promise, "I *will* be as harsh as truth, and as uncompromising as justice. On this subject I do not wish to think, or to speak, or write, with moderation." Such passion may be useful, even necessary, if great evils are to be corrected, but only if a Lincoln should become available to supervise what finally happens and to deal prudently with others (zealous friends and sincere enemies alike) with a remarkable, even godlike, magnanimity.[41]

Last but not least, the classical emphasis on the ethical implications of all political arrangements reminds us conversely that every political arrangement presupposes certain qualities in the populace that is to live under that arrangement. Free government based on enlightened consent is not going to survive if its citizens are regarded as unworthy of such government and if they are incapable of making it work. The cultivation of excellence, or, more euphemistically, liberal education for leadership, may be indispensable for the survival of such government. If it should be that capacities for liberal education are not created equal in all men, religious education for all the people must supplement liberal education. Did the Founding Fathers rely on the virtues of a religiously trained populace without taking provision for the continuance of that training?[42] However that may be, although they did concentrate more on the structures of government, they did not forget the character of the people. "As there is a degree of depravity in mankind which requires a certain degree of circumspection and distrust, so there are other qualities in human nature which justify a certain portion of esteem and confidence. Republican government presupposes the existence of these qualities in a higher degree than any other form."[43] Classical and American thought seem to come together most in their reliance on "moral principles grounded in thoughtfulness," political prudence, that is, the avoidance of unreasonable expectations and the concern for enlightenment, for liberal education.

Summary and Conclusion

The modern notions of nature and freedom, I have argued, replacing the classical dependence of morality on purposive nature have led finally to the "exaltation of human 'creativity' coupled with despair of finding a rational source of ends to guide that 'creativity.'" This I understand to be what Leo Strauss spoke of as "the deepest reason for the crisis of liberal democracy." "The theoretical crisis," Strauss goes on, "does not necessarily lead to a practical crisis, for the superiority of liberal democracy to" its currently practical alternatives, "is obvious enough. And, above all, liberal democracy, in contradistinction to communism and fascism, derives powerful support from a way of thinking which cannot be called modern at all: the premodern thought of our western tradition."[44]

In my brief discussion of Aristotle I focused on what might be thought to provide some of that "powerful support" directly and as a corrective.

The third section deals with two thinkers who have, with the aid of Leo Strauss and others, liberated themselves from the powerful dogma that a return to classical thought is impossible and devoted themselves to studies in depth of American thought and institutions. In interesting and complementary ways the principles, problems, and virtues of the modern American polity have been shown to require for their clarification not only modern philosophy but also the "premodern thought of our western tradition." We note that when Strauss speaks of our western *tradition*, he refers not only to classical philosophy but also to the Bible. This side of the tradition is more conspicuous in the work of Jaffa, but it is not ignored by Anastaplo.

It may not be amiss here to sketch out some of the intervening steps between the philosophy of freedom and history and the coupling of creativity with despair as it bears on the crisis of liberal democracy. History, that limit and product of human freedom, was conceived by Hegel as a rational process. The rationality of the process in the post-Hegelian development is either transformed as in Marxism or denied as by Nietzsche.

The Marxist-Leninist position looks forward to a transformation of man's moral and political being such as to make moral discipline and the compulsory side of political life dispensable. Liberal democracy, at least in its original American version which denies that the recalcitrance in nonangelic human nature that requires government will ever disappear, is to be replaced by the dictatorship of the self-chosen representatives of the proletariat, the Communist Party. The required transformation of humanity and the universalization of Communist rule do not seem to be coming closer; the supposedly temporary dictatorship turns stale and takes on many of the odors of traditional despotism. To the extent that measures are adopted that go against the grain of "traditional" human nature, such as the collectivization of agriculture and industry, the despotic powers of government are correspondingly extended and intensified. Unreasonable hopes and expectations produce their opposites. The practical superiority of liberal democracy over communism does seem to be obvious. Yet questions of justice in connection with market conditions and the extent of private property rights under modern liberal democracy deserve notice. A Xenophontic, that is, elementary and nonideological, approach might prove useful.

From the point of view of the ordinary concerns of most men it might be said without too much oversimplification that the most prevalent and persistent forms of injustice are bullying and cheating. Cheating, it has been argued, cannot be eliminated from free market systems. The liberal democracies through the rule of law seem to have concentrated most on preventing men from bullying one another. Like our Communist rivals we are also greatly concerned with preventing cheating, but have taken the precaution of dealing with this problem in such a way as to avoid concentrating too much power in the hands of our governmental protectors, so as to avoid putting our protectors in a position to bully us. A prudent decision has been made to accept slippage with one evil in order to prevent more suffering from a greater evil. The reasoning behind this choice seems to be that, although the two are often connected, injury to dignity is usually worse than injury to material well-being. Furthermore, he who is in a position to bully is usually also in a position to cheat, whereas the converse is not true.[45]

The rationality of the historical process is denied by Nietzsche, yet he remains a historicist; that is, he believes that human thought becomes meaningful only as an expression of the psyche of an individual thinker in the context of the given historical conditions of his existence. He rejected all teleology in favor of a doctrine that was to lead to a nobility beyond all past nobilities. He rejected all metaphysics as nothing but personal expressions of its "makers" will to power, and expanded the doctrine of the will to power to cover the whole of existence, that is, into a metaphysical doctrine. We admire Nietzsche for intrepidly carrying through the deepest tendencies of modern philosophy: its repudiation of teleology; its critique of reason; its religious devotion to finding a home for man of his own making in the world. We appreciate as well his refusal to give up the riches modern thought has repudiated. We are amazed by the ingenuity of the fantastic notion through which he proposes to hold on to what he has repudiated: the willing of the eternal return of the same. We wonder about what he might have had to endure in making that desperate notion credible to himself.

Arguments for the rule of living reason were called "aristocratic" by Aristotle and Plato. The politically practical counterpart to the rule of living reason is the rule of the liberally educated, of the men of higher education. The liberally educated man in the Aristotelian "polity," or "mixed regime," moderates between oligarchic and democratic extremes. His awareness of natural limitations, the powers of the passions, the obstacles to knowledge, the moral disguises of selfish ambition make him cautious and moderate, a center of opposition to demagoguery, extremism and fanaticism.

The large middle class that dominates public opinion in the United States and increasingly in liberal democracies throughout the world has so far proved a great anchor of political stability.[46] It can be thought of as consisting of three combinable elements, distinguished in terms of their political objectives: a democratic element aiming at freedom and equality, based on the notion of equal rights, especially the right of each to be free from personal subjection to the will or authority of any other man; an oligarchic element aiming at wealth (the acquisition of property or "the maximization of income"), based on the notion of equality of opportunity; and an aristocratic element aiming at virtue, or excellence, or "improving the quality of life."[47] Freedom from subjection is easily interpreted as living as one likes, and the pursuit of wealth aims, it seems, at living as one likes on a larger scale. In the polity or mixed regime of the United States the political or social function of the aristocratic element might be said to educate people to like what they ought to like. The aristocrats may be defined by the primacy of learning and teaching and self-improvement for their lives. In concrete terms we are speaking of educators, artists, writers, clergy, operatives of the mass media, the "communications industry," and government officials in their educative capacities.

Because of unprecedented educational opportunities in the modern industrial world, technological society's need for a technically educated work force, and the increased accessibility of television and radio, the power and influence of what we have been calling the "aristocratic element" increases exponentially. At this point the theoretical crisis does become a practical crisis. Moral, spiritual, and intellectual autonomy, "authenticity", the reigning standard among modern intellectuals, whose potential nobility might be appreciated by those few willing and able to work for it, seeps into the mass consciousness as the *right* to live as one likes. "License plucks liberty by the nose." Can free institutions survive if the aristocratic element abandons its traditional vocation? Who is to educate the educators? This is now a pressing political, but not only political, question. The future of liberal democracy may indeed depend on our ability to avail ourselves of the resources of the premodern thought of our western tradition.

Notes

1. *Du Contrat Social*, Bk. I, chap. 8.

2. (New York: E. P. Dutton, 1950) chap. 21, p. 183.

3. Chap. 14, pp. 108-9.

4. *Leviathan*, chap. 15.

5. *Second Treatise of Government*, sec. 54. Cf. Martin Diamond, "The American Idea of Equality: The View from the Founding," *The Review of Politics*, vol. 38, no. 3 (July 1976), 328-31. Cf. the Aristotelian critique of Locke by John Gillies, *The Politics and Economics of Aristotle*, Bohn's Classical Library (London: George Bell and Sons, 1894), intro., pp. xxxi–xxxix.

6. Letter to Henri Grégoire, 25 February 1809. Would the political bearing of Jefferson's remark be as compelling if Newton's superiority were a superiority in "wisdom to discern," coupled with "virtue to pursue, the common good of. . . society"?

7. Bk. I, chap. 6.

8. Thus, Rousseau could conclude that direct democracy is the only truly legitimate form of government.

9. Leo Strauss, "The Three Waves of Modernity," *Political Philosophy: Six Essays by Leo Strauss*, ed. Hilail Gildin (Indianapolis: Bobbs-Merrill, 1975), 91-92.

10. *Grundlegung zur Metaphysik der Sitten; Foundations of the Metaphysics of Morals*, sec. One. Donald Meiklejohn makes the interesting argument that "rigidity" is precluded from the Kantian doctrine on lying by taking into account the empirical question as to whether in any particular case rational or some other kind of communication is taking place. Lying is prohibited when "communicating rationally with another moral being." When dealing with drunks, the insane, would-be murderers et al., other principles properly come into play. Review of Sissela Bok's "Lying: Moral Choice in Public and Private Life," *Ethics*, (January 1980), 296-300. Meiklejohn's reformulation of Kantian doctrine does not yet address the question of how to deal with those who are both rational and evilly inclined. Pisanio and Cornelius in Shakespeare's *Cymbeline* avert gross injustice and tragedy by, as they put it, being false (to the bad) in order to be true

(to the good) (I.5.43–44 and IV.3.42). (One may sophisticate or avoid facing the problem by departing from the generally accepted understanding of rational and defining rational and evil as mutually exclusive.)

11. *The City and Man* (Chicago: Rand McNally, 1964), 38.

12. The other eye is directed inward to the *ego cogitans*. See Swifts' Laputans in *Gulliver's Travels*.

13. Francis Bacon, *Novum Organum*, I, aphorism 3; Descartes, *Discourse on Method*, pt. VI; cf. Laurence Berns, "Francis Bacon and the Conquest of Nature," *Interpretation: A Journal of Political Philosophy* (January 1978), 1–26; and Richard Kennington: "Descartes and Mastery of Nature," *Organism, Medicine, and Metaphysics*, ed. S. F. Spicker (Dordrecht, Holland: D. Reidel, 1978), 201–23.

14. *Essay on Human Understanding*, Bk. II, chaps. xx, esp. no. 6, and xxi.

15. Leo Strauss, *Natural Right and History* (Chicago: University of Chicago Press, 1953), 250–51.

16. See *Idee zu einer allgemeinen Geschichte in weltbürgerlicher Absicht*, "Idea of a Universal History with Cosmopolitan Intent."

17. Strauss argued that the hard core of these modern doctrinal "secularizations" of Biblical faith is to be found in the development of modern political philosophy, more than in the Bible itself. Cf. Strauss, "The Three Waves of Modernity," 82–83 and 95, and Strauss, *Natural Right and History*, 60–61 n. 22.

18. "Progress or Return? The Contemporary Crisis in Western Civilization," *Modern Judaism* I (Baltimore: The Johns Hopkins University Press, 1981), 32–33. This was understood by Strauss as the linkage between the first and second "waves of modernity" in "The Three Waves of Modernity," 89–90.

19. Kant's separation of "self" (autonomy=self-legislation) from nature appears paradoxical. The "self" referred to here is not the whole person or soul of the individual, which includes "nature," but the will or the pure practical reason itself: "It is heteronomy ("another's legislation") because the will does not give itself the law." *Kritik der praktischen Vernunft*, 32–35, 40–41; *Critique of Practical Reason*, Lewis Beck, (trans.) (New York: Library of Liberal Arts), 32–35, 41–42.

20. The return to nature and natural science as a possible source of ethical and political standards by biologists like Konrad Lorenz, Adolph Portmann, and E. O. Wilson should be noted. Wilson (a prodigious synthesizer with a gift for clear exposition) looks forward to a "genetically accurate and hence completely fair code of ethics." Although he has not yet considered Aristotle's *Physics*, Book II, *De Anima*, and the *Nicomachean Ethics*, he seems to be groping towards a framework for synthesis something like what might be provided by the Aristotelian scheme of four causes and the distincton between potency and act. *Sociobiology: The New Synthesis* (Cambridge, Mass.: Harvard University Press, 1975), 575; *On Human Nature*, (New York: Bantam Books, 1978), 58 and 67. In application to human affairs, the scheme could be understood as follows: Nature (Evolution) provides the material (Material Cause), the potencies ("genotype"): Every potency is a potency for something. The potencies point to the purposes and ends (Final Cause) that would actualize and fulfill the potencies. On the basis of

the conditions provided by nature and chance or circumstance, man, (Efficient Cause) the habit- and ("culture-") convention-forming animal, through habituation, training, custom, law, art and education forms the given materials and powers into behavior (Formal Cause) ("phenotype") that either fulfills, perverts, frustrates, or corrupts (or some combination thereof) those powers and materials. (This is not to minimize fundamental differences between Aristotelian and modern biological sciences. See, for example, Marjorie Grene, "Aristotle and Modern Biology," *The Understanding of Nature: Essays in the Philosophy of Biology* [Dordrecht, Holland: D. Reidel, 1974), 74–76; see also the very helpful article on Portmann, pp. 254–93; and Leon R. Kass, *Toward a More Natural Science: Biology and Human Affairs* [New York: Free Press, 1985], 247ff.) The poverty of most inferences from animal behavior for substantive questions of ethics and politics—Portmann conspicuously excepted—is striking for students reasonably acquainted with classical ethical or political philosophy. The combination of the study of modern biology with serious study of the ethical and philosophical tradition seems to be required; for example, Grene and Kass, op. cit.; Hans Jonas, *The Phenomenon of Life: Toward a Philosophical Biology* (New York: Harper & Row, 1966); Erwin Straus, *Phenomenological Psychology* (New York: Basic Books, 1966), esp. the celebrated article "The Upright Posture," 137–65; et al.

21. *Politics*, Bk. VI, chap. 2, 1317a40ff.

22. Cf. also *Politics*, Bk. V, 1310a26–35.

23. Cf. Yves Simon, *Freedom of Choice*, (New York: Fordham University Press, 1969), esp. 158.

24. Cf. *Politics*, 1325b5ff. and 1333a30–1334a10.

25. Ibid., 1253a1–18. Cf. my "Rational Animal-Political Animal: Nature and Convention in Human Speech and Politics", *Essays in Honor of Jacob Klein* (Annapolis: St. John's College Press, 1976), 29.

26. *Politics*, 1278b3ff., 1289a13–20, 1295a40–b1.

27. "Liberal Education and Responsibilty," *Liberalism, Ancient and Modern* (New York: Basic Books, 1968), 16.

28. No. 57. Cf. nos. 63 and 71. Cf. Martin Diamond, "The American Ideal of Equality," 320–22, and especially "Ethics and Politics: The American Way", *The Moral Foundations of the American Republic*, ed. Robert H. Horwitz (Charlottesville: University Press of Virginia, 1977), 39–72.

29. *Nicomachean Ethics*, Bk. II, chap. 4 1105a17ff.; Bk. I, chap. 8, 1099a4ff. et al.

30. This classification of democracy overlaps with "polity." Cf. the elaborate discussion in Paul Eidelberg, *The Philosophy of the American Constitution* (New York: Free Press, 1968). I regret that this important book, arguing that the American Constitution establishes and was intended to establish a "mixed regime," came to my attention too late to be reviewed here.

31. *Politics*, Bk. VI, chap. 4, 1318b6ff., especially 1318b28–1319a6; cf. Bk. III, chap. 11, 1281a39ff.

32. *Politics*, Bk. IV, chap. 11, 1296a7ff. Cf. Robert Licht, "On the Three Parties of America," *Political Parties in the Eighties*, ed. Robert A. Goldwin (Washington, D.C.: American Enterprise Institute for Public Policy Research, 1980), 67–96.

33. In *The Conditions of Freedom: Essays in Political Philosophy*, (Baltimore: The Johns Hopkins University Press, 1975), 149–60. I shall not discuss here Jaffa's remarkable book on Lincoln, *The Crisis of the House Divided*. For a criticism and appreciation of Jaffa's Lincoln book, which moves on a philosophical plane commensurate with Jaffa's plane, see George Anastaplo, "American Constitutionalism and the Virtue of Prudence: Philadelphia, Paris, Washington, Gettysburg," *Abraham Lincoln, the Gettysburg Address and American Constitutionalism*, ed. Leo Paul S. de Alvarez (Irving, Tex.: University of Dallas Press, 1976), 165–68 n. 64.

34. George Anastaplo, "The Declaration of Independence," *St. Louis University Law Journal* (Spring 1965), 390.

35. *Liberalism Ancient and Modern*, 11–16. Cf. Harry Jaffa, *Equality and Liberty* (New York: Oxford University Press, 1965), 50–52. Cp. Hamilton's arguments against ancient political thought and practice in Harvey Flaumenhaft, "Alexander Hamilton on the Foundation of Good Government," *The Political Science Reviewer* (Fall 1976), 143–214.

36. *Human Being and Citizen* (Chicago: Swallow Press, 1975), essay V. Cf. also *The Constitutionalist: Notes on the First Amendment* (Dallas: Southern Methodist University Press, 1971). chap. 8.

37. See *The Constitutionalist*, chap. 8, sec. ix, and Thomas Jefferson's letter to John Adams, 28 October 1813.

38. *Equality and Liberty*, p. 139, *Crisis of the House Divided*, (New York: Doubleday & Co., 1959), 227, 232, and 239.

39. *Human Being and Citizen*, essays III, X, and XVI.

40. See Anastaplo on "Citizenship, Prudence and the Classics," *The Artist as Thinker* (Chicago: Swallow Press, 1983), 279–83; and Strauss, *Natural Right and History*, chap. 4.

41. "Abraham Lincoln's Emancipation Proclamation," *Constitutional Government in America*, ed. Ronald K. L. Collins (Durham: Carolina Academic Press, 1980), 439. In the context of a discussion of the right and the wrong way to argue against censorship, Anastaplo gives voice to what has become a growing concern in his recent writings: "Indeed, we may have more to fear from a lack of concern about abuses of our considerable liberties than we have from threats of immediate restrictions upon them." "Human Nature and the First Amendment", *University of Pittsburgh Law Review* (Summer 1979), 746. Cf. "Censorship," *Encyclopaedia Britannica, Macropaedia*, 15th ed. (1985), vol. 3,634–41.

42. "Heaven grant that it may be the glory of the United States to have established two great truths, of the highest importance to the whole human race; first that an enlightened community *is* capable of self-government; and, second, that the toleration of all sects does *not* necessarily produce indifference to religion." Daniel Webster, speech, reception at Pittsburgh, 8 July 1833. Cf. Toc-

queville, *Democracy in America* II, Bk. 2, chap. 15, and Xenophon, *Memorabilia*, Bk. IV, chap. 3.1 and 2. See also the remarkable biologist's account of "the distress of the modern soul" by Jacques Monod in *Chance und Necessity* (New York: Vintage Books, 1972), 164–173.

43. *The Federalist*, no. 55, end.

44. Strauss, "The Three Waves of Modernity," 98.

45. Adapted from my "Speculations on Liberal and Illiberal Politics," *The Review of Politics* (April 1978), 231–54. (Correction to p. 231, line 6 from bottom should read: "And even those causes which are neither judgments nor reasons, like appetites, passions and desires, are rarely unmixed with judgments or reasons.")

46. Large middle classes were rarities in premodern times. Large, even more so very large, middle classes presuppose widespread affluence. The existence of these conditions in the modern world evidently depend on the prodigious productivity unleashed by the technological powers discovered in association with modern natural science and its "conquest of nature." We cannot here discuss the unprecedented dangers, now journalistic commonplaces, brought about by the technological development. Modern science, we have argued, following Leo Strauss, has proved inadequate for the articulation of the meaning of human life. Despite this opposition, Strauss did not simply reject the science upon which the conditions for modern liberal democracy depend. Science, "man's attempt to understand the whole to which he belongs," incorporates what is true in modern as well as ancient science. Strauss looks forward to "the true universal science into which modern science will have to be integrated eventually." From "Social Science and Humanism," *The State of the Social Sciences*, ed. Leonard D. White (Chicago: University of Chicago Press, 1956), 415–25; reprinted, *The St. John's Review* (Annapolis: Spring 1985).

47. See Robert Licht, "On the Three Parties of America," op. cit., n. 32, above; and Laurence Berns, "Two Old Conservatives Discuss the Anastaplo Case," *Cornell Law Review*, vol. 54, no. 6 (July 1969), 925.

Judith A. Best

THE INNOCENT, THE IGNORANT,
AND THE RATIONAL:
THE CONTENT OF LOCKIAN CONSENT

"The political problem," Leo Strauss tells us, "consists in reconciling the requirement for wisdom with the requirement for consent."[1] He goes on to distinguish the classic or ancient view in which "wisdom takes precedence over consent," from the egalitarian or modern view in which "consent takes precedence over wisdom." The ancients' proposal does indeed give precedence to wisdom because consent is merely the vehicle through which wisdom may rule. Since law (what the many posit) is an empty vehicle, its quality depends upon its passenger. The distinction between law and justice remains. Law may be just, when its passenger is wisdom, but there are other possible passengers. For the ancients the conflict of wisdom and consent (or of justice and law) can be mitigated but never totally eradicated. It is a perennial political problem.

Hobbes, seeing the danger in the distinction between justice and law, proposes an absolute sovereign created by contract as a solution. This not only gives preference to consent; it also makes it the sole condition of law because the sovereign is a vessel into which almost all natural rights are poured. Since the sovereign has a monopoly of rights, is the full vessel, his will is law. Hobbes thus impales himself on the consent horn of the dilemma, but in so doing he apparently solves the problem by making law and justice identical. Justice is keeping one's contracts.

John Locke does not accept Hobbes's solution to the problem. He rejects the absolute sovereign, the rule of men, and he proposes instead the rule of law, but a rule of law in which consent is the sole condition of legitimate government. What is Locke's concept of consent? Why can he at once agree with Hobbes that consent is the sole condition of legimate government and disagree with Hobbes regarding absolute government?

An answer to these questions is not easily found, for one of the obvious and frequently noted problems in Locke's *Second Treatise of Government* is that Locke's argument does not move with mathematical precision. In a word, he is not consistent. He does not, as does Hobbes, begin with first principles, and then carefully deduce from those first premises. Rather, he often employs the technique of gradually retracted assertion. The most obvious case is his initial assertion that the state of nature is a state of plenty and his retraction through the chapter on property to the point where he contradicts his original premise and asserts that the state of nature is a state of penury. In analyzing Locke it is important, therefore, to find a base point, a position from which he never retracts. There is, I believe, general agreement that Locke never retracts from his assertion that absolute government is worse than the state of nature. This is the most obvious point of his disagreement with Hobbes. Further, Hobbes, following Machiavelli's advice that we learn most from the worst case, deduces his entire political prescription from his own worst case, the state of nature. If we focus on Locke's base position and worst case, absolute government, we may find the answers to these questions.

In the beginning of his chapter on the state of nature, Locke asserts that there is a natural law and, on the implicit principle that every real law must be enforced, that there is an executive power in the state of nature. This is followed by a fairly extensive argument that the executive power is universal, "put into every man's hands."[2] After describing and defining the executive power of nature, Locke calls it a "strange doctrine,"[3] one that is not only foreign, belonging to a different place, but also one that excites astonishment and objection because of its apparent unreasonableness, because it makes men judges in their own cases. Since he attributes the objection to others, "those who make this objection,"[4] one expects a defense and a rebuttal to this charge.

Locke's response is that absolute monarchy is more unreasonable. This response is not a rebuttal; it is a retort! You think I'm being unreasonable! Talk about the pot calling the kettle black! However, to say that B is more unreasonable than A does not make A reasonable. Locke, of course, knows this, and, therefore, he silently concedes that the objection to the universality of the executive power is correct.

But is absolute government actually more unreasonable? Are many bad judges better than one? Are a thousand tyrants better than one? We can almost hear Hobbes's voice leading the objections. If there is only one bad judge, there is only one source of danger. A man has only one flank to protect. He doesn't have to worry about a multifront war. If there are many bad judges, a man has an unlimited problem of defense; he has to watch all comers. The range and the distribution of the problem is mind-boggling. It would appear that Hobbes was right: Conditions are improved when the number of bad judges is reduced. But Locke points out that the Hobbesian proposal to reduce the extent of the problem necessarily intensifies it. Of course, everything else being equal, many bad judges are worse than one. If it were possible to reduce the number of bad judges without increasing or without multiplying the power of the remaining bad judges, every rational man would elect to do so. But it is not possible. Hobbes's solution multiplies the power of the remaining judge, "one man commanding a multitude."[5] Things were bad enough in the state of nature where we played one on one, but under absolute government we play one man against a whole team. The chances that the individual will prevail in the latter case are little and none.

The defenders of absolute monarchy are hoist on their own petard when they object that the universality of the executive power is unreasonable. It is unreasonable that men should be judges in their own cases, but it compounds the irrationality to increase the natural power of anyone who judges in his own case by giving him the command of multitudes. This is not just a rebuttal of Hobbes's solution to the problem; it is a clarification of the problem. The problem is not simply the number of the judges; it is the nature of the judges. The problem is the enforcement of private will, private judgment. Any solution that relies on private will is the wrong solution. Locke asserts that absolute government is most unreasonable and is the worst possible condition.

The absolute monarch commands multitudes, "and may do to all his subjects whatever he pleases."[6] But why? On what basis? And how does absolute government come to be? Hobbes had argued that the state of nature was the worst possible condition, the *summum malum*, but also that it was the beginning, the original, the given; therefore, he did not have to account for it. Since Locke agrees with Hobbes that the state of nature is the original condition and since Locke's *summum malum* is not the original condition, he must account for it. A full understanding of what is worse than the state of nature and how it comes to pass may give us some insight into what is better than the state of nature.

It would seem that absolute government cannot be by any right of nature, for nature gives no man more authority than another, "in one community of nature, there cannot be supposed any such subordination among us that may authorize us to destroy another, as if we were made for one another's uses."[7] If absolute government comes not from nature, it would follow that it must come from compact. Yet in his analysis of the despotical power, "an absolute, arbitrary power one man has over another to take away his life whenever he pleases," Locke asserts that, "that is a power which neither nature gives. . .nor compact can convey."[8]

In both his chapters on slavery and on the despotical power, Locke finds the source of the despotical power to be forfeiture, to be a penalty for offense. In the chapter on slavery, Locke declares flatly that absolute government is not based on consent, "for a man not having the power of his own life *cannot* by compact or his own consent enslave himself to any one, nor put himself under the absolute arbitrary power of another to take away his life when he pleases."[9] He repeats the point later in his chapter on the despotical power:

> For man, not having such an arbitrary power over his own life, cannot give another man such power over it; but it is the effect only of forfeiture which the aggressor makes of his own life when he puts himself into the state of war with another.[10]

An aggressor, one who makes war on another, literally gives up his own property rights. To put it in Locke's more legalistic language, the executive power of nature, belonging to all and including the right of reparation, permits "the injured person and the rest of mankind that will join with him in the execution of justice," to destroy the aggressor.[11] As an example he cites "captives taken in a just and lawful war" and concludes, therefore, that the despotical power does not arise from compact.[12]

This argument, which is fairly convincing regarding compact, tends to undermine the assertion that nature gives no right of despotical power since it is based on the natural right of reparation and the executive power of nature. Rather than be captious, we can solve this problem by qualifying the assertion: Nature gives no despotical power over the innocent. In fact this is Locke's point, and he is quite insistent that the rights of nature are the rights of the innocent. Nature, he says, prefers the innocent. After asserting that the executive power is universal, he states that this is to "preserve the innocent and restrain offenders."[13] In his chapter on the state of war, he mentions the innocent four times. In the first case he declares their value: "By the fundamental law of nature, man being to be preserved as much as possible when all cannot be preserved, the safety of the *innocent* is to be preferred."[14] Later in the chapter he speaks of the "right to the *innocent* party to destroy the other whenever he can, until the aggressor offers peace and desires reconciliation on such terms as may repair any wrongs he has already done and secure the *innocent* for the future."[15] Finally, he directly connects the civil law with the innocent, "For wherever violence is used and injury done, though by hands appointed to administer justice, it is still violence and injury, however colored with the name, pretenses, or forms of law, the end whereof being to protect and redress the *innocent*."[16]

Initially one is rather troubled by Locke's claim that nature places a higher value on the innocent, because it seems to patently contradict his basic premise of natural equality. How can there be a natural equality and a natural priority at the same time? Inconsistent or not, the assertion is appealing because it appears to introduce a qualitative element. It appears that nature prefers a certain quality of life over mere life.

Who are the innocent? And why is it that the innocent are to be preferred: why not the good or the just? The innocent are the law-abiding, those who abide by the law of nature. Locke's use of the word *innocent* here is precise and fully in keeping with his definition of the law of nature: "The state of nature has a law of nature to govern it, which obliges everyone; and reason which is that law, teaches all mankind who will but consult it, that being all equal and independent, no one ought to harm another in his life, health, liberty, or possessions."[17] The innocent are those who do no harm, who are not disposed to do harm, and thus who are free from guilt and not deserving of suffering. Under this first definition, the law does not prescribe positive action; it does not require that one assert one's self or perform any deeds of beneficence. It merely proscribes actions that harm others. It requires that one forbear and abstain. The term *innocent* is much more appropriate to describe those who have priority of nature than either the good or the just, terms that suggest excellence or virtue in a positive-active rather than a negative-passive sense.

At the end of this section, Locke restates the law of nature, this time giving it a slightly more active, less passive prescription.

> Everyone, as he is bound to preserve himself and not to quit his station wilfully, so by the like reason, when his own preservation comes not in competition, ought he, as much as he can, to preserve the rest of mankind, and may not, unless it be to do justice to an offender, take away or impair the life, or what tends to the preservation of the life, the liberty, health, limb, or goods of another.[18]

Whereas the initial passive prescription (harm no one, thou shalt not be an aggressor) is unconditional, the second and more active prescription (help others, punish aggressors) is conditional upon one's own safety. Since the act of punishing aggressors must usually if not always involve risk to one's safety, the obligation to actively, as opposed to passively, preserve others is insubstantial.

The innocent are not the peacemakers; they are the peaceful. The innocent are preferred not because nature esteems the actively worthy or noble, a qualitative form of life, but rather because nature wills preservation, mere life, and peace (harm no one) is the condition of preservation. Nature prefers the peaceful to the peacebreakers because of the equality of the natural right to life.

Even if we accept nature's preference for the innocent and agree that the despotical power arises by the forfeiture of the aggressors, it still does not solve the problem of how an absolute ruler comes to be. The tempting solution is that it is some kind of compact, but not a political compact. Locke, indeed, argues that "it is not every compact that puts an end to the state of nature between men, but only this one of agreeing together mutually to enter into one community and make one body politic; other promises and compacts men may make one with another and yet still be in the state of nature."[19] Since Locke's clearly stated purpose in the *Second Treatise* is to define political power and to distinguish it from all other kinds of power, it might follow that an absolute sovereign is created by compact, but this compact is not a political compact.

A political compact properly so called has the common good as its end, not the private good of the ruler. It is tempting to conclude that an absolute monarch is created by those "other promises and compacts men may make with one another." This, however, is a dead end. Such a contract, according to Locke, cannot be made. It is irrational to worsen one's condition. The creation of an absolute sovereign does worsen one's condition. Such a contract is not a real contract; that is, it is not obligatory. By such a contract the innocent enslave themselves; they subject themselves to the despotical power. Nature permits that only the guilty be subject to the despotical power. The innocent cannot and do not forfeit their rights.

An absolute government over the innocent does not exist by any right of nature, certainly does not exist by political compact properly defined, and cannot exist by any kind of compact. Locke's argument seems to have led to the absurd conclusion that absolute government over the innocent does not exist. The simple solution is that the innocent may be under absolute government by natural power as distinguished from natural right, that is, by unjust conquest. However, the conqueror having no right or title, the innocent are not bound to obedience. The practical problem is that the innocent often believe themselves bound. The innocent often give either direct or tacit consent to an absolute ruler. Locke's statements that they cannot do so seem to be contrary to fact. They do do so. It is unreasonable to consent to absolute government, but that doesn't make it impossible. Locke, of course, knows that they do and sees that as the essential problem.

In his extended analysis of absolute government in the chapter on political society, he suggests that absolute government may have begun when "chief rule" without "caution" devolved out of the deference given to and the faith in "some good and excellent man."[20] This lack of "caution," he ascribes to "the negligent and unforeseeing innocence of the first ages."[21] The innocent are not merely the harmless, the nonaggressors; they are also those lacking in worldly knowledge and common sense. In a word, they are the ignorant. The law of nature forbids consent to absolute government, but men are "ignorant for want of studying it."[22] This answers the question of how absolute monarchs come to be. They come to be on the basis of unsuspecting innocence; absolute monarchs command multitudes of ignorant, nay foolish, men.

> As if when men, quitting the state of nature, entered into society, they agreed that all of them but one should be under the restraint of laws, but that he should still retain all the liberty of the state of nature, increased with power and made licentious by impunity. This is to think that men are so foolish that they take care to avoid what mischiefs may be done them by polecats or foxes, but are content, nay, think it safety, to be devoured by lions.[23]

At this point one is inclined to wonder if absolute government is the penalty for ignorance. Criminals incur the penalty of subjection to the despotical power because of their aggression. The ignorant incur the penalty of subjection to absolute government because of their want of study. Still, it does seem rather harsh! Absolute government being worse than the state of nature, the penalty for ignorance would be more severe than the penalty for willful violation of the law of nature. Nature's preference for the innocent does not seem to have given them any real advantage. It is on a par with God's gift of the earth to all mankind—worthless.

Even if the innocent can be said to break the law of nature by consenting to absolute government, they do this out of ignorance. Isn't ignorance an excuse? Ignorance is an excuse if the law of nature is not promulgated, available to everyone. No man can be expected to obey a law he cannot know. Locke begins by asserting that the law is available to everyone and, then characteristically, gradually retracts the assertion. In his chapter on the state of nature, he says, "It is certain there is such a law, and that, too, as intelligible and plain to a rational creature and a studier of that law as the positive laws of commonwealths, nay possibly plainer."[24]

This assertion is immediately followed by his critique of Hobbes's proposal for absolute government. Hobbes was surely a studier of the law of nature and just as surely was an intelligent and logical man. If the law of nature is so "intelligible and plain" and so easily understood by a studier, why does Hobbes make such a grievous error in interpreting it? Few man have studied it as diligently as he. If he could misinterpret it, what hope is there for the rest of us? The law of nature is a defective law; it is not fully known to all, and it is not fully known even to all studiers. Locke eventually concedes that the law is not fully promulgated. When he lists the things wanting in the state of nature, he lists first the lack of "an established, settled, *known* law."[25] Ignorance of the law of nature is indeed an excuse.

In his chapter on the paternal power, Locke says that children, because they are born "ignorant and without the use of reason, they were not presently under the law, for nobody can be under a law which is not promulgated to him."[26] But how is the law promulgated? Locke answers that "it is made known by reason only."[27] Those who are without reason are not under the law. "He that is not come to the use of his reason cannot be said to be under this law."[28] The law of nature is reason, and it is promulgated by reason. Reason is only known to those who have it. Only those who have reason are rational. It would seem that Locke is begging the question with a vengeance. Why does he beg the question? What is the point of this circular argument? What do we learn from it? We learn, I believe, that the law of nature is not only defective; it is also not a real law; that is, it is not prescriptive, but rather descriptive: Rational men act rationally. We learn that nature's greatest preference is not for the innocent, who have been transformed before our eyes into the ignorant, rather, *nature prefers the rational*. The rational are the free. Or freedom is a product of rationality. "We are born free as we are born rational, not that we have actually the exercise of either; age that brings one brings with it the other too."[29] The will is bound; rationality is a condition of freedom. "The freedom then of man, and liberty of acting according to his own will, is grounded on his having reason."[30]

The innocent are the "law-abiding," but the law they keep is a defective law. Innocence is not enough; like the law of nature itself, innocence is defective. It is negative-passive, and because it is, it cannot fulfill the will of nature—"the peace and preservation of all mankind."[31] Only the rational can actualize, or actualize as much as possible, nature's will. The law of nature is inherent in the rational. Rationality is positive-active; it directly affirms nature's will.

The argument is indeed circular, but there is method in its superficial madness. Nature wills the preservation of all men, but if all men cannot be preserved, then the preservation of the innocent has priority. However, the innocent cannot preserve themselves because they are largely ignorant. They are unlikely "to be free from restraint and violence," from the "arbitrary will of another." The real issue is not who is to be preserved, but how are men to be preserved. The innocent may be the "law-abiding," but the rational are the true lawmakers. The rational are preferred because they create the rule of law that fulfills the will of nature.

Nature's preference for the rational is not a contradiction of natural equality, nor does it indicate a greater esteem for a certain quality of life. Nature's preference for the rational is merely the means or method by which nature "enforces" its law, by which nature allows for the observance and actualization of its law. Just as the possibility of human labor converts a worthless gift, the earth, into a plenty, so the possibility of human rationality converts a worthless freedom into an actual freedom.

Consent to absolute government is the heart of the problem for Locke. If all legitimate government rests on consent and if, further, the historical fact is that men have consented to absolute government, then it would follow either that consent is not a sufficient basis for government (the conclusion of the ancients) or that absolute government is legitimate (the conclusion of Hobbes). Neither of these two conclusions is acceptable to Locke. His answer is to collapse the distinction between rationality and consent. He merges and fuses reason into consent. Men have the liberty (the right) to consent to what is rational and only to what is rational. Consent is not simply a procedure; it has a substance. It is not just form, a manner of acting, of decision making. It also has matter; it includes the content of the decisions to be made. Its matter, or substance, is natural rights. Consent is more than agreement; it is more than an act of will. It is an act of determinate will, an agreement to a specific thing: the protection of natural rights. Consent is, therefore, both the necessary and sufficient condition of legitimate government.

The ancients faced with the conflict of wisdom (knowledge of the good) and consent (the power of the many) tried to bring off a compromise in which the status of law (the condition of being law) is consent, and the quality of law is its relative degree of wisdom. Thus, the ancients drew a distinction between good law and bad law. Consent, for the ancients, is a service the power of the many provides to wisdom. Locke, faced with a conflict of reason (natural rights) and consent (the individual will), tried to fuse the status and quality by making reason a prerequisite, an antecedent of the will. He injects reason into consent, thereby making a distinction between law and no law. All true law, law properly so called, is good law. "For law in its true notion is not so much the limitation as the direction of a free and intelligent agent to his proper interest, and prescribes no further than is for the general good of those under that law.''[32] This welding of reason and consent that gave real law, consent, a content was very functional for Locke's purpose of justifying a revolution and identifying the limits of government.

When Locke, in his attack upon Hobbes, raises the rhetorical question, ''I desire to know what kind of government that is, and how much better it is than the state of nature, where one man commanding a multitude has liberty to be the judge in his own case, and may do to all his subjects whatever he pleases,'' he does not imply, as some have suggested, that the answer is that this is bad government. Locke's answer is that this is not government at all. In his chapter on political society, Locke states ''Absolute monarchy, which by some men is counted the only government in the world, is indeed inconsistent with civil society, *and so can be no form of civil government at all*.''[33] Government, Locke clearly believes, is the appointed remedy for the ''inconveniences'' of the state of nature.

Since absolute government is not government at all, it is clear that men are not bound to obey it. Men are bound only when they have consented. They cannot consent to absolute government; thus, they did not do so. ''Revolution,'' resistance to a ''government'' that does not protect natural rights, does not have to be justified because it is not revolution. There is no government overthrown because there was no true government in the first place. There is no duty to obey; men have not reneged or rebelled because true consent could not have been given.

In preaching resistance to kings, Milton at one point argued that revolution may be much the lesser of two evils. To counter the suggestion that the people's consent to and election of a king is a sign of divine will and therefore that revolution is a sin, Milton said, ''If it needs must be a sin in them to depose, it may as likely be a sin to have elected.''[34] Under this justification, revolution may be a form of penance for a prior offense. But Locke absolves the people completely. Ignorance of the law of nature is not simply an excuse; it is an exculpation. The people cannot sin in this way.

The collapse of the distinction between reason and consent was functional for Locke's purposes and remains functional as long as men recognize Locke's point that consent has a content, and that mere procedural agreement *and* the preservation of natural rights are both conditions of legitimate government. Our Founders knew it and did not forget it. They knew that to be rightful (to be true and actual) the consent of the people must be reasonable. They knew that the proposition cannot be converted; they knew that what the people agree to is not necessarily reasonable. The problem inherent in Locke's collapse of the distinction between reason and consent is that men may forget that consent has a content, that they may come to believe that democratic majoritarianism or popular sovereignty is the sole condition of legitimacy.

The clearest illustration of the fact that men do forget that consent has a content is Stephen Douglas' position on popular sovereignty. His proposal that the inhabitants of a territory should decide the slavery question for themselves is an endorsement of the Hobbesian principle that there are no inherent limits on consent, that consent is an act of sheer will. Fortunately for us all, Abraham Lincoln was alive, and he understood the natural rights content of consent. It was Lincoln who agreed with Locke that it is *salus populi suprema lex*, not *vox populi suprema lex*. And so it was he, above all men of his time, who fought against the debasement of the concept of consent, who argued that no man had the right to agree to slavery for himself or others. It was Lincoln who recognized the difference between choosing and choosing well.

The danger of incorporating reason into consent is compounded by the advent of public opinion polls and computers. It is now relatively easy to determine the personal preferences of the majority. That those personal preferences possibly may be uninformed and unreasonable escapes those who see government as no more than a problem of arithmetic. Our Founders, of course, knew better, which is why they chose the republican form of popular government over the purely democratic form. Because they knew that majority rule can be tyrannical, they saw the necessity of refining and enlarging public opinion, of developing public spiritedness, of inculcating the true principles of liberty, and of establishing complex, balanced, and even rival institutions to protect natural rights. The Founders knew that the process of adding together purely personal preferences does not of itself make those preferences rational. An adding machine is not the philosophers stone—it cannot turn lead into gold or even convert the innocent and the ignorant into the rational.

As Louis Hartz, and Tocqueville before him, correctly observed, America has been a liberal community from its inception. Yet today many observers believe they see a crisis in the liberal democracy, an apparent confusion in or loss of public purpose. There seems to be some question as to who the liberals are and what the liberals are for. The old quarrel, between Hobbes and Locke, about the definition of consent is pertinent to the issue at hand because consent is the foundation stone of the liberal theory of government. The liberalism of Hobbes is a deeply flawed political theory because, as Locke demonstrates, it attempts unsuccessfully to ignore or finesse the perennial political problem—the tension between wisdom and consent—by basing legitimacy on will alone. The liberalism of Locke is, in my judgment, a more successful theory, in part because it addresses the political problem and bases legitimacy on the determinate will.

Nonetheless, the Lockian theory has generated problems of its own. By meshing and infusing reason into consent, by making reason an implicit condition rather than an explicit one, it has had the unfortunate effect of obscuring the political problem—it has made it possible for some of us to overlook and disregard that problem or even deny it exists. If there is a crisis or conflict in liberalism today, it may be because some of us have forgotten that consent is more than an act of sheer will. It may be time, and past time, to reconstruct the distinction the ancients found to be so useful. It may be time to recognize that consent is one thing and rationality quite another. Only then may we be prepared to face the perennial political problem of "reconciling the requirement for wisdom with the requirement for consent."

Notes

1. Leo Strauss, *Natural Right and History* (Chicago: University of Chicago Press, 1953), 141.

2. John Locke, *The Second Treatise of Government* (Indianapolis: Bobbs-Merrill, 1952), sec. 7.

3. Locke, sec. 13.

4. Ibid.

5. Ibid.

6. Ibid.

7. Locke, *The Second Treatise of Government*, sec. 6.

8. Ibid., sec. 172.

9. Ibid., sec. 23, emphasis added.

10. Ibid., sec. 172.

11. Ibid.

12. Ibid.

13. Ibid., sec. 7.

14. Ibid., sec. 16, emphasis added.

15. Ibid., sec. 20, emphasis added.

16. Ibid., emphasis added.

17. Ibid., sec. 6.

18. Ibid.

19. Ibid., sec. 14.

20. Ibid., sec. 94.

21. Ibid.

22. Ibid., sec. 124.

23. Ibid., sec. 93.

24. Ibid., sec. 12.

25. Ibid., sec. 124, emphasis added.

26. Ibid., sec. 57.

27. Ibid.

28. Ibid.

29. Ibid., sec. 61.

30. Ibid., sec. 63.

31. Ibid., sec. 7.

32. Ibid., sec. 57.

33. Ibid., sec. 90, emphasis added.

34. John Milton, "Tenure of Kings and Magistrates," *John Milton, Complete Poems and Major Prose* (New York: Odyssey Press, 1957), 759.

*Thomas L. Pangle**

NIHILISM AND MODERN DEMOCRACY IN THE THOUGHT OF NIETZSCHE

This essay is meant to help prepare a confrontation with the philosopher who is the most penetrating and thoroughgoing opponent of liberal democratic civilization. Nietzsche characterizes the modern democratic spirit, in all its forms, as "decadence." This decadence he understands, however, as the final, catastrophic emergence into broad daylight of a previously hidden historical process that has been unfolding in all Western history: the "nihilism" of Athens and Jerusalem, of scientific rationalism and Judeao-Christian monotheism. Nietzsche understands himself as the thinker through whom this process finally attains self-consciousness. Now, by Nietzsche's own testimony, *Thus Spoke Zarathustra* is the published writing in which his mature philosophy finds its fullest expression.[1] Yet because *Zarathustra* comprises the "Yes-saying part" of Nietzsche's project and because in it "the eye is spoiled by the tremendous need for seeing far," it possesses a "remoteness" that makes it the most difficult to approach of all his finished works (cf. *EH*, 1141).[2] It seems to presuppose, rather than supply, an account of how Nietzsche understands the cultural crisis to which Zarathustra is responding. My purpose here is to attempt to gather from Nietzsche's diverse pronouncements a synoptic, consistent statement of his critique of the West and of its present, deepest political and spiritual tendencies.

*The author thanks the John Simon Guggenheim Memorial Foundation. Pages 180–201 are a slightly modified version of "The Roots of Contemporary Nihilism and Its Political Consequences According to Nietzsche," University of Notre Dame, *Review of Politics*, 45:1, pp. 180–201 (1983).

The Clearest Symptom of Nihilism and the Full Significance of That Symptom

It is true that near the beginning of *Zarathustra* Nietzsche has Zarathustra announce the fundamental problem in its most arresting and succinct form: "God is dead!" But initially this chilling asseveration is barely intelligible. From the immediate context we gather that what Zarathustra refers to primarily is the alleged fact that the Judaeo-Christian God is no longer generally believed in. To the extent this is true, it of course signals a profound dislocation of our culture. But why should this imply that our predicament differs, except in degree, from that of periods such as the late Athenian and Roman empires, which experienced the overturning of religious traditions and even the widespread desuetude of faith?

To say that God is dead is not the same as saying that God does not exist, or even that men have lost their faith. Many prophets and moralists have lamented widespread loss of faith; many philosophers have said, in their hearts and sometimes with their lips, that there is no God. Nietzsche says God died. God did once exist, but has now ceased to exist ("for only something that can live can be dead"—*WP*, 581). In other words, God's existence, like every other meaningful existence, is temporal or historical. Just as Marx is not simply a materialist, insofar as he is a historical materialist, so Nietzsche is not simply an atheist, insofar as he is a historical atheist: Zarathustra is "the most pious of all those, who do not believe in God" (p. 372). Zarathustra's piety is not, then, belief in God. For Zarathustra, God never existed in the same way he did for those who have "believed in" Him: "Is not precisely this divinity, that there are gods, but there is no God?" (p. 294).

Nietzsche's "disbelief" in God stems from a new way of thinking that means to escape from, or altogether recast, the age-old philosophic distinction between opinion and knowledge, nature and convention. The proclamation of the death of God is only the most gripping expression of the paradoxical insight that *all* standards of significance and coherence are in the last analysis temporary. It is this awareness that sets Nietzsche apart, in his own estimation, from all previous philosophers and our era from all earlier eras; for the first time thought can be liberated from what Nietzsche calls "lack of a historical sense," the *"Hereditary Defect of the Philosopher."*[3]

But what is, from the point of view of philosophic truthfulness, the curing of a defect, is for mankind at large—and therefore for the philosopher himself—the advent of a lethal danger. To leave it at saying that modern man questions with incredulity all moral absolutes, or can no longer believe in God, is to remain at too vague and superficial a level. If we are to grasp what Nietzsche means by "nihilism," we must first secure a clear conception of what Nietzsche understands man to have been or to have possessed in the past that is now annihilated. Then we must trace the process, the specific forces, of annihilation in order to arrive at a precise account of the outcome these forces have shaped—the present condition of humanity and the options available to it.

Let us begin with a provisional sketch of what in Nietzsche's view distinguishes man, and human history, from the rest of existence. Against Plato, Nietzsche denies that man is in all times and places, or even by nature, a social being (cf. *GM*, I, 11; II, 8,9,16,17; III, 18). Yet unlike Rousseau, Nietzsche is certain sociality is coeval with man and may be said to be a proclivity of many men from the beginning; "at all times, as long as there have been human beings, there have also been herds of men" (*BGE*, 199). Like other herds the human herd seeks the preservation and strengthening or expansion of the herd. But the human herd came gradually to differ form all other types of herds, in that it came to seek something more, and through this seeking, human herds evolved from mere clans, packs, and tribes into "peoples" (*Volker*: for what follows, see Z, "On The Thousand and One Goals"). Peoples cannot survive—they begin to undergo physical and emotional disintegration—if their only conscious goal is bodily strength and well-being. Peoples must experience a *meaningful* existence: Their physical being must be understood as dedicated to, and in some circumstances sacrificable for, some *way* of life that makes demands far beyond what is required for security and creature comforts. It is this need that defines the human, setting man apart from all other existence: "That is why he calls himself 'man,' which means: the esteemer" (p. 323). Each people devises for itself a way of life that is "heavy" or difficult; in its feelings, thoughts, and actions, a people confronts an ordered hierarchy of increasingly arduous challenges that culminates in tests that few if any of its members can pass. Each individual member is thus called upon, in more or less subtle ways, to "overcome" himself, to go beyond what he has been or done previously. These challenges, inbred from earliest youth, are experienced as "needs." A people's system of such higher needs is the product of a long history of imaginative, if groping, invention and experiment fraught with pain and danger—including the dangers of collective madness and self-destructive moral conflict. It is likely that only a minority of nascent peoples survives this long period of gestation (cf. BGE, 156). But in the successful cases there eventually comes a time of "codification"—the era of the Homeric epics among the Greeks, of the Torah among the Jews, of the Law of Manu among the Brahmins—when an exemplary articulation of the people's "way" takes place (*A*, 26, 57). A "horizon" is constructed, a comprehensive if ultimately limited interpretation of the past, and indeed of the whole universe, that distorts and enshrouds all phenomena in order to prove the eternal significance of the people and its goals (*UM*, II, 1). For a people seeks to establish its tasks as "heavy " not only in the sense of difficult but also in the sense of anchored and lasting. A people needs to believe that it, itself, as well as what it treasures, is permanent. Each individual needs to believe that he partakes of an existence that can defend itself against oblivion and thus forever find opportunity for enhancement. This need is a manifestation of what Zarathustra will call the "Spirit of Heaviness" or the "Spirit of Gravity" (*der Geist der Schwere*). There is an obvious connection between the Spirit of Gravity and man's drive to create and worship gods, but Nietzsche denies that the "religious instinct" must be understood as solely or even necessarily derivative from the Spirit of Gravity; many passions—fear, gratitude, resentment, anger, the desire for spectators who make human suffering meaningful, the need for symbolic embodiments of one's highest overcomings—can inspire or help inspire the creation of gods. Nevertheless, in all previous historical expressions of the "god-forming" impulse, the Spirit of Gravity has been at work: "The gods" have been synonymous with "the immortal ones."

The revering or esteeming that distinguishes human history is thus imbedded in a fundamental paradox, which prevents it from ever becoming fully self-conscious. A culture, when healthy, is plastic and dynamic, but must hide from itself much of its dynamism and, hence, become all the more dynamic, but in more subtle ways. As each people confronts the surprises of nonhuman nature and engages in spiritual and physical conflict with other peoples, it encounters "facts"—including human possibilities and rival interpretations of the world—that compel it to reweave its own saga of itself and its tasks (often redefining and enlarging the latter). But this reweaving must be carried out in such a way as to allow the people to insist that nothing of consequence has been altered, or that, at most, new implications of the ancient, eternal verities have been uncovered. The process of stretching and contracting the "horizon" continues until there is encountered a rival people possessing an interpretation so comprehensive and rich with new challenges that the first people feels itself dwarfed and compeled to assimilate or until physical causes bring disintegration or until a time when the people can find among itself none of the rare, visionary individuals who are the only source of the dramatic reinterpretations that a people must repeatedly create in order to take account of its new experiences.

For the truth is that "the people" is itself something of an abstraction and illusion, created by the Spirit of Gravity. A people is a herd of changing individuals, each of whom has a slightly different, unique, and competing perspective that unconsciously contributes to shaping the cultural horizon. That horizon is a kind of shifting average of the outlooks of all the members, some of whom have a great deal more influence than others. The vast majority of the members of the herd differ little from one another and effect at most only marginal changes. Insofar as a people comes to possess and then to reshape a powerfully convincing understanding of itself, it is indebted to a historical sequence of a very few individuals who feel the holy needs, and the doubts they provoke, with unusual urgency and are able to elaborate answers in an impressively coherent and captivating way (cf. BGE, 126). These few, most creative, men are originally the prophets, lawgivers, and poets, but eventually it is the *philosophers* who come to be the hidden geniuses behind "peoples." Even the philosophers, however, have been unable to acknowledge the true source of "values," because they like other men have been under the spell of the Spirit of Gravity that prevents men from seeing that the source of all meaning is the mutable inventiveness or creativity of man (Z, "On Self-Overcoming").

Our epoch, as the first to divine the subjectivity and historicity that is the hitherto hidden nature of peoples, renders impossible the belief in any people's values or gods and hence sounds the death knell of the only forms of reverence and aspiration man has known. Modern man can behold and admire past piety and dedication; he cannot share in it. Man as man, "the esteeming animal," is threatened by extinction. The "death of God" would seem to herald the death of man.

The obliteration of the possibility of "peoples" does not imply the literal extinction of the human race, or even the physical dissolution of society, but instead something in a way more nauseating and horrifying. The modern historical consciousness possesses a specific character pointing to a narrow range of possible outcomes, and that specific character is determined by its genesis out of the confluent evolution of the two great streams of Western civilization—Socratic rationalism and Judaeo-Christian religion. Nietzsche's "historical philosophizing" implies the jettisoning of the idea of a fixed human nature: What man is (beyond his lower physical needs) differs from one epoch to another. In order to understand the "nature" of the *human* in a given epoch, one needs a historical analysis of the chief spiritual forces that cause man to *become* what he "is"; one needs a "genealogy" that will unearth the buried presuppositions and the hidden alternatives that frame a particular era's humanity (cf. Heidegger, *Nietzsche*, II, 69–70. It follows that to grasp the character of our modern impasse, we need to bring into focus the genealogy of the dual tradition Nietzsche claims has shaped our spirits.

The Roots of Modern Nihilism

Western Rationalism

Although Socrates was by no means the first philosopher,[4] or even the first Greek philosopher, it was in and through him that the shattering impact of philosophy on man's moral, religious, and political existence became manifest. Socrates was "the one turning point and vortex of so-called world history" (BT, 15). For he was the first to press intransigently the demand that all moral principles governing life be judged for validity before the tribunal of dialectical reason. His life was devoted to challenging men to justify their lives in terms of clearly articulated arguments, governed by universal rules of discourse, and grounded in shareable experiences that can in principle be made transparent to rational men in all times and places. With these demands Socrates confronted a culture that, like that of all other peoples, based its commitments not on reason but on "instinct." Prior to Socrates, Greek judgments concerning the noble and base were matters of taste, breeding, habituation, and faith. The poets, whose images dominated life, drew their wisdom from the inspiration they experienced in various kinds of visionary dreaming and intoxication; reason entered only as a supplement, ordering and expoudning this overflowing of the "unconscious." But Socrates found such a subordination of reason intolerable. The attack on life governed by instinct is the fulcrum of his thought: "'Only by instinct': with this expression we touch the heart and midpoint of the Socratic tendency. With it Socratism condemns existing art as well as existing ethics: wherever it turns its searching gaze, it sees lack of insight and the power of illusion and infers from this lack the essential perversity and reprehensibility of what is present" (*BT*, 13; cf. *BGE*, 191). Socrates thus began the revaluation not only of Greek values but of the values of all peoples who were to be touched by his legacy: "The influence of Socrates, down to the present moment, yes, into all future time, has spread itself over posterity like a shadow that keeps continually growing in the evening sun" (*BT*, 15). The success of Socratism is due in part to the senescence of some of the peoples it encounters, but it also discloses a true weakness in all pre-Socratic cultures. Peoples wish to believe that their values have roots in what is permanent, but those roots can be made to seem shallow once they fail to lead to anything universal—and dialectical reason advances an overwhelming claim to be the only sure path to the universal. The Socratic demand for rational universality is a radicalization of the preexisting Spirit of Gravity. Socrates surely did not invent either logic or philosophy; the Greeks, like all peoples, felt keenly the need to ground their instinctual values in gods whose existence they sought to defend and explain through prosaic and poetic myth as well as argument. But until Socrates, dialectic usually subordinated itself to poetry when it entered the sphere of religion and morality; Socrates was the first in whom there appeared a "hypertrophy" of the "logical urge" (*BT*, 13).[5]

Nietzsche's repeated attempts to explain the new "theoretical life" Socrates represented evince an alternating mixture of repulsion, awed fascination, and frank puzzlement. First and foremost, Socrates was a "symptom of degeneration, a tool of the Greek dissolution" (*TI*, "The Problem of Socrates," 2). The feebleness of his religious faith and poetic impulse, as well as his distrust of and antagonism to the instinctual, took their genesis from the Athens of his time, in which for various reasons all possibilities for strong, unified action within the traditional ordering of the passions had been exhausted. The prevailing climate was one of increasing dissoluteness, hypocrisy, mob rule, and competition among magnificent "savage egoisms" typified by Alcibiades (*BGE*, 190, 200, 212, 262; *BT*, 14; *TI*, "The Problem of S.," 9; *TI*, "What I Owe to the Ancients," 3). But Socrates, like all genuine philosophers, cannot be understood as merely the child of his time; as a philosopher, he was the "stepchild" who turned against his time (*UT*, III, 3-end; *BGE*, 212). In his insistence on the tyranny of reason over instinct, Socrates acted as the "physician" of his culture, striving to restore measure and honesty. Moreover, he discovered in dialectical argumentation a new task, a fresh form of self-overcoming and spiritual competition, that gave the Greek agonistic spirit a new lease on life (*BGE*, 212; *TI*, "The Problem of S.," 9–11).

But Nietzsche insists on questioning both the public spirit and the constructiveness of Socrates' doctoring of souls. He finds strong evidence indicating that resentment against the power of a poetic creativity Socrates could not share and the opportunity to take revenge against contemporary, fatigued heirs of the poetic tradition, played no small role in Socrates' motives (*TI*, "The Problem of S.," 7). Nietzsche stresses that the massive foreground impression is of Socrates as a negating, debunking power: "The most acute word, however, about this new and unheard of high value set on knowledge and insight was spoken by Socrates, when he found that he was the only one who acknowledged to himself *that he knew nothing*" (*BT*, 13). Nietzsche forces us to wonder: Did Socrates stand for anything other than a penetrating critique of all life? He surely lacked almost completely the "creative-affirmative force of instinct" that characterizes "all productive men" (*BT*, 13).

Nevertheless, "Socrates was also a great erotic" (*TI*, "The Problem of S.,"; *BT*, 13,) who claimed to know or divine a truth, in man and in the cosmos, that was lovable and inspiring. Is Socratic *eros* not a kind of instinct? "The logical drive that appeared in Socrates . . . shows a natural force, such as we encounter to our awed amazement only in the greatest instinctive forces" (*BT*, 13). Nietzsche is keenly aware that Socrates did not merely condemn existing art and ethics; "Socrates believes that he must correct existence . . . as the precursor to a wholly different culture, art, and moraltiy" (*BT*, 13). Socrates held out the promise of a new understanding of virtue based on a rational insight into the true, permanent needs of human nature, hence guaranteeing the happiness and fulfillment of that nature.

To Nietzsche, however, "that Socratic equation of reason, virtue, and happiness" is the "most bizarre of all equations" (*TI*, "The Problem of S.," 4). From the beginning Nietzsche doubted whether Socrates possessed an account of the soul or of nature that gave convincing content to this equation, and he came to doubt whether Socrates himself believed in this illusion. What Nietzsche finds more credible is Socrates' skepticism or "knowledge of ignorance," and Nietzsche is thus alive to the irony in the Socratic dictum that "virtue is knowledge" (*BGE*, 202, 208). If the knowledge that is supposed to equal "virtue" is a "human wisdom" constituted by an awareness of ignorance concerning the "good and noble" (cf. Apology of Socrates, 21d, 23a–b), then what is left of virtue? And how can whatever is left make men "happy"?

I believe it is fair to say the Nietzsche never succeeded, even to his own satisfaction, in fully explaining the felicity Socrates claimed to find at the heart of his unfinished quest for wisdom. In his earliest analysis, Nietzsche is inclined to view Socrates as "the type of a form of existence unheard of before him: the type of the *theoretical man*" (*BT*, 15). Insofar as such a man is animated by the "instinct-disintegrating" logical impulse, it is the "*search*" for truth rather than truth itself that consumes him. For there is not "truth," but only meaningless chaos once one casts aside (if a human ever could wholly cast aside) the form-giving "illusion" of creative art inspired by the instincts. But the theoretical type as represented by the Platonic Socrates and his heirs in fact subordinates the logical impulse to a new and peculiar sort of faith and instinct: "A profound *illusion*, which first came into the world in the person of Socrates—that unshakeable faith that thought, guided by the thread of causality, reaches into the deepest abysses of Being, and that thought is capable not only of knowing Being but even of *correcting* it. This sublime metaphysical illusion accompanies science as an instinct and leads it again and again to its limits, where it must turn into *art: at which it is really, by this mechanism, aimed*" (*BT*, 15). Even here, in the *Birth of Tragedy*, Nietzsche voices his suspicion that on occasion the historical Socrates had some inkling of the instinctual basis of his own "purely rational" existence (*BT*, 14 end); in his later writings Nietzsche advances with increasing pertinacity the suggestion that Socrates' irony was, at its deepest level, an expression less of greatness of soul than of a dishonest and even self-deceptive concealment of the fact that his life was set in motion by "plebian" resentments and fears he could not justify or even examine very carefully. Nietzsche's last word on Socrates is to the effect that Socrates came to regard life as a sickness he could not cure and from which he escaped with relief (*BGE*, 190–191, 208, 212; *GS*, 340; *TI*, "The Problem of S.," passim).

Accordingly, Nietzsche comes more and more to attribute the positive, cheerful, and noble image of Socrates to the artistry of Plato. Relying on Diogenes Laertius or his sources, Nietzsche tries to understand Plato as a man who in his youth was a tragic poet of great promise, "corrupted" by the influence of Socrates. Through Plato a new alliance was effected between art and reason, in which art now willingly accepted a drastically subordinate position: "The Platonic dialogue was as it were the barge on which the shipwrecked ancient poetry saved herself together with all her children" (*BT*, 14). As a poet and a man of noble, if perverted, instincts, Plato sought the beautiful (*kalon*); in other words, he conceived of the good as an end in itself, as an inspiring and uplifting object of dedication and sacrifice. Socrates, in contrast, was probably a utilitarian. Socrates' insistence that men give reasons why any good thing is good, and his claim that vice is merely ignorance of what truly benefits a man—and virtue merely knowledge of the same—reveals a perspective that seeks to reduce the noble or beautiful to the good understood as the useful, useful in the most common or universal sense (*BGE*, 190–91). Whether Socrates followed this line of thought consistently or not, Nietzsche detects in it the fundamentally plebian origins and instincts of the "rabble" that—sublimated to be sure—underlies all

"*Socratism*" or strict rationalism, inasmuch as it seeks to ground values in what is universally valid. Utilitarian ethics are rooted in fear. They bespeak an existence that focuses on the universal animal longings for security and comfort and resents those who, scorning such cravings, heighten insecurity by sacrificing the useful for the noble and uncommon. The utilitarian ethos has an overwhelming tendency to reduce all goals to material welfare. In some of his mature writings, especially *Beyond Good and Evil*, Nietzsche tries to distinguish sharply the essentially Platonic aspects of the dialogues from this Socratism: "There is something in the morality of Plato that does not really belong to Plato, but is only found in his philosophy—one may say, in spite of Plato— namely, the Socratism, for which he really was too noble" (*BGE*, 190.

Plato's greater "innocence" (cf. *TI*, "Skirmishes," 23) made him instinctively avert his eyes from what the life of Socrates revealed about the character of rationalism and its effects on life; instead, Plato created an adulterated and beautiful version of rationalism: "Plato did all he could to interpret into the proposition of his teacher something refined and noble—above all himself" (*BGE*, 190). The result was the theory of the Ideas and the Theory of the Good. Plato invented a realm of permanent order and beauty beyond this world of the senses, a realm that constitutes true being in contrast to the ambiguous, deceptive, and imperfect world of mere appearances. He taught that this higher world may be attainable insofar as men cultivate its reflection within them—the "pure mind." In depicting Socrates as the new hero of this theoretical way of life, Plato aimed in part at erecting an exemplar to inspire new peoples and civilizations. He was thus the source of a metaphysical dogma, which in manifold and sometimes even barely recognizable forms has dominated the entire subsequent history of the West (*BGE*, preface, 2, 4, 14).[6]

The new kind of civilization that issues from the Platonic revaluation of Greek values departs strikingly from all previous values and "peoples": To a degree never before known, the new values are monotheistic, cosmopolitan, and otherworldly. The nonutilitarian good that is understood to be behind all existence is conceived of as a single ruling idea, a monarchic force that dominates the other fundamental elements or ideas and *a fortiori* all human beings in all times and places. But the Good cannot rule in any way analogous to human rule, for it cannot manifest the individuality, mutability, and moral ambiguity that frames human existence. The highest existence is understood to be free from suffering, self-overcoming, and transformative action; instead God seems to call upon men to transcend their humanity and imitate his serene measure of moderation (cf. *Laws*, 716c–d).

The historical momentum engendered by Plato's thought is ac-
celerated and twisted in a new direction through the fateful encounter of
Platonic classicisim with Judaism. Despite the misleading impression
conveyed by some of his shrill polemics, especially in the sometimes
rather feverish *Antichrist*, Christianity represents for Nietzsche much
more than a vulgarized version of Platonism: Weighed carefully as a
whole, his account makes it clear that in his opinion Christianity has
contributed to Western man's development a level of spiritual depth
almost entirely absent in the classical world.

Judaeo-Christian Ideals

To understand the nature of that contribution, we must turn to a
feature of Nietzsche's understanding of "peoples" that has been thus
far left out of account. According to Nietzsche, "every enhancement of
the type 'man' has hitherto been the work of an aristocratic
society . . . a society that believes in a long ladder of rankordering and
differences in value between man and man, and needs slavery in some
sense" (*BGE*, 257). As a consequence there underlies and pervades all
morality and politics, either as a direct reflection of existing society or as
the cultural inheritance from previous stages of history, a dichotomy
between the "master" perspective and the "slave" perspective (cf. *D*,
112; *BGE*, 19, 257, 259). Nietzsche emphasizes that these two perspec-
tives are far from being mutually exclusive: "In all the higher and more
mixed cultures there also come to sight attempts at mediation between
the two moralities, and still more often interpenetration and mutual
misunderstanding; and at times they occur right alongside one
another—even in the same man, in a single soul" (*BGE*, 260). But Nietzsche
seeks, provisionally, to distinguish the features of each so as to lay bare
the duality at the basis of all moral and political life.

Nietzsche finds in the prephilosophic Greeks and Romans a
developed and sublimated, but nonetheless highly revealing, example
of a predominantly master morality. The "good" is here identified with
the "noble," which means above all military prowess, pride, self-control,
capacity for sound political speech and judgment, and relative freedom
from and contempt for economic considerations. Within the ruling
caste, nobility demands a sense of brotherhood that entails frankness,
trust, simplicity, generosity, gratitude, and respect, envigorated by
sharp competiton for preeminence and honor, as well as a capacity for
unveiled anger and revenge. In relation to the oppressed, nobility expresses itself in an attitude of contempt mingled with some pity. The
"bad" the masters identify with the "base," that is, the shameful ways

of the oppressed class: weakness and herdlike insecurity, humility, lack of self-confidence, petty selfishness and narrow calculation, haggling and overly precise self-justification (*HTH*, 45; *BGE*, 257–62; *GM*, passim).

The moral ethos of the slave, far from being an affirmation of what he is and does, is born of his resentful reaction against his situation and the masters who control it. What is vivid and primary for the slave is the "evil," meaning not the "contemptible" but rather the awesome force and pride of the masters. The good is whatever opposes this "evil." The slave values especially those qualities that allow him to elude or ameliorate the oppression of the evil masters: humility, endurance of aggression without retaliating, compassion and a willingness to help fellow sufferers, shrewd calculation of material advantage, and security. Yet since the slave is at bottom a frustrated master, his whole outlook is stained with hypocrisy. The "evil" includes an element of the enviable, while the good is always accompanied by a tinge of disdain and self-contempt.

Deprived of opportunity for reflection and expression, the slaves remain, in most cultures, relatively inarticulate and goalless. Slave morality finds a goal, and attains world-historical significance, insofar as it becomes linked to a group and an outlook within the master class: the priests.[7] Although the nature of the priesthood varies greatly from one people to another, generally the "masters" who constitute healthy peoples tend to look upon the gods with gratitude, as grander images and sources of themselves.[8] Still, no religion ever entirely shakes off vestiges of a more primeval religiosity that grew out of the savagery of prehistoric man. Before the gods became "noble," Nietzsche suggests, they were simply terrifying—reflections of the original human "packs." Where a separate priesthood exists, the fear that remains lurking within civilized conceptions of god lends it a peculiar sort of authority. Moreover, the idleness of a distinct sacerdotal class gives much opportunity for reflection, and this together with the priest's relative political impotence promotes longings for modes of prestige distinct from the military and political action of the leading "warrior" masters. Asceticism, which may well have originated as an unwelcome necessity, perhaps out of a supposed need to placate the gods' cruel demand for sacrifice, comes to be held up as an emblem of rarer tasks and higher overcomings. And thus a new moral opposition, between the "pure" or "holy," and the "impure" or "polluted," joins and begins to rival the masters' original opposition between "noble" and "base": The priests, out of resentful or straightforward competitiveness, increasingly stress the relative impurity of the active life, military bloodshed, and sexual self-indulgence of the "nobles" (*GM*, I, 6-7; II, 19; III, 10; conside here *Iliad* I).

Where the priests gain the upper hand, this signals the decline of a people's faith in itself and a subsequent loss of its capacity for action (cf. *GM*, III, 17). Therer are rare cases, such as that of the "noble" Brahmins who created the Law of Manu,[9] where the priests establish a new regime that does not undercut but rather gives protection and new stimulation to men of action. But for the most part (and in the Vedanta generally) the life devoted to idleness, contemplation, and asceticism arises out of, and strengthens, a pessimistic rejection of action and change—and thereby life itself (*A*, 20; *GM*, I, 6; III, 17, 27; *BGE*, preface).

This predominant syndrome of priestly nihilism bespeaks a weariness with life; a very different situation may develop when the priests' dissatisfaction with their lot finds expression not in a will to passive withdrawal but in an active will to negate and transform, fueled by a resentment against the successes of nonpriestly political superiors (whether native masters or foreign conquerors). In this case the priest not only makes a display of his asceticism in the hopes of shaming and outshining his worldly masters but also, within his own soul, his ever more ghastly self-denials become the avenue by which he gives vent to a will to cruelty and domination that has turned inward, in lieu of the missing opportunities for outward manifestation. The most remarkable and influential moral consequence is a vast heightening of the sense of responsibility, culminating in the invention of the notion of "sin." For originally, Nietzsche claims, man had only a minimal sense of responsibility and no conscience whatsoever (*BGE*, 32). The "bad conscience," the sense of *guilt* that says that the source of our failings is altogether under our control, has its origins, Nietzsche "hypothesizes," in civil society's suppression of man's brutal will to struggle against and conquer others. The will to cruelty compensated for its frustration by turning inward and forming itself into the conscience, which is man's way of tyrannizing over himself by labeling part of himself ugly and demanding that that part be repressed or eliminated (*GM*, II, 16ff.). Through their notion of "sin" the priests take over and exploit this preexisting sense of guilt, enlarging its range and elevating the importance of the ugly inner qualities, the "sins." Eventually, if their rivalry with the warriors intensifies, the priests may take the step of starting to suggest or hint that the "sinful" in man includes many of the most powerful attributes of the ruling masters. The unfolding of this priestly alternative thus leads the priests closer and closer to the outlook of the slaves, and a stage may finally be reached at which a revolutionary alliance of priests and slaves becomes conceivable.

Precisely this is the key to the history of the Jews, "the strangest . . . the *most catastrophic* people of world history." Nietzsche advances the suggestion that the Jews were originally a people whose morality and god were "noble" and even "pagan," sharing "the logic of every people that is in power and has a good conscience." But eventually "anarchy within and the Assyrian without" foreshadowed the death of *this* Israel. Israel fell under the sway of "priestly agitators" who at the head of the lower strata of the demoralized society forged a new people of an unheard-of type: a slave people (*A*, 11, 25–26, 36–38, 55; *GM,*, I, 8; *BGE*, 248).

The synthesis created out of priest and slave resentment has three principal elements. There is in the first place the promulgation of new, extreme versions of "sin," guilt, and bad conscience. Under the leadership of their priests, the Jews as a people dedicate themselves to uncovering and rooting out the "evil" master-impulses within their hearts. But this means that they are engaged in an attempt to erase or suppress the direct, "natural" expression of all human existence. In fact, the project they are embarked upon is an endlessly tormenting attempt to root out life itself. For even the psychic energy behind their self torment is only a redirected form of the masters' will to cruelty and conquest and each new level of psychological introspection is bound to reveal new, hitherto unsuspected guises and recesses of the soul in which "sin" resides.

The ultimate hopelessness of their self-imposed task is alleviated by the new Jewish god. The image of the gods that the priest-slave morality places above itself cannot be, in analogy to master morality, a grander version of the priests or slaves—for the divine must be mastering, a promise of eventual revenge against the worldly masters (*GM*, I, 13–15). Yet, on the other hand, thought the divine must inspire fear, it obviously cannot be "god" in the masters' sense—for the highest must legitimate the slave's revolt against what the masters stand for. The Jewish founders respond to this dilemma by conceiving of a divinity that is radically *other* than man, utterly beyond human experience and human expectation: the *Holy* God. This new divinity is an omnipotent and therefore single despot before whom *all* are slaves, but against whose rule the masters—and all men insofar as they find the master-impulse within them—are in rebellion. Men are indebted to God, but with a burden of defaulted debt that eclipses anything the master peoples imagine in their notions of "gratitude" (*GM*, II, 20). God holds men responsible for their present sinful condition and demands that they struggle to suppress their nature in the name of His "holiness"—a quality of absolute purity that fulfills in barely imaginable ways what is but faintly adumbrated in the priests' attempt to free themselves from pollution (*GM*, II, 22). By introducing new, extreme versions of sin and holiness and the concomitant love of man *for the sake of God*—namely, the love not of what man *is*, but of what he might *become*, through his contempt for what he is and his aspiration directed toward an utterly superior being—Judaism ushers in a realm of demands and dreams that is the most fertile source of creative self-overcoming mankind has yet known (*BGE*, 52,60,250; *GM*, 18; III, 28). At the same time, however—to consider the other side of this "absolutely unexampled madness of the will"—the Holy God is understood to have revealed that man's own unaided efforts will never suffice to overcome sin in the world or even in the sinner's heart. Jehovah, who for the time being rules principally over the single, "chosen" people, therefore holds out the hope of an apocalyptic future intervention by which his undeserved love will transfigure existence and restore the unity between creator and creature that the evil creature has sundered.

This enormous consolation illustrates the third major feature of the new religion, its concern with ameliorating (though not curing) human suffering. Judaism is a religion of slaves as much as of priests, and the priests of Judaism are anxious to minister to the insecurity and frustration of the masses. They therefore temper the sternness of their religion's asceticism by joining to it most of the slaves' compassionate and humanitarian impulses, elevating these into attributes and commandments of holiness (*BGE*, 61; *GM*, III, 15ff.; *A*, 23).

In Nietzsche's view, Christianity "is *not* a countermovement to the Jewish instinct; it is its very consequence, one inference more in its awe-inspiring logic" (*A*, 24). Almost inevitably the time comes when the hierarchy within Judaism and the proud Jewish contempt for the Gentiles is finally no longer tolerable to those Jews who feel most acutely the Jewish religious instinct: "The little rebellious movement that is baptized with the name of Jesus of Nazareth is the Jewish instinct *once again*—in other words, the priestly instinct, which no longer endures the priest as reality" (*A*, 27). Jesus was evidently infused with the idea that God's promise was to be fulfilled in and through him. But Nietzsche doubts whether we can ever know what this meant for Jesus himself (*A*, 27–28, 31, 42; cf. Morel, *Analyse de la maladie*, 14ff). Just as a great writer among Socrates' disciples succeeded in shrouding the historical figures, so in Jesus' case the writings of disciples have almost totally effaced the original. The leader of this movement was Paul, "the greatest of all apostles of vengeance" (*A*, 45), who sought revenge not only against his Roman and priestly rulers but also against the Law, whose commandments he found impossible to fulfill. Following his example, Jesus's subtlest followers constructed a revised Judaism colored by Platonic influences (*D*, 68).

Pauline Christianity extends the central demands of Judaism to all mankind. In the process those demands are of course altered, but their essential character as a synthesis of slavish and priestly is in no way diminished. On the contrary, guilt is intensified, the call for inner examination and confession, as opposed to external action, is sharpened, and man is made to feel even more profoundly his radical inadequacy. In addition, the New Testament provokes more vivid and immediate hopes for "the next world" and thus incites a stronger denial of *the* world. What Christians are exhorted to is the imitation (within their powers) of the asceticism and private charity of Jesus: on the one hand, active compassion for the weak, the suffering, and the untalented; on the other hand, condemnation of the strong, the successful, and the gifted insofar as they do not exhibit humility and do not devote themselves to the service of their inferiors. The effect, for most men, is to reduce their sense of earthly social responsibility to "love of the neighbor," a rather tepid, indiscriminating, pitying, herd mentality.

After a protracted struggle with the "Stoic enlightenment" (A, 42, 47–49, 59), Christianity finally succeeded in bending the tradition of Platonic philosophy, including Aristotelianism and the Stoics, into its service. The common ground shared by Christianity and Platonism certainly helps explain the intellectual victory of Christianity, and frequently Nietzsche speaks as if this, together with Christian seizure of political and social power within the various "peoples," suffices as an explanation of how Christianity transformed the philosophic tradition into a theological tradition. But in his most probing explorations of the relation between the philosophers and Christianity, Nietzsche confronts more squarely the question posed by the apparent gulf between reason and revelation, or faith in reason and faith in the "absurd": What can explain the respect or obedience Christianity has won from philosophers down through the centuries? One begins to discern the answer when one takes note of the fact that the Christian religion is *post*philosophic; it poses to the theoretical man a challenge different from that of any previous religion. Acknowledging the existence and attractiveness of philosophy, Christianity dares the skeptical rationalist to attempt a kind of self-overcoming unknown previously: "The faith which original Christianity demanded, and not infrequently attained, ...This faith is *not* that . . . with which, say, a Luther or a Cromwell, or some other northern barbarian of the spirit, clung to his god and to Christianity. It is much closer to the faith of a Pascal, which resembles in a gruesome way a continual suicide of reason" (*BGE*, 46). In other words, Christianity appealed to the philosopher's will to dramatic self-transformation or self-cruelty: "There is a cruelty and religions Phoenicianism in this faith that is expected from an over-ripe, manifold, and much-over-spoiled conscience; its presupposition is, that the subjugation of the spirit *hurts* indescribably, that the whole past and habituation of such a spirit defends itself against the *absurdissimum* which "faith" represents to it" (*BGE*, 46). Nietzsche understands philosophy to be not the quest for truth for its own sake, but an exquisitely refined expression of the urge to reshape the world and oneself, "the most spiritual will to power" (*BGE*, 9): Hence, "The seeker after knowledge . . . acts as an artist and transfigurer of cruelty; indeed, any insistence on profundity and thoroughness is a violation, a desire to hurt the basic will of the spirit" (*BGE*, 299; cf. 230). This is what makes him certain that the ascetic Christian saint must have tempted and intrigued the philosopher from the beginning: "No other type seems to have interested men, even philosophers, more" (*BGE*, 47). Why did they bow? They divined in him—and as it were behind the question mark of his fragile and miserable appearance—the superior force which wanted to test itself in such a conquest; the strength of the will in which they recognized and wished to honor their own strength and joy in mastery: they honored something in themselves, when they honored the saint" (*BGE*, 51).[10]

The conversion of philosophers to Christianity, or the adoption of philosophic methods by Christians, produces more than enormously refined apologetic theology. In the hands of scientifically trained theologians (the greatest example being Pascal), the Judaeo-Christian insistence on probity takes on a new dimension of penetrating cruelty and begins to scale new heights of meticulous psychological dissection and self-awareness. By inducing philosophy to direct reason's critical gaze upon reason itself, and its possible roots in "sin," Christianity compels philosophy to begin to rediscover—with more self-consciousness than ever before—the dubiousness of reason's claim to be the voice of objectivity. Thus, the advent of Christian theology, signals from afar the beginning of the end of Western man's belief in Plato's illusion of the "pure mind." Granted, the Christian faith does not deny the existence of the "pure mind"; it rather removes that mind to another world and postpones our participation in it to a future life (TI, "How the 'True World' Finally Became a Fable"). But in doing so it begins to reveal the frailties and mutability of the human mind that Plato was probably too naive to recognize and Socrates too devious to acknowledge.[11]

Only very gradually, and with a bashful and frightened hesitancy, does mankind under the aegis of Christianity unravel the implications of the demand for total probity and confession. The culminating stages in this historical development are dominated by modern philosophy. In the context of responding to the question "Why atheism today?," Nietzsche describes the whole of modern philosophy since Descartes as covertly in rebellion against its subordination to Christian "doctrine." He immediately adds, however, that while this struggle has been "anti-Christian," it has been "by no means antireligious." "It seems to me that the religious instinct is indeed in the process of growing powerfully—but the theistic satisfaction it refuses with deep suspicion" (*BGE*, 53–54). What Nietzsche means becomes somewhat plainer in the next aphorism. The atheism of modern philosophy has a spirit altogether different from, say, the cool skepticism of Epicureanism: Not only is it animated by a *faith* in the value of unpleasant truth but, what is more, it has its source in an advanced version of the "religious cruelty," which in its post-Christian manifestation finally demands the "sacrifice" of "whatever is comforting" in our illusions about ourselves. It is this originally Christian conscience, turning upon itself, that gradually forces modern man to eye with suspicion the objects as well as the motives behind every "faith" until he arrives at the point where the awareness dawns that all conceptions of good and evil, god, and order are the creations of his own changing human subjectivity: "It is in one particular interpretation, the Christian-moral one, that nihilism is rooted. The end of Christianity—at the hands of its own morality (which cannot be replaced) which turns against the Christian God (the sense of truthfulness, developed highly by Christianity, is nauseated by the falseness and mendaciousness of all Christian interpretations of the world and of history . . .)" (*WP*, 1). "Even we knowers of today, we godless ones and antimetaphysicians, still take *our* fire from the flame that a centuries-old faith has kindled: that Christian faith, that was also Plato's faith . . . " (*GS*, 344; cf. *GM*, III, 23–27).

Nihilism as the Spirit of Our Age

We are now in a position to understand better the full psychological devastation implied in the inanition of the Platonic-Christian God. The cause of God's death is a historically acquired disposition of the soul that renders untenable *all* beliefs in *any* objective and transhistorical spiritual values, and the world that remains before man in the wake of this destruction of permanence is not a value-neutral flux of data and subjective ideals. To the men of our time who experience in an awakened way the death of God, the world that remains is repellent in its ugliness and baseness. For the particular rationalistic-religious psychological constitution within us that produced the honesty that lays to rest the soul's claim to partake of some permanent order was not engaged in a neutral quest for knowledge; it hunted down the soul's self-assertion in order to overcome that self-assertion. Socratic rationalism and Christian other-worldliness, in denigrating the shifting, subjective will (the only source of meaning and order), intensified man's rejection of human existence itself; so when man is forced finally to recognize this as the whole of existence, he necessarily confronts his own existence with revulsion (cf. *WP*, pt. 1, esp. 6, 7, 8, 12, 32, 55, 58). It is this experience of ugly emptiness that constitutes the specific nihilism or "pessimism" that Nietzsche diagnoses as the sickness of the modern West. Contemporary man's gloomy awareness of the historicity and subjectivity of all meaning is not so much his discovery of the situation of thought in the world as it is his expression of the basis on which *his* thinking *must* interpret experience—so long as his epoch and his historical configuration of consciousness endures.

This experience has provoked and will continue to provoke a variety of responses, exhibiting a great diversity of depth and honesty. Among the strongest thinkers and artists, Nietzsche finds what he calls "active nihilism" or the "*German* form of skepticism"—a determined will to complete the process of criticizing and even ridiculing our inherited values. The counterpart of such men on the political plane of action is the type of an Alcibiades, who finds in the release from tradition and the confusion of all standards an exhilarating opportunity to assert his individuality against the prevailing democracy, in a magnificent but fundamentally aimless urge to dominate.[12] Among other thoughtful contemporaries (the most serious example here is Schopenhauer), there is emerging, according to Nietzsche, a more passive pessimism, still strongly infected with Christian moralism and yearning for a state of calm and complete withdrawal from the world—a "new Buddhism" or a new opening to the East (*GM*, preface, 5; *WP*, 1, 10, 17, 22, 23, 31, 55, 56; *BGE*, 202).

But what Nietzsche identifies as by far the most prevalent attitude among modern intellectuals and opinion leaders is a contradictory melange of anemic skepticism and eqalitarian moralism. The skepticism is anemic inasmuch as it is incapable of either a strong affirmation or a strong negation. It expresses itself in a tolerant curiosity that studies the various religious, metaphysical, artistic, and moral-political values of the past—and frequently mimics or playfully adopts them—without ever becoming seriously committed to any of them. In its heart this egalitarian "open-mindedness" feels the self-contempt that comes from knowing one possesses nothing high of one's own. As a result, what in the long run wins the respect of the man of modern education, and alone gives reason for pride in the "contemporary mind," is the self-denying diligence of modern scientific research and scholarship (*UM*, II, III; *BGE*, 200, 208, 224).

Insofar as the modern scientist or scholar is true to his own ideal, he is a human being who strives to be the perfectly objective observer, claiming to possess a "method" that frees him, qua scientist, from personal as well as cultural or historical commitment and bias. He thus embodies a bloodless and highly self-protective version of the priestly ideal, taking pride in retreat from life, but in fact reacting resentfully against life and its "impossible" demand that one make value judgments. In fact, Nietzsche argues, the scholar/scientist unconsciously imposes on the phenomena a specific type of moral interpretation that represents merely a more mathematical, "sensualist," and unidealistic version of the rationalism first promoted by Socrates. The result is visible in physics, but is more palpable in the sciences of man. The scholar equates understanding with predictive explanation in terms of efficient material causality and general or universal processes. He thus reduces the radical diversity and mutability of man to homogeneous, abstract, supposedly transhistorical categories; he tries to account for the effects of an essentially elusive and unpredictable creativity by referring to putative "fundamental" needs, so called because the vast majority of human beings can be seen to feel them; he doubts the historical significance of rare individuals as opposed to mass movements and finally, he approaches with deep suspicion any claims to qualitative, incomparable superiority and uniqueness. In short, Nietzsche insists that the modern scientist unreflectively imposes "plebian," democratic values on all of existence. The scientific man mirrors the leveling political movement that Nietzsche holds to be the dominant and potentially triumphant outcome of the modern crisis (BGE, 6, 22, 45, 58, 202–14; GM, preface 7; I, 1, 4; III, 23–27).

For the death-throes of the Western tradition produce something even worse than the alienation of man from his life as a creative "esteemer"; they proffer an escape, a purpose or goal that leads man away from authentic confrontation with the crisis. The false goal is liberal-democratic socialism, or the "religion of pity"—the triumph of "the herd" (BGE, preface, 44, 199, 202–3, 253; A, 53, 57; TI, "Skirmishes," 39; WP, 125, 753, 755). Only when one views modern democracy in the light of the geneaology of Western morals does one come to comprehend, according to Nietzsche, its true nature and future tendency; it then becomes clear that the hotly disputed differences among the various factions in the democratic camp—liberals, socialists, communists, anarchists—are of secondary or even tertiary significance (BGE, 202; WP, 51, 753, 755, 864). The democratic movement as a whole is the psychological-historical outcome of the tradition we have sketched above and, as such, is irremediably tainted with its decay. Why and how this is so as regards Christianity transpires from the reconsideration of a few key points. Prior to Christianity, the human animal herd's will to survive was subordinated, among all vital peoples, to a will to preserve a specific way of life and to promote those who manifested the excellence of that way of life. But for two thousand years the Christian slave ethos has heightened man's concern for the herd's *physical* well-being by elevating that concern into divinely commanded "love of thy neighbor" and making compassion a holy duty. Christianity did more than strengthen the merely animal side of the herd instinct; in honoring humility and castigating pride, it fostered an especially resentful and leveling version of the herd. And by demanding that the weak be sustained, while removing the stigma from confessions of weakness, Christianity increased the number of those who are weak or conceive themselves to be so. Of course, so long as the original spirit of the religion was maintained, this strengthened herd instinct was sublimated in a self-denying otherworldliness that precluded determined efforts in favor of earthly prosperity and individual comfort and spurred man to feats of artistic creativity and self-overcoming. But the gradual eclipse of that "other world," together with the spread of rationalism, opened the way to a secularized charity, dedicated exclusively to the "abolition of suffering" through technology. Today, in the grasping for meaning that attends the storm of nihilism, compassion for suffering and for the herd as a whole (including oneself) seems not only "natural" but also appears as the only plank remaining from the ship of Christianity; it thus inherits whatever is left of the psychological legacy of Christian idealism (*BGE*, 62; *TI*, "Skirmishes," 34; *A*, 43, 46, 51; *WP*, 30, 51, 209, 253, 339, 373, 765, 1017).

Modern democracy is inspirited by only a relic of Christianity, but it can claim with some plausibility to be the first unqualified political expression of rationalism. There is, as we have seen, an implicit harmony between the interpretation the scientific method imposes on life and the leveling homogeneity fostered by democracy. The roots of this harmony Nietzsche claims to have uncovered at the very fountainhead of rationalism, in the utilitarian and plebian bent of the Socratic Spirit of Gravity: Reason seeks out and regards as "true" what is permanent and universally evident, but the creativity that is the essence of the human is unique, changing, temporary, and local in all its expressions and felt needs. The human experience of esteeming and creating remains opaque, or merely formal and abstract, to any strictly rationalist way of thinking. Since all human actions, ideals, and needs that transcend the body and economics partake of precisely such creativity, they come before the tribunal of reason as suspect or simply unjustifiable when they compete (as they always do) with material needs.

Despite the spiritual banality of the democratic goal, the lack of a real "countermovement" allows it to loom impressively on the barren contemporary landscape. The "conservatives" Nietzsche regards as outdated, blind, and helpless (TI, "Skirmishes," 43; WP, 755). In the camp of the progressives, he admits, are to be found "clumsy good fellows whom one should not deny either courage or respectable decency" (BGE, 44); Nietzsche is aware that there are democrats who still experience a need for objects of devotion and sacrifice, who still suffer from shame or self-contempt and hence still feel the need for self-overcoming. But these qualities are active in the service of an unworthy goal. The world such men strive to bring into being is one without suffering, shame, or sacrifice, devoid of vigorous competition and the need to take responsibility for agonizing choices, and lacking in reverence for what is rare among men and within the democrat's own heart. The inhabitants of the future society aimed at by the democratic movement are to be contented, peaceful, hedonistic beings who feel none of the tension and discord that form the springboard to self-transforming creativity. And what gives this vision its nightmarish quality is the fact, stressed by Nietzsche in a more unqualified way than by his opponents on the Left, that man can be so remade. According to Nietzsche, all man's human characteristics are the inherited products of his own historical action; they are guaranteed neither by "nature" nor by God, and they could be erased or altered by a few generations of social and genetic engineering. Nietzsche sums up in an unforgettable way the character and the extent of the danger from democratic progressivism through Zarathustra's first speech, in which he portrays the future as the era of the "Last Man."[13]

The Future of Nihilism: The Last Man as the True Goal of Social-Democratic Man

Zarathustra's speech on the "Last Man," the most famous and influential of all his—or Nietzsche's—speeches, forms one part of a longer public discourse whose main purpose is not the description of the Last Man but rather the exhortation to the "Super-man."[14] The very word "Super-man" bespeaks the alien character of what Zarathustra calls his "teaching" (Lehre, see esp. 341). As the crowd's reaction shows, Nietzsche (though not his Zarathustra, at least not at first) is aware that the term will provoke ridicule and laughter; he would not have been altogether shocked to learn that in the next century the word, in English translation, was to figure in the title of a famous comedy and even of a comic strip. But among the few listeners who cock up their ears, the word *Super-man* is clearly meant to make a more chilling impression. In German, *Super-man* (*übermensch*) is most obviously connected with the old word *superhuman* (*übermenschlich*; see *GS*, 143),[15] of which adjectival form it is the "missing" noun. But Zarathustra immediately links his new word also to *überwinden*, "overcoming," and in particular to the "overcoming" of humanity: "Man is something that must be overcome." Mankind has reached a point in its historical evolution where it can no longer orient itself by a vision of some fixed being or principle higher than man—"God is dead!" But precisely for this reason, "Humanity," insofar as it was ever a virtue, and "Humanism," insofar as it was ever a worthy cause, are also dead. For humanity's self-esteem and spiritual vigor were constituted by aspiration and striving upward toward God or gods (cf. esp. *BGE*, 60). If the human species is to retain dignity or worthy purposefulness in its own eyes, it must learn to reorient itself and its aspiration toward a future "super-species" (*Über-Art*, cf. 279 and 337), which a few human beings will create out of themselves or their offspring through self-overcoming and therefore self-destruction: "What is great in man, is this, that he is a bridge and not an end (*Zweck*)." Those who truly manage thus to reorient themselves will by this very fact have taken a long step toward the Super-man, for what will most obviously distinguish the Super-man from all earlier "higher men" will be the Super-man's radical sense of responsibility (*guiltless* responsibility)—not only for themselves but also for the *whole* present and future, the latter conceived as the justification of the entire past. As Nietzsche was later to say in the *Antichrist*, there has existed in previous history "a kind of Super-man" (e.g., Goethe), but only "a kind": "The higher-valued type has often enough existed; but as a fortunate accident, as an exception, never as *willed*" (*A*, 3–4). To be sure, this hardly suffices to give us an adequately clear picture of what it is we are to strive for if and when we hearken to Zarathustra's call. But about this we have no right to complain, according to Zarathustra; he insists that we, or his audience, are not yet capable of understanding much about the Super-man, even if he were to tell us: "What is the greatest, that you can experience? The hour of the great contempt." At least at the outset of our study of *Thus Spoke Zarathustra*, we will gain clarity about the Super-man, not so much by looking beyond ourselves for some "other" kind of life as by looking incisively at what we ourselves are—in a spirit that plunges us into passionate and fully honest self-contempt.

But what is so discouraging, and indeed most contemptible, about contemporary democratic man is his increasing lack of capacity for self-contempt—and thus for self-transforming longing or love. In the second part of his oration, Zarathustra tries passionately to evoke such love by proclaiming the objects of his own love. A careful consideration of what one is tempted to call Zarathustra's "Amatitudes" would be almost as revealing in the case of Zarathustra as is consideration of the Beatitudes in the case of Christ. But the audience is in no way inclined to such meditation. Once again they greet Zarathustra's imploring speech with laughter or indifference. It is at this point that Zarathustra begins to realize just how extraordinary is the spiritual distance between him and the civilization around him. Yet he cannot easily abandon his political hopes; he cannot easily give up the attempt to find some common ground with the *mass* of his contemporaries. A moment's intense reflection on the crowd's reaction brings him to the realization that what stands in the way of his even beginning to communicate his "teaching" is the audience's "cultivation" or sophisticated education (*Bildung*). We are thus given to understand that the "people" (*Volk*) Zarathustra first seeks to arouse are not made up of peasants ("goatherds") or workers, but rather of the middle and upper classes, led by what we would nowadays call "the opinion leaders" or "intellectuals." Education or "culture" is *the* source of pride for such men and women, and the education on account of which they preen themselves, the education or spirit of cultivation that more and more dominates the modern universities and "educated opinion" at every level, has, according to Zarathurstra, a very well-defined if semihidden and semiconscious directedness. Zarathustra stakes his hopes on the possibility that this directedness is as yet unperceived by those who serve it; if he can bring the as yet unseen goal vividly before modern man, he will succeed finally in shattering—in some hearts at least—the barrier that separates him, with his sense of crisis, from complacent "enlightened opinion."

Zarathustra therefore proceeds to sketch a portrait of what human life will be like when man has finally succeeded in reaching all the targets at which the most progressive political and scientific thought aims. Zarathustra speaks here of the *last* man; he does not refer merely to men of the next century or even of the century after the next; the era that completely realizes the way of life Zarathustra envisages may be many centuries away. In other words, Zarathustra does not speak here as a "futurologist," trying to guess "what's coming next." He means rather to unveil for us the ultimate practical consequences and therewith the true human meaning of the historical process that is now unfolding and that will continue to unfold unless some cataclysmic interruption occurs.

First and foremost, the human type now being unwittingly bred is one that will lack the experience of love: "What is love? . . . asks the Last

Man, and he blinks." The love of which the Last Man is ignorant is the love that arises from self-contempt, conflict, and inner "chaos," the love that seeks to express itself in the creation of new ways of life that shine like stars above the creative, and therefore self-destructive, lover. In contrast, the only love the man of the future will know is "love of the neighbor"—the reassuring or placid warmth of indiscriminate fellowship; the Last Man will be incapable of "values" in the precise Zarathustrian sense (cf. "The Thousand Goals and a Goal"). Sexuality will have become merely "a little pleasure for the day and a little pleasure for the night." Every important difference between male and female human beings will have disappeared: "Everybody wants the same, everybody is the same—whoever feels differently goes voluntarily into the asylum." The family, it seems, will have been dissolved in a herd of equal and independent individuals. Zarathustra does not directly speak to the question of whether unborn children will still need to be carried by women, but he makes it clear that sexual pleasure of both men and women will be absolutely inconsequential, unencumbered by the risks, responsibilities, and what we today call the "cruel choices" nature once foisted upon humans.

There is one and only one concern that will temper the pursuit of sexual and other pleasure: "one honors health." And the science of medicine will have achieved such mastery over the body that becoming sick will be considered, as Zarathustra ironically says, a "Sin"—the only Sin. Only the culpably careless will allow themselves to fall prey to the debilities that once haunted human existence. It is true that Zarathustra apparently does not believe technology could ever abolish the fact of death (though life can be very much prolonged: "the Last Man lives longest"). Still, the Last Man will live out his many days secure in the knowledge that when the long-postponed day of doom does arrive, it will be utterly painless and even mildly pleasing. For the drug-Nirvana that removes the sting from death will be only a continuation of the "little poison now and then" that filled all of life with "pleasant dreaming."

To the extent that sex, drugs, and herdlike feelings of community fail to fill the Last Man's idle days, there will always be work, "since work is a form of entertainment." As long, that is, as it does not challenge us so far as to force us to risk our health, comfort, and sense of security: "One is careful, however, that the entertainment does not become too trying." Implicitly agreeing with Marx, Zarathustra foresees the time when the proper organization of the modes of production will afford such material abundance that work will cease to be a necessity, let alone a danger. Meanwhile education will have bred a race of men who see no point in gaining more wealth than others once luxury is available to all without effort: "One no longer becomes poor and rich: both require too much exertion." The Last Man is an altogether reasonable (i.e., utilitarian) creature. Why struggle, he asks, to achieve a position that is in no way needed to secure one's material welfare? For a time, one might suppose, the need to acquire property and defend it against others would still prevail on the international level, yet Zarathustra sees no reason why the conquest of the realm of necessity should not eventually spread, along with rational "culture," over the whole globe, rendering war, competition among nations, and finally the nation-state itself obsolete. As Zarathustra describes it, in the final and longest historical epoch the state and the whole apparatus of coercive administration has withered away: "Who still wants to rule? Who still wants to obey? Both require too much exertion."

Having transformed himself and his environment so as to cancel out every lasting or significant form of contradiction and alienation, man has become totally at home on this earth, totally reconciled with what "now is"; accordingly, he experiences no need whatsoever for any gods or heaven. Political, religious, and ethnic sources of diversity and discord will have gradually lost all evident justification: "No herdsman and *one* herd!" As a consequence the classless, universal, and homogeneous society need fear no violence of any kind, and eventually law enforcement and punishment will have become unnecessary. "Everybody wants the same, everybody is the same: whoever feels differently, goes voluntarily into an asylum." The part-time psychotherapists will have replaced the policeman and soldiers, just as the part-time doctors and part-time economists or administrators will have replaced the priests and the statesmen.

But in a way the most ghastly attribute of the future homunculus is his "refinement," or knowledge of and attitude toward all previous human history. It is here especially that Zarathustra locates the future civilization's pride or *amour-propre*; he thus makes it clear that the Last Man will not be devoid of some desire for superiority, some need for rank and triumph. It is not the absence or disappearance of the Will to Power that arouses Zarathustra's hatred and contempt; it is the form the Will to Power threatens to assume. The Will to Power, as such, surely does not provide a sufficient basis for choosing between Last Man and Super-Man.

The Last Man's "refinement" is grounded in his scientific, historical scholarship, which will have carried its researches to the point where one can "know everything that ever happened." The point of this zealous intellectual history will be to learn about, not from, what has gone before. Not for one moment will the Last Man look upon tradition with awe, or feel the inner demand to test himself by attempting to create a new moral code that incorporates, while enlarging and deepening, some of the most comprehensive and difficult moral challenges of the past. Evincing an advanced and purified version of the spirit that even now predominates in Western scholarship, the Last Men will study the "ancients" wholly from above, as amusingly curious beings whose concerns a refined intellectual could not possibly take "personally" or seriously. Earlier cultures will stand revealed as either the lisping precursors of the civiliation that has "invented happiness," or else as the foolish and fanatic obstacles that once obstructed the rational process of history. In either case there will be "no end of ridicule," mixed with a continual reassuring affirmation of the Last Man's collective sense of superiority: "'Formerly, all the world was mad,' say that most refined, and they blink." In this context Zarathustra notes that there will still be some differences of opinion; individual vanity will find that the facts allow for endless petty "quarrels" over schools of interpretation. But such outbreaks of competition will not be permitted to disturb the fundamental, communitarian consensus that insists on reconciliation before dinner time.

Zarathustra's chilling depiction of the Last Man helps, perhaps more than anything he has said thus far, in clarifying what he means by the Super-man. For the Super-man is the antithesis of the Last Man; as such, he is first of all the sworn enemy of attempts to abolish human suffering. His aim is to intensify rather than diminish one's dissatisfaction with himself and others, to heighten man's painful awareness of unfinished tasks and unmet challenges—all involving the need to rank and choose. To prepare the way for the Super-men is to seek to deepen those feelings of inferiority and superiority, of shame and pride, of loneliness and distinction that arise out of intense struggles among groups and individuals dedicated to conflicting, comprehensive ways of life: "We new philosophers . . . also want exaclty the opposite of an assimilation, an equalization: we teach alienation (*Entfremdung*) in every sense, we tear open gulfs such as have not existed before" (*WP*, 988; cf. *BGE*, 44). As Zarathustra later makes more explicit in his speeches on marriage, reproduction, and death, he does not oppose or even, in the final analysis, regret the future, almost boundless power promised to man by medical technology. He sees in this the promise of opportunities for new choices of a sterner, more comprehensive sort than men and women have ever had to make before. Above all, the Super-men take upon themselves the nigh impossible task of comprehending, and in some sense reviving, in new and unforeseen ways, the whole history of "the noble"—the *kalon*, the *Edle*, or the *Vornehm*—with all its spiritual challenges.

Just as Marx and Engels, in the *Communist Manifesto*, unveil the true direction of present-day civilization in order to compel their readers to confront the choice between bourgeoisie and proletariat, so Zarathustra attempts to compel us to confront the choice between Last Man and Super-man. In both cases the choice is presented as inescapable. But the correct choice, or the crisis, as Marx interprets it necessarily becomes obvious to vast numbers of modern men, including an entire class that awaits and can supposedly be counted on to act according to the message. This means, though, that in the case of Marx one has to wonder whether the most fundamental choice really still exists, or whether it has not been already made for us, by history. The bourgeoisie is destined for extinction, and the triumph of the proletariat is either inevitable or, as Marx sometimes suggests, has as its sole alternative some kind of anarchy. For Nietzsche the choice is presented as wholly our responsibility. One may go so far as to wonder whether the very alternatives are not in some part at least the product of a free human creation rather than a necessary historical process ("The opposite of the Super-man is the *Last Man*: I created the latter together with the former").[16] Zarathustra surely declares that the weight of history does not support, but rather inclines against, the advent of the Super-man: "Alas! the time of the most contemptible man is coming" And Zarathustra himself proves not to have realized, at first, how difficult it is for most modern men even to perceive the crisis of which he speaks.

Through these considerations Nietzsche supplies the justification for (and implicitly asks us to join in) his reckless rhetoric and his willingness to risk or foment any and all upheavals that might derail present civilization. As he presents it, the choice is *not* whether to preserve civilization as we know it or to venture the destruction of that civilization in an attempt to create the Super-man. Civilization or humanity as we know it and have known it is in the process of total transformation; unless the momentum of history is broken, man will evolve steadily in the direction of the Last Man, and degeneration will proceed to the point where the very possibility for an alternative will have disappeared. It is on this grim estimation of the human prospect that Zarathurstra's whole project —not only its tone but also its substance—is predicated. If the decay of modern democracy into the culture of the Last Man is not necessary, if a less total decadence is in the offing, if there is a possibility of preserving the essentials of contemporary life with all its contradictions or reviving some earlier stage of the West, or of discovering some compromise or synthesis, then the attempt to bring into being the Super-man, fraught as it is with awesome dangers, would have to be thoroughly rethought.

Nietzsche's philosophy of man, insofar as it is a truly historical philosophy, is a meditation not on the permanent nature of man, but rather on the fate of man as that fate unfolds in time. Nietzsche's philosophy is concerned with, and its validity depends on, not only a quasi-theoretical explanation of the human historical situation as a whole but also a convincing "prudential" or political assessment of the deepest tides of contemporary society. Nietzsche's keen awareness of his need to provide such an assessment is a major reason why so many of Zarathustra's subsequent speeches are devoted to a detailed criticism and analysis of the most influential and honored cultural forces he finds in the world around him. Nietzsche's "aristocratic radicalism" is not meant as a new beginning "from scratch." Nietzsche intends to initiate a *post*nihilistic, *post*democratic, "countermovement" that begins by defining and creating itself dialectically, against the entire tradition of the West, and thereby presupposes and claims to possess the deepest possible understanding of that tradition. If we are to try to meet Nietzsche's challenge on its own level, we must then try to summon the strength to carry out two awesome tasks. We must undertake a painstaking and truly open-eyed reconsideration of both the Socratic and the Biblical roots of the tradition; in the light of such a reconsideration, we must rethink our own deeply democratic prejudices and commitments.

Because Nietzsche is such an extreme opponent of modern democracy and because he places his enmity for democracy at the very center of his thought, he is a peculiarly painful thinker for us, the adherents or friends of liberal democracy. Nonetheless, we must avoid the temptation to which almost all contemporary "scholars" fall prey, the temptation to try to explain away or sweep under the rug Nietzsche's utterly unconservative atheism of the Right. For what makes Nietzsche's hatred of liberal as well as all socialist democracy so extreme is also what transfigures that hatred: Nietzsche is a "philosopher," in his own strict sense of the term (*BGE*, 212). As such, he poses a challenge of a rare and high order—a potentially liberating challenge. The more deeply we penetrate Nietzsche's critique, the more irresistably we are compeled to reexamine, from a strange and startling perspective, the promises and the threats and the vices and the virtues of our democratic way of life and, indeed, of modern egalitarianism in all its forms.

Notes

1. Martin Heidegger in his *Nietzsche*, 2 vols. (Pfullingen: Neske Verlag, 1961) has taught us to add immediately that in the years subsequent to the completion of Part Four of *Zarathustra*, Nietzsche described himself as at work on a philosophic edifice for which *Zarathustra* was merely the "vestibule." Only fragments—if elaborate and rich fragments—of this *magnum opus* were left behind; in what sense Nietzsche's philosophy remains, in his own estimation, decisively unfinished can become clear only through a careful study of the *Nachlass* in the light of *Zarathustra*.

2. Reference is to Nietzsche's works by aphorism or section number wherever possible; where a page number is indicated, it refers to the Schlechta edition of the *Werke* (Munich: Carl Hanser, 1966). I have made use of the Kaufmann translation, altered in minor ways to make them more strictly literal. Abbreviations used for titles of the major works are as follows: BT (*Birth of Tragedy*), UM (*Untimely Meditations*), HTH (*Human, All Too Human*), GS (*Gay Science*), BGE (*Beyond Good and Evil*, GM (*Genealogy of Morals*), TI (*Twilight of the Idols*), EH (*Ecce Homo*), A (*Antichrist*), WP (*Will to Power*), Z (*Thus Spoke Zarathustra*).

3. "All philosophers have in common the defect, that they proceed from contemporary man and through an analysis of him think they reach their goal. Involuntarily they conceive 'man' as an *aeterna veritas*, as something permanent in every whirlpool, as a sure measure of things. Everything that the philosopher says about man is at bottom, however, nothing more than the testimony concerning the man of a *very limited* period of time. Lack of a historical sense is the hereditary defect of all philosophers. . . . They will not learn that *historical philosophizing* is necessary from now on and with it the virtue of modesty." (HTH, 2; cf. GM, I, 2, II, 4; TI, "Reason in Philosophy," 1).

4. In what follows I am indebted to Werner J. Dannhauser, *Nietzsche's View of Socrates* (Ithaca: Cornell University Press, 1974). Among other things, I accept, and will not here rehearse, his detailed refutation of Walter Kaufmann, *Nietzsche*, 4th ed. (Princeton: Princeton University Press, 1974).

5. This is not to deny that Nietzsche finds strong stirrings of "Socratism" in pre-Socratic thought, and even in Sophocles: Dannhauser, *Nietzsche's View of Socrates*, 100, and Georges Morel, *Nietzsche*, 3 vols, *Analyse de la maladie* (Paris: Aubier-Montaigne, 1971), 2: 278–79.

6. Doubtless Nietzsche is somehow aware that this characterization does not begin to do justice to "Plato's secrecy and sphinx nature": After all, Plato slept with a volume of Aristophanes at his side (BGE, 28). This "royal and magnificent hermit of the spirit" did not write "books for all the world" because he understood what Nietzsche calls "the difference between the exoteric and the esoteric, formerly known to philosophers—among the Indians as among the Greeks" (BGE, 30). "The hermit does not believe that any philosopher—assuming that a philosopher is always first of all a hermit—ever expressed his real and ultimate opinions in books" (BGE, 298). Despite these dazzling flashes of in-

sight, Nietzsche does not approach Plato's texts with the hermeneutic caution that would seem to be implied: "Plato becomes a caricature in my hands" (*WP*, 374). The charm of such regal frankness cannot dispel our disappointment. Nietzsche does not seem concerned with the task—perhaps impossible—of understanding Plato as Plato understands himself, or even with the more manageable task of trying to understand Plato exactly as he intended himself to be understood. This can be partially, but only very partially, explained by noting that Nietzsche is interested in Plato's legacy, his historical influence, as much as in Plato's thought itself. That legacy, Nietzsche was sure, has been highly dogmatic and moralistic: "Even the most sublime ethical deeds, the stirrings of pity, self-sacrifice, heroism, and that so difficult to attain calm sea of the soul which the Apollinian Greek called sophrosune, were derived from the dialectic of knowledge by Socrates and his like-minded successors, down to the present, and accordingly designated as teachable" (*BT*, 15).

7.   The ignoring of this cardinal feature of Nietzsche's analysis, and all that we shall see is implied, has led to some rather simplistic and distorted renditions of Nietzsche's view of Christianity. A recent striking example is Philippa Foot, "Nietzsche: The Revaluation of Values," *Nietzsche*, ed. Robert C. Solomon (New York: Doubleday, 1973), 156–68. The soundest discussion I have found is Paul Valadier, *Nietzsche et la critique du Christianisme* (Paris: Editions du Cerf, 1974), 181ff.

8.   *HTH*, 114; *BGE*, 49; *GM*, II, 23; *A*, 16, 25; *WP*, 135–37; Morel, *Analyse de la maladie*, 126–32, obscures the significance of gratitude in Greek piety according to Nietzsche.

9.   *A*, 55–57; *WP*, 142, 143, 145; Letter to Gast of 31 May 1888 (pp. 1296–97).

10.   Cf. Pascal's remark: "Philosophers, they astonish ordinary men who are less educated; Christians, they astonish philosophers": Quoted in Karl Löwith, "Man Between Infinities," *Nature, History, and Existentialism* (Evanston, Ill.: Northwestern Univeristy Press, 1966), 115. In his campaign to rationalize Nietzsche, Kaufman characteristically ignores Nietzsche's affinity with Pascal, going so far as to claim that Nietzsche's "whole conception of historical Christianity hinges on Luther"; as a consequence Kaufmann obscures the religious roots of "honesty" and modern philosophy—even though he quotes *GS*, 344 (*Nietzsche*, 348–58).

11.   Cf. Letter to Overbeck of 23 February 1887 (p. 1250): "These *Greeks* have much on their conscience—falsification was their true trade, the whole of European psychology is sick with Greek superficialities; and without the little bit of Jewishness etc. etc. etc."; and *TI*, "Skirmishes," 23: "Plato . . . says with an innocence possible only for a Greek, not a 'Christian,' . . ."

12.   *BGE*, 55, 199–200, 209, 229, 262; *WP*, pref., 10, 22, 23, 41, 56, 112, 751, 1017, 1026; cf. Richard Schact, "Nietzsche and Nihilism," in Solomon, *Nietzsche*, 60–65; Karl Löwith, *From Hegel to Nietzsche* (New York: Doubleday, 1967), 188–89, 258.

13. As will become clear in what follows, Zarathustra's notion of the "last man" is misunderstood if it is taken as a critique of the "petty bourgeois" (Solomon, *Nietzsche*, 5): Zarathustra is describing *not* a type that exists in the present, but one that *may* predominate in the future, in a society where "work is a form of entertainment . . . one no longer becomes poor or rich . . . everybody is the same . . . "—that is, the *classless* society. I respectfully differ, on this crucial point, with both George Grant, *Time as History* (Toronto: CBC Systems, 1969), chap. 4, and Heidegger, *Nietzsche*, I, 284–85 (which seems to be contradicted by the Nietzschean passage quoted earlier and cited in note 16).

14. The limited space at my disposal does not permit me to do justice to the context of this first, and sole, Zarathustrian public oration; on the other hand, I have not ignored the context, and reflection on it shapes the invisible background of my remarks.

15. Compare also the ordinary German word *untermensch* ("brute, thug, subhuman").

16. Quoted by Heidegger in *Nietzsche*, I, 241. Heidegger comments: "Das will sagen: Das Ende ist als Ende erst sichtbar aus dem neuen Anfang. Umgekehrt: Wer der Übermensch ist, wird erst klar, wenn der letzte Mensch als solcher gesehen wird."

Robert Eden

WHY WASN'T WEBER A NIHILIST?

> . . . It is essential to political philosophy to be
> set in motion, and to be kept in motion, by the
> disquieting awareness of the fundamental difference
> between conviction, or belief, and knowledge.[1]

More than thirty-five years have passed since Leo Strauss published his critique of Max Weber's social science.[2] It is perhaps his only essay that is "well-known" in being "widely read." To be "well-informed" today in social science one must know that Strauss's thought can be summed up in his high-toned charge that Weber was a nihilist. Critics of social science, no less than friends, are confident of this. At no point, however has Strauss's critique been subjected in print to the most minimal scrutiny as an argument in the philosophy of social science or in political philosophy. So far as the public traces tell, no one has so much as outlined the main steps of that argument, yet everyone knows its gist.[3] Almost twenty years ago, as a graduate student fresh from Berkeley and from Sheldon S. Wolin's graduate seminar in the philosophy of social science, I sat down to make an outline of Strauss's argument. I was amazed to discover what I shall demonstrate below: that Strauss did not argue that Weber was a nihilist, but rather sought to determine why Weber was not. This thesis will initially strike most readers, as it then struck me, as contradictory to received opinion that I had taken to be authoritative, thus paradoxical in the strongest sense.[4]

To establish this paradoxical thesis, my analysis will begin with Strauss's initial contention and trace his effort to determine why Weber was not a nihilist. Strauss's argument leads us, by stages, to reflect on Weber's moral resistance to nihilism. It is a difficult argument to digest because it exhibits a painful contradiction between Weber's moral resistance to nihilism and his quest for self-knowledge. It helps or compels us to question the roots of Weber's indignation, and if it is digested, it can bring us to a vantage point from which we may look down not only upon Weber's indignation but also upon our own. There, admittedly, few of us wish to be.

Beyond outlining Strauss's argument, I have tried to revive Strauss's critique as an introduction to the highest task of understanding Weber,

212

the task of taking Weber's measure as a human being. Perhaps the fitting apology for Strauss's occasonal high-handedness is that he brings Weber to life, enabling us to converse with and question Weber at the height of his powers, as Socrates would converse with the heroes in Hades.[5]

Liberal Democracy Between Weber and Strauss

The crisis of liberal democracy is a touchy subject, as it ought to be. What constitutes that crisis, and how it should be resolved, are matters of partisan opinion, on which the constitutional democracies of the West are deeply divided.[6] Since spirited partisans will in all likelihood stick by their views, it would be imprudent to assume that the clash of opinions on this controversial subject will foster much common sense, informed consent, or a common perspective.[7]

Yet to a remarkable degree we do share a common perspective on the crisis of liberal democracy, a view universal enough that most university graduates know its rudiments and can recite them back like a catechism. It is the perspective originally conveyed, through the social sciences, as the distinctive contribution of Max Weber and now transmitted, through the media, as the distinguished contribution of this evening's pundit. We scholars are by no means all Weberians. Yet, with remarkably few exceptions, the academically educated agree that Weber's is the most comprehensive and realistic view of the crisis of liberalism yet advanced by a proponent of liberal democratic institutions. Even the attempts by Marxists and the New Left to make Weber's perspective their own reinforce this consensus; such attempts indicate that opponents of liberal institutions also believe Weber's account will survive the onslaughts of skepticism and disillusionment.[8] Sharing such a perspective in no way ameliorates the crisis of liberal democracy, of course. It could not do so without contradicting Weber's doctrine of the separation of politics from science.[9]

According to this common perspective, science "serves moral forces" by compelling or helping us to render ourselves an account of the ultimate meaning of our own conduct (that is, of the ultimate values with which our course of conduct is consistent.)[10] Weber's view enables us to accommodate the crisis of liberal democracy while making no claim to resolve it. Indeed, anyone who claims to resolve it is, from Weber's standpoint, highly suspect. For if it is liberal to accommodate and tolerate ultimate commitment or devotion to a cause in practice, it is illiberal to propose any resolution to the crisis of liberal democracy at the level of science. Only someone who covertly intended to dissolve liberal institutions would do so.[11] If reason and science could side with common sense and informed consent against any ultimate commitment or devotion to any cause, the open society could close itself. It could refuse, in practice, to tolerate any politics that rejected informed consent. On this view only a proponent of a totalitarian or closed regime would propose to resolve the crisis of liberalism at the level of science. So long as liberal democracy remains the truly open society it is fated to suffer a crisis that must be in principle without resolution.[12]

This "common knowledge" forms the background against which most students first read Leo Strauss's critique of Weber in *Natural Right and History*. Because Weber's doctrine, in many popularizations, had become a *lingua franca* within the academy, it usually supplied the frame of reference of efforts to understand Strauss's alternative perspective on the crisis of liberal democracy.[13] In this essay I explore Strauss's attempt to turn our attention toward the origin of this frame of reference or toward the origin of our common perspective on the crisis of liberal democracy. Strauss approaches Weber, as I shall argue, in the spirit of Socratic inquiry, trying to turn our gaze toward the fire that illuminates our cave. According to Strauss, Weber's quest for critical distance on the crisis of liberal democracy was inseparable from Weber's quest for self-knowledge.[14] The adequacy of that quest for self-knowledge is Strauss's subject; he does not directly address the crisis of liberal democracy. But because these subjects are in practice inseparable, Strauss's critique of Weber is necessarily a critique of Weber's perspective on the crisis of liberal democracy. It adumbrates Strauss's own analysis of that crisis. Strauss argues, in passing, that Weber misunderstood this problem because he gave too little thought to the causal role of modern, liberal political philosophy and political economy.[15] *Natural Right and History* eventually traces the crisis of liberal democracy to its roots in the thought of John Locke. The most radical critique in Strauss's book is not the critique of Weber, but the discussion of Locke.[16] *Natural Right and History* includes a radical critique of the philosophic founder of the liberal democratic regime. To reach the roots of the modern liberal project, however, the reader must first work through a critique of Weber. Strauss made us weigh his reasons for abandoning Weber's perspective before going on to his own account of the roots, or principles, of liberal democracy and its current crisis. I shall therefore try to indicate how this chapter sets us in motion toward a consideration of the crisis of liberal democracy, one that does justice to its principles, as Weber and his social science could not.[17]

These prefatory remarks may suggest why Strauss never makes explicit the problem of the chapter on Weber; we must deduce what that problem, Weber's problem, was. Strauss began by remarking that

no one since Weber has devoted a comparable amount of intelligence, assiduity, and almost fanatical devotion to the basic problem of the social sciences. Whatever may have been his errors, he is the greatest social scientist of our century."[18]

This unstinting praise seemed to imply that Strauss's study would disclose "the basic problem of the social sciences." But the phrase never recurs in his critique, and the chapter ends without a statement of what constituted that basic problem.[19] Strauss almost immediately noted that Weber held the doctrine that "the substance of social science is radically historical."[20] Yet, precisely if that were true, it is doubtful that one could speak sensibly of *the* basic problem. If its substance is historical, no problem can be the basic problem of social science; there is only a multiplicity of problems succeeding each other in time—unless *the* basic problem is nothing other than the radical historical substance of social science. From the outset, however, Strauss denies that this was Weber's view or can be squared with his conception of the basic problem.[21] It certainly does not square with what Strauss presents as social science and its problems.[22] In the course of Strauss's analysis it becomes increasingly clear that Weber thought an adequate view of the basic problem was unattainable.

In an adequate view, the fundamental and permanent alternatives would become visible as paths or ways of life open to man as man.[23] Strauss indicates that philosophy, and in particular political philosophy, were closed to, or for, Weber. Despite or because of his distinction between science and politics, the political life and the philosophical life do not come to light in Weber's thought as ways of life open to us. This may indicate the bearing of this chapter on Strauss's main inquiry in *Natural Right and History*: In Strauss's perspective on the crisis of liberal democracy, both politics and philosophy again become visible as permanent possibilities for man. Weber's perspective instead enables us to cultivate our indignation as a matter of ultimate concern; that is why diverse partisans can share his view of the crisis of liberal democracy while occupying opposed points on the political spectrum. Weber's perspective is agreeable to partisans because it heightens the importance of devotion to a cause and hence their own importance as devotees or leaders.[24] Weber's perspective is a defense of politics, and as Strauss attempts to demonstrate, any defense of politics that abstracts from ranking the causes for which we fight is necessarily a defense of politics *against philosophy*; its root dogma must be the impossibility of political philosophy.[25] My suggestion is that indignation in defense of politics is the basic problem of the social sciences, which Weber ultimately personified.

With this preface the reader may be prepared to consider how Strauss proves, that is, abandons, his initial contention.

The Contention that Weber's Thesis Leads to Nihilism

Strauss contends "that Weber's thesis necessarily leads to nihilism or to the view that every preference, however evil, base, or insane, has to be judged before the tribunal of reason to be as legitimate as any other preference."[25] This should remind one immediately of Weber's most famous contention: that Calvin's doctrine of predestination led to the spirit of capitalism or to its distinctive acquisitive asceticism.[27] Strauss turns to *The Protestant Ethic* several pages after proving his own initial contention. He argues that Weber failed in *The Protestant Ethic* (and indeed in all his scholarly work) to practice the most legitimate, important, and elevated kind of nonevaluating objectivity. In identifying the essence of Calvin's doctrine with its historically influential part, Weber failed to consider that the essence might well have been what Calvin himself thought it was. Weber should have distinguished between the original and its corruption:

> What Weber should have said was that the corruption of Calvinist theology led to the emergence of the capitalist spirit. This would have implied an objective value judgment on vulgar Calvinism: the epigones unwittingly destroyed what they intended to preserve.[28]

Let us call the error Strauss has identified "the fallacy of unexamined originals." One cannot show that "the results of an action" stand in "a wholly inadequate or even paradoxical relation to its original meaning" unless one has access to an adequate account of that original meaning.[29] Nor can one speak sensibly about "unintended consequences" unless one can establish the original intention. The fallacy of unexamined originals is therefore one of the errors that Weber's social science can least afford, and its repeated commission has been crippling. Strauss advances his higher nonevaluating objectivity in order to preclude this error.

Yet Strauss himself has just, rather flagrantly, committed this very fallacy. Toward the end of his proof he had conjured up the (plausible) objection that the thesis leading to nihilism was not what Weber meant, that it was not Weber's essential thesis or teaching. Strauss's brusque reply is amazing, in view of his criticism of *The Protestant Ethic* thesis. What counts, he says, is only the actual doctrine "which dominates present-day social science."[30] (If you find this outrageously brusque, ask whether there is anything better than the sting of an injustice, paraded as matter-of-factness, to make one appreciate the justice of nonevaluating objectivity.) Once one does appreciate the demands of nonevaluating objectivity, however, and applies its standard retrospectively to Strauss's initial indictment of Weber, one discovers that Strauss has committed a fallacy that could not be allowed to stand.

Strauss accordingly goes on at considerable length to explore "what Weber really meant."[31] He attempts a portrait of Weber's thought in all its original pathos and agony. Just as Strauss corrects Weber's argument about Calvin, he compels us to qualify his own contention that Weber's thesis leads to nihilism, in the light of his more searching interpretation of what Weber actually thought. It is primarily in this much longer, second part of his argument, that Strauss explores the character of Weber's resistance to nihilism and thereby sheds light on the question before us.

Weber's Opposition to Vulgar Nihilism

For those readers who greet his initial proof with a patient shrug, Strauss makes a fresh start that moves the argument to a new plane.

> Many social scientists of our time seem to regard nihilism as a minor inconvenience which wise men would bear with equanimity, since it is the price one has to pay for obtaining that highest good, a truly scientific social science. . . .We have to consider, therefore, whether social science as a purely theoretical pursuit, but still as a pursuit leading to the understanding of social phenomena, is possible on the basis of the distinction between facts and values.[32]

These wise readers regard the main result of Weber's titanic labors, apparently, as a solution to the basic problem of the social sciences, a solution that makes possible a good so great as to assure Weber's immortality, regardless of the nihilism to which that solution leads. Strauss's argument seems to be an ascent, from these neo-Weberian lowlands to the highest problem that strained Weber's every nerve. The ascent entails a more searching articulation of Weber's thought than Strauss's initial "proof" that Weber's thesis leads to nihilsm. We find that it did not lead Weber to nihilism. Weber is gradually revealed as a passionate antagonist of what Strauss has described as nihilism. In displaying this contradiction between the spirit of much Weberian social science and Weber's own pathos of inquiry, Strauss exposes the difference between the regime Weber intended and the regime that satisfies Weber's epigones. This regime is an offspring of the morganatic alliance between social science and vulgar nihilism, to which Strauss draws our eyes in the passage just quoted. We are therefore tempted to modify Strauss's initial contention along the following lines. What Strauss should have said was that the corruption of Weber's teaching led to the emergence of a social science collaborating with vulgar nihilism. This would have implied an objective value judgment on vulgar Weberianism: The epigones unwittingly destroyed what they intended to preserve.[33]

But there are insuperable objections to the suggested modification. The parallel to Calvin is untenable. Weber had argued that Calvin's doctrine was influential because of its incomparable logical rigor.[34] Strauss is in agreement with Weber on this score, even when we include his reservations as to the adequacy of Weber's grasp of Calvin's original teaching. If the spirit of ascetic acquisitiveness resulted from Calvin's doctrine, this disastrous outcome could not have been avoided by an improvement in the rationality or coherence of Calvin's essential doctrine. The consequences annihilated Calvin's worldly efforts, but the nihilistic consequences had to be made visible through an empirical social science, like Weber's, that was not at Calvin's disposal. The contrast with Weber could not be greater. Weber made his main concern the study of the "routinization" of ethical and religious doctrines; he could not possibly have overlooked the problem entailed in the vulgarization of his own doctrine of values.[35] Indeed, Strauss shows Weber haunted by dread of contributing to the degradation that Strauss describes as nihilism. The main alternatives, in Weber's view, were mechanized petrification or spiritual renewal, as Strauss makes elaborately clear.[36]

To understand Weber's dilemma, we must ask what a consistent rejection of vulgar nihilism in both theory and practice would entail. The view Strauss describes as "nihilism" was portrayed in roughly the same terms well before Weber. Nietzsche regarded it as a modern democratic orthodoxy, the logical outcome of modern egalitarianism. Nietzsche argued that a consistent opposition to this democracy of all preferences was indeed possible. But it would entail radical and revolutionary aristocratic politics.[37] What Strauss initially portrays as nihilism is, after all, one of the dominant persuasions in the liberal democracies today. In practice, if one defends constitutional democracy, one must be resigned to defend a regime in which "the view that every preference, however evil, base, or insane, has to be judged before the tribunal of reason to be as legitimate as any other preference" will have a large following and will periodically dominate key institutions of government. "Liberalism" today has a bad name in many circles because it is seldom distinguishable from such vulgar nihilism. As Strauss's defense of Weber unfolds, it becomes evident that Weber was an opponent of such "liberalism." At the same time, Weber ruled out any return to natural right. Strauss had remarked that

> there is a tension between the respect for diversity or individuality and the recognition of natural right. When liberals became impatient of the absolute limits to diversity or individuality that are imposed by even the most liberal version of natural right, they had to make a choice between natural right and the uninhibited cultivation of individuality. They chose the latter.[38]

This choice eventually yielded "liberal" policies that made decent citizens detest and disavow "liberalism" and look for "new ideas." It is this vulgar nihilism that many social scientists found livable because it made the uninhibited cultivation of their highest hobby a remunerative pursuit. But it was not Weber's choice. Like Nietzsche, and later Heidegger, Weber rejected both natural right and vulgar nihilism, or the democracy of all preferences. Did Weber, then, discover an Archimidean point for social science that would provide leverage against this democratic nihilism, and yet keep social science from joining Nietzsche and Heidegger altogether?

It has become evident that we must distinguish between two forms of nihilism and acknowledge that our initial question divides into two. Strauss began by identifying nihilism with a view that can become a popular democratic prejudice (as we know from abundant recent experience).[39] Ordinary citizens may invoke this view to defend their actions or assert their rights, without thinking through the implications of nihilism as a consistent political or philosophical doctrine. It may lead them to follies or crimes they would not commit under the restraint of another belief, depress their powers of reasoning below the threshhold of the common sense of the average working man, and thrust upon them the greatness and misery of uninhibited self-assertion. This naive view is distinct, however, from that resolute, intrepid, circumspect experiment with knowledge, or from nihilism as exemplified by Nietzsche and Heidegger.[40] Our twofold question, therefore, is why Weber was not a nihilist in either sense. One of the charms of Strauss's essay is that it enables us to clarify Weber's resistance to both these opposed and distinct forms of nihilism.

Strauss methodically compels us to modify his initial contention in the light of Weber's opposition to vulgar nihilism. His graver criticism is adumbrated by his claim that in order to "see why Weber could conceal from himself the nihilistic consequences of his doctrine of values, we have to follow his thought step by step."[41] Weber's thought somehow made it possible for Weber to conceal from himself the necessary consequences of his doctrine: He was prevented from thinking through the necessities of the progression in question because he could not think nihilism through to the end. To paraphrase Weber's criticism of half-hearted dialectical materialists: Nihilism is not a cab to be taken at will.[42] The implications of Weber's doctrine of values can be concealed only by means of inconsistency. If Calvin was not subject to this line of criticism, it was because he was a more *konsequent* thinker.[43]

The regime of constitutional democracy may permit vulgar nihilism to thrive, and because social science may for a time thrive alongside it, many social scientists do not share the revulsion that vulgar nihilism generates among most citizens (who are not charmed by "that highest good, a truly scientific social science"). That revulsion is at a high pitch, however, in Weber's original thinking. One can thus see why it might be difficult for Weberian social science to defend constitutional democracy when it becomes inseparable from vulgar nihilism.[44] Once shaken from his smug patience with "the democracy of all preferences," the complacent social scientist must be divided against himself. If he ascends to Weber's original position, he should share precisely the revulsion that makes liberal democracy repellent. This may explain why attacks on liberal democracy from the existentialist and Nietzschean Left have confounded Weberian social scientists: Such attacks confront them with what sounds like Weber's original teaching or with their own bad conscience. When we are compelled to choose between "mechanized petrification" and spiritual renewal in the forms of commitment proposed by the Nietzschan Left, we Weberians are hard put to choose. The possibility that Weber holds out an alternative depends on whether it is possible to join Weber's revulsion against vulgar nihilism with a strict rejection of philosophical nihilism. This combination has proved elusive, despite ever-renewed efforts by several generations of Weberians.[45] Is the Weberian regime of "critical rationalism" and "an ethics of responsiblity" (to use Schluchter's formulation) a coherent project, or merely a noble lie?[46] To answer this practical question, we must have a coherent answer to Strauss's question: Why wasn't Weber a nihilist?

To distinguish Weber's social science from philosophical nihilism, Strauss would have been obliged to show how, and why, Nietzsche and Heidegger reached the conclusion that nihilism was a fatality to be borne by resolute thought. To exhibit the progression to this conclusion in the form that Nietzsche and subsequently Heidegger formulated the progression, would be equivalent to rendering an historicist account of the origin of the most radical historicism. One peculiarity of Strauss's argument in *Natural Right and History*, however, is that it treats nihilism and radical historicism in separate chapters. The systematic connection between them (if *systematic* is a proper term here) is not discussed.[47] Nonetheless, Strauss's awareness that historicism and philosophical nihilism were closely and perhaps indissolubly bound together may be said to underlie Strauss's critique of Weber: It obtrudes repeatedly and in unexpected ways. For example, Strauss uses Nietzschean and Heideggerian terms of criticism against Weber with devastating effect.[48] Together, Chapters 1 and 2 of *Natural Right and History* demonstrate that Weber's greatness certainly did not rest on his coming to terms with nihilism.[49] How can one accept radical historicism (as described in Chapter 1) to the point of claiming that the substance of social science is radically historical,[50] without thinking nihilism through to the end?

The Possibility of a Truly Scientific Social Science

Strauss's critical analysis undermines the complacency of those "wise" social scientists who rest their hopes upon Weber's distinction between facts and values. Strauss argues that a truly scientific social science cannot arise on that basis.[51] Despite this disappointment (and Strauss's unconcealed disdain for this contemporary wisdom), there are several perplexing features to the discord that Strauss brings to light between Weber and his more complacent epigones. Although Weber defends the nobler cause, his cause is ultimately shown to be indefensible. Contrary to these epigones, Weber took the position that the life dedicated to science as the highest good was without foundation; science is incapable of rendering a clear and certain account of itself[52] Yet the apparent ignobility of their cause does not deter Strauss from responding thoroughly, carefully, and ultimately respectfully to the desire or aspiration of Weber's epigones. He liberates the desire for a truly scientific social science, pointing the way toward one more worthy of serious devotion as a highest good. Strauss's reasoning severs the aspirations of social science from Weber's doctrine, as well as from the concerns that undergirded Weber's doctrine. Toward the end of the chapter on Weber (or in the locus of rhetorical hyperbole), Strauss even discloses a ravishing vista, an untouched wilderness waiting to be mapped and explored by adventurers whose highest good is a truly scientific social science.[53] It ought to give one pause that Strauss should take the part of these evidently amoral, socially irresponsible idlers and time-servers, when Weber's heroic agony is the main alternative.

It becomes impossible, in any event, to avoid the task of understanding Weber's nature and character, since Weber's resistance to nihilism only becomes fully visible when Strauss explores the harmony between his reasoning and his moral preferences.[54] In this respect Strauss's critical analysis resembles a Platonic dialogue, and a few points of comparison to *The Republic* may advance our inquiry.

The unabashed nihilism of the "many social scientists" (who think they are *sophoi*) is akin to Thrasymachus's outspoken cynicism about justice in *The Republic*. Thrasymachus insists that justice is bound to the ruling group or regime; he falls silent when he discovers that he could not support his conviction with adequate reasoning, or that he lacks a sufficient political science.[55] Speaking in the political mode of violent assertion, as if he were the city itself, seems to be Thrasymachus's bliss. However, he blushes when what he took for political wisdom proves indefensible. Strauss tries to elicit a similar blush. But he does not frustrate the desire of the "wise" for a purely theoretical quest as their highest good. The counterpart of Max Weber in *The Republic* would seem to be Glaucon, who demanded that justice should be shown as the good in itself, independent of rewards, punishments, or other consequences. Glaucon turned to Socrates claiming to be in despair that anyone could give a clear or certain account, an adequate defense, of justice in itself.[56] Weber's parallel demand is that science must be shown to be the highest good, regardless of extrinsic consequences; Weber despaired of the possibility that science could give a clear and certain account of itself.[52]

The dialogue with Glaucon, as Strauss understood it, illuminated the limits of politics and the problem of justice because Glaucon's nature was insatiable within those limits. Glaucon had needs that defied political satisfaction and could not be met by any city without deranging the city. His demand for an account of justice reflects this: Glaucon is bound to conceive justice as something good in itself, which he can possess, and be possessed by, or in which his nature can be entirely fulfilled.[58] There will always be a remnant of Glaucon's nature that no city or justice can answer.

The dialogue with Weber (if we may call Strauss's chapter that) illuminates the limits of science, the problem of the basis of science, because Weber's needs defy scientific satisfaction and could not be met without deranging science. In both dialogues these limits do not become evident until we see how they are transcended. Glaucon's nature can only be fulfilled by partaking of the philosophic life and its satisfactions. Weber's need cannot be satisfied by a science at odds with common sense and committed to the practical transformation of the world of common sense or of public affairs. Above all, Weber's sense of tragedy rebels against science: In sharp contrast to Machiavelli, Weber was endowed with a strong natural sense of the sacredness of the common.[59] Weber's efforts to render what he understood through the means of modern science proved to be futile because those means were designed, as Strauss emphasizes, to dissolve and reconstitute the world of common sense perception.[60] Hence, the distinction between science and politics that Weber refined was inadequate to describe why the life of science could not fulfill Weber's nature. Both science and politics had been transformed by that radical break with common sense initiated by Machiavelli and Hobbes; as a consequence of this complex transformation, the political world no longer articulates the sacredness of the common, and science makes no effort to comprehend and interpret the prescientific perception of the human and natural world.[61] Glaucon needed to leave the cave for a time, to transcend the horizon of the prescientific city; Weber need to recover it. Weber's need for a clear and certain account of science could no more be satisfied by his social science than Glaucon could be satisfied by politics or justice. If one were to infer Weber's need from what Strauss subsequently holds out to satisfy Weber's quest, one might speak of a prescientific or natural need for an adequate perceiving and judging of political and moral things. Weber's need, if this inference is correct, was for *phronesis*, practical wisdom in the ancient, pre-Machiavellian sense. This need was bound to be equally frustrated by the modes and orders of modern politics and by the limitations of modern science. By pointing beyond the limits of Weberian science, to the step Weber was unable to take, Strauss almost leaves the genre of critical analysis in order to delineate a Weber fulfilled and returned to his natural element.[62] Weber viewed Plato's attempt to disclose the limits of politics in The Republic as a paradigm of the disenchantment of the world by science.[63] For Strauss it was also the disclosure (and in this sense a disenchantment) of the natures of Glaucon and Adeimantus. Socrates describes how the cave becomes enchanted with imagery cast upon the walls by firelight. He also helps us to take Glaucon's measure, and to attain critical distance upon Glaucon's potentially tyrannical *eros* or charm.[64] Strauss enables us to understand why Weber was not a nihilist by showing us his soul and his moral preferences. In exhibiting them critically, he dispels their charm, their potential hold over us. Strauss could not have questioned Weber's moral resistance to nihilism so relentlessly had he not broken the spell of Weber's insistent moral concern.[65]

Ever More Fundamental Alternatives

The comic resolution I have sketched in this comparison to *The Republic* is evidently unattainable. It postulates a possible harmony between those social scientists who love the pursuit of truth as the highest good and a social scientist, such as Weber, who hates intellectualism as "the worst devil."[66] The disclosure of Weber's moral preference is therefore darkened by the potential for endless and tragic conflict, which is inseparable from Weber's position. Strauss's quest takes the form of a continuous descent in which we are compelled to abandon all hope as we spiral down in pursuit of the basic problem of the social sciences or the most fundamental disclosure of Weber's moral preferences. At every circle of this inferno we are assured that the conflict, opposition, or distinction under consideration is fundamental. Then the descent goes on; we discover to our despair that *fundamental* means nothing more than "provisionally and for the most part."[67] Then suddenly (and for no apparent good reason), when we have reached what seems to be the bottom of things, Strauss summons us to an inglorious, Falstaffian retreat, "from these awful depths to a superficiality which, while not exactly gay, promises at least a quiet sleep."[68]

This retreat, as well as the logic of every preceding step we have taken, is bound to make us skeptical that the fundamental alternative has been clarified. Let us briefly recapitulate. Strauss had asked for a demonstration of Weber's premise:

> Weber's whole notion of the scope and function of the social sciences rests on the allegedly demonstrable premise that the conflict between ultimate values cannot be resolved by human reason. The question is whether that premise has really been demonstrated, or whether it has merely been postulated under the impulse of a specific moral preference.[69]

In each case Strauss examines or reconstructs Weber's attempt to demonstrate his basic premise, but in each case the demonstration culminates in a dramatic assertion of Weber's moral concerns and spiritual anxieties. The most important of these descriptions of Weber are as follows:

(Weber) needed the necessity of guilt. He had to combine the anguish bred by atheism (the absence of any redemption, any solace) with the anguish bred by revealed religion (the oppressive sense of guilt). Without that combination, life would cease to be tragic and thus lose its depth.[70]

Weber refused to bring the sacrifice of the intellect; he did not wait for a religious revival or for prophets or saviors; and he was not at all certain whether a religious revival would follow the present age. But he was certain that all devotion to causes or ideals has its roots in religious faith and, therefore, that the decline of religious faith will ultimately lead to the extinction of all causes or ideals. He despaired of the modern this-worldly experiment, and yet he remained attached to it because he was fated to believe in science as he understood it. The result of this conflict, which he could not resolve, was his belief that the conflict between values cannot be resolved by human reason.[71]

It was the conflict between revelation and philosophy or science in the full sense of the term and the implication of that conflict that led Weber to assert that the idea of science or philosophy suffers from a fatal weakness. He tried to remain faithful to the cause of autonomous insight, but he despaired when he felt that the sacrifice of the intellect, which is abhorred by science or philosophy, is at the bottom of science or philosophy.[72]

The last of the demonstrations is the weightiest, but its result is less certain. The preceding two lead to a reassertion of Weber's basic premise, to his belief in ultimate and irreconcilable conflict. The last leads rather to an assertion of fatal weakness in the idea of science and to a profession of despair. Unlike the preceding demonstrations, the last is not taken from Weber's writings. For most contemporary social scientists (including those most familiar with Weber's thought), Strauss's articulation of what Weber had in mind is almost certain to come as a novelty. For it discloses a problem that does not normally become visible within the horizon of Weberian social science. This remoteness from Weber confirms Richard Kennington's observation that the final demonstration owes less to Weber's final thoughts than to Strauss's own itinerary and most to his early formulations in *Spinoza's Critique of Religion*.[73]

At the beginning of the last demonstration, Strauss proposes this more precise account of Weber's thought:

The fundamental question. . .is whether men can acquire that knowledge of the good without which they cannot guide their lives individually or collectively by the unaided efforts of their natural powers or whether they are dependent for that knowledge on Divine Revelation. No alternative is more fundamental than this: Human guidance or divine guidance.[74]

If these were the options, Weber's rejection of nihilism would have to be a clear choice between them, and it would be necessary to identify nihilism with one or the other. This proves difficult if not impossible to do. I propose to examine the demonstration in order to establish more precisely what Weber had in mind, and what light the passage can shed upon his rejection of nihilism.

On first inspection it would seem that Weber's position or cause is that of autonomous insight. Weber articulated the best argument for the autonomy of science from revelation and affirmed its autonomy even when the argument itself proved inconclusive. But (as Kennington has observed) Weber's account establishes the supremacy of revelation in the conflict:

> Revelation is unable but also not obligated to refute the possibility of philosophy, whereas philosophy, to show its own reasonableness, is obligated but unable to refute the possibility of revelation. The choice of philosophy cannot satisfy its own requirement that the choice be reasonable choice. Weber was wrong: the conflict is not insoluble but decides in favor of revelation. . .philosophy is vanquished by revelation.[75]

Yet when philosophy or science is defeated, Weber nevertheless stands by the cause of autonomous insight, desperately, "because he was fated to believe in science as he understood it,"[76] or because he was determined to remain true to himself and to the inescapable condition of "our historical situation."[77] Weber's deed is consciously done, and Strauss has provided an articulation of the coherent basis for it in the preceding chapter: The deed is a confirmation of the radical historicist argument that thought is ultimately governed by fate.[78] To see that the ground for thought is not reason or that even the decision for science is a blind decision is to abandon the possibility of philosophy as indefensible. It is, therefore, not possible to argue that Weber's affirmation of the cause of scientific autonomy is a choice between the fundamental alternatives: Submission to fate, or to thought as a fatality, is neither human nor divine guidance. It is guidance by whatever fate turns out to be: chance, accident, or another riddle of being.[79] If Weber's demonstration is wrong, his action is right, yet only by the standard of a fully thought-out radical historicism. In the perspective of that standard, Weber's affirmation of the cause of science makes sense, but not as a rejection of nihilism: The standard is the standard of philosophical nihilism.[80]

Intellectual probity or honesty should lead philosophers to acknowledge the supremacy of revelation, according to Weber's account. The issue is not whether to make an intellectual sacrifice, but which one to make. Both honest philosophy and Weberian social science, when taken to their ultimate consequences, lead to such a sacrifice. The only difference, then, is between the forms of rule or guidance that result. Weber's analysis leads directly to the conclusion that every purported return to the self-confidence of ancient philosophy (or the ranking of the philosophic life as *the* good life) is merely an *entr'acte* along the path toward a closed society governed by priests, that is, toward "a hierarchical ordering of values unequivocally prescribed by ecclesiastical dogmas."[81] Against this threat, an autonomous science that cannot defend itself with arguments or reason must fall back upon power; the fundamental alternatives were really between the open and closed societies, and because the philosophic quest is indistinguishable from the prophetic or priestly quest, the open society must be defended against the closed society with all the intensity and indignation one can muster.[82]

We have already mentioned the weakness of this formulation of the ultimate conflict. Defense of the open society (as it is) means defending a constitutional framework in which vulgar nihilism is always possible and may flourish. One cannot be a Weberian with a good conscience and embrace the democracy of all preferences. One's life would cease to be tragic and lose its depth. Weber's polemic posture requires that his regime hold forth a coherent and intellectually defensible project distinguishable from the nihilist projects of Nietzsche or Heidegger.[83] When Weber's position is examined as a choice for science, however, we discover as we just did that it becomes indistinguishable from radical historicism.

According to "Weber's" final demonstration of his basic premise (an invention by Strauss), philosophy cannot remain free, nor resist the claims of revelation, if it remains bound to unassisted reason. All previous philosophy and science seem to point to the supremacy of transcendent values: Revelation is only the most consistent expression of that ranking of otherworldly values. When we examine the case for revelation, however, it proves to say nothing of otherworldly values at all. Transcendence plays no discernible part in "Weber's" demonstration. The case against human guidance is put forward as a natural and secular, "this-worldly" account of an historical struggle between theology and philosophy.[84] It is not a case for divine guidance, but a case against philosophy as heretofore conceived and for a mode of thought that can do justice to the complexities of the struggle between revelation and reason as that struggle bears upon the alternatives for social science. The struggle between theology and philosophy is only the remote

ancestor of the present struggle, just as the struggle between ecclesiastical (or closed) and modern (or open) political orders is only the
remote precursor of the present struggle. The fundamental alternatives
are between any orientation toward transcendant values (whether in the
name of philosophy or revelation), on the one hand, and thought that
turns resolutely away from transcendance toward this world as the
home of the riddle of being, on the other.[85] Consistent nihilism accepts
the defeat of philosophy in the contest with revelation, while remaining
intransigently opposed to divine guidance. It seeks guidance from this
world, while granting the entire force of the phenomenon that have
made divine revelation irresistible to man in the past. It seeks to account
for these phenomena without appeal to transcendance. The two most
decisive points in "Weber's" demonstration of the case for revelation
can both be accommodated by existentialism. First, there is the openness or yearning for a solution to the riddle of being:

> Man is so built that he can find his satisfaction, his bliss, in free investigation,
> in articulating the riddle of being. But, on the other hand, he yearns so
> much for a solution of that riddle and human knowledge is always so
> limited that the need for divine illumination cannot be denied and the
> possibilty of revelation cannot be refuted.[86]

For both Nietzsche and Heidegger, thinking nihilism through to the end
required an adequate interpretation of this human yearning and of this
hiddenness of the solution from human knowledge. The second
decisive point is the confirmation of "the thesis of faith, that there is no
possibility of consistency, of a consistent and thoroughly sincere life,
without belief in revelation."[87] That possibility of an authentic life
without appeal to revelation or transcendance is, of course, one theme
of Heidegger's *Being and Time*.[88] Thus, thinking through the case against
"philosophy" to the end can lead not to the superordination of revelation, but rather to that radical historicist presentation of the human condition and human possibilities, which replaces revelation. Insofar as
Weber's final demonstration is an attempt to defend the highest human
possibilities (or devotion to causes and ideals), it appears to be an inconsistent attempt to hold open the possibility of revelation. Here, once
more, as soon as we remove the inconsistency, we arrive not at a
defense of vulgar nihilism or of liberalism in alliance with Weberian
social science, but rather at the philosophic politics of Nietzsche and
Heidegger.[89] That is why, from every point of view, when we follow
Weber's thought step by step, we find that:

> In following this movement toward its end we shall inevitably reach a
> point beyond which the scene is darkened by Hitler. Unfortunately, it does

not go without saying that in our examination we must avoid the fallacy that in the last decade has frequently been used as a substitute for the *reductio ad absurdum*: the *reductio ad Hitlerum*. A view is not refuted by the fact that it happens to have been shared by Hitler.[90]

Weber's final demonstration points toward more basic alternatives that are unfortunately of a grim political character. Weber's resistance to nihilism is a moral matter that cannot survive a step by step disclosure of the necessary implications and consequences of the doctrine that he tried to take eclectically, or halfway. The result is awful, but it is not exactly pandemonium or a war of all against all.[91] Weber's inability to provide a coherent and rational basis for his resistance to nihilism signals the end of the regime of pragmatic toleration within the sciences, or more broadly, within the Republic of Letters. The result seems to be a rebirth of the school-wars, or of the academic and intellectual versions of what Machiavelli had called "pious cruelty"—on Weber's reading, the struggle between the proponents of Weberian social science and, say, its Nietzschean opponents, is a struggle against "the worst devil," or intellectualism.[92] Strauss's analysis indicates why the struggle to separate science from politics, which Weber conducted with such moral fervor, was lost at the level of science before it was begun. It could only be prosecuted by means of rhetoric, force, and fraud, because far too much had been conceded to Nietzsche at the outset at the level of science.[93] As between Nietzsche and Weber, the choice is between two forms of *amor fati* guiding thought, not between human and divine guidance.

A Thucydidean Weber

Strauss's critical analysis traces Weber's attempt to go to the basis of the social sciences, to take the problem of science with the utmost seriousness. But Weber's attempt seems to leave us at a depth where science degenerates into a war of weasels fighting in a hole. With Weber, social science apparently becomes so fixated with its basis as to lose all peripheral vision of the surface of social life, including the surface requirements of moderation in the governance of science. Strauss's comic demeanor returns us to these requirements. He is willing to play the fool to Weber's gravity and to return jestingly to the surface, but not because he underestimated Weber's moral stature. Weber remained a question mark for Strauss. His moral resistance to nihilism is ultimately unintelligible on the basis of the arguments Weber himself adduced. It is even doubtfully intelligible through the additional arguments that

Strauss reconstructs as Weber's amanuensis. In light of what we have seen, we may anticipate that the philosophical quest that commences at the end of Strauss's chapter on Weber would never fully satisfy Weber's needs. Weber remains as a monument and reminder of the incompleteness of *Natural Right and History*, of the inquiry's inability to respond adequately to the need of a certain kind of man. It is essential that Strauss sympathized with that need and was capable of sharing it. He does not question, or contradict, one thesis regarding the character of reality that informed Weber's work:

> When he demanded, for example, that interpretive understanding be subservient to causal explanation, he was guided by the observation that the intelligible is frequently overpowered by what is no longer intelligible or that the lower is mostly stronger than the higher.[94]

This is a thesis that Socrates, as Strauss understood Socrates, did not embrace as a guiding insight; insofar as *Natural Right and History* is guided by the intention to recover the possibility of Socratic political philosophy, the inquiry was bound not to satisfy Weber's soul or his highest aspiration. In the course of discussing a man he compared to Weber, Strauss repeated Weber's thesis and pointed to what I am tempted to call Weber's "unfulfilled vocation":

> In pondering over Riezler's highest aspiration, I had to think more than once of Thucydides—of Thucydides' quiet and manly gentleness which seeks no solace and which looks in freedom, but not in indifference, at the opposites whose unity is hidden; which does not attempt to reduce one opposite to the other; and which regards the higher of the opposites not, as Socrates did, as stronger but as more vulnerable, more delicate than the lower.[95]

Perhaps Weber could have told us reasonably why he was not a nihilist if he had understood himself through Thucydides instead of Jeremiah.[96]

Weber's Historical Perspective

Strauss's book consists of philosophical inquiries into the history of natural right. The critical analysis of Weber seems to suspend such inquiry while digressing upon its possibility; the explicit theme of the chapter on Weber is to defend the possibility of philosophy and of Strauss's subject, natural right. Natural right is a nonentity if political philosophy, in particular, is impossible.[97] There is also an implicit theme that I have highlighted in my commentary, anticipating the main alternatives that ancient political philosophy had explored: politics and philosophy as competing ways of life.[98] When we look at Weber from Thucydides forward, these rival ways stand forth, or Strauss brings us to the threshhold where they become visible. If philosophy is no longer eligible, or if it is "the inescapable condition of our historical situation," that science must no longer "partake of the contemplation of sages and philosophers about the meaning of the universe",[99] then only the alternative to the *vita contemplativa* remains, the *vita activa*. From the classical standpoint, the rich diversity of ways of life within the active life are reduced to one way, because they are variants within the political way of life.[100] Strauss, as it were, brings Weber to the threshhold of the classical formulation of the permanent alternatives. With some care, he follows Weber's arcane and roundabout rejection of philosophy, which entails a prolonged digression on method because Weber made the methodological distinction between fact and value focal.[101] I have given that focus shorter shrift while arguing that it does not lead us to the fundamental problem of the social sciences. Since Strauss wrote, of course, the dichotomy between fact and value has lost its vogue. My experience has been that indignation in defense of politics can and does impose a ceiling upon inquiry long after social scientists and political theorists have abandoned the fact-value distinction as untenable. Experience with related defenses of politics enabled Strauss to anticipate this, and he, therefore, insisted that the first step should not be a retreat from Weber's distinction—which is the main course the social sciences have taken in abandoning Weberian canons of objectivity—but an advance beyond it toward a more rigorous form of nonevaluating objectivity than Weber practiced.[102] Strauss also gave Weber his due; he recognized that the fact-value dichotomy was intended as a clarification as well as a defense of spiritness and indignation in defense of politics. Such spiritedness was the fundamental problem of the social science that Weber embodied. Hence, Weber's doctrine was at least a partial remedy against the blindness of subcritical or subscientific indignation. The dichotomy served Weber's effort to separate science from politics. It was a means of critique against ideological politics disguised as science, a means of combatting what Benda called "the betrayal of the intellectuals."[103] Weber's rejection of philosophy was integral to his defense of the *vita activa* against intellectualism. Since Weber spoke candidly of his personal hatred of intellectualism as "the worst devil," we are on firm ground in arguing that Weber personified indignation against it.[104] But if Weber personified indignation against intellectualism in defense of the practical life, the *vita activa*, or of politics, Weber also transformed that indignation by devoting himself "with almost fanatical devotion" to the clarification of the ultimate meaning of his own conduct: He made it a fundamental problem of the social sciences.[105]

One dimension of that problem was articulated in Weber's history of the intellectuals in politics, or his sociology of knowledge. It is primarily in these inquiries, and only secondarily in his methodological writings, that Weber unfolded his perspective on the crisis of liberal democracy.[106]

The first impression we get from the chapter on Weber is that Strauss's thought can be reduced to the charge that Weber was a nihilist. This powerful rhetorical first impression has led most readers to dismiss Strauss's further inquiry or to content themselves with the illusion that Strauss was merely a true believer in natural law, perhaps even a Jeffersonian fundamentalist of some kind.[107] The charge is one that is bound to awaken indignation in defense of Weber or against him, indignation that was almost certain to impose a ceiling beyond which many readers would never ascend. This is to say that Strauss's critique of Weber was bound to obscure his own perspective on the crisis of liberal democracy and to postpone the day when most readers would have to reckon with Strauss's own perspective. As I have tried to demonstrate, Strauss interposed an argument for a higher nonevaluating objectivity. The centerpiece of that argument, and the chief instance of the fallacy of unexamined originals in Weber's scholarship, was Weber's *Protestant Ethic*. Strauss's critique of that work clears the path toward Strauss's thoughts on the crisis of liberal democracy by suggesting that Weber looked in the wrong place to understand the origins of the liberal commercial republic. The alternative to Calvin's rationalization of theology, which Weber never adequately scrutinized, was liberal political economy.[108] In later chapters of *Natural Right and History*, Strauss sought to demonstrate (without explicitly mentioning Weber) that Weber failed to come to terms with the prudence of John Locke. On Strauss's showing, Locke's prudence is coextensive with and inseparable from his philosophizing in public, that is, with the entirety of his published writing. Locke's *Essay* is integral to his political philosophy, and not merely because it was a highly politic work.[109] *Natural Right and History* is necessarily a study in prudence because classical natural right was exercise of prudence, and modern natural right was championed by a man of superior prudence; the most influential and effectual (or consequential) prudence in the purview of *Natural Right and History* was not the prudence of Edmund Burke but that of John Locke.[110]

John Gunnell is probably right to contend that any survey of Strauss's remarks on liberal democracy that abstracts from Strauss's studies of the philosophic founders of modern liberal politics is bound to leave the

topic somewhat in the dark.[111] The question I would raise for consideration is why Strauss constructed his books to frustrate that abstraction.
One cannot speak as Gunnell does without qualification of an "intellectualist" premise, because the explicit purpose of *Natural Right and
History* is to attain critical distance upon that category or distinction.[112]
Strauss shows why Locke was not an "intellectual" as Weber and Gunnell understand that term.[113] The claim Strauss advances is that Locke's
far-reaching practical influence was the intended effect of his foresight,
or that in Locke's case the most important consequences of his activity
do not stand in a paradoxical relation to his original intentions. Strauss
proceeded circumspectly on the view that liberal democracy in its present crisis might not be adequately understood unless one could encom-
pass Locke's accomplishments. But by Strauss's account these were acts
of superior prudence, and to understand superior prudence at all one
must rise at least for a time to the height from which superior prudence
sees.[114]

Toward the end of his critique of Burke, Strauss proposed that

> "doctrinairism" and "existentialism" appear to us as the two faulty ex-
> tremes. While being opposed to each other, they agree with each other in
> ignoring prudence, "the god of this lower world."[115]

Natural Right and History is as reserved as the ancient classics Strauss
held up for emulation. In it his perspective on the crisis of liberal
democracy is withheld while we remain animated by indignation in
defense of politics. Strauss goes out of his way to disclose that we are so
animated by provoking precisely that indignation. And his perspective
is peculiarly conditional in coming to light only when we have decided
no longer to ignore prudence, especially not to ignore the full scope of
John Locke's prudence.

Notes

1. Leo Strauss, *What is Political Philosophy? and Other Studies* (New York: Free
Press, 1959), 12.

2. The chapter entitled "Natural Right and the Distinction Between Facts and
Values" first appeared in Leo Strauss, "The Social Science of Max Weber,"
Measure: A Critical Journal, vol. 2, no. 2 (Spring 1951), 204–30. The version in
Natural Right and History (hereafter cited as *NRH*) differs in including footnotes,
well over a third of which are to Weber's *Wirtschaft und Gesellschaft: Grundriss der
verstehenden Soziologie*. The other differences are that paragraphs one, two, four
and the final paragraph, appear only in the book version; paragraph four is the
link to Strauss's preceding discussion of historicism (*NRH*, 9–34). According to

Richard Kennington, the critique of Weber was first presented as a lecture at the New School for Social Research. See Robert Eden, "Bad Conscience for a Nietzschean Age: Weber's Calling for Science," *The Review of Politics* 45 (July 1983): 366ff.

3. The only exception, to my knowledge, is Stephen P. Turner and Regis A. Factor, *Max Weber and the Dispute Over Reason and Values: A Study in Philosophy, Ethics, and Politics* (London: Kegan Paul, 1984), 208–13.

4. It is a measure of the authority of this received opinion that Roth and Bendix could class Strauss's essay among "political critiques of Weber" as late as 1971. See Reinhard Bendix and Guenther Roth, *Scholarship and Partisanship: Essays on Max Weber* (Berkeley: University of California Press, 1971), 62–64.

5. Plato, *Apology of Socrates*, 41a1–c4. Compare "The Journey to Hades," *Human, All-too-Human*, II, 408, in Friedrich Nietzsche, *On the Genealogy of Morals and Ecce Homo*, trans. Walter Kaufmann and R.J. Hollingdale (New York: Vintage Books, 1967), 179.

6. On Weber's view of the crisis, see Robert Eden, "Doing Without Liberalism: Weber's Regime Politics," *Political Theory*. 10 (August 1982): 379–407, and *Political Leadership and Nihilism: A Study of Weber and Nietzsche* (Gainsville: University of South Florida Press, 1984).

7. Consent and not merely consensus is at stake in the crisis. That dispirited liberalism is consequently beset on all sides, even the inside, by spiritedness, is brought out in Harvey C. Mansfield, Jr., *The Spirit of Liberalism* (Cambridge, Mass.: Harvard University Press, 1978).

8. A Weberian Marx or Marxian Weber is adumbrated in Bryan S. Turner, *For Weber: Essays in the Sociology of Fate* (London: Kegan Paul, 1981).

9. For a valiant attempt to escape this contradiction and resolve the crisis, see Guenther Roth and Wolfgang Schluchter, *Max Weber's Vision of History: Ethics and Method* (Berkeley: University of California Press, 1979), 65–118.

10. See Hans H. Gerth and C. W. Mills, *From Max Weber: Essays in Sociology* (New York: Oxford University Press, 1958), 152.

11. Weber's influence was disseminated in two different versions. The softened version was propagated by Arnold Brecht, who made the fact/value distinction more moderate and mushier. See Allan Nelson, "'Science' and 'Values': Arnold Brecht's *Political Theory* Revisited," *The Political Science Reviewer* 10 (1980): 139–88. The hard-edged version was Karl Popper's, which declared war on the enemies of incremental social engineering through social science as opponents of an open society. See Karl R. Popper, *The Open Society and its Enemies*, 2 vols. (New York: Harper & Row, 1962).

12. Max Weber, *The Methodology of the Social Sciences*, ed., Edward Shils and Henry Finch (New York: Free Press, 1949), 19.

13. See Turner and Factor, *Max Weber and the Dispute over Reason and Values* 180–233.

14. Compare *NRH*, 67, 74, 76.

15. *NRH*, 60–61 n. 22.

16. Compare *NRH* 249–51 with 165–66. *NRH* identifies Hobbism as the core of Lockean liberalism and radically strips away the natural law garments in which Locke cloaked his Hobbism.

17. Weber's failure to do justice to the principles on which liberal institutions are based is discussed in detail in Eden, "Doing Without Liberalism: Weber's Regime Politics," *Political Theory* 10 (August 1982): 379–407, and Eden, *Political Leadership and Nihilism: A Study of Weber and Nietzsche* (Gainesville: University of South Florida Press, 1984).

18. *NRH*, 36.

19. See note 67, below. On the connection between Strauss's careful use of the term *idea* and his use of the term *problem*, consider Kennington's observation that in *NRH*, "The term 'idea' is normally used in the chapter where it becomes problematic. . . .And 'the idea of science,' which is expounded at length in connection with Hobbes in chapter 5, where it is absent, occurs only in the chapter devoted to Max Weber." Richard Kennington, "Strauss's Natural Right and History," *Review of Metaphysics* 35 (September 1981): 68. Kennington's observation would suggest that "the basic problem of the social sciences," in its connection to the modern idea of science, is articulated more fully in the Hobbes chapter. Consider *NRH*, p. 8, "The fundamental dilemma, in whose grip we are, is caused by the victory of modern natural science." For Strauss's use of the terms *basic* and *basic problems* see *NRH*, 39, 60 n., and 64. "Fundamental" alternatives and problems are discussed on pages 35, 36, 74 and 78.

20. *NRH*, 38.

21. *NRH*, 39.

22. *NRH*, 9–34, 35–36, 53–54, 61–62, 67, 71, 73, 77–78.

23. *NRH*, 35–36.

24. For reasoning to support this formulation see Eden, *Political Leadership and Nihilism*, 1–2, 6–8, 37–38, 42, 74, 99, 134–35, 208–10, 211–23.

25. *NRH*, 35–36. See Eden, "Bad Conscience for a Nietzschean Age: Weber's Calling for Science," *The Review of Politics* 45 (July 1985): 389–92.

26. *NRH*, 42.

27. Max Weber, *The Protestant Ethic and the Spirit of Capitalism*, trans. Talcott Parsons (New York: Scribners, 1958), 27, 98–128.

28. *NRH*, 62.

29. *From Max Weber: Essays in Sociology*, trans. Hans H. Gerth and C. W. Mills (New York: Oxford University Press, 1958), 117. Surely the most important case of the fallacy of unexamined originals is Weber's failure to justify his account of the origins of modern science by an investigation of Bacon, Hobbes, Descartes, or Spinoza. See Eden, *Political Leadership and Nihilism*, pp. 157–66, and Eden, "Weber's Historical Perspective," *Review of Politics* 46 (January 1984): 142–45.

30. *NRH*, 49.

31. *NRH*, 63, 65–66, 70, 74, 75–76.

32. *NRH*, 49.

33. For an argument along these lines see Sheldon S. Wolin, "Max Weber: Legitimation, Method, and the Politics of theory, *Political Theory* 9 (August 1981): 401–24, in combination with his "Political Theory as a Vocation," cited above. See also Leo Strauss, "An Epilogue," in his *Liberalism Ancient and Modern* (New York: Basic Books, 1968), 203–23.

34. Weber speaks of the doctrine's "magnificent consistency" as the "logical conclusion" of the elimination of magic from the world of religion, *The Protestant Ethic*, 104, 105.

35. His awareness of the problem is most evident in the essay on ethical neutrality, Max Weber, *The Methodology of the Social Sciences*, ed. Edward Shils and Henry Finch (New York: Free Press, 1949), 1–47. Routinization or vulgarization was in a sense the whole point of Weber's original statement on objectivity, in the *Methodology*, pages 49–112, which was intended to set the course for a scholarly journal. Nevertheless, Weber's own empirical studies did not treat the problem of the routinization of comparable doctrines in philosophy or science: No sociology of science or philosophy emerged or could emerge on the basis of Weber's work. See note 66 and Strauss's remarks on the absence of a sociology of philosophy in contemporary social science, Leo Strauss, *Persecution and the Art of Writing* (New York: Free Press, 1952), 7–8.

36. For some reason, Weber's tripartite formulation is reduced by Strauss to these two alternatives, in apparent disregard of Weber's preoccupation with new prophets or a rebirth of prophecy in its untrammeled, original, revolutionary form. In accordance with this, Strauss compresses Weber's triad of the three types of legitimacy, treating charismatic legitimacy as an afterthought. Furthermore, in *NRH* Strauss almost entirely ignores Weber's study of ancient Judaism, which is cited only once (p. 59 n. 21) and slightingly. We must therefore be stunned when the most fundamental alternative *for Weber* turns out to be between philosophic and prophetic guidance or between reason and revelation. (*NRH*, 42, 49, 57–58, 69–70, 73–74, 74–76.) I am inclined to say that Strauss distances Weber from Jerusalem and Jeremiah in order to draw him toward Athens and Thucydides.

37. See the essay by Thomas Pangle in the present volume, and Eden, *Political Leadership and Nihilism*, 43–44, 53–54, 63–68, 103–33.

38. *NRH*, 5.

39. See Eden, *Political Leadership and Nihilism*, 99–103, 144–48, 189–94, and esp. 68–71.

40. See Martin Heidegger, *Nietzsche*, vol. 1, pt. 3 (Pfullingen: Neske Verlag, 1961), "The Will to Power as Knowledge," 473–658. On the epigram-page of this volume, Heidegger says, "Nietzsche himself names the experience which determines his thought: 'Life . . . more full of secrets—from that day forward, when the great liberator came over me, that thought, that life should be an experiment of the knower.'"

41. *NRH*, 42.

42. Gerth and Mills, trans., *From Max Weber*, 125.

43. Consider Strauss's analysis of how Calvin eludes Spinoza's critical attack, in *Spinoza's Critique of Religion*, trans. E. M. Sinclair (New York: Schocken Books, 1965).

44. For examples of this difference see Mansfield. *the Spirit of Liberalism*.

45. See Turner and Factor, op. cit.

46. See Guenther Roth and Wolfgang Schluchter, *Max Weber's Vision of History: Ethics and Method* (Berkeley: University of California Press, 1979), 65–112, and Eden, "Weber's Historical Perspective," *Review of Politics* 46 (January 1984): 142–45.

47. See Mark Blitz, "Radical Historicism and the Meaning of Natural Right," *Modern Age* (Spring 1984), 245–46.

48. Strauss discusses the thesis of historicism, that no thinker can transcend the horizon of his age or that all thought is essentially historical, then turns this mode of critique against Weber. Compare *NRH*, pages 9–34, with pages 57, 64–65, 77, 78. Strauss also makes clear that his criticism of the historical school and its characteristic presumptions applies to Weber, page 62. He also follows Nietzsche's lead in seeking the moral concern at the core of Weber's thought: compare Friedrich Nietzsche, *Beyond Good and Evil: Prelude to the Philosophy of the Future*, trans. Walter Kaufmann (New York: Vintage Books, 1966), aphorism 6, with *NRH*, page 64. We should wonder, as John Gunnell has suggested, whenever Strauss does this: "It is indeed strange that Strauss's account . . . seems to reflect the very historicism he so vehemently repudiates." John C. Gunnell, "The Myth of the Tradition," *The American Political Science Review* 72 (March 1978): 133.

49. The opening discussion of Weber's relation to historicism, (*NRH*, 36–39), raises the question as to whether Strauss's study is exclusively concerned with Weber's doctrine of values or with his historicism: "It is the recognition of timeless values that distinguishes Weber's position most significantly from historicism. *Not so much historicism* as a peculiar notion of timeless values is the basis of his rejection of natural right" (p. 39). But that doctrine of irreconcilably opposed timeless values that cannot be ranked, or respect no hierarchy, proves upon closer inspection to be "peculiar" in the sense that it is inseparable from an unexplained moral preference: it is Weber's idiosyncrasy, his ipsissimity (*NRH*, 48, 52, 65). Moreover, the key themes of radical historicist thought, especially the notion that there is an essential connection between thought and fate, play a lively role in Weber's thought as Strauss expounds it (cp. 44,48, 73,74). Strauss's study seems to imitate the intellectual motion he anticipated, a progressive estrangement of contemporary social science from its original positivism toward an increasing awareness that only a more radical form of historicism can provide it with an adequate or intellectually satisfying "basis."

50. *NRH*, 38.

51. *NRH*, 49–79. Bear in mind Kennington's observations, in note 19 above.

52. *NRH*, 74,76ff.

53. *NRH*, 76ff. Compare Leo Strauss, *Thoughts on Machiavelli* (Seattle: University of Washington Press, 1958), 62–63, 74, 80, 91).

54. *NRH*, 49. Is "barren truths which generate no conclusion" a quotation that has a source? Compare Leo Strauss, *Socrates and Aristophanes* (New York: Basic Books, 1966), 14–15.

55. Plato, *Republic*, 336b–354c, 358b–d.

56. Ibid., 358b–d.

57. *Republic*, 360a–b. Similarly, Weber "tried to remain faithful to the cause of autonomous insight" (*NRH*, 76): Weber seems bound to conceive the idea of science in terms of devotion to a cause, finding and obeying the demon who holds the fibres of one's very life (Gerth and Mills, trans., *From Max Weber*, 156). Compare Nietzsche, *The Gay Science. With a Prelude in Rhymes and an Appendix of Songs*, trans. and with a commentary by Walter Kaufman (New York: Vintage Books, 1974), aphorism 1.

58. Compare Leo Strauss, *The City and Man* (Chicago: Rand McNally, 1964), 105, bottom.

59. See Strauss, *Thoughts on Machiavelli* (Seattle: University of Washington Press, 1958), 292.

60. *NRH*, 77–80, 172–79. See Gerth and Mills, trans., *From Max Weber*, 78,139, 155. Weber's most dramatic statement of what the prescientific or natural world looked like is also almost unique, in his writings, in making the attempt. It is marvelous, but violates all his methodological canons, and it does justice only to the tragic vision of that world without accounting for Aristophanes' comic vision (see ibid., 148). Weber's accounts in *Economy and Society*, of the magical world of primitive man, are curiously Baconian. The basic language of primitive man appears to be the language of power, rather than the language of custom or ancestral practice. See Max Weber, *Economy and Society*, vol. 2, ed. Guenther Roth and Claus Wittich (New York: Bedminster, 1968), 399–403.

61. Gerth and Mills, trans., *From Max Weber*, 148,151–52.

62. Compare the curious praise and criticism at *NRH*, page 76: All intelligent readers of Weber's writing on method have felt that is it philosophic; Strauss can supply an articulation of that feeling, but to do so he must go away from "what he himself thought about his methodology."

63. Gerth and Mills, trans., *From Max Weber*, 141.

64. Strauss, *The City and Man*, 137.

65. See Eden, "Bad Conscience for a Nietzschean Age," 391–92.

66. Gerth and Mills, trans., *From Max Weber*, 152. Strauss does not mention Weber's animus toward intellectualism or connect it to his animus toward philosophy. He does note that Weber systematically conflated intellectuals with philosophers (*NHR*, 58) and somewhat earlier that "the politicization of philosophy consists precisely in this, that the difference between intellectuals

and philosophers—a difference formerly known as the difference between gentlemen and philosophers on the one hand and the difference between sophists or rhetoricians and philosophers on the other—becomes blurred and finally disappears" (p.34). See note 33 above.

67. NRH, 39,40,41,43,50,51,62,70,71-72,74. compare the occurrences of "fundamental" in the previous chapter, pages 11,12,19,23,27,29,31.

68. NRH, 76.

69. NRH, 64.

70. NRH, 66.

71. NRH, 74.

72. NRH, 75-76.

73. Kennington, Strauss's Natural Right and History," 70.

74. NRH, 74.

75. Kennington, "Strauss's Natural Right and History," 69.

76. NRH, 74.

77. Gerth and Mills, trans., From Max Weber, 152.

78. NRH, 21,27.

79. Consider NRH, 21,25,26,27,28,29.

80. It should be emphasized that Strauss has supplied the final argument for Weber. Earlier he had turned away from the suggestion that Weber's true thought was a Nietzschean thought elevating the imperative "become what you are," the doctrine of amor fati (NRH, 48). Later in the argument it becomes evident that Weber's moral resistance to the nihilistic implicatoins of this thought kept Weber from embracing it. How does Weber then differ from Locke, whose influential doctrine was influential because it was evidently more moral or more consistent with decency than the Hobbesian core of his thought? See below, "Weber's Historical Perspective," pp. 230-233.

81. The Methodology of the Social Sciences, 19.

82. Ibid.; Gerth and Mills, trans., From Max Weber, 152,156, 127-28.

83. For an attempt to describe Weber's defense of science and democratic politics against Nietzsche's philosophic politics see Eden, Political Leadership and Nihilism, 134-210.

84. NRH, 75: "The secular struggle between philosophy and theology." When Strauss says "This state of things would appear to be but natural," it may recall his previous "bird's eye view" on page 22, preceded by the first statement about what is natural to man that Strauss makes in NRH: "But dogmatism . . . is so natural to man that it is not likely to be a preserve of the past" (p.22).

85. See Strauss's "Preface to the English Translation," Spinoza's Critique of Religion, trans. E. M. Sinclair (New York: Schocken Books, 1965), 9-12.

86. *NRH*, 75.

87. Ibid.

88. Mark Blitz, *Heidegger's "Being and Time" and the Possibility of Political Philosophy* (Ithaca: Cornell University Press, 1981), 111ff.

89. See Eden, *Political Leadership and Nihilism*, 227–44.

90. *NRH*, 43.

91. *NRH*, 45.

92. See Eden, "Bad Conscience for a Nietzschean Age," and Richard Rorty, "Philosophy in America Today," *The American Scholar*, vol 51, no.2 (Spring 1982), 200.

93. Compare *NRH*, page 76, with Friedrich Nietzsche, *On the Genealogy of Morals and Ecce Homo*, trans. Walter Kaufmann and R.J. Hollingdale (New York: Vintage Books, 1967), essay III, nos. 24–27, 148–61.

94. *NRH*, 77.

95. Strauss, *What is Political Philosophy?*, 260.

96. Compare Marianne Weber, *Max Weber: A Biography*, trans. Harry Zohn (New York: John Wiley & Sons, 1975), 593–94. Weber's own attempt to take his distance toward Jeremiah is Max Weber, *Ancient Judaism*, ed. and trans. Hans H. Gerth and Don Martindale (New York: Free Pres, 1952), 267–334.
The tension to which I have referred, between Socrates and Thucydides, is a theme to which Strauss returned in *The City and Man*, especially in beginning and ending the chapter on Thucydides. I cannot enter in any detail here into the difficulties of Strauss's treatment of that tension. The first problem is to identify where the chapter on Thucydides begins. My hunch is that it is set in motion when we recognize the utter inadequacy of the last lines of Strauss's chapter on Plato, when measured by the problem mentioned in the body of the paragraph preceding these lines (pp. 137–38).

One index of the seriousness of the obstacles that stood between Weber and a fresh, untrammeled reading of Thucydides is the location of Strauss's fullest study of Thucydides. It stands at the end of his most comprehensive exposition of classical political philosophy. The problem of working back to Thucydides is thus broached by Strauss's less comprehensive exposition, which begins where Weber, and Strauss's chapter on Weber, left off (*NRH*, 76–80).

Thucydides is one of six illustrations of the "fallacy of unexamined originals" discussed by Strauss (*NRH*, 58). The error Weber repeats was authorized by no less a philologist than Nietzsche himself (see *Human, All-too-Human*, vol. 1, no. 92). One may say that Thucydides was claimed by the Historical School as the originator of scientific history and by Nietzsche as the precursor of his own tragic vision. The difficulty of working back to Thucydides was therefore inseparable from the difficulty of swimming against the tidal current of radical historicism, the difficulty Strauss tries to begin working through in *NRH*. Strauss unobtrusively announces that understanding natural right in its ancient and modern forms might be necessary to recover the Thucydidean meaning of history, by the title of the first chapter, "Natural Right and the Historical Approach[7]' (compare *NRH*, 34).

The bearing of Strauss's description of Riezler for Weber may require slight amplification.

The initial opposites in question are obviously war and peace. Strauss has shown in his critical analysis of Weber that he did not hold a steady gaze embracing these opposites; he treated peace as phoney and war as real (*NRH*, 64–65), then elevated the duty toward universal peace to the level of an ultimate cause (*NRH*, 65). Strauss recalls this account in his essay on Riezler when he compares Riezler and Weber (*What is Political Philosophy?*, 239–40). Weber's failure to understand the perspective of the city at peace, or to comprehend the perspective of peace as a coherent political perspective—his compulsion to dismiss the horizon of peace in favor of a horizon of conflict or war—needs to be compared with Thucydides's success. According to Strauss, Thucydides's accomplishment as an historian lay in preserving both the perspective of the city at peace and the perspective of war, while enabling the reader to recapitulate Thucydides's own conversion from the horizon of peace to the perspective of war (*The City and Man*, 230).

As Strauss's most sustained inquiry into *physis*, his chapter on Thucydides constitutes his most sustained reply to Heidegger and thus his own most reasonable account of why Strauss was not a nihilist.

97. *NRH*, 35–36. See note 19.

98. Compare the account of the two ways of life in Leo Strauss, *On Tyranny* (Ithaca: Cornell University Press, 1969), 80–94.

99. Gerth and Mills, trans., *From Max Weber*, 152.

100. This is not to say that ancient political philosophy ignored the diversity of souls or of human types; Strauss remarked that "A stupendous contraction of the horizon appears to Machiavelli and his successors as a wondrous enlargement of the horizon," (Leo Strauss, *Thoughts on Machiavelli*, 295). Obviously, a Burkean state pursuing the greatest variety of ends and concerned with individuality will promote an impressive diversity (*NRH*, 322). It does so, however, by making lives increasingly interdependent, socialized and interwoven with politics, and by reducing the scope of rule. The place of great political ambition or of the natural political man, and of the solitary philosophic life, become precarious. See Strauss's deepening of Tocqueville's theme of tyranny over the spirit rather than over the body, in *On Tyranny*, pages 27,201–2,211–20.

101. *NRH*, 36,38–42,46–48,50–57,59–62,64–65,76–78.

102. Strauss's review of Schmitt's defense of the political (against liberalism) was originally written for the *Archiv fur Sozialwissenschaft und Sozialpolitik* in 1932; see Leo Strauss, "Comments on Carl Schmitt's *Der Begriff des Politischen*," *Spinoza's Critique of Religion*, trans. E.M. Sinclair (New York: Schocken Books, 1965), 331–53. Consider also Eden, "Bad Conscience for a Nietzschean Age, 391–92.

103. *NRH*, 34.

104.   Gerth and Mills, trans., *From Max Weber*, 152.

105.   See *NRH*, 36.

106.   See note 6. Weber's most famous statement of his perspective, the lectures on science as a vocation and politics as a vocation, were condensations of the perspective secured through his empirical studies, especially *The Economic Ethics of the World Religions*. See Gerth and Mills, trans. *From Max Weber*, 77–156,172,176, 267–301,323–24,327–30,333–40,350–59.

107.   See Roth's account under the rubric, "Political Critiques of Max Weber," *Scholarship and Partisanship: Essays on Max Weber*, ed. Reinhard Bendix and Guenther Roth (Berkeley: University of California Press, 1971), 62–64.

108.   *NRH*, 60–62 n.22.

109.   *NRH*, 202 n. 46, 203 n. 48, 204 n. 49, 204 n. 50,206–7. See also Richard Kennington, "Nature and Natural Right in Locke" (Paper prepared for delivery at the colloquium on John Locke, Department of Government, Harvard University, 15–16 March 1985).

110.   *NRH*, pp.7,133–4,135–7,141–42,147,152–53,159–63,165–66,206–7.

111.   See Gunnell's essay in this volume.

112.   *NRH*, 34, and see note 66.

113.   *NRH*, 34,58,202–3, and note 110.

114.   *NRH*, 202–3. Compare Eden, *Political Leadership and Nihilism*, 58.

115.   *NRH*, 321.

Part 3

LIBERALISM AND THE AMERICAN EXPERIENCE

First Section

PRIVATE INTEREST AND PUBLIC CHOICE

Stephen G. Salkever

THE CRISIS OF LIBERAL DEMOCRACY: LIBERALITY AND DEMOCRATIC CITIZENSHIP

Introduction: Liberal Democracy as Incoherent Theory

What if there is no crisis of liberal democracy? But the question hardly seems discussable; to pose it is almost to identify oneself as irretrievably *infra dig*, or at any rate wholly ignorant of the deepest insights of modern political analysis. For well over a hundred years the best social theorists, whatever their political orientation, have agreed that to say liberal democracy is to say crisis, that a fundamental instability or incoherence is built into this most characteristic of modern regimes. For Marx, liberal democracy represents the illusory sociality of actually isolated individuals ("monads"), a regime whose essence is inseparable from its evanescence. For Nietzsche, human life after the death of God signifies nothing less than the presence of the two most fundamental alternatives: We must either sink below the level of humanity and become Last Men or, should this plausible nightmare yield to desperate hope, transcend ourselves and become more than human. For Weber, we moderns, trapped in the iron cage of an ethic absurdly separated from its ground, must tragically resign ourselves to the increasing domination of specialists without spirit or look forward, with mixed feelings, toward the triumph of some new and mindless religious awakening.

This assessment of liberal democracy as a mixture of fundamentally incoherent and hence unstable principles is not limited to the nineteenth century critics of liberalism (or their twentieth century heirs, like Habermas and MacIntyre). Reflection on the first great justifications of this regime, such as those of Hobbes and Locke, suggests that they, too, thought that there was a fundamental paradox at the heart of liberal democracy, a paradox deriving from the meaning of the terms such a regime seeks to harmonize.

Democracy is understood in these works as meaning simply rule by the people, or rule by a majority of naturally equal individuals, without any

245

further consideration of the personality characteristics or ways of life or virtues that might distinguish such individuals from others. Democracy, then, is simply popular rule. But how does the adjective *liberal* qualify that rule? For Hobbes and Locke, the answer is clear: Liberal democratic rule is rule that is both popular and directed toward the protection of individual rights or liberties. But given this understanding of the key terms, liberal theorists are confronted with a puzzle concerning both reason and motive: Why should a majority—for what reasons—consider the protection of private rights to be the chief political goal? And what can motivate a popular majority to place such a goal (or any public good) first when it conflicts with other interests? In this way the theorists of liberal democracy, from Hobbes through Rawls and Nozick, have conceived a crisis of political obligation as the central element of the problem of liberal democracy: For what reasons and for what motives will any given aggregate of free individuals agree to accept a political agenda that may conflict with the preferences even of a majority of their number?

This theme of the radical incoherence of liberal democracy persists and flourishes in our own time. Formal or positive political theorists articulate their conception of the central problem of democracy in terms of the various paradoxes of voting, devices designed to capture the absurdity of democratic political action or political choice. Politics is conceived as a sort of Prisoner's Dilemma game, a form of interaction pointing to the conclusion that the most reasonable political choice is that of the free rider, the person who attempts to secure the benefits of political cooperation without paying any of its costs, a strategy whose eventual (though not short-run) futility is illustrated by the Tragedy of the Commons. More empirically oriented social scientists, concerned with motives rather than reasons, very frequently perceive a similar dilemma at the heart of American political life. Lester Thurow's *Zero-Sum Society* diagnoses our relative failure to solve economic problems as a consequence of our incapacity to be concerned with public goods, rather than of any possible injustice or lack of economic intelligence.[1] Lasch's *Culture of Narcissim* attempts to expose a similar incapacity and explains it in terms of the psychoanalytic picture of a nation of self-absorbed, short-sighted, and thoroughly dissociated individuals.[2] Janowitz's *The Last Half-Century* more temperately reaches a similar conclusion, identifying the central tendency of American and Western European democracies as the progressive erosion of all mechanisms of social control.[3] In different modes and melodies, these and other writers lend voice to the pervasive sense that to understand our regime is to see the way in which the conditions of modern political life self-destructively undermine the possibility of any effective social order.

The way in which the first great theorists sought to solve the paradox of liberal democracy was to derive a political obligation from undifferentiated self-interest through the imagery of the state of nature and the social contract. Hobbes labored to show that only an extreme failure of natural reason could prevent a person from grasping the evident rationality of yielding one's power of private judgment in political matters. Tellingly appropriating, as it were, religious language, and with palpable irony, he asserts that only "[t]he fool hath said in his heart, there is no such thing as justice; and sometimes also with his tongue."[4] And yet, as his work indicates, it is by no means foolish to wonder how the more extreme demands of democratic citizenship, like military service, can be seen as a rational means to the end of personal survival.

Clearly some more powerful motive than enlightened self-interest is required to cause (in the sense of motivation or efficient cause) citizens to take risks and forswear crimes for the sake of the public good. Hobbes and Locke were surely aware of this problem (as was Hume; it is what he means by saying that *ought* cannot be derived from *is*), and it is in this way, among others, that their work is so much more interesting than that of later democratic theorists. "The sciences," Hobbes says, "are small power; because not eminent. . . . For science is of that nature, as none can understand it to be, but such as in good measure have attained it."[5]

Hobbes was not so foolish as to be a blind optimist about the efficacy of political enlightenment; in his role as universal legislator he, no less than Rousseau's figure, is compelled to place his teachings in the mouth of the biblical God, in hopes that the rules of reason will become binding natural laws. Locke, too, insists upon the need for a civil religion of sorts, even while (in the *Letter Concerning Toleration*) denying its legitimacy. And yet these appeals to a religious motive have a hollow ring. The god of Hobbes and Locke is little more than a big stick or great enforcer in the sky, called in at need to buttress the shaky foundation of civil authority (like Rousseau's "Poul-Serrho" in *Emile*, Book 4); religion here is a patchy remedy rather than part of a plausibly attractive way of life. I think it is not unfair to say that these gestures toward divinity call attention to a perceived crisis of liberal democracy rather than propose means of alleviating it.

A similar difficulty attends the other great attempt to overcome the tension between liberty and democratic equality, that of asserting an essential connection between democratic politics and a particular sort of personality.[6] For Hobbes, those people who love ease and fear wounds will be inclined to obey a common power, but not so for those "needy men, and hardy" and all those "ambitious of military command," who would rather take the risks of internal war, since "there is no honour military but by war; nor any such hope to mend an ill game, as by causing a new shuffle."[7] Locke is even more distinct in specifying the character of those who can be good citizens: "And the commonwealth, which embraces indifferently all men that are honest, peaceable, and industrious."[8] But why should the commonwealth embrace these and not the pious, charitable, and merciful, or the bold and patriotic, for example? If liberal democracy is simply popular rule for the sake of securing particular interests, then how can some ways of conceiving and pursuing those interests be granted special status, especially given the evident diversity of interests? As is the case with the appeal to civil religion, the preference for some ways of life rather than others seems forced, externally imposed. It is in fact a symptom rather than a cure for the theoretical "crisis" of liberal democracy, since as a response to the problem it violates the definitions of the terms through which the problem is set: democracy as the sovereignty of *any given* people and liberty as the interest of *any given* individual.

Once this way of conceptualizing liberal democracy as inherently problematic has been accepted, it is but a short step to the empirical claim that modern political life is characterized by a crisis of public motive, a crisis of authority. It is as if our tradition of social science were saying that since no rational justification for identifying private interest with public need is possible, no structures of public authority can in fact exist, or if they do exist, their presence can be accounted for by "mere" custom and may therefore be treated as accidental and ephemeral: Once the old saint in the forest has heard that God is dead, his dancing too must cease. It thus becomes second nature for us, as theoretical interpreters of political life, to see alienated, privatized, lonely crowds wherever we look (and not, say, injustice).[9] I am suggesting that it is precisely because our categories of analysis generate the conclusion that reconciling private and public interest is, in Rousseau's words, like attempting to square the circle that we are inclined to see modern public life as radically incoherent and to overlook those patterns and events that run counter to our theoretical expectations.

But what of Leo Strauss? Isn't it the case that a central part of his political philosophy is the disclosure of the essential and critical weakness of liberalism or liberal individualism? I think that it is not and that the greatest care must be taken to distinguish between the Straussian understanding of liberalism from that of those philosophical movements he called historicism and radical historicism; it was the popularization of these doctrines, and not liberalism, that seemed to him to embody the deepest threats to the possibility of decent political life in our times. This interpretation of Strauss is not obvious, and it is beyond the scope of this essay to argue for it. I can here only express my agreement with Nathan Tarcov, who argues as follows concerning Strauss' account of the crisis of liberal democracy: "Not modern liberalism but loss of confidence in it constitutes the crisis. . . . Strauss's purpose is not to undercut liberalism practically but to find a theoretical solution to the problem posed by its having already been undercut. The opposite impression may underlie much of the political hostility to his work."[10] For Strauss, the crisis of liberalism is not a crisis *in* liberalism; that is, it is not a crisis essential to or inherent in the liberal regime, not a paradox from which we can be redeemed only by the proletariat (Marx) or by a god (Nietzsche, Heidegger). Liberalism is the name of that *Weltanschauung* through which a society "tolerates indefinitely many *Weltanschauugen*" and so allows them to come into being as ways of life.[11] As such, it is a very valuable thing, even though not the most valuable (since it is necessary though not sufficient for the very best sorts of lives). This makes liberal democracy very difficult to talk about, especially for those whose rhetorical equipment is limited to terms of unmitigated praise or damnation. As Frost says of the oven bird, "The question that he frames in all but words/Is what to make of a diminished thing."[12] The problem of liberal democracy for us is, then, both theoretical and rhetorical and may be stated thus: How to find a theoretical vocabulary that accurately reflects the spirit of liberal democracy, that allows us to speak with tolerable precision of its specific possibilities and limits, and that at the same time can provide the ground for resisting the practically universal inclination of theorists to dismiss utterly the attractiveness of our form of government?

My proposal is that "the crisis of liberal democracy" may be more of an iatrogenic disease than is often supposed. Admittedly, this is an empirical question. But one may at least hypothesize that "crisis" analysis is as premature as it is pessimistic. It must at least be granted that individual liberties are protected by liberal democracies to a far greater degree than in any other regime.[13] It would also be hard to ignore the difference in the degrees of difficulty that confront liberalism as a practical matter, as opposed to theoretic. Harvey Mansfield's conclusion is apt, "In our day liberals and liberal causes have prospered, but liberalism is in trouble."[14] We may also notice that forms of social order indeed persist—in families, churches, universities, firms, unions, political parties, and so on—but that their significance may be overlooked because their foundation is understood as irrational and hence unstable. As Richard Flacks notes, "Appeals to Americans to shake off their apparent moral indifference and critiques of American moral callousness often miss the point that to be concerned about 'humanity' may be thought of as contradicting one's felt moral obligations to those whom one actually knows, loves, and must care for."[15]

Perhaps, then, the "crisis" is not the appropriate diagnosis of contemporary liberal democracy. If our only political problem is of the sort represented by Prisoner's Dilemma games or the Tragedy of the Commons, then the word "crisis" seems a theorist's overstatement—a pleasant and diverting paradox derived from an abstract conceptual world in which customary attachments and prerational commitments don't count. But to say this is not to propose an end to analysis, a blithe endorsement of things as they are. Rather, it is to suggest that we try to articulate a more appropriate basis for critically (or teleologically) understanding modern liberal democracy in terms of its inherent possibilities and purposes. In the rest of this essay, I will attempt to develop such an alternative conception of liberal democracy, one drawn not from the early modern liberal theorists or from their nineteenth and twentieth century critics, but from the thought of less abstract social scientists: Aristotle, Tocqueville, and the authors of the *Federalist Papers*. The central points of this conception are that democracy is to be understood not as popular rule simply, but as rule by people who are primarily concerned with income and security and that such rule can be called liberal not when it aims at protecting individual rights, but when the members of the ruling people are marked by the characteristic virtues of liberality or generosity or moderation. The two pairs of definitions are not antithetical: My proposal about the meaning of democracy only makes "popular sovereignty" more specific, and it is not unreasonable to suppose that liberal or generous people will be inclined to care for, or at least be tolerant of, the rights and interests of others.

America: Liberal Democracy as Historical Fact

The starting point of this analysis is to treat liberal democracy as an historically specific phenomenon, rather than a theoretical possibility. For Tocqueville, the emergence of democratic politics, the rule of the many dominated by a passion for equality, is intelligible only by reference to that regime that democracy rejects and supercedes, the hereditary aristocracy in which a few families rule and in which the dominant motive is honor. Like Tocqueville, Aristotle characterizes the major alternative to democracy as a rule by the wealthy (oligarchy), by those who are so secure in their wealth and power that their major concern is the acquisition of honor. Democracy, for Aristotle, is only accidentally the rule of the many; essentially, it is the rule of the poor—poverty understood here not as a condition of destitution, but as the situation of people who have to earn their livelihood by work of some kind and who will, therefore, be primarily concerned with acquiring the wealth they lack rather than honor or military glory. Aristotle's preference for democracy over oligarchy derives from his empirical assertion that the poor who love wealth present greater possibilities for education in virtue than do the wealthy who love honor.

Aristotle's democracy differs from the modern regime in several ways, size being the most obvious; perhaps the principal difference concerns the mode of acquiring wealth: agricultural in ancient democracies, commercial or industrial in modern ones. Nonetheless, Tocqueville, for whom modern democracy is essentially commercial democracy, agrees with Aristotle concerning the preeminent democratic passion: "Men living in democratic times have many passions, but most of these culminate in or derive from the love of wealth. That is not because their souls are smaller but because the importance of money is really greater then."[16] Tocqueville is surely critical of our democratic lives, in a manner that seems to anticipate Nietzsche and Weber: Our unceasing quest for wealth produces much pointless agitation and, in the observer, boredom. However, his explanation of the preoccupation with money and security does not rest upon attributing to democracy any peculiar irrationality or weakness; rather, the love of wealth is an appropriate and perhaps inevitable response to the conditions of life in a world in which birth or rank provides no security, in which lives must be lived without the guarantee of familial ties. Any serious attempt to understand the possibilities of democratic politics must begin by assuming the persistence of this motive and considering the ways it might be (or is) shaped and directed in particular places, rather than dreaming of its extirpation. Democracy, for Tocqueville, is the name of a relatively definite potentiality that is susceptible to a variety of actualizations, some compatible with liberty and some resembling a new industrial despotism.[17] The work of political reflection or science is to identify those *mores* and laws that affect the way democracy is actualized in different times and places and so in effect to produce policy agenda, which will vary from country to country, rather than to establish a science of universal rules or natural laws.

For Tocqueville, then, the love of wealth can have a variety of outcomes, depending on the context in which it operates. But the predominant attitude of early modern political thought toward this motive was less nuanced. As Hirschman in *The Passions and the Interests* shows, the early political defense of capitalist or commercial enterprise was that it *always* encouraged—in spite of itself perhaps—a form of life that produced peace and widespread social welfare.[18] This praise of commercial activity and of the love of wealth was frequently accompanied by a not very hidden contempt for those whose energies were directed toward gain rather than glory, notably in the case of Adam Smith's use of the invisible hand metaphor.[19] This combination of a contemptuous tone with a theoretical claim about the inevitably beneficial consequences of the despicable love of wealth is nicely illustrated by Alexander Pope's "Epistle to Burlington,"[20] which gives an account of the poet's visit to the estate of a tasteless *nouveau riche* who is assigned the name of the misanthropic Timon:

> At Timon's Villa let us pass a day,
> Where all cry out, "What sums are thrown away!"
> So proud, so grand; of that stupendous air,
> Soft and Agreeable come never there.
> Greatness, with Timon, dwells in such a draught,
> As brings all Brobdingnag before your thought.
> To compass this, his building is a Town,
> His pond an Ocean, his parterre a Down:
> Who but must laugh, the Master when he sees,
> A puny insect, shivering at a breeze!
> Lo, what huge heaps of littleness around!
>
> [ll.99–109]

After cataloguing the details of Timon's grossness, the poet angrily departs but his anger is undercut by his recognition that all these private vices yeild undoubted social benefits:

> In plenty starving, tantalized in state,
> And complaisantly helped to all I hate,
> Treated, caresed, and tired, I take my leave,
> Sick of his civil Pride from Morn to Eve;
> I curse such lavish cost, and little skill,
> And swear no Day was ever passed so ill.
> Yet hence the poor are clothed, the Hungry fed;
> Health to himself, and to his infants bread
> The Laborer bears: What his hard Heart denies,
> His charitable Vanity supplies.
>
> [ll.163–172]

From the perspective of the most pressing public needs, moral education and traditional liberal culture now seem entirely beside the point;

for the present, the thoughtful observer can only withdraw, perhaps to dream of a better age (ll.173ff), and allow avarice and "charitable vanity" to have their way. As long as the needs of the poor (broadly defined) are the measure of good government, the only public policy required is that which liberates and encourages the private pursuit of wealth.

The founders of the American republic were of course familiar with this argument, but it is equally clear that they did not accept the proposition that private vices are public benefits. As Storing says, "The Federalists did not, it should be emphasized, rely on some unseen hand to produce public good out of individual selfishness."[21] Hamilton, in arguing the case for a strong national government in *Federalist* 6, rejects the thesis that "the spirit of commerce has a tendency to soften the manners of men" and asks, "Has commerce hitherto done anything more than change the objects of war? Is not the love of wealth as domineering and enterprising a passion as that of power or glory?"[22] The Federalist solution to the problem of the conflict between private and public interest is to establish a complex legal-institutional system, expressed in the Constitution, by which interest may be made to counter interest and/or to correspond with public duty. This system, when combined with the "multiplicity of interests" that in fact characterize an extended commercial republic, will be sufficient to insure that American democracy will be liberal in effect, that is, that "the rights of individuals, or of the minority, will be in little danger from interested combinations of the majority."[23] Given the adequacy of this solution, it would be unnecessary to attempt to provide support for the project of "giving to every citizen the same opinions, the same passions, and the same interests."[24] The hand that channels the pursuit of private wealth will by no means be unseen, but it will be sufficient to obviate the need for any direct policy measures to moderate that pursuit and direct it toward liberality. It will, in other words, circumvent the need for any public attention to civic or moral education.

Disagreement as to this last point, rather than any more fundamental quarrel about the appropriate ends of government, formed the central controversy between the Federalists and their opponents. For most Anti-Federalists, individual rights could be adequately protected only in small republics and only when citizens shared certain fundamental opinions and virtues. The means by which these opinions and virtues were to be secured was not the subject of extensive discussion, but reliance seems to have rested principally on avoiding extremes of wealth and poverty and on maintaining the prevalence of certain commonly shared religious beliefs.[25] It is important to note here that the virtue that most concerned the Anti-Federalists was not liberality or generosity, but patriotism or public spiritedness, a commitment reflected in their general suspicion of the large states as cosmopolitan and hence corrupt. This way of conceiving the fundamental alternatives of American political life, in terms of the opposition between legally regulated avarice and fully committed republican citizenship, and the concomitant neglect of the possibility of shaping a democratic people in the direction of liberality or generosity rather than courageous patriotism is a predominant feature of our contemporary debate about the quality of modern liberal democracy. I will assume here that such neglect is undesirable; at any rate, it follows from and reinforces the habit of treating the problems of American democracy in the light of the sort of "crisis" criticized above. In what follows I will attempt, through a brief examination of Aristotle and Tocqueville, to suggest that this neglect is unnecessary, and in fact, misleading about the possibilities of contemporary American politics.

According to the Federalists, the best democracy is one that will limit the scope of unmediated popular rule: "If every Athenian were Socrates, the Athenian assembly would still have been a mob."[26] Hamilton goes so far as to say that conscience has less purchase on people acting in their capacity as citizens than when acting as separate individuals: "Has it been found that bodies of men act with more rectitude or disinterestedness than individuals? The contrary of this has been inferred by all accurate observers of the conduct of mankind; and the inference is founded upon obvious reasons. Regard to reputation has a less active influence when the infamy of a bad act is to be divided among a number than when it is to fall singly upon one."[27] The claim that a large commercial republic is the best democracy because it limits the scope of popular rule and thus removes the temptation of illiberal popular tyranny is not altogether unlike Aristotle's praise of agrarian democracy in *Politics* III (with the important difference that Aristotle praises such a regime because it allows the laws [*nomoi*] to rule, not the representatives). But doesn't this violate the basic Aristotelian notion of the rationalizing or humanizing character of political activity? Is it necessary to conclude that the political activity of democrats—of people primarily concerned with wealth and security—will inevitably be illiberal?

Aristotle: Democracy as Potentiality

For all his differences, Aristotle's connection with the problem of the modern, liberal democratic regime can be seen in his thought, shared with Plato, that the central human problem—the inclination that leads us away from our own happiness and interest—is a tendency toward unlimited acquisition (*pleonexia*). In his discussion of the economic art in *Politics* I, he says that some people mistakenly think that the function of this art is to increase one's property without limit: "The cause of this disposition is anxiety [or being serious, *spoudazein*] about living, but not about living well. As the desire for life is unlimited, so also the desire for things productive of life is unlimited."[28] However natural in one sense our inclination to *pleonexia* may be (it is not a form of corruption peculiar to the lower classes), the fact remains that we can only be happy insofar as we live according to a reasonable order of the sort that may be provided by the *nomoi* of our city or culture. The *paideia* provided by the *nomoi* will be adequate insofar as it causes us to choose not "to have more (*pleonektein*) either of money or of honor or of both."[29]

The reference to these two possible objects of unlimited desire, money and honor, indicates Aristotle's characteristic way of identifying the problems that are characteristic of those two chief rivals for political power, the poor (or *dēmos*) and the wealthy. In several places he asserts that democracy is preferable to oligarchy, on grounds that the characteristic passions of the *dēmos* are less dangerous than those of the wealthy.[30] In Book IV, he argues for the potential superiority of democracy in a related way. After remarking that many of those who wish to establish an aristocracy (rule of the truly best) make an important mistake by giving too much power to the wealthy, Aristotle explains why this is an error by stating that "the graspings (*pleonexiai*) of the wealthy subvert the regime more than those of the *dēmos*."[31] The basis for Aristotle's position is not a romantic idealization of the virtues of every *dēmos*, but the empirical claim that the wealthy will tend to be motivated by the love of honor and the *dēmos* by the love of gain (*kerdos*) and that the greatest crimes, the greatest *pleonexiai*, are consequences of the unlimited love of honor and preferential regard.[32] The form of *pleonexia* that infects the *dēmos* is easier to check than that which drives the wealthy, so that under certain circumstances a democracy can be a regime in which a substantial degree of political virtue is realized.

The problems and possibilities of democracy are approached from a slightly different perspective in Book III, in the discussion of whether the best *polis* should be ruled by the few people who are best or by the multitude (*to plēthos*, a term synonymous with *dēmos*).[33] It would seem obvious that the best should rule, but Aristotle initially sets out an argument that denies this. His claim is that while each individual member of the many (*hoi polloi*) may not be a serious man (*spoudaios anēr*), the many, "when coming together, admit of being better than those who are best, not individually, but as a whole." The argument for this is a series of analogies. First, it is said that just as a dinner paid for out of everyone's pockets will be better than any one person can provide, so the combined virtue and wisdom of *to plēthos* may add up to a greater whole than the good qualities of the best. But this analogy is hardly decisive since, Aristotle says, it could be used to make a case for the superior judgment of a large number of beasts. He concludes that while it has not been shown that every *plēthos* is superior to the few best, it is still possible that some given *plēthos* may be superior. This possibility is immediately reinforced by noting that not allowing *to plēthos* to share in the regime is a frightening thing, since a city full of poor and disenfranchised people is a city full of enemies. Since a *polis* has several functions and must provide for the security as well as the virtue of its citizens, a city in which the many are mixed with the better may be capable of the best judgments; this is supported by another analogy that relates that impure (*mē kathara*) food mixed with pure is more nourishing than a small amount of pure food alone. The discussion concludes (1283b) with the tentative assertion that nothing stands in the way of the possibility that the many may sometimes be better than the few, "not as individuals, but as a whole." We are left to wonder about the circumstances in which a *dēmos* is such that it can be made more *katharos*, and about the agency through which this *katharsis* occurs.

These circumstances are primarily economic (broadly speaking), having to do with both the amount and the kind of wealth the citizens possess. Democracies can be the most measured or reasonable of those regimes that do not aim explicitly at education in virtue, because in the best democracies the laws are permitted to rule rather than the citizens, thus reducing the occasions for pleonectic vice.[34] These democracies are those in which the dominant element is composed of farmers or herdsmen of middling wealth;[35] such people have substance enough to live as long as they work, but not much leisure and so will be inclined to rule according to laws,[36] and thus will be open to the sort of reason that good laws or customs (the Greek *nomos* includes both these English terms) approximate, given the impersonality of the *nomoi* and their braking effect on *pleonexia*.[37] A good democracy is thus one in which a certain opinion about the best life prevails among the citizens, an opinion that gives highest marks to industrious *and* law-abiding people. The easiest way of securing this opinion is not by direct instruction, but by economic regulations that favor farming, limit the amount of property that may be held, reduce poverty, and separate political office from financial reward.[38] This opinion, which forms or shapes (and hence actualizes) the best *dēmos*, does not insure but at least opens the possibility that the political leadership will be composed of decent people (*hoi epieikeis*) and so avoids the charge that every democracy is necessarily corrupt.[39]

What we can learn from Aristotle's discussion of the problem of democracy is less a set of substantive conclusions (given the commercial character of modern democracies) and more a style of analysis:[40] The quality of any given democracy should be seen as adverbial, as it were— it depends on the attitude democrats take toward the pursuit of wealth, income, and security, a pursuit that is a necessary feature of our lives. This attitude in turn is primarily determined by the nature of the customs or traditions that inform democratic life in particular places. Unlike the route prescribed by modern theory, the Aristotelian political scientist interested in democracy will not abstract from these particulars by attempting to formulate a universal decision procedure that makes obligation rational or reconciles interest and duty. Nor, for that matter, will such a political scientist attempt to translate the Aristotelian understanding of the best human life into a set of universally binding rules (such as, "Always prefer the superior in virtue") to be somehow or other impressed upon an understandably dubious democratic populace. Rather, the task of this political science is twofold: to articulate forms of life that reflect the best and worst possibilities inherent in a particular context and to examine the laws and customs of the place with an eye to determining how they do or do not moderate the pursuit of wealth intrinsic to all democracies. The outcome of all this will be distinctly context-specific policy agenda, rather than universally valid algorithms for maximizing preferences (or, for that matter, virtues).

Tocqueville: An Aristotelian Approach to American Democracy

Tocqueville's *Democracy in America* is an example of this kind of political science. It is concerned, in the language of William T. Bluhm's essay in this volume, not with the summation of preferences but rather with the formation of preferences, and its focus is not universal but relative to the specific context of American democracy. It is in a sense less democratic than more familiar political science, at least insofar as Tocqueville is correct in saying that "democratic men love general ideas because they save them the trouble of studying particular cases."[41] This characterization of Tocqueville as Aristotelian may appear to conflict with Tocqueville's claim for the novelty of his work, which he introduces by saying that a "new political science is necessary for a world wholly new."[42] But Tocqueville's new political science is not, like Hobbes's or Machiavelli's, based on a confident rejection of ancient philosophy or political philosophy. The novelty Tocqueville claims is not for his method, but for the object of his study: The problem of modern democracy, a regime in which rule is by the poor, who passionately love money and equality of status,[43] and one in which connections among individuals over time and space are continually at risk.[44]

The greatest danger here is that the democratic character will become marked by what Tocqueville calls "individualism," "a considered and peaceable sentiment that disposes each citizen to isolate himself from the mass of his fellows and withdraw into the circle of family and friends, in such a way that after having created a little society for his own use he willingly abandons society at large to its own devices."[45] If such an opinion becomes predominant, the regime will become stagnant,[46] and degenerate either into anarchy or, more probably, into servitude.[47]

But these dangers are not sufficient grounds for despairing of the possibilities of democracy. The democratic character may tend toward a dissipating individualism, but democrats are at the same time more compassionate and gentle than their aristocratic predecessors who, like Aristotle's oligarchs, love honor more than wealth and so are prone to inhumanity and war.[48] In the new world of commercial democracy, "Mores are gentle and laws humane. Though heroic devotions and any other other very high, very brilliant, and very pure virtues are few, habits are orderly, violence rare, cruelty almost unknown. Human life becomes longer and property more secure. Life is not very glamorous, but very easy and very peaceable."[49] Though democracy tends toward such a desirable outcome, it does not always achieve it, since it also contains contrary tendencies in the direction of individualism and despotism. These contrary potentialities set the task for Tocqueville's political science. The problem "is no longer to preserve the particular advantages that inequality of conditions procures for men, but to secure the new goods that equality can offer them. We should not try to make ourselves like our fathers but should strive to attain the sort of greatness and happiness that is proper to us."[50] Tocqueville's intention, then, is not to find a way of reconciling interest and duty in the abstract, nor to discover a rule for public choice to which all rational beings must accede, but to identify those attitudes and practices that have the greatest bearing on the particular possibilities that define democratic life.

Tocqueville's solution to the problem of democracy is deceptively simple: "I maintain that there is only one effective remedy against the evils that equality can produce, and that is political liberty![51] Political liberty is the key, but the meaning of this term is difficult to ascertain, for us at any rate, because it does not correspond to the way the term is used by either of the two great modern traditions with which we are familiar. It is immediately apparent that Tocqueville does not mean the opportunity to pursue one's own good in one's own way, in J. S. Mill's terms; limitless independence is frightening,[52] and the aim of democracy should be to regulate and legitimize power, rather than to destroy it.[53] But if Tocqueville's understanding of freedom is not that of early modern liberalism, it is equally clear that he did not set forth a conception of true freedom as committed republic citizenship, on the model of Machiavelli or Rousseau.[54] He was as little attracted to idealized images of republican life in Periclean Athens and republican Rome as were the authors of the *Federalist*, and for similar reasons:[55] The code of honor that shapes the civic culture of republican citizens, a code that exalts courage above all the other virtues, is inseparable from a taste for turbulence and war.[56] To embrace such an ideal is to neglect the distinctive moral possibilities of a poor man's democracy in which "everybody works, and work opens all doors."[57]

Those moral possibilities pertain to a way of life that embodies certain genuine virtues, but ones very different from those of committed or instinctive patriotism: "Commerce is the natural enemy of all violent passions. It loves moderation, delights in compromise, and is most careful to avoid anger. . . Commerce makes men independent of one another and gives them a high idea of their individual worth; it leads them to want to manage their own affairs and teaches them how to succeed therein. Hence it makes them inclined to liberty but disinclined to revolution."[58] The life of acquisitive enterprise is, of course, not by itself sufficient to realize those virtues that justify and define it; unchecked and untempered it can, in Tocqueville's view, lead to the despotism of an atomized mass society. But possibility is not necessity; the importance and the distinctiveness of Tocqueville's analysis lies in his characterization of the spirit of acquisitive enterprise, the spirit that is the driving force of the new democratic majority, as neither a deformity (as for Rousseau, Marx, Weber, and Nietzsche) nor a panacea, but a potentiality. Democracy needs to be educated in the light of its own best possibilities and not, as the imagery of crisis would lead us to believe, utterly transformed. Thus, I think it is misleading to see Tocqueille as struggling toward a radical vision of civic republicanism, but held back by his commitment to the categories of liberal thought.[59] Perhaps it would be better to say that Tocqueville manages to avoid the literary attractions of republican radicalism (such as rhetorical vividness and force) in presenting a thoroughly liberal critical understanding of the problem (and not the crisis) of liberal democracy. The poor—in his sense—whose competitive desires rule democracy need to be educated in a manner appropriate to their own genius and not transformed into citizens: "It is therefore essential to march forward and hasten to make the people see that individual interest is linked to that of the country, for disinterested love of country has fled beyond recall."[60]

The education in liberty Tocqueville proposes has nothing to do with direct teaching or manipulation by political philosophers who stand above the fray. It consists, rather, in identifying (very much in the manner of Books IV–VI of the *Politics*) those factors that have in fact contributed to giving American democracy a liberal or generous direction. Its principles and limits are clearly stated in the context of a discussion of the doctrine of self-interest properly understood:

> No power on earth can prevent increasing equality from turning men's minds to look for the useful or disposing each citizen to get wrapped up in himself.

> One must therefore expect that individual interest will more than ever become the chief if not the only motive behind all actions. But we have yet to see how each man will interpret his individual interest.[61]

Tocqueville's intention is not to legislate, or even to show the need for fundamental legislation, but rather "to show, by the American example, that laws and above all mores can allow a democratic people to remain free."[62] The whole of the inquiry is an attempt to explain the reasons for the liberal quality of American democracy, by distinguishing the sources and supports of liberality from those aspects of American life that threaten it.

Some of those sources are economic in the narrow sense, such as the absence of any large class of propertyless and destitute persons,[63] the fact that "wealth circulates there with incredible rapidity,"[64] and the expenditure (contrary to official proclamations of economy in government) of "enormous sums" on "maintenance of the needy and free education."[65] One of the great threats to American liberty is posed by the possible increase of economic inequality in an industrial society,[66] a development that for Tocqueville, as for Aristotle,[67] threatens the possibility of liberality and tends to give rise to a polity composed only of masters and slaves. The character of economic life is therefore a significant item on the political agenda whose aim is the encouragement of a liberal interpretation of private interest among democrats. But it is by no means the only, or perhaps even the most, important one.

Much of Tocqueville's attention, and perhaps his most famous teaching, is that active participation in local political associations is the "free school" through which the democratic personality becomes inclined toward liberality.[68] Speaking of universal suffrage, he says that it "is certainly not the elected magistrate who makes the American democracy prosper, but the fact that the magistrates are elected."[69] This is to say that the most important (though generally overlooked) feature of any method of summing preferences is the effect such a method has on the *formation* of preferences. But Tocqueville's stress on the need for political participation and on the critical importance of decentralized political life is not aimed at producing republican citizens on the model of an idealized or romanticized classical antiquity.[70] The virtuous habits of mind and heart to be acquired through political activity are clearly and specifically liberal: "The free institutions of the United States. . . provide a thousand continual reminders to every citizen that he lives in society. . . . Having no particular reason to hate others, since he is neither their slave nor their master, the American's heart easily inclines toward benevolence."[71] In spite of the importance of local politics, Tocqueville does not tend toward the Jeffersonian (or Arendtian) view that increasing the importance of local control will be sufficient for democratic education in virtue; administrative centralization is a powerfully dangerous democratic tendency,[72] but at the same time it is (not accidentally) the case that "the federal government is more just and moderate in its proceedings than those of the states" since—because of the Constitution—legislative power is less likely to rule unchecked there.[73] Participatory politics is not an inevitably desirable means of combating illiberal individualism; it can be such a means, but only insofar as it is informed by certain attitudes that do not always accompany it, but which happen to do so in the American case.

One of the indispensable forces shaping political life and attitudes in America, for Tocqueville, is the set of standards and institutions connected with the common law. The fact that there "is hardly a political question in the United States which does not sooner or later turn into a judicial one" is, for Tocqueville, decidedly a good thing,[74] since it enforces a disciplined search for authoritative standards and so serves as a counterforce to both individualism and the "ill-considered passions of democracy."[75] The common law perspective is introduced into the language of every-day political life through the institution of jury trials, a practice whose importance can hardly be overestimated: "Juries, especially civil juries, instill some of the habits of the judicial mind into every citizen, and just those habits are the very best way of preparing people to be free."[76] If local participation is a school of freedom, it is so only for people whose minds have been shaped and prepared by something like the discipline of judicial reflection: "I do not know whether a jury is useful to the litigants, but I am sure it is very good for those who have to decide the case. I regard it as one of the most effective means of popular education at society's disposal."[77]

Tocqueville's treatment of the political significance of American religion (which should "be considered as the first of their political institutions") has much the same bearing as his discussion of common law institutions and practices.[78] Liberal democracy needs some sort of religion, but not, as for Locke, a device for frightening or enticing democrats into keeping their promises: "I have known zealous Christians who constantly forgot themselves to labor more ardently for the happiness of all, and I have heard them claim that they did this only for the sake of rewards in the next world. But I cannot get it out of my head that they were deceiving themselves. I respect them too much to believe them."[79] The function religion can perform in democracies is much less apparent and much more like the implicit work of the common law vocabulary: It can educate, unobtrusively, those who must love wealth in the habits of even-tempered benevolence and liberality, which are the measure of the best democratic lives. Religion does this by combatting the spirit of individual independence,[80] but not all religions—nor religion as such—can perform this task in the appropriately democratic and liberal manner. So much at least is clear from the way in which Tocqueville's teleological account leads to unfavorable judgments about a wide variety of religions, including Islam (and by implication, Judaism), pantheism (or transcendentalist unitarianism), and fundamentalist evangelical Protestantism.[81] Like every other institution, religion in America is discussed from the perspective of the question of the extent to which it can lead to the development of those liberal attitudes and ways of life that are the actualization of the peculiarly democratic virtues.

All the Tocquevillian analyses I have considered here seem to point in a common direction: Mores and institutions are democratically valuable insofar as they develop habits of mind *or* dispositions that lead to rule without tyranny and to obedience or subordination without slavishness. This is similarly true of his discussion of the structure of the American family and his consideration of the doctrine of self-interest properly understood, which is presented not as a theoretical truth, but as a more or less ennobling myth.[82] These analyses also point, by implication, to the immense subtlety that liberal democracy requires, insofar as the most important agents of democratic education seem to matter in ways different from, and generally concealed by, their official justifications: welfare spending is not a mode of economic efficiency; universal suffrage not a way of electing the best people, jury trials not a means for reaching the best verdicts; religion not an otherwordly sanction for good conduct; self-interest, properly understood, not a way of maximizing self-interest. Democracies can be made more liberal, but the problem of liberal democracy admits of no simple solutions, either theoretically or rhetorically: "It is difficult to make the people participate in government; it is even more difficult to provide them with the experience and the feelings they lack to govern well."[83]

Conclusion: Articulating the Liberal Democracy

What can we learn about liberal democracy from Tocqueville? Our political order is surely different in several important respects from the one he saw. Perhaps the most significant difference is that it can no longer be said that we have no great wars to fear.[84] Another key difference is that by the emancipation of blacks we have had to confront "the most formidable of all the evils that threaten the future of the United States";[85] here we may have done better than Tocqueville expected. Economic development has also changed the prospects of democracy in ways that are impossible to characterize simply. These changes suggest that mechanical applications of Tocquevillian conclusions are generally out of place. But what remains is the fact that we are still a democratic people, individuals who must work to earn a living, and that the moral poles that define our activity are those that measure the space between liberality and narrow individualism (or majority tyranny). This articulation of the problems and possibilities of democratic life can focus our political thought by emphasizing the importance of the sources of indirect education in generosity and liberality as central to the survival of a genuinely liberal democracy.

If we adopt something like this articulation we will be in possession of an alternative to "the crisis of liberal democracy," a way of thought that leads us to understand ourselves in the misleading light of a contrast between some Nietzschean or Marxian nightmare of a radically privatized present and a dream of a republican community of virtuous citizens. Such a contrast is as dangerous as it is distorting, because the virtues of public spirited citizens are not those of a liberal democracy; as George Kateb says in a similar context, "We have left the world of constitutional democracy behind when we affirm community."[86]

Seeing American politics through the lenses of the "crisis" formulation concentrates attention on political movements that are sporadic, episodic, and generally directed against the national government. As a result, our very idea of politics takes on the color and characteristics of war and thus subverts Tocqueville's hopes for the salutary operation of the myth of self-interest properly understood.

Following Tocqueville's lead, we might attend more carefully to the hidden springs of liberal democracy, such as the way the character of the language in which political proposals are made shapes the formation of democratic preferences towards and away from the liberal disposition. One very important, and threatening, phenomenon is the way in which the traditional language of the common law is being translated into the vocabulary of economic efficiency (a la Richard Posner), or into that of cybernetic or psychoanalytic jargon (as we express our inputs into conflict resolution).[87] But not all the signs are dark; the remarkable expansion of liberal education, for all its problems, surely presents capital opportunities that did not exist in Tocqueville's America where "primary education is within reach of all; higher education is hardly available to anybody."[88] The same is true of what we call "popular culture," which Tocqueville could see only as a potential force held in check by residual Puritanism.[89]

Liberal democracy is not a crisis to be resolved so much as a regime or culture to be preserved and enhanced—although as much may depend on luck as on thoughtful care. But as a regime it is perhaps uniquely problematic in that its definitive virtues, generosity and moderation, are particularly hard to identify and defend, because they are quiet virtues. Indeed, most of our political rhetoric (left, right, and center), as well as our political science, calls forth images of a militant democracy—America reconceived as Athens or Sparta—as if these were the only ones worth praising. Hidden from ourselves by our most articulate spokesmen, our real crisis may be one not of insufficient public energy but of inadequate self-regard.

Notes

1. Lester C. Thurow, *The Zero-Sum Society* (New York: Basic Books, 1980.

2. Christopher Lasch, *The Culture of Narcissism* (New York: W. W. Norton, 1978).

3. Morris Janowitz, *The Last Half-Century* (Chicago: University of Chicago Press, 1978).

4. Thomas Hobbes, *Leviathan*, ed. Michael Oakeshott (Oxford: Basil Blackwell, n.d.), chap. 15.

5. *Ibid.*, chap. 10.

6. A good programmatic statement of how this might be done is found in William Galston's "Defending Liberalism," *American Political Science Review*, 76 (September 1982): 621–629.

7. *Hobbes, Leviathan,* chap. 11.

8. John Locke, *A Letter Concerning Toleration* (Indianapolis: Bobbs-Merrill, 1950), 56–57.

9. For the significance of the replacement of justice by alienation in the contemporary political vocabulary, see Joseph Cropsey, "'Alienation' or Justice," *Political Philosophy and the Issues of Politics* (Chicago: University of Chicago Press, 1977).

10. Nathan Tarcov, "Philosophy and History: Tradition and Interpretation in the Work of Leo Strauss," *Polity,* 16 (1983): 5–29, p. 9.

11. Leo Strauss, "Philosophy as Rigorous Science and Political Philosophy," *Studies in Platonic Political Philosophy* (Chicago: University of Chicago Press, 1983), 37.

12. Robert Frost, "The Oven Bird," *The Poetry of Robert Frost,* ed. Edward Connery Lathem (New York: Holt, Rinehart & Winston, 1969), 120.

13. See George Kateb, "The Moral Distinctiveness of Representative Democracy," *Ethics,* 91 (1981): 357–74.

14. Harvey C. Mansfield, *The Spirit of Liberalism* (Cambridge, Mass.: Harvard University Press, 1978), 114. The tension between the relative abundance of social and political activity in American and the failure of the categories of American political language to express and defend that activity is the subject of Robert N. Bellah, Richard Madsen, William M. Sullivan, Ann Swidler, and Steven M. Tipton, *Habits of the Heart: Individualism and Commitment in American Life* (Berkeley: University of California Press, 1985), esp. chapters 7 and 8.

15. Richard Flacks, "Moral Commitment, Privatism, and Activism: Notes on a Research Program," *Social Science as Moral Inquiry*; ed. Norma Haan et al. (New York: Columbia University Press, 1983), 343–59, 346.

16. Alexis de Tocqueville, *De la Democratie en Amerique, Oeuvres Completes,* vol. 2, ed. J. P. Mayer (Paris: Gallimard, 1951), pt. 3, chap. 17, p. 236. Translations from Tocqueville are my modifications of the George Lawrence translation of *Democracy in America* (New York: Doubleday, 1969). Hereafter, citations will refer to volume, part, and chapter in the work, and to the page numbers in both the Gallimard and the Doubleday editions. Thus, the present reference is to Tocqueville, 2, 3, 17 (*O.C.* 2: 236; *D. in A.,* 614).

17. Ibid., 2,2,20 (*O.C.* 2: 164–67; *D. in A.,* 555–58).

18. Albert O. Hirschman, *The Passions and the Interests* (Princeton: Princeton University Press, 1977).

19. See Joseph Cropsey, "The Invisible Hand: Moral and Political Considerations," *Political Philosophy and the Issues of Politics,* op. cit., 76–89, 82–83.

20. Alexander Pope, "Epistle to Burlington," *Epistles to Several Persons (Moral Essays),* ed. F. W. Bateson (London: Methuen and Co., 1951), 134–56.

21. Herbet J. Storing, *What the Anti-Federalists Were For* (Chicago: University of Chicago Press, 1981), 73.

22. Alexander Hamilton, James Madison, John Jay, *The Federalist Papers* (New York: The New American Library 1961), 57.

23. Ibid., no. 51, p. 324.

24. Ibid., no. 10, p. 78.

25. Storing, *What the Anti-Federalists Were For*, 15–23.

26. Hamilton et al., *The Federalist Papers*, no. 55, p. 342.

27. Ibid., no. 15, pp. 110–11.

28. Aristotle, *Politics* I: 1257b. Translations from Aristotle are mine; citations refer to the book of the *Politics* and to the standard pagination of the Bekker edition.

29. Ibid. II: 1266b. For a good discussion of the Aristotelian use of the difficult term *pleonexia*, see Bernard Williams, "Justice as a Virtue," *Essays on Aristotle's Ethics*, ed. Amelie Oksenberg Rorty (Berkeley: University of California Press, 1980), 189–99.

30. *Politics* III: 1286a.

31. *Politics* IV: 1297a.

32. *Politics* II: 1267a.

33. *Politics* III: 1281a.

34. *Politics* IV: 1289b, 1292b.

35. *Politics* VI: 1318b; IV, 1292b.

36. *Politics* IV: 1292b.

37. Ibid., 1295b.

38. *Politics* VI: 1318b.

39. Ibid., 1319a.

40. See Tocqueville, 2,2,19 (*O.C.* 2: 160–63; *D. in A.*, 551–54).

41. Ibid. 2,1,3 (*O.C.* 2: 23; *D. in A.*, 440).

42. Ibid. 1, author's Introduction (*O.C.* 1: 5; *D. in A.*, 12).

43. Ibid. 1,2,6 (*O.C.* 1: 252; *D. in A.*, 241); 1,1,3 (*O.C.* 2: 50; *D. in A.*, 54); 2,2,1 (*O.C.* 2: 102; *D. in A.*, 504).

44. Ibid. 2,2,2 (*O.C.* 2: 105–6; *D. in A.*, 507).

45. Ibid. (*O.C.* 2: 105; *D. in A.*, 506).

46. Ibid. 2,3,21 (*O.C.* 2: 269; *D. in A.*, 645).

47. Ibid. 2,4,1 (*O.C.* 2: 295; *D. in A.*, 667).

48. Ibid. 2,3,1 (*O.C.* 2: 174–75; *D. in A.*, 564–65).

49. Ibid. 2,4,8 (*O.C.* 2: 337; *D. in A.*, 703).

50. Ibid. (*O.C.* 2: 338; *D. in A.*, 705).

51. Ibid. 2,2,4 (*O.C.* 2: 112; *D. in A.*, 513).

52. Ibid. 2,1,5 (*O.C.* 2: 29; *D. in A.*, 444).

53. Ibid. 2,3,12 (3*O.C.* 2: 220; *D. in A.*, 601).

54. See *Prince*, chap. 5, and *Discourses*, bk. I, chap. 16.

55. Tocqueville, 2,1,15 (*O.C.* 2: 67–68; *D. in A.*, 475–77); 2,3,18 (*O.C.* 2: 242; *D. in A.*, 620); *Federalist Papers*, no. 6.

56. Tocqueville, 2,3,18 (*O.C.* 2: 242–49; *D. in A.*, 620–27).

57. Ibid. (*O.C.* 2: 245; *D. in A.*, 623).

58. Ibid. 2,3,21 (*O.C.* 2: 261; *D. in A.*, 637).

59. For an interesting view somewhat to the contrary, see William M. Sullivan, *Reconstructing Public Philosophy* (Berkeley: University of California Press, 1982), 216.

60. Tocqueville, 1,2,6 (*O.C.* 1: 246–47; *D. in A.*, 236).

61. Ibid. 2,2,8 (*O.C.* 2: 129–30; *D. in A.*, 527).

62. Ibid. 1,2,9 (*O.C.* 1: 329; *D. in A.*, 315).

63. Ibid. 1,2,6 (*O.C.* 1: 249; *D. in A.*, 238).

64. Ibid. 1,1,3 (*O.C.* 1: 50; *D. in A.*, 54).

65. Ibid. 1,2,5 (*O.C.* 1: 222 and n. 10; *D. in A.*, 214 n. 11).

66. Ibid. 2,2,20 (*O.C.* 2: 165–66; *D. in A.*, 556–57).

67. *Politics* IV: 1295b.

68. Tocqueville, 2,2,7 (*O.C.* 2: 123; *D. in A.*, 522).

69. Ibid. 2,2,4 (*O.C.* 2: 112; *D. in A.*, 512).

70. Ibid. 1,1,8 (*O.C.* 1: 166–67; *D. in A.*, 162).

71. Ibid. 2,2,40 (*O.C.* 2: 112; *D. in A.*, 512).

72. Ibid. 1,1,5 (*O.C.* 2: 88,97; *D. in A.*, 88,96).

73. Ibid. 1,1,8 (*O.C.* 1: 158; *D. in A.*, 155).

74. Ibid. 1,2,8 (*O.C.* 1: 281; *D. in A.*, 270).

75. Ibid. (*O.C.* 1: 275; *D. in A.*, 264).

76. Ibid. (*O.C.* 1: 286; *D. in A.*, 274).

77. Ibid. (*O.C.* 1: 286; *D. in A.*, 275).

78. Ibid. 1,2,9 (*O.C.* 1: 306; *D. in A.*, 292).

79.   Ibid. 2,2,9 (*O.C.* 2: 131; *D. in A.*, 529).

80.   Ibid. 2,1,5 (*O.C.* 2: 34; *D. in A.*, 449).

81.   Ibid. (*O.C.* 2: 30; *D. in A.*, 445); Ibid. 2,1,7 (*O.C.* 2: 37–38; *D. in A.*, 451–52); Ibid. 2,2,12 (*O.C.* 2: 140–41; *D. in A.*, 534–35).

82.   Ibid. 2,3,12 (*O.C.* 2: 219–22) *D. in A.*, 600–603); Ibid. 2,2,8 (*O.C.* 2: 127–30; *D. in A.*, 525–28).

83.   Ibid. 1,2,9 (*O.C.* 1: 329; *D. in A.*, 315).

84.   Ibid. 1,1,8 (*O.C.* 1: 174; *D. in A.*, 169–70).

85.   Ibid. 1,2,10 (*O.C.* 1: 356; *D. in A.*, 340).

86.   George Kateb, "On the 'Legitimation Crisis'," *Social Research* 46 (1979): 695–727, 719.

87.   An extended development of a similar diagnosis of the problem of contemporary self-understanding is found in Bellah et al., *Habits of the Heart*, where it is argued that "[b]etween them, the manager and the therapist largely define the outlines of twentieth-century American culture" (p. 47). The authors of that work argue that the decay of Biblical and traditional republican language, and the corresponding growth of economic and psychotherapeutic ways of thinking and speaking, are political dangers of the greatest significance. (They perhaps have too little to say about the possible importance of traditional legal culture.) A not dissimilar point is developed in Laurence Berns's compact and provocative essay, "Speculations on Liberal and Illiberal Politics," *Review of Politics* 40 (1978): 231–54. Berns puts the issue in the following way: "Where can liberal rationalism turn to find political allies of sufficient strength to ensure its survival? The best allies for liberal rationalism, I suggest, are traditional patriotism and the revealed religions" (p. 241 n. 13).

88.   Tocqueville, 1,1,3 (*O.C.* 1: 51; *D. in A.*, 55).

89.   Ibid. 2,1,19 (*O.C.* 2: 84–88; *D. in A.*, 489–93).

William T. Bluhm

LIBERALISM AS THE AGGREGATION OF INDIVIDUAL PREFERENCES: PROBLEMS OF COHERENCE AND RATIONALITY IN SOCIAL CHOICE

INTRODUCTION: BENTHAMITE BEGINNINGS

Since the time of Bentham, a central concern within liberal political culture has been how to aggregate individual utilities (more lately called simply "preferences," or "preference schedules") in a fair and efficient way in the creation of public policy. The language of preference aggregation is found abundantly in the writings and talk of *academia* (embracing philosophers, economists, political scientists, and students of public policy) and in the communications of policy analysts and public decision makers. In the writings of academics (e.g., Rawls, Buchanan, and Tullock), it is interesting that utilitarian concepts are frequently put together with social contract metaphors and with language about rights (in a sense more fundamental than merely legal rights), despite the fact that Bentham dismissed social contract theory and held for a purely positivist conception of individual rights.[1]

Whether thinkers of the sorts I have mentioned stand at the left (Welfare or Egalitarian Liberal) end or at the right (Libertarian) end of the spectrum of liberal democratic culture, they are concerned with the construction of a "social welfare function," though they may not always call it that. Also, recommendations about its ideal form and the process of its generation will vary markedly with one's ideological position.[2] We are concerned here with the question of whether individual preferences, which figure centrally in this literature, can, as such, be aggregated either theoretically or practically in a way that will ensure a coherent and rational welfare function. Can individual perferences be the starting points for the construction of public order?

For Bentham, as for the modern liberal who employs utilitarian notions, life was a business of utility-seeking, and a rational man was a maximizer of utility.[3] Bikhu Parekh paraphrases Bentham thus:

269

> Since pleasure alone is good, . . . it is only rational to have as much of it as possible. To pursue less of it when more is available, or to forego opportunities of pursuing it is patently irrational. It is an action without a reason.

Government is a service agency whose purpose it is to help us, collectively, achieve abundance. In doing so, government will create legal rights and obligations, by virtue of the power vested in it by a community. But, as Parekh paraphrases Bentham's thought, "Government never should create rights, 'instruments of felicity,' . . . unless it can be absolutely certain that their probable advantages would more than compensate for their certain disadvantages."[5] In the language of modern policy analysis, decision makers should pay careful attention to cost-benefit ratios in making public policy. But whose benefit is to be served if interests—or preferences—clash? And is "benefit" a measurable quantity at all?

Bentham thought that "benefit" was quantifiable, and perhaps justifiably so in his time, when we consider the very basic benefits that he and the Philosophical Radicals sought for an impoverished and hard-pressed people through their schemes of political and social reform. Hence, his concept of the "felicific calculus." But ours is a different age, with different problems and one, at least in the postindustrial west, in which "felicity" is not readily equatable with the measurable quantities of economic growth and the distribution of economic benefit. Bentham also believed it meaningful to say that one can make interpersonal comparisons of utility (just as some welfare economists, such as John Harsanyi, still maintain today, though this is a matter of considerable conflict at the moment). And he thought it possible to convince people that they should have regard for other people's utilities as well as for their own, so that achieving the general welfare might be some kind of additive or summing process.[6] It was, indeed, a central part of Bentham's educational program to make people sociably minded, by teaching them to serve one another. Thus, if "pleasure alone is good" (his major premise), "it is good irrespective of whether it is your pleasure or mine."

> If an action of mine gives you two units of happiness and me only one, it is irrational of me to prefer my own happiness to yours. Bentham therefore concludes that a moral agent should aim to promote the greatest happiness in the aggregate, this being the only rational and right end of human action.[7]

One frequently has the impression, in reading Bentham, that while he was concerned with the problem of bringing individual preferences into harmony in order to make them aggregable, he tended to lose sight of individuals as persons altogether and came to think of the idea of abundance as the primary social goal in the abstract, in purely quantitative terms. And it is certainly the case that modern utilitarianism does the same thing. As R. M. Hare puts it: "Utilitarianism sees persons as locations of their respective utilities—as the sites at which such activities as desiring and having pleasure and pain take place. Once note has been taken of the person's utility, utilitarianism has no further direct interest in any information about him." Judgments of all sorts are "ultimately based exclusively on the amounts of utility and disutility generated. Persons do not count as individuals in this any more than individual petrol tanks do in the analysis of the national consumption of petroleum." This way of looking at things finally "reduces the collection of diverse information about the n persons in that state into n bits of utility, with the totality of relevant information being given by an n-vector of utilities."[8]

One wonders what the result of such exercises might mean in human terms, for preferences are never simply given, as so many welfare economists and theorists of individual rights assume. As Charles Fried has pointed out, "Philosophers and theorists are not precluded from discussing with each individual, on a personal basis, how he should perceive his values, preferences, and needs, even though for reasons of principle we leave him the last word when it comes to formulating a social rule." And he asks whether "the commitment to leaving the consumer the last word in the public arena has not obscured . . . the educational and philosophical task of debating with individuals about what their values should be as they enter the marketplace."[9] If the principle of "consumer sovereignty," which underlies most aggregative exercises today, is to be a principle that incorporates the idea of rationality, it must assume that the consumer can reflect on, discourse about, and perhaps alter his preferences. If we do not make these assumptions, "what we have," argues Fried, "cannot even be described as a choice or as a system of preferences, but only as random behavior."[10] Hence, the aggregation of preferences as "brute facts" lacks coherence and rationality at the outset—within the individual whose preferences are its point of departure. Fried's argument substitutes for the idea of mere "preference" a concept of the person as a stable and continuous reality, whose rational *needs* are to be served both by market operations and by the political provision of services. But this may lead away from the model of preference aggregation into an entirely different kind of philosophical system.[11]

Let us come back to Bentham. What if pleasure and preferences clash, despite Bentham's processes of socialization? Or what if interpersonal comparisons prove more difficult than he supposed? What is to be done if society must choose between individuals and groups, instead of simply summing up the greatest happiness of the aggregate, whose abstract or generalized character the lover of pleasure—regardless of whether it is his or the other's—could appreciate? Bentham himself faced up to questions such as these only in part and never quite satisfactorily. In the *Fragment on Government* (1776) he employed a majoritarian formula, "the greatest happiness of the greatest number," which he had borrowed from Joseph Priestly. But we do not find this expression in the *Introduction to Principles of Morals and Legislation* (1789), nor in any of his writing from then down to 1816. During this period Bentham writes utopianly of the "univeral interest" and the "interest of all," and of the "happiness of the community as a whole."[12] From 1816 to 1829, the radical period in which he was ready to attack the interest of an unenlightened elite on behalf of the downtrodden many, the "greatest happiness of the greatest number" is found again in Bentham's writings. But in 1829, in his "Article on Utilitarianism," the philosopher abandons the expression as self-contradictory; Bentham was not a majoritarian. (He spoke eloquently of the plight of a hypothetical exploited minority of slaves in his "Article on Utilitarianism.")[13] But if one starts with the idea of policy making as some kind of problem in addition, how does one proceed when confronted with a need to add "apples and oranges"?

Welfare Economics

From Bentham, the way to the present broad currency of concepts of utility aggregation among philosophers and political scientists as well as economists and public servants lies chiefly through the history of welfare economics. This is a branch of economic thought devoted to the study of market efficiency and is chiefly concerned with the "question of how an economic system can produce the maximum quantity of the specific goods and services people want."[14] Its exponents, like Bentham, have sought to combine the basic institutions of a capitalist economy with the activities of government as a service agency that stands ready to compensate for market failures by providing public goods as the need arises. With the principle of Pareto optimality as a cornerstone of their theory, these economists have sought to show that a just balance of the two (i.e., market and governmental activities) can produce an increasingly abundant and therefore happy (because pleasure-filled) society.

Building on the earlier work of economists such as Alfred Marshall, Leon Walras, and Vilfredo Pareto, Arthur Cecil Pigou founded the new field in 1920 by publishing *The Economics of Welfare*. Two propositions were central to his theory.

1. Any cause which, without the exercise of compulsion or pressure upon people to make them work more than their wishes and interests dictate, increases productive efficiency, and, therewith, the average volume of the national dividend [income], provided that it neither injures the distribution, nor augments the variability of the country's consumable income, will, in general, increase economic welfare.

2. Any cause which increase the proportion of the national dividend received by poor persons, provided that it does not lead to a contraction of the dividend and does not injuriously affect its variability, will, in general, increase economic welfare.[15]

Thus, at its outset welfare economics had an egalitarian tendency, and we can hear echoes of Pigou's second proposition today in the theory of justice of John Rawls, who works with concepts from this field. One writer on welfare economic theory goes so far as to state that "assuming the law of diminishing utility and competitive prices, welfare would be maximized when the income of society was uniformly or equally distributed."[16] And E. J. Mishan, another welfare economist, tells us that an "appreciation of the methods of welfare economics can do much to mitigate some of the more blatant ills of the affluent society by combating conservative presumption in favor of commercial criteria and by revealing manifest injustices in any price system that has not been corrected to make allowance for visible and widespread external diseconomies." In another place Mishan remarks that "the theoretical discussion of the diversity and implications for welfare of . . . external effects have thus been growing with the years, along with skepticism about the virtues of the competitive market as an allocating mechanism."[17]

On the other hand, working from similar philosophical assumptions about the nature of utility and its measurement, a libertarian wing has been developing influence within the field of welfare economics among political scientists, among economists working in the theory of public choice, and among policy makers. Extremists at this end call themselves "Liberals" and are ready to repudiate what they term "the Paretian approach" in welfare economics (e.g., Charles K. Rowley and Alan T. Peacock in *Welfare Economics: A Liberal Restatement*, 1975). In their social elitism and in their insistence on the minimization of the role of government, kindred souls are scholars such as James Buchanan and Gordon

Tullock, who are regarded by the extreme right as members of the Paretian "heretic fringe." William H. Riker, whose recent book, *Liberalism Against Populism*, we discuss below, should be ranked with this group because of his Libertarian views. Rowley and Peacock, in characterizing the "heretics," say that this group attempts to "apply the Wicksellian unanimity rule to its logical extremities and nothing more, with the inference that moves commanding universal consent and such moves alone, can be said unambiguously to improve social welfare."[18]

Harsanyi's Moral Utilitarianism: An Effort to Link Moral with Personal Preference

While Paretian welfare economists generally have assumed, unlike Bentham, that the subject of their study must be treated as a solipsistic pleasure seeker, whose pleasure cannot be compared with those of others, and as someone who is not necessarily interested in the welfare of others, this is not universally the case.[19] Some, like John Harsanyi, in agreement with Bentham, build ethical theories on the assumption that utilities can be interpersonally compared and that there is a moral aspect to human nature that seeks the good of society as a whole, "defined in terms of impersonal and impartial criteria."[20] Harsanyi defines ethics, in terms reminiscent both of Bentham and of Rousseau, as "a theory of rational behavior in the service of the common interests of society as a whole."[21] The "general will" of this *moi commun* (my analogy, not Harsanyi's) is concretized by Harsanyi as "*maximizing the average utility level* of all individuals in the society." "Utility" measures purely personal preferences, "welfare" measures moral preferences.[22] In this fashion utilitarian ethics becomes for Harsanyi a part of the general theory of rational behavior.

Harsanyi links moral preference to personal preferences by the Pareto requirement that "a prospect *x* be morally preferred to a prospect *y*, if some individual personality prefers *x* to *y*, and no individual personality prefers *y* to *x*." As David Gauthier summarizes the argument:

> From this, and the requirements that both personal and moral preferences be capable of representation by vNM utility functions, Harsanyi proves the surprisingly strong theorem that each person's welfare function, representing his moral preferences, must be a weighted sum of all the individual utility functions representing personal preferences, and that all weights must be positive . . . Hence only utilitarian theories can be impartial, optimizing with respect to individual utility, and consistent with the maximizing conception of rationality.[23]

In a telling critique of Harsanyi's thesis, David Gauthier questions Harsanyi's assumption "that moral preferences parallel personal preferences in being capable of representation by a vNM utility function."[24] Just as plausible, he asserts, is that a public official, or moral agent,

> acts impartially, impersonally, and sympathetically to the interests of all, insofar as one's judgment expresses a *fair compromise* among the preferences of different individuals when their preferences do not agree in ordering all prospects in the same way.[25]

He suggests that the appropriate model for ethical theory is "the *theory of rational bargaining.*"[26] Harsanyi has not demonstrated that there is a linear relationship between ethical worth and individual utility.[27] Crucial to Gauthier's argument is the observation that

> in dealing with the preferences of several persons we are dealing with independent claims. Satisfaction accrues, not to the persons collectively, but to each individually. A single quantitative measure obscures the difference among persons. And although this may be of ethical significance, we cannot simply *assume* that it is not relevant. That ethics requires the maximization of a single quantitative measure must be the utilitarian's *conclusion*, and not his premise.[28]

We are again face-to-face with the problem of a Benthamite reduction of personality, with all its uniqueness, to generalized and abstract quantitative "utility." And this calls into question the possibility of making interpersonal comparisons of utility that Harsanyi's approach assumes. If we do not wish to raise the question, however, we may still ask whether it is ethically appropriate to begin the analysis, as Harsanyi does, with preferences taken as given, both personal and moral, rather than with preferences that represent needs reflected upon by persons capable of ethical development, as earlier suggested. If that is an appropriate place to begin then Gauthier's view of bargaining theory no more than Harsanyi's approach will yield an adequate welfare function that is formally or mathematically expressible.

Harsanyi has a second argument, which attempts directly to operationalize the concept of impartiality in individual choice. It is one that seems to be a variant of Rawls's use of the "veil of ignorance" in deciding on rational strategy (see below, pp. 277–278). It also seems to reduce Harsanyi's *moi commun*, who thinks in ethical (i.e., for him, social welfare) terms, to the *moi particulier*, concerned only with private or personal preferences (albeit in terms of enlightened self-interest). Harsanyi argues that the

> requirements of impersonality and impartiality would always be satisfied if he [the individual expressing an ethical choice] had to choose between

the . . . alternatives on the assumption that he had the same *probability* of occupying any of the existing social positions from the very highest to the very lowest (. . . the *equiprobability model* of moral value judgments).

According to modern decision theory, a rational individual placed in this hypothetical choice situation would always choose the alternative yielding him the *higher expected utility*—which, under this model, would mean choosing the alternative yielding the *higher average utility level* to the individual members of society. Thus . . . making a moral value judgment involves trying to maximize the arithmetic mean of all individual utilities.[29]

Gauthier asserts that Harsanyi's equiprobability argument is unsound, because any individual (*i*), making the calculation Harsanyi's model calls for, in thinking himself into the position of person *a* in situation *x* and person *b* in situation *y*, would have to possess preferences depending "*solely* on the utilities received by *a* and *b*" in their situations. "But person *i*'s preferences need not depend solely on these utilities—or on the strength of the preferences of *a* and *b*; his preferences may also depend on the personal characteristics of *a* and *b*." "We may not incorporate into our interpersonal measure of utility any evaluation of the preferences on which utilities rest."[30] (Gauthier accompanies this with a discussion of J. S. Mill's example of Socrates dissatisfied and the fool satisfied.)[31] One might add that the preferences of *i* may depend also on his *own* unique characteristics, which is probably implied by the idea of the importance of his assessment of the personal attributes of *a* and *b*. Thus, once more, interpersonal comparison of utilities breaks down, and, with it, Harsanyi's thesis.

In choosing among prospects without knowing what one's characteristics and circumstances will be, one will rationally maximize *not* the average utility to be received by the various persons in their situations, but the average of one's own utilities for being each of these persons. Since these averages need not be identical, Harsanyi's proposed operationalization of rational and impartial individual choice does not require that such choice be based on the utilitarian principle. And indeed, since each individual will choose in accordance with his own preferences, we may deny that true impartiality has been achieved. Harsanyi's operationalization is therefore *irrelevant* to ethical choice.[32]

Preference Aggregation as Constitution-Making: Center-Left

Considerable attention has been paid by economists, philosophers, and political scientists during the last two decades to the problem of selecting a general framework for rational individual choice, such that each person, in maximizing his own utility, is also constrained to maximize general welfare. In this fashion the problem of preference aggregation becomes a problem of constitution-making. (Gauthier points out that Bentham understood the welfare-maximizing requirement of utilitarian theory in this way in his *Introduction to the Science of Morals and Legislation*.) Thinkers such as John Rawls have built constitutional orders with an egalitarian thrust, which envisage an active and broadly competent state with redistributive functions. Others, such as James Buchanan and Gordon Tullock, Robert Nozick, and William H. Riker, working with similar if not identical basic concepts (e.g., individual rationality as strategic choice, maximization; authority as based on contract, efficiency), build systems that minimize the role of the state in society and emphasize the market as aggregator and allocator par excellence. Yet neither egalitarian nor libertarian approaches have proven successful as persuasive theoretical and practical efforts.

In *A Theory of Justice* John Rawls has attempted to show that self-interested individuals can cooperate socially in such fashion as to combine the efficiency norms of welfare economics (the maximization of welfare) with deontological principles of justice that value the autonomous person more than the welfare of society. Viewed in the context of American social myth, Rawls's intention can be expressed as an effort to establish the logical congruence of American hedonic individualism and American moralism.[33]

Rawls' starting point consists of three "intuitive" assumptions about human motivation that stand for the common but contradictory values of American liberal democrats. These are: (1) that every individual is a "maximizer" who wants to satisfy as many individual preferences as possible. (We all want more rather than less of anything, and as much of everything as possible.) (2) that in the general case, the maximization of social benefits as a whole (undistributed) through careful economic behavior will serve the ends of self-interested individuals; and (3) that every individual has (or can be educated to have) a sense of justice, defined as the sense that "each person possesses an inviolability founded on justice that even the welfare of society as a whole cannot override."[34]

The central problem of Rawls's theory is to deduce from premises of self-interest, mutual disinterest, rationality, and a sense of justice (as Kantian fairness) the basic rules of social organization that members of a model political society will adopt. In order to do this he places his model people behind a veil of ignorance in what he calls "The Original Position" (the world prior to political contract). This is a model world whose inhabitants are ignorant of their particular assets, talents, and social, economic, and political statuses in the empirical world. In such a condition Rawls concludes that his citizens will adopt two principles of justice:

1. Each person is to have an equal right to the most extensive basic
    liberty compatible with a similar liberty for others.
2. Social and economic inequalities are to be arranged so that they are
    both:
    (a) to the greatest benefit of the least advantaged, consistent with
         the just savings principle, and
    (b) attached to offices and positions open to all under conditions
         of fair equality of opportunity.[35]

Rawls's book focuses on explaining why selfish individuals will find it
rational (in their interest) to adopt the second of these principles. His
problem can be stated as follows: How can the pure individualists of
Kant's phenomenal world, motivated only by selfish desires, be convinced, to act like the noumenal persons of Kant's Kingdom of Ends,
who are motivated by the pure idea of law and right (the Categorical Imperative)—a problem Kant never solved? Rawls accomplishes the solution by reducing the significance of individualism through robbing it of
all particularity (the "Veil of Ignorance") and by requiring that the
members of his model world think atemporally—like Kant's noumenal
men. At the same time, he presents the second principle as one that individualists can accept on the basis of their selfishness by introduction of
the maximin rule, which specifies that "we rank alternatives by their
worst possible outcomes: we are to adopt the alternative the worst outcome of which is superior to the worst outcomes of the others."[36] It is interesting (but also sad and ironic) that the only way Rawls finds to make
persuasive the deontological values of the second principle of justice
(elite advantage only if the least advantaged are compensated) is with an
individualist appeal to enlightened self-interest in the form of the maximin rule.

Much criticism of Rawls has focused on his use of the maximin
strategy in motivating his model men to adopt the second principle of
justice. The most significant criticism charges that (a) maximin is not
psychologically realistic (Americans in particular are risk-acceptant, not
risk-averse); and (b) that it would not accomplish "justice" in Rawls's
terms, because to apply it would make it possible "to benefit the poorest
at the expense not of society's most privileged but at the expense of the
nearly poor."[37]

Characteristic of Rawls's political philosophy is his failure to begin
with first principles. He argues *from* them, not *to* them, and has been
severely criticized for doing this by other political philosophers. Thus,
Allan Bloom wonders whether Rawls's teaching is "meant to be a permanent statement about the nature of political things, or just a collection
of opinions that he finds satisfying and hopes will be satisfying to
others." He thinks Rawls "takes it for granted that we are all

egalitarians." "We start from what we are now and end there, since there is nothing beyond us. At best Rawls will help us to be more consistent, if that is an advantage. The distinctions between opinion and knowledge, and between appearance and reality, which made philosophy possible and needful, disappear."[38]

The last charge of Bloom's is a misstatement of the problem, since it is clear that Rawls does not think that we all *are* egalitarians, but rather that our desire to be enlightenedly self-interested (the maximin principle) can lead us, through reflection on his argument, to *become* egalitarians. But Bloom is right about neglecting first principles, which fits well the Benthamite tradition. We all remember that in criticizing the theory of an original social contract Bentham declared that "the indestructible prerogatives of mankind have no need to be supported upon the sandy foundation of a fiction."[39] But he nowhere gave us an ontological foundation for the "indestructible prerogatives of mankind."

The appearance of a detailed egalitarian theory of justice, which attempted to give due regard to the value of efficiency, within the parameters of capitalist economic order, at a time when welfare liberalism was dying the death in practical politics, gave renewed hope to welfare liberals that their cause was not, after all, moribund. Efforts were made to use Rawls's theory to resolve problems of a practical order in the real world of political decision, especially in the area of health policy, where debate has raged for some time over the question of whether and in what terms a universal "right to health care" should (can) be defined. Tom Beauchamp and Ruth Faden, two well-known scholars in this field, have commented in these terms about the result:

> Reservations about the power of moral philosophy to handle these problems may be rooted in the all too general character of moral principles when applied to such issues. Philosophers have long thought that general theories of justice could be applied with consistency, rigor and substance to the formulation of public policies. This hope has recently been butressed by the publicatons of philosophers interested in such work, for example, those interested in applying Rawls's (1971) account of justice to concrete problems. These efforts have for the most part, we suggest, been failures. They have served principally to show that policies governing practical matters of great complexity cannot be directly and consistently derived from highly abstract principles. Such derivations cannot be achieved in law, and even less can they be achieved in philosophy. There is also no single consistent set of material principles of distributive justice that reliably applies when concrete issues of justice arise.[40]

It seems unfortunate that entirely deductive, logically rigorous, but metaphysically ill-grounded and empirically empty utilitarian theories of social choice, like that of John Rawls, should be taken today as the paradigm of moral philosophy by scholars beset by philosophical puzzles in dealing with concrete policy issues in a society in which "preference" has become sovereign. Moral philosophy as such is discredited by the failure of empty (but popular) deductivism. One wonders whether Beauchamp and Faden would be ready (or able) to make the same critical comment say, of Aristotelian practical reason if that moral philosophy were carefully applied to issues in health policy.

Preference Aggregation as Constitution-Making: Models on the Right

We also have constitution-building on the right. One of the best known contributors to the libertarian literature of social choice is Robert Nozick, whose *Anarchy, State and Utopia* like Rawls's *Theory of Justice* has been much commented on and will therefore receive minimal treatment here.[41] Nozick is a pure individualist, who has no concern with the problems of the "least advantaged," nor with the amelioration, for any reason, of their position. His fundamental assumption is that "individuals have rights, and there are things no person or group may do to them (without violating their rights). So strong and far-reaching are these rights that they raise the question of what, if anything, the state and its officials may do."[42] But he presents not a line of philosophical defense of these rights. Like the political theory of Rawls, that of Nozick is ontologically empty. Nozick avoids all discussion of first principles and simply invokes the name of Locke, though he is careful to avoid realiance on theories of "Natural Right" or "Natural Law." "Rights," in the way he uses the term, without definition or justification, figure simply as "preferences" in the franker language of welfare economics. Nozick's "rights" have no more philosophical grounding than Bentham's "indestructible prerogatives of mankind." And Nozick's occasional invocation of the Kantian idea that the person is inviolable is empty.[43] To be specific, Nozick never attributes to individuals a "sense of justice," which implies an ability to comprehend and act upon a general rule of right, quite independently of the demands of self-interest. Consider how poorly the following social program that Kant himself derives from his noumenal conception of right fits with Nozick's free market system.

> The General Will of the people has united itself into a society in order to maintain itself continually, and for this purpose it has subjected itself to the internal authority of the state in order to support those members of the

society who are unable to provide the most necessary needs of nature for themselves. The money should be raised not merely through voluntary contribution, but by compulsory exactions as political burdens, for here we are considering only the rights of the state in relation to the people.[44]

Though Rawls would obviously agree with the sentiment that Kant expresses here, while to Nozick it would be anathema, Nozick's failure to give any substantial grounding to his idea of the inviolability of persons does little to help us distinguish his ethical position—hedonic individualism—from that of Rawls, since Rawls makes no practical use of the Kantian "sense of justice" that he attributes to the people of his model world, because the centrality of the maximin rule in the calculation of these people in "the original position" reduces Rawlsian justice to "enlightened self-interest," as we have seen.

Nozick's model person is an individualist who is simply more self-confident than Rawls's risk-averse model people. He espouses an ultralibertarian social and political program in which all values except protection are to be realized through market exchange rather than through collective action (i.e., through the state). Nozick's language of self-interest is contradicted only by his arbitrarily opting (after hundreds of pages of tedious argument) to erect a minimal state for the supply of protection, all other values being left to the magic "unseen hand" of the market and to voluntary associations. He never makes it clear, in view of his description of the main features of human nature and especially of the logic of individual choice, why this theory does not culminate in a "dominant protective" association rather than in a "minimal state."

It is tragic that in the hour of crisis of American liberal political culture, our society's most prestigious academic institution is unable to do better than produce an abstract and sterile debate between two of its most eminent philsophers who represent our dual traditions of libertarian and egalitarian individualism, a debate that in no way addresses itself to the pressing problems of social welfare, environmental policy, educational policy, criminal justice, and defense policy, whose solution requires resolving contradictions between claims of individual right and justice on the one hand and dispassionate recognition of the fact of scarce resources and the need for efficient management of those resources for the common good on the other.

The most recent contribution to the libertarian literature of constitution-building is William H. Riker's *Liberalism Against Populism: A Confrontation Between the Theory of Democracy and the Theory of Social Choice.*[45] The first sentence of the book capsulizes for the reader the conceptual system within which its argument is presented: "The theory of social choice is a theory about the way the tastes, preferences, or values of individual persons are amalgamated and summarized in the choice of a collective group or society.''[46] Within this general area of interest, Riker focuses on voting methods, because every social choice theory must include a theory of voting, and because "voting is . . . an indispensable feature of democracy," the political form that is authoritative in our political culture.[47]

The book argues in great technical detail that different "fair" voting systems produce different results in social choice, "when applied to the same profile of individual preferences," and that there is "no obvious way to choose between" systems.[48] The sole escape from this "nihilistic conclusion is to find that some method is uniquely fairest" and thus superior to others on moral grounds.[49] Simple majority decision between two alternatives, Riker notes, is "said to be just that," since it is the sole method that can satisfy at once three important criteria of fairness, "monotonicity, undifferentiatedness, and neutrality."[50] However, Riker argues, it is "probably extremely rare for binary alternatives to occur naturally without any human intervention."[51] And the political process of making this reduction (e.g., primaries, nominating conventions, double-stage elections) "is often (probably always) in itself unfair."[52] Thus, no voting method of broad practical use that is also universally and univocally "fair" can be found.

This poses large problems for the viability of democracy, understood as government by popular will. In addition, Riker finds that the processes of democratic social choice are infinitely manipulable, both by self-interested elites and by the common voter, through strategic voting and agenda control (Chapters 6 and 7), which present still another aspect of the problem of fairness. Also, building on the implications of Kenneth Arrow's "Impossibility Theorem" or "General Possibility Theorem," there is no way to insure rationality (logicality) in social choice. And to cap all this, there is "an unresolvable tension between logicality and fairness."[53]

> To guarantee an ordering or a consistent path, independent choice requires that there be some sort of concentration of power (dictators, oligarchies, or collegia of vetoers) in sharp conflict with democratic ideals. . . .
>
> . . . The unavoidable inference is . . . that, so long as a society preserves democratic institutions, its members can expect that some of their social choices will be unordered or inconsistent. . . .
>
> . . . The possibility of a lack of meaning in the outcome is a serious problem for social judgment and social choice. It forces us to doubt that the content of 'social welfare' or the 'public interest' can ever be discovered by amalgamating individual value judgments. It even leads us to suspect that no such things as the 'public interest' exists, aside from the subjective (and hence dubious) claims of self-proclaimed saviors.[54]

The upshot of all this is a condemnation, as unworkable, of that form of democracy Riker labels *populist* (or "Rousseauist"), a form in which "liberty and hence self-control through participation are obtained by embodying the will of the people in the action of officials."[55] The "will of the people" does not exist because it may either be meaningless (consisting of a series of intransitive choices) or it may be unfairly assessed and manipulated. In its place Riker opts for a "liberal" (or Madisonian) system, in which "the function of voting is to control officials, *and no more.*"[56] By *control* the author here means nothing better than "an intermittent, sometimes random, even perverse, popular veto."[57] "Liberal democracy is simply the veto by which it is *sometimes* possible to restrain official tyranny," "a veto at the margin."[58]

The book concludes with a brief positive appraisal of the major institutions of divided and separated consitutional government based on regular elections that characterize the American Federal system.[59] Riker's preference that this government function minimally is implied in his celebration of the economic market in contrast with political collective choice processes in a section entitled "Voting Disequilibrium: What It Means to Lose," and on a closely subsequent page.[60] His ideal government would be one of very strictly limited powers indeed, a "night-watchman" state.

Having laid out Riker's critique of "populist democracy" by reviewing his effort, through the application of social choice theory, to show that the concept produces neither "fair" nor rational government, let us proceed to a critique of the critique. It is my judgment that Riker's use of social choice theory to understand governmental process "proves" not only that populist government but also what he terms *liberalism* are equally unworkable, a mockery. If the function of government is conceived primarily and centrally, in perfectly predictable, "fair," and "logical" ways to aggregate the momentary and arbitrary preferences of individuals into social policy, then neither efforts at direct embodiment of a popular will nor efforts at the systematic popular control of officials are possible. "Democratic government" in each case will be nothing but arbitrary manipulation and random process.

Let me illustrate first by looking at one of the examples Riker uses to answer the question he raises at the beginning of Chapter 2, as to whether "social summaries of citizens' decisions . . . are . . . coherent," and whether they are "imposed by manipulation."[61] In dealing with the problem of different summarizing methods producing different choices from identical values, Riker presents a case study of "experimental evidence." This was drawn from the story of preparations for a project to launch two Mariner spacecrafts in 1977 for a Jupiter and Saturn flypast in 1979 and 1980; for this launch, teams of outside scientists, each concerned with a different aspect of planetary observation, were asked by the managing agency of the project to select pairs of trajectories for the two craft by cardinal ranking of 32 pairs selected by the scientists for final consideration. Riker says of the rankings made, "The members of the teams took their task very seriously and calculated their preferences according to their own self-interest rather than according to any kind of general interest (as assumed in some populist theories)."[62]

This language seems inappropriate, since what each team apparently did was to order trajectories for optimality in making the particular observations with which the team was charged in the over-all project. Apparently no one was given the task of working out scientifically a trajectory that optimized all desired observations, which was evidently impossible. Yet there was plainly present a sensed common good—the need to get the vehicles launched in a manner that would accomplish as well as possible multiple scientific measurements. Four "well-known and well-rationalized methods of summation" were employed to arrive at a decision, on the basis of the ten cardinal rankings.[63] It is remarkable to me that only two winners, #26 and #31, came from this process, each winning twice since each of the four methods evidently emphasized different features of "fairness" in summation, and the scientific objectives numbered ten. This seems a substantial movement toward consensus in a complex enterprise incapable of exact scientific determination. (It is not clear why the Delphi technique was not used to obtain consensus.)

Riker reports that the managing agency, "after some adjustment and improvement of pair 26, persuaded the teams to adopt it."[64] This last part of the choice process—rational persuasion in the light of scientific calculation—is not duplicated in political choice conceived simply as preference summation, but it may well have an anaologue in the work of political leadership, which need not necessarily be mere manipulation in the interest of the rulers. Presumably, in the trajectory case, the managing agency used scientific knowledge in making "adjustments" and "improvements" in pair 26 and rational persuasion supported with scientific evidence, not mere rhetoric, in getting a final consensus on the adoption of this pair as the trajectory to be employed. They might just as well have adapted and adopted pair 31, as Riker suggests. Just so, a populist community may have a sensed common good, analogous to that of the scientific enterprise, plus a variety of opinions about how to optimize that common good viewed from special angles. It is also possible that voting in such a situation may yield two different "solutions" to the problem of the common good, either one of which, when modified by responsible political leadership in the context of information and of political dialogue and persuasion, could yield a satisfactory solution. Much will depend on the strength of the sense of a common good, on the effort of the citizenry to develop honest and informed opinions that are not simply arbitrary preferences, and on the quality of the information, good will, and moral quality of the leadership. In the social choice model of preference summation used by Riker for evaluating populist democracy, none of these factors are considered to be operative. Nor are they considered operative in his "liberal democracy." But unless they *are* operative there is just as much opportunity under "liberalism" as in the populist model (perhaps more) for manipulative machinations by entrenched elites through strategic voting, agenda control, and unfair methods of narrowing down to binary choices the alternatives that they present to the atomistic electorate of purely self-interested individuals who periodically elect and reject them. In the atomized and hoodwinked society assumed to be the typical electorate, why could a clever elite not adequately manipulate the electorate to insure the permanence of its tyrannical position, under the pessimistic assumptions Riker lays down? And how is the possibility of a "random" or "perverse" rejection of a corrupt elite by a happenstance majority of the fragmented electorate of Riker's "liberal" system any different from the possibility in his populist model of a similar rejection, since the populist similarly makes devices of popular electoral control a central institution? Rousseau in fact emphasized short terms and popular vigilance, and suspicion of rulers, who were given a mere administrative function in implementing the "general will." This required that the regular meeting of his popular assembly open with the questions:

> The first: Does it please the sovereign to preserve the present form of government?
>
> The second: Does it please the people to leave the administration in the hands of those who are currently responsible for it?[65]

How does this differ at all from the emphasis placed by Riker in maintaining his "liberal" regime (quoting Madison) through "a dependence on the people . . . [as] the primary control on the government"?

In his last paragraph Riker writes, "Liberal democracy almost guarantees some circulation of leadership so that great power is usually fleeting and no vested interest lasts forever."[66] The same guarantee is certainly present in the populist model, through elections. But if in each case the electorate is fragmented, a mere bundle of rationally unaggregable preferences the existence of "auxiliary precautions" (the institutions of constitutionalism) will be of little avail in preventing a clever elite from manipulating and hoodwinking its electorate. Without moral consensus in the body of the people, civic alertness against elite machinations, and the possibility of responsible leadership—none of which figure in Riker's model of summation— the operation of the *machinery* of the government alone would not allow us to make distinctions about the adequacy of their functioning since *both* models centrally feature voting by popular bodies.

Let us look briefly at the way Riker deals with the implications of Arrow's Theorem about transitivity in social choice. (*Transitivity* means that if person (or society) (i) prefers *x* to *y* and *y* to *z*, then he (it) prefers *x* to *z* as well. The relationship would be intransitive (irrational) and would create a cycle if one were to change the last term to read: "prefers *z* to *x*.") Arrow holds that if the following conditions of "fairness" obtain in social choice, then transitivity (i.e., logicality, rationality, meaningfulness) cannot be guaranteed: 1–universal admissibility of orderings, 2–unanimity (or 3–monotonicity, and 4–citizens' sovereignty), 5–independence from irrelevant alternatives, and 6–nondictatorship.[67]

I think it is important to point out, first of all, with reference to the Arrow theorem, that it does *not* hold that positing the conditions of fairness *insures* intransitivity. It just does *not* insure or guarantee transitivity. As Riker puts it: "Arrow's theorem . . . is that every possible method of amalgamation or choice that satisfies the fairness condition *fails to ensure a social ordering*. And if society cannot, with fair methods, be *certain* to order its outcome, then it is not clear that we can know what the outcome of a fair method means."[68] But, one might ask, who but utopians *ever* look for *certainty* in political outcomes? The world of a model (logical necessity) is not the same as the empirical world, which is replete with indeterminacy, which yields not only unpredictability, but also human freedom. Therefore, Riker's remark seems unwarrantedly dismal and cynical when he writes:

> This conclusion appears to be devastating, for it consigns democratic outcomes—and hence the democratic method—to the world of arbitrary nonsense.[69]

It is interesting that he quietly qualifies this large statement with the phrase *at least some of the time*.[70] But then *what* system can avoid falling into arbitrary government "at least some of the time"? Certainly Riker's preferred "liberal" system—by his own admission— cannot guarantee against arbitrary measures, "at least some of the time" (*see also* pp. 244, 245).

We need to note that Riker takes account of real-world democratic politics in which some of Arrow's abstract conditions are significantly modified. In one kind of democratic situation, an electorate's preferences reveal "single-peakedness."[71] Riker defines this as "a condition or a preference profile such that the profile contains a Condorcet winner when every curve representing a preference order (with alternatives on the horizontal axis and degree of preference on the vertical axis) is single-peaked."[72] And he writes that "single-peakedness implies transitivity and hence ensures the existence of a Condorcet winner."[73] Riker continues by telling us that "the fact that a profile, D, is single-peaked means the voters have a common view of the political situation, although they may differ widely on their judgments."[74] Now this means that condition #1—universal admissibility of orderings—does not obtain in this case. Preferences under the circumstances described fit a pattern, and something like value consensus exists. This means that in *practice* not all *logically* admissible orderings enter into democratic decision. Riker even takes note of the importance of factors that do not exist in Arrow's abstract theorem of "fair" social choice that modify the problem of intransitivity. He writes:

> If, by reason of discussion, debate, civic education and political socialization voters have a common view of the political dimension (as evidenced by a single-peakedness), then a transitive outcome is guaranteed.[75]

If the condition of single-peakedness obtains, and we assume the existence of a consensual democracy, whether "populist" or "liberal" in Riker's understanding of those terms, the problem of irrationality and meaninglessness in choice is itself a meaningless bugaboo. If single-peakedness does *not* exist, then *neither* the decision of populist *nor* of liberal government (electoral decisions or those by representative elites) will be guaranteed to be rational and meaningful.

I do not understand why Riker immediately follows the sentences on which we have just been commenting with the statement:

> So if a society is homogeneous in this sense, then there will typically be Condorcet winners, at least on issues of *minor* importance. The fact will not prevent civil war, but it will ensure that the civil war makes sense.[76]

It is not at all clear why the Condorcet results should obtain only for minor issues or why a consensual society (characterized by "value restrictions") should face the threat of civil war. MacKay's illustration of single-peakedness (presented in footnote 75) describes a functioning "Downsian" democracy, in which voters cluster toward a centrist position. This is not a society on the brink of civil war.

Riker attempts an explanation of his puzzling statement by arguing that "when subjects are politically important enough to justify the energy and expense of contriving cycles, Arrow's result is of great practical significance. It suggests that, on the very most important subjects, cycles may render social outcomes meaningless."[77] But this seems incomplete as an explanation of Riker's position, because it implies the destruction of single-peakedness—the situation we have been considering—and therefore the destruction of value homogeneity in a society by manipulative elites. Such an assertion takes us beyond the model world into the empirical world and to consideration of a variety of possible but unspecified dynamics of an economic, demographic, social, or cultural character that would reduce a homogeneous, single-peaked society to a fragmented one. But this means that the factors relevant to a determination of whether meaningful democratic decision making is possible have nothing to do with Arrow's abstract logical world. And if this is so, then Riker's very general dismal conclusion, both about "populist" and "liberal" democracy, seems unwarranted. The factors governing the results Riker predicts do not seem to be in the logical models he manipulates, but rather in the moral, economic, demographic, and cultural circumstances of the empirical world.

Conclusion

There is a large value to Riker's work in social choice theory, and to social choice theory generally. It alerts us, in deciding how fruitfully to conduct the science of politics, to the questionableness of assuming that the primary problem of government, as the Benthamite tradition holds, is the summation of given and infinitely various preference orderings into a fair and meaningful whole—into social policies for the common good.[78] If we look only at the assumptions of the model world of Arrow's theorem, we indeed would despair of operating a viable liberal democracy. No "true" summation seems possible.[79]

The assumptions we have reviewed remind us of Plato's model world of the "social contract," as recounted by Glaucon in *Republic*. In Glaucon's model, the citizens "set down a compact among themselves neither to do injustice nor to suffer it. And from there they began to set down their own laws and compacts and to name what the law commands lawful and just."[80] However, since each citizen was a radically self-interested individual, "we would catch the just man red-handed going the same way as the unjust man out of a desire to get the better; this is what any nature naturally pursues as good, while it is law which by force perverts it to honor equality." Plato then recounts the story of the ring of Gyges. And he concludes that:

> if there were two such rings, and the just man would put one on, and the
> unjust man the other, no one, as it would seem, would be so adamant as to

stick by justice and bring himself to keep away from what belongs to others and not to lay hold of it. . . .And in so doing, one would act no differently from the other, but both would go the same way. Men do not take it to be a good for them in private, since wherever each supposes he can do injustice he does it.

A very striking parallel to the behavior of the people in Glaucon's model is found in the machinations of agenda-riggers described by Riker in a recent article on the study of disequilibrium in majority rule: "There is some way by which *any* point can beat the status quo. . . .Hence, an official or participant who can control the agenda can bring about the adoption of his or her desired alternative â. But, of course, there is also a path by which à may then beat â. So a second participant may foil the first."[82] And so on, *ad infinitum*. The article seems to evidence a certain disenchantment with the mathematical pursuit of the implications of abstract models of social choice. Riker urges us in the article to turn to the study of institutions:

We cannot leave out the force of institutions. The people whose values and tastes are influential live in a world of conventions about both language and values themselves. These conventions are in turn condensed into institutions, which are simply rules about behavior, especially about making decisions. . . .Interpersonal rules, that is, institutions must affect social outcomes just as much as personal values.[83]

Plato and Aristotle would surely agree with this, as their political science so clearly shows. The world of preference summation, like the world of Glaucon's "social contract," excludes things like good will, education to civic virtue, trust, responsible leadership, community, and value consensus. And the production of all these things requires, of course, good institutions, as Plato and Aristotle both knew. This does not mean that modern political science should speculate about the establishment of philosopher kings, though we might learn something important from a study of the moral makeup of Aristotle's statesman of "practical reason." It means that modern political science, to avoid cynicism and sterility, needs to address itself to questions about the nature of the good life, the character of trust and how it can be nurtured, the meaning and fostering of responsible leadership, community, and a vital and noble value consensus.

That we need such a political science is revealed by the present condition of our political system. The authors of a recent report by a presidential commission on the quality of American life in the 1980s remark that

This is a time of unusual turbulence. Many Americans have genuine doubts about the capability of political processes to deliver solutions to our most pressing problems. Despite all the prescriptions for governmental philosophy and action put forth during the recent campaign (1980), there does not appear to be a great deal of popular confidence in any of them. Americans are between idea systems. Just as the problems of the Depression led to a redefinition of the role and scope of the government in the 1930s, the trials of the 1970s caused much of the support for New Deal liberalism to erode. What is not yet clear is whether a new public philosophy—the successor to New Deal liberalism—will emerge in response to the new realities of the 1980s.

Therefore we raise . . . the most basic questions about the American political process: How much government does the nation need, and how much are the nation's citizens willing to pay for? What is the proper role of the public sector? Why has this nation recently experienced so much trouble in building coalitions in support of new initiatives?[84]

Questions of this order will not be answered by a political science that is centrally concerned with the summation of preferences. An adequate science must rather be concerned with the formation of preferences. It must seek to answer the question of how we can develop, in democratic fashion, a rational understanding of the problems before us and a rational and agreed upon approach to the solution of those problems. It will be a political science concerned with the definition and implementation of the common good.

Notes

1. See Jeremy Bentham, *A Fragment on Government*, par. 39. John Rawls does not see himself as a utilitarian, but as a critic of utilitarian thought. In Rawls's *Theory of Justice*, for example, he criticizes extensively the utilitarianism of Sidgwick, and attempts in numerous places to associate his own fundamental assumptions with those of Kant. Jan Narveson in "Rawls and Utilitarianism," in H.B. Miller and W.H. Williams, eds., *The Limits of Utilitarianism* (Minneapolis: University of Minnesota Press, 1982), 128–43, however, argues that Rawls's two principles of justice can be derived from the understanding of utilitarianism embraced by Rawls. This writer agrees. See above pages 13–15.

2. "The theory of social choice studies aggregation devices (sometimes called social welfare functions) with a view to deciding whether there is a perfect, or rational, or acceptable design, and what constraints such a thing should meet." Alfred MacKay, *Arrow's Theorem: The Paradox of Social Choice* (New Haven and London: Yale University Press, 1980), 13–14. "Social welfare functions are mathematical expressions showing the relationship between social welfare and the different factors that create social welfare. They stand in the same relationship to a society as utility functions do to an individual." Lester C. Thurow, et al *Markets and Morals*, eds. Gerald Dworkin (New York: Hemisphere Publishing, 1977), 90.

3. Some political scientists argue for the less greedy sounding idea of "satisficing." See, for example, the work of Herbert Simon.

4. Bikhu Parekh, ed., *Bentham's Political Thought* (New York: Harper & Row, 1973), 15.

5. Ibid., 35, citing *Works* III: 184, 220, 221.

6. R. M. Hare defines utilitarianism as "a species of *welfarist consequentialism*—that particular form of it which requires simply *adding up* individual welfares or utilities to assess the consequences, a property that is sometimes called *sum-ranking*." In Amartya Sen and Bernard Williams, eds., *Utilitarianism and Beyond* (New York: Cambridge University Press, 1982), 4.

7. Parekh, ed., *Bentham's Political Thought*, 15.

8. Hare, *Utilitarianism and Beyond*, 4,5.

9. Dworkin et al., eds., *Markets and Morals*, p. 184.

10. Ibid.

11. Ibid., 185ff.

12. Parekh, *Bentham's Political Thought*, 16.

13. Ibid., 14-15, 309-10.

14. Patricia Bowers, *Private Choice and Public Welfare* (Hinsdale, Ill.: Dryden Press, 1974), 18.

15. A. C. Pigou, *The Economics of Welfare*, 4th ed. (London: Macmillen, 1932) 47, 53; quoted in Maurice Dobb, *Welfare Economics and the Economics of Socialism* (New York: Cambridge University Press, 1969), 28.

16. John F. O'Connell, *Welfare Economic Theory* (Dover, Mass.: Auburn House, 1982), 5.

17. "Welfare Economics," *Encyclopedia of the Social Sciences* 16 (New York: Macmillan, 1968): 508, 511.

18. Charles K. Rowley and Alan T. Peacock, *Welfare Economics: A Liberal Restatement* (New York: John Wiley & Sons, 1975), 10-11.

19. Leading assumptions of what Rowley and Peacock term the "Paretian orthodoxy" in welfare economics are the following:

  1. That "the underlying analytical structure is static, with decisions to take place at a point in time and to be implemented costlessly and instantaneously . . . . Uncertainty as to the future does not exist . . . . Perfect knowledge about the present is commonly assumed."

  2. "Each individual's preference ordering over states of the economy is characterized by selfishness or, more precisely, by solipsism; i.e., his preference ranking is defined over the commodity bundles that he receives and is not influenced by the commodity bundles allocated to other individuals . . . . Neither malevolence nor benevolence is recognised as having any relevance for individual welfare."

  3. "It is assumed that individuals seek to maximise their individual utilities, that producers seek to maximise their profits, and that all parties rationally pursue respective objectives" (pp. 11, 12).

20. John C. Harsanyi, "Nonlinear Social Welfare Functions: Do Welfare Economists Have a Special Exemption from Bayesian Rationality?," *Essays on Ethics, Social Behavior and Scientific Explanation* (Dordrecht, Holland D. Reidel, 1976), 96–98; cited in David Gauthier, "On the Refutation of Utilitarianism," *The Limits of Utilitarianism*, ed. Miller and Williams, 150.

21. "Morality and the Theory of Rational Behavior," *Social Research*, 44 (Winter, 1977): 625–56; cited in Ibid.

22. Ibid.

23. Ibid. A vNM utility function is a technical device defined by John von Neumann and Oskar Morgenstern, which transforms ordinal utility for an ordered set of alternatives to cardinal utility. See glossary of key decision-theory terms in William H. Riker, *Liberalism Against Populism* (San Francisco: W. H. Freeman, 1982), 293–98. See also Riker's critique of cardinal utility measurements in politics, ibid., 97.

24. Ibid., 151.

25. Ibid., 152–53.

26. Ibid., 153.

27. Ibid., 154.

28. Ibid.

29. John C. Harsanyi, "Rule Utilitarianism and Decision Theory," *Erkenntnis* 11 (May 1977): 28; quoted in Gauthier, "On the Refutation of Utilitarianism," 155–56.

30. *op. cit.*, p. 157.

31. *Ibid.*, 156–57.

32. Ibid., 158.

33. John Rawls, *A Theory of Justice* (Cambridge, Mass.: Belknap Press, 1971).

34. Ibid., 3.

35. Ibid., 60, 302.

36. Ibid., 152–53.

37. See Benjamin Barber, "Justifying Justice: Problems of Psychology, Measurement, and Politics in Rawls," *American Political Science Review* 69 (June 1975): 663–74; John C. Harsanyi, "Can the Maximin Principle Serve as a Basis for Morality? A Critique of John Rawls' Theory," *American Political Science Review* 69 594–606; Douglas Rae, "Maximin Justice and an Alternative Principle of General Advantage," (June 1975): 630–47.

38. In *American Political Science Review* 69 (June 1975?: 648, 649.

39. Bentham, *A Fragment on Government*, par. 36.

40. Tom L. Beauchamp and Ruth R. Faden, "The Right to Health and the Right to Health Care," *The Journal of Medicine and Philosophy* 4 (June 1979).

41. Robert Nozick, *Anarchy, State and Utopia* (New York: Basic Books, 1974).

42. Ibid., ix.

43. See pp. 91–93 for a discussion of Herbert Hart's natural rights theory. For references to Kant see pages 32, 228, 337n4, 338nl.

44. Immanuel Kant, *The Metaphysical Elements of Justice*, (Indianapolis: Bobbs-Merrill, 1965), 93–94.

45. (San Francisco: W. H. Freeman, 1982).

46. Ibid., 1.

47. Ibid.

48. Ibid., 58, 59.

49. Ibid.

50. Ibid. For definitions of these terms see Riker's glossary, pages 293–98.

51. Ibid., 59.

52. Ibid.

53. Ibid., 136. In his glossary Riker gives the following brief statement of the "General Possibility Theorem": "The proposition that, if a social choice function satisfies universal admissibility, unanimity (or monotonicity and citizens' sovereignty), independence from irrelevant alternatives, and nondictatorship, then the social choice may not satisfy transitivity" (p. 293).

54. Ibid., 136, 137.

55. Ibid., 11.

56. Ibid., 9.

57. Ibid., 244.

58. Ibid., 245, emphasis added.

59. Ibid., 250–53.

60. Ibid., 201–6, 210. Towards the beginning of the section he offers mild praise of the workings of Pareto optimality in an expanding market economy: "Pareto optimality does not necessarily mean that inequalities or profound unfairness are either created or erased; it means merely that, relative to a given initial endowment, everybody is better off in some amount, however small." He then goes onto the following pronouncedly negative comparison of the political with the economic market:

> However real and politically significant is the resentment of a poverty not alleviated by the operation of the market, still the market does not make people worse off,

unless as in the case of unemployment—they are politically excluded from participation. Since exclusion is temporary unless politically imposed, losing in the market is a remarkably mild kind of losing compared with losing in politics. Losing politically is typically much worse than losing economically. [p. 202]

If this is the truth of the matter, one is led to wonder why economic distress has so often led to what Treitschke called "politics *kat exochen*"—politics in the highest degree": war and revolution.

A few passages further along, Riker presents another economic-political comparison:

Economic scarcity forces the use of a rationing device such as market prices or planning allocations. . . .

But that is all it means. Simply, those who do not have must go without. Economic scarcity does not also require that the nonpossessor suffer additional punishment for nonpossession, nor does it mean that the nonpossessor is legally prohibited from gaining possession. Economically, it is enough that the poor go hungry; politically and morally the poor may—perhaps must—also be publicly ridiculed for starving and permanently condemned to starvation. [p. 204]

Conversely, Riker neglects to point out that politics can also fill the bellies of the poor that pure market economics has emptied; redistributive measures and new laws of ownership enable the nonpossessor to gain possession.

A few paragraphs further on the author makes another comparison:

To lose on issues of political and moral scarcity (which issues are the stuff of politics) is much worse thatn to lose in the market. One must suffer outcomes in which one is economically or emotionally deeply deprived. Truly, it is politics, not economics, that is the dismal science. [p. 206.]

But one could adduce innumerable examples that political action is frequently the only means available for rectifying economic and emotional deprivation. But my intention here is not to engage in a polemic against free market economics, for I, too, am a capitalist, though not of the libertarian persuasion. My purpose is simply to highlight the libertarian thrust of Riker's constitution-building effort.

61. Ibid., 21.

62. Ibid., 30.

63. Ibid.

64. Ibid., 31.

65. Jean-Jacques Rousseau, *On the Social Contract*, trans. R. J. Masters (New York: St. Martin's Press, 1978), 107.

66. Riker, *Liberalism Against Populism*, 253.

67. This is Riker's restatement of the conditions. See his glossary for definition of the terms. In his original statement of the conditions, Arrow presents them as five, rather than six; does not give a label, but simply a technical formulation to condition 1; gives a different label to condition number 3; and apparently subsumes Riker's condition number 2 under 4. See Kenneth J. Arrow, *Social Choice and Individual Values* (New York: John Wiley & Sons, 1951), 22-23. Alfred F. MacKay presents the conditions as fourfold: (1) unlimited scope, (2) Pareto Prin-

ciple, (3) independence of irrelevant alternatives, (4) nondictatorship. His #2 apparently embraces Riker's numbers 2, 3 and 4. *Arrow's Theorem: The Paradox of Social Choice* (New Haven: Yale University Press, 1980).

68. Riker, *Liberalism Against Populism*, 119, emphasis added.

69. Ibid.

70. Ibid.

71. Ibid., 297.

72. Ibid.

73. Ibid., 126. See Riker's glossary for a definition of *Condorcet Winner*.

74. Ibid.

75. Ibid., 128. See Alfred F. MacKay's comment on the implication of single peakedness.''

> A group of preference rankings is single-peaked if there is some one of the choice alternatives concerning which all the voters agree that it is not worst. This can be illustrated by a situation in which the candidates or issues line up along the standard liberal-conservative spectrum. Suppose that there are three candidates, one leftist (L), one centrist (C), and one rightist (R). Single-peakedness means that the electorate view these candidates in the "reasonable" manner, each voter ranking them according to their "distance" from his favorite. Thus left-of-center voters rank them L, C, R. Right-leaning voters rank them R, C, L. Centrist voters prefer C to the other two. Notice that in the situation described, the voters do not docilely all agree. There is "fruitful" competition between left and right, with the centrists exerting a moderating influence. Still, they all do agree that candidate C is not the worst. There is no voter, for example, whose first choice is R, but if he cannot have R would prefer L to C; no one, that is, who prefers both extremes to the middle . . . A glance at the cyclical majorities pattern in the paradox of voting [Arrow's paradox] shows that no such special, limited agreement obtains there. . . . Hence, a restriction to single-peakedness has as a consequence the barring of cyclical majorities patterns. [*Arrow's Theorem*, 28–29]

76. Riker, *Liberalism Against Populism*, 128.

77. Ibid.

78. See MacKay's discussion of Arrow's conditions, especially of condition (1) unrestricted scope in MacKay's language, *Arrow's Theorem*, pages 1–48. MacKay applies the conditions to scoring the results of a decathlon competition. He asks rhetorically in one place: "Should we expect an acceptable scoring system to be applicable to every conceivable setting of events, competitors, and every possible way a group of competitors might finish in an event? Well, maybe it would look nice. But it does not look *pressing*. Unrestricted scope does not appear to be implicated in the very concept of holding a decathlon, or in the point of doing same" (p. 26). One might say the same of holding an election in a democratic society, where unrestricted domain does not exist by the fact of basic consensus. To be fair in politics thus does not require unrestricted domain.

79. Cf. William H. Riker, "Implications from the Disequilibrium of Majority Rule for the Study of Institutions," *American Political Science Review* 74 (June 1980): 442.

80. *The Republic of Plato*, trans. Allan Bloom (New York: Basic Books, 1968), 37.

81. Ibid., 37, 38.

82. Riker, "Implications from the Disequilibrium of Majority Rule," 442.

83. Ibid., 432.

84. President's Commission for a National Agenda for the Eighties, *Report of the Panel on the Quality of American Life in the Eighties* (Washington, D.C.: 1980), 128–29.

Editors and Contributors

Kenneth L. Deutsch (Coeditor) is professor of political science at SUNY College at Geneseo. He has published three books: *Political Obligation and Civil Disobedience, Constitutional Rights,* and *Modern Indian Political Thought* (Sage Publications, 1986). He has also published a number of articles and reviews in such journals as *The American Political Science Review, Polity,* and *The Review of Politics.* He is presently working on a book on Aquinas' political and legal philosophy.

Walter Soffer (Coeditor) is professor of philosophy at SUNY College at Geneseo. He has published a number of articles on Descartes, Kant, and Husserl. He recently completed a book on Descartes entitled *From Science to Subjectivity: An Interpretation of Descartes' "Meditations"* (Greenwood Press, 1987). He is presently at work on a study of the relation between sexuality and politics in Plato's *Republic.*

An augmented edition of **Michael Platt's** *Rome and Romans According to Shakespeare* appeared in 1983 from the University Press of America; its sequel, *Shakespeare's Christian Prince,* will appear from the same press in 1987. He is currently working on a book on Nietzsche on a fellowship from NEH. His essay on the high point in *Zarathustra* will appear in *Nietzsche Studien* for 1987.

Victor Gourevitch is professor of philosophy at Wesleyan University. His earlier study of Strauss's thought, "Philosophy and Politics I-II," appeared in the *Review of Metaphysics* 22 (1968), pp. 58–84 and 281–328; his annotated translation of Rousseau's First and Second *Discourses,* together with the *Replies* to Critics of the *Discourses,* and the *Essay on the Origin of Languages,* appeared last year (Harper & Row, 1986).

Roger D. Masters is professor of government at Dartmouth College. His publications on Rousseau have included *The Political Philosophy of Rousseau* (Princeton, 1968) and two volumes of translations: *First and Second Discourses* (St. Martin's Press, 1964) and *Social Contract, with Geneva Manuscript and Political Economy* (St. Martin's Press, 1978). He has just completed *The Nature of Politics* (forthcoming), the first of several books assessing the philosophical implications of evolutionary biology.

John G. Gunnell is professor of political science at SUNY at Albany. He is editor of the Political Theory Series of SUNY Press. He is the author of numerous books, including *Political Philosophy and Time, Political Theory: Tradition and Interpretation,* and *Philosophy, Science and Political Inquiry.* He has recently published a study of the relationship between philosophy and political theory, entitled *Between Philosophy and Politics: The Alienation of Political Theory* (University of Massachusetts Press, 1986).

Hilail Gildin is professor of philosophy at Queens College and editor-in-chief of *Interpretation: A Journal of Political Philosophy.* He is the author of *Rousseau's "Social Contract": The Design of the Argument.* Currently he is preparing a book on the political philosophy of Aristotle.

Richard H. Cox is professor of political science at SUNY at Buffalo. He has published *Locke on War and Peace* and edited *The State in International Relations* and *Politics,* and *Ideology and Political Theory.* He also has published a number of articles on the history of political philosophy and an essay on Shakespeare's *A Midsummer Night's Dream.* He is currently working on a study of the problem of war and peace in Plato's *Republic.*

Laurence Berns is a senior tutor at St. John's College, Annapolis. He is the author of numerous papers and articles on such authors as Aristotle, Xenophon, Shakespeare, Francis Bacon, and Hobbes. He is completing a literal annotated translation of Aristotle's *Politics.*

Judith A. Best is distinguished teaching professor of political science at SUNY College at Cortland. She is the author of *The Case Against Direct Election of the President* (Cornell University Press, 1975), *The Mainstream of Western Political Thought* (Human Sciences Press, 1980), and *National Representation for the District of Columbia* (University Publications of America, 1984). She is also the author of several articles, including "What is Law: The *Minos* Reconsidered," *Interpretation* (May 1980), and "The Item Veto: Would the Founders Approve?," *Presidential Studies Quarterly* (Spring 1984). Currently she is contributing to *The New Federalist Papers, This Constitution,* and other projects commemorating the bicentennial of the Constitution.

Thomas L. Pangle is professor of political science and fellow, St. Michael's College, at the University of Toronto. He has been a National Endowment for the Humanities senior fellow and a Guggenheim fellow.

Among his writings are *Montesquieu's Philosophy of Liberalism* (University of Chicago Press, 1973), *The Laws of Plato* (Basic Books, 1979), and a monograph in *Nietzsche-Studien* (1986), "The 'Warrior Spirit' as an Inlet to the Political Philosophy of Nietzsche's Zarathustra." Pangle is the author of the introductory essay to Leo Strauss's last, posthumously published work, *Studies in Platonic Political Philosophy* (University of Chicago Press, 1983).

Robert Eden teaches political philosophy at Dalhousie University in Halifax, Nova Scotia. He is the author of one book, *Political Leadership and Nihilism: A Study of Weber and Nietzsche* (University of Florida Press, 1984) and is presently at work on a second, *Is a Constitutionalist Political Realignment Possible?*, a study of American politics and Tocqueville's political science.

Stephen G. Salkever is professor of political science at Bryn Mawr College. He has published articles and essays on Rousseau, Hume, Plato, and Aristotle, and on the concepts of virtue, rationality, and interpretation. He is presently working on a book on Aristotelian political philosophy.

William T. Bluhm is professor of political science at the University of Rochester. He is the author of *Theories of the Political System* (Prentice-Hall, 1965; 3rd ed. 1978), *Building an Austrian Nation* (Yale University Press, 1973), *Ideologies and Attitudes* (Prentice-Hall, 1974), and *Force or Freedom?: The Paradox in Modern Political Thought* (Yale University Press, 1984). Bluhm is also the editor of *The Paradigm Problem in Political Science* (Carolina Academic Press, 1982), and the author of two chapters of that volume. He has contributed numerous articles to symposia and to scholarly journals. At present he is doing research for a book in the field of ethics and public policy.

Index